FORGING BUSINESS–LABOUR PARTNERSHIPS:
THE EMERGENCE OF SECTOR COUNCILS IN CANADA

EDITED BY MORLEY GUNDERSON AND
ANDREW SHARPE

Forging Business–Labour Partnerships: The Emergence of Sector Councils in Canada

Published in cooperation with
the Centre for the Study
of Living Standards by

UNIVERSITY OF TORONTO PRESS
Toronto Buffalo London

© University of Toronto Press Incorporated 1998
Toronto Buffalo London

Printed in Canada

ISBN 0-8020-0904-2 (cloth)

Printed on acid-free paper

Canadian Cataloguing in Publication Data

Main entry under title:

Forging business-labour partnerships : the emergence of sector councils in Canada

ISBN 0-8020-0904-2

1. Sector councils – Canada – Congresses.   2. Industrial relations – Canada –
Congresses.   3. Labour policy – Canada – Congresses.   I. Gunderson, Morley, 1945– .
II. Sharpe, Andrew.   III. Centre for the Study of Living Standards.

HD8106.5.F67 1998   331'.0971   C97-932232-4

University of Toronto Press acknowledges the financial assistance to its publishing
program of the Canada Council for the Arts and the Ontario Arts Council

For Brady, Jesse, Rory, and Brendan

MG

For Sandra and Brendan

AS

Contents

Foreword

The Canadian experience with sector councils, examined in this book, bucks the dominant trend of recent years towards decentralization of employment-relations institutions. Consequently this collection of papers analysing experiences with these councils is welcome. Together, these contributions allow us to place the decentralizing trend in historical perspective, with an eye to assessing the role that intermediary institutions can play in improving employment relations today and in the future.

What has been the role of sectoral institutions in the past? At one time industry-wide collective bargaining structures were created to 'take wages out of competition' and thereby stabilize employment conditions. But this becomes harder to do in an economy in which markets no longer conform to national boundaries and an 'industry' may include a multitude of products with different price, labour cost, and technological features. At other times, industry-wide efforts provided forums for organizing discussions around specific technologies. However, here too the growth of micro-electronics, general-use manufacturing technologies such as computer-driven machine tools, and, more recently, computer-aided design and manufacturing systems crosses industry and sector boundaries. Moreover, at one point, industry-occupation cells served as a useful analytical category in analysing employment trends and projections. However, the growing trend to contract out the non-core functions of businesses means that jobs which in the past would have been classified within the manufacturing sector are now counted in the service or construction sector.

Given these developments, what can sector councils add to the performance of a labour market and employment system? The material in this book provides a number of interesting answers.

If structures for standardizing wages were the critical focus for raising workers' incomes and living standards in the past, human-capital development and mobility are the critical factors today. Thus it is not surprising that most of the councils deal with one aspect or another of skill development, adjustment, or redeployment of labour in the face of changing technological and market conditions. These are natural functions for institutions that transcend firm boundaries, since they are needed to address one of the most important market failures observed in modern economies – namely, the difference between the social and private returns to workforce training and skill upgrading. All around the world, policy-makers are searching for appropriate ways to mix public and private investments in workforce development. Understanding what role sectoral institutions can play is therefore vitally important.

The organizations examined here illustrate the blurring of industry lines in the modern economy. Indeed, truth in labelling would suggest a need to call these institutions something other than 'sector' councils, although I have no alternative term to suggest. Only about two-thirds of the councils described here in fact conform to traditional industry boundaries such as steel, textiles, trucking, and so on. The other third suggest a variety of new venues for aggregating and coordinating interests: technologies that cut across industries, such as software development or graphic arts; gender groups, such as the women's network in trades and technology; services relevant to all types of businesses such as logistics; and some new industries, such as tourism and environmental concerns. The implication is that labour markets and careers increasingly cross industry lines; therefore our institutions need to be fluid enough to support this type of mobility, and flexible enough to adapt to future unforeseen changes in career paths and opportunities.

The respective roles of the government and the private sector in forming and sustaining these councils is also reflective of the changing relationships among these actors in employment relations. The government is neither a regulator in the traditional command and control mode nor a simple third-party mediator or arbitrator of labour and management differences. Instead it is a catalyst or institution-builder, stepping in where there are identifiable externalities or market failures that require cross-firm coordination. It does so presumably because no individual firm, acting alone, finds it in its interest to address the relevant issue, and there is not sufficient private-sector indigenous leadership to mobilize sector participants to act collectively for their common interest. In this case, government officials need a keen analytical eye to know when there is a real need or market failure worth overcoming, and they need to develop a new vision and strategy of how to work with both market forces and private actors to get the job done efficiently.

The role of the labour movement is also instructive. Labour doesn't have the muscle, as the Steelworkers or the Teamsters unions did in an earlier era, to insist on creation of industry-wide bargaining structures or pattern agreements. Instead it needs to rely on government to initiate and help fund these institutions and then needs to negotiate a seat(s) at the table and the rules of joint governance. And given the diversity of occupations and the limited membership of unions, labour must be represented increasingly by multiple voices, some of which are not part of the labour movement. Employment-related institutions of the future are therefore likely to be composed of more diverse interests than the typical labels of labour, management, and government suggest.

I find these lessons instructive. They suggest that we are likely to see demand for institutions above the level of the firm but below the national level. Some of these may be temporary and some may have enduring roles and functions. But their utility and effectiveness depend on their ability to generate and coordinate actions of organizations at more micro and macro positions in the economy. They need to generate support and action on the part of individual firms, thereby internalizing the externalities or overcoming the market failures that motivate their creation. And they need to motivate and help coordinate government policies that facilitate and support, rather than just regulate and enforce, private behaviour. Where such functions can improve performance, sectoral or some intermediary institutions are likely to emerge.

As I read these chapters, I repeatedly experienced a sense of *déjà vu*. While I accept that it is difficult to take wages out of competition through industry patterns or formal structures as in the past, I wonder if some interactions at sectoral levels would not still be useful. In that way broad principles or norms could be established that set limits on acceptable terms and conditions of employment in industries and occupations. Perhaps we have witnessed one swing of the pendulum in the past two decades as wage-setting moved to more decentralized levels to allow firms to adapt to increasing diversity and price competition in product markets. Will we now witness a social reaction and a call for principles and/or standards that might bring some discipline to the setting of terms and conditions of employment? Obviously this cannot be done simply by attempting to reconstruct industry-wide bargaining structures or pattern agreements. However, there may be some role for the creation of common benefit funds, professional norms and standards of practice and ethics, and the common socialization needed to enforce such norms, or use of modern communications technologies to disseminate rapidly and widely information needed for labour market competition to perform its standardizing role. If this is true, the sectoral level of interaction may re-ascend in importance in the years ahead.

There is another reason to believe that the need for some external institutions, tied either to the labour market or the sector level, will re-emerge if, as some predict, worker attachment to firms declines in the future. If mobility increases or firms continue to externalize more of the employment functions, the demand will grow for professional associations, craft unions, or other coordinating and labour-market institutions to ease job mobility across firms. While there is no guarantee that the sector is the best level for such institutions, the lessons from the sectoral studies contained here are relevant to whatever institutions emerge.

Finally, there is a more intangible, but long-standing and indispensable, function that forums such as those described in this book serve. They produce the contacts among labour, management, and government officials needed to build the personal ties that will be instrumental in resolving the problems that cannot easily be anticipated but are certain to arise in the future.

For all these reasons, the information and analysis presented here provide good food for thought about the institutions found in Canada's employment-relations systems today, as well as those that we may need to create to meet the needs of tomorrow.

THOMAS A. KOCHAN
George M. Bunker Professor of Management
Massachusetts Institute of Technology

Acknowledgments

The editors would like to thank Human Resources Development Canada for financial support for the Centre for the Study of Living Standards' project on sector councils, which led to this volume. In particular, we would like to thank Harvey Lazar, then senior assistant deputy minister, strategic policy, for his leadership role in securing funding.

Earlier versions of the papers contained in the volume were presented at a conference on sector councils organized by the Centre for the Study of Living Standards and held in Montreal on 12–13 January 1997. The conference took place in conjunction with the annual meeting of sector council officials, and we would like to thank Lenore Burton and Ken Gelok of the Canadian Labour Force Development Board for facilitating this arrangement. We believe that the resulting interaction between practitioners and researchers greatly enriched the volume. We would like to thank participants in the conference, particularly the discussants and session chairs.

Two anonymous referees provided valuable comments on all papers in the volume and we owe them a debt of gratitude.

Finally, at the University of Toronto Press, we would like to thank Virgil Duff for the commitment he has shown this project since its inception and Darlene Zeleney for efficient management of the production process.

MORLEY GUNDERSON
ANDREW SHARPE

List of Sector Councils

Note: Updated lists of sector councils, including website addresses, can be found at the website of the Sector Councils' Steering Committee (www.councils.org).

Apparel Human Resources Council.
Automotive Parts Sectoral Training Council
Biotechnology Human Resources Council
Canadian Aquaculture Industry Alliance Sector Council
Canadian Automotive Repair and Service Council (CARS)
Canadian Aviation Maintenance Council
Canadian Council for Human Resources in the Environment Industry
Canadian Council for Professional Fish Harvesters
Canadian Grocery Products Council
Canadian Professional Logistics Institute
Canadian Steel Trade and Employment Congress (CSTEC)
Canadian Technology Human Resources Board
Canadian Tourism Human Resource Council
Canadian Trucking Human Resources Council
Cultural Human Resources Council
Forum for International Trade Training (FITT)
Graphic Arts Training Council
Horticultural Human Resource Council
Human Resource Sector Council for the Electronic and Appliance Industry
Mining Industry Training and Adjustment Council (MITAC)
National Seafood Sector Council
Sectoral Skills Council of the Electrical / Electronics Industry (SSC)
Software Human Resource Council
Textiles Human Resources Council
Women in Trades and Technology (WITT) National Network

FORGING BUSINESS–LABOUR PARTNERSHIPS:
THE EMERGENCE OF SECTOR COUNCILS IN CANADA

Introduction

MORLEY GUNDERSON and ANDREW SHARPE

The Canadian experience with sector councils is unique in the world. Councils have been or are being established in over twenty-five sectors to achieve a number of objectives, including delivery of adjustment programs, administration of training funds for skills upgrading, and establishment of industry standards. The federal government and certain provincial governments see the development of sectoral activities, and sector councils in particular, as a key component of their human resource and adjustment strategies and have devoted considerable resources to support these activities. Sector councils, as a new form of labour-management cooperation, represent a major innovation in our industrial relations system.

The objective of this volume is to provide an overview of the Canadian experience with sector councils, with particular attention to the lessons emerging from this experience. The book represents the first attempt to bring together a wide range of views on various aspects of the sector council experience. Contributors include both academics and practitioners. The perspective here is interdisciplinary, with contributions from economists, political scientists, and industrial relations specialists, as well researchers in other disciplines.

The volume is divided into six sections. The first part provides historical and economic perspectives on sector councils. Part II looks at labour and business approaches to sector councils, while Part III discusses sectoral initiatives in Quebec and Ontario. Part IV examines the contribution sector councils have made to the advancement of the concept of joint governance, and Part V looks at the evaluation of sector councils. The final section discusses the relationships between corporatism, the industrial relations system, and sector councils.

Pressures for Adjustment

The pros and cons of sectoral councils as adjustment mechanisms must be viewed in the broader context of the adjustment pressures to which they are a response.[1] The inter-related adjustment pressures emanate from the demand and supply side of the labour market as well as from institutional pressures.

On the demand side, both external and internal labour markets of firms have been dramatically affected by global competition, trade liberalization, techno-logical change, and deindustrialization. While the efficiency gains from these forces should provide the means to compensate those who are adversely affected, there is no automatic mechanism to ensure that this will occur. Unfor-tunately, these forces have led to greater polarization in the labour market with respect to wages as well as 'good jobs and bad jobs.' The technological change has tended to be biased towards skilled labour, and the import competition from developing countries has had its most adverse effect on low-wage workers in developed countries. The deep and prolonged recessions of the early 1980s and 1990s have also left their legacy, with unemployment rates ratcheting up to new and sustained higher levels.

The demand side of the labour market was affected by other forces, includ-ing mergers and acquisitions, privatization, deregulation, subcontracting and restructuring – often to get the economies of scale necessary to compete in the world market. Mass layoffs and plant closings became common, creating severe adjustment consequences in particular communities and industries. The contin-gent workforce became more prominent in various forms, including part-time work, limited-term contracts, homework, and self-employment. Public concern over the deficit, and reluctance to raise taxes to reduce it, meant tight monetary and fiscal policies as well as retrenchment in public expenditures. This affects not only public sector employment but also the infrastructure for the private sector. The retrenchment also means that it will be difficult to pay for equity-oriented programs and the social safety net to deal with the downside adjust-ment consequences.

External and internal labour markets of firms were also affected by equally dramatic changes on the supply side. The participation of women in the work-force, especially those with pre-school-age children, continued to increase so that the two-earner family became the norm and not the exception. The baby-boom population moved through the labour market, creating adjustment prob-lems of clogged promotion opportunities, retraining, life-long learning, and an 'expensive' workforce, especially as pension benefit accruals become more prominent. Pension and retirement issues are now coming to the fore. The workforce has also become more diverse with respect to age, ethnicity, gender, and minority groups status.

In many cases, the supply side adjustment pressures exacerbated those aris-ing from the demand side. The continued influx of women and their segregation into low-wage jobs enhanced the pressures placed on jobs by import competition and technological change. Displaced older workers had severe adjustment problems, especially given the high unemployment rates of the recessions and the fact that technological change often required completely new skills. In other cases, however, the supply side forces were complementary to the demand side ones and eased the adjustment consequences. The need for flexible working hours in two-earner families often created a demand for voluntary part-time work and even self-employment. The aging workforce often created windows for voluntary retirement as a mechanism of adjustment. The restructuring that occurred created some upside adjustment problems (e.g., skill shortages, vacancies) that could be met by some of the downside adjustments (layoffs, plant closings).

In essence, these economic forces in the labour market created problems, but they also created opportunities – opportunities to match the supply side preferences with demand side needs, and upside adjustment needs with downside adjustments that were occurring. Evidence of the mismatching became conspicuous in numerous areas: organizations often worked much of their workforce long hours and overtime, while other individuals were laid off; many workers facing the family 'time crunch' wanted reduced work time, while others wanted to increase their work time; many older workers would willingly accept retirement if a modicum of income security could be provided, while numerous younger workers wanted jobs and middle-aged workers wanted the promotions that would be vacated by retirees; some organizations faced chronic skill shortages that created severe bottlenecks in production, while many individuals were willing and able to fill those jobs or take the requisite training. The mismatches became conspicuous and anomalous given the high unemployment, time pressures of the dual-earner families, and pressures for competitiveness. Nevertheless, conventional mechanisms (e.g., the market, collective bargaining, and government regulations and programs) did not seem to dissipate the mismatches.

The demand and supply side adjustment pressures were occurring at the same time as dramatic change in the institutional environment in which external and internal labour market adjustments were taking place. In many circumstances these institutional changes were influenced by the demand and supply side forces. Increased capital mobility and the threat of plant relocation and investment decisions have put pressure on governments to compete for business investment and the jobs associated with that investment. That competition has often taken the form of reducing the regulatory and legal environment in which employers operate. Governments have paid as much attention to the bond market as to public opinion polls. These pressures have led to increased scrutiny of equalization payments and adjustment programs, as well as the social safety net in general. Even progressive employers who are willing to pay a fair share of the cost of such programs may be constrained by having to compete against employers in other countries where such programs are non-existent or not enforced. In an increasing competitive world where prices are set by international competition and capital is mobile, payroll taxes to pay for these programs cannot be shifted forward to consumers or backward to stockholders; they can be shifted to the only immobile factor – labour.

The adjustment consequences facing labour are further exacerbated by the decline of unionization throughout the world, and especially in the United States. Adjustment consequences can be dealt with by any combination of the three main mechanisms for dealing with the employment relationship: the market, collective bargaining, and government legislation and regulation. Given the decline of collective bargaining and the pressures to reduce government regulation and legislation, market mechanisms have become the prime adjustment mechanism. This is certainly valid for the external labour market, but it is also true internally, as more emphasis is placed on the viability of separate business units, subcontracting, pay for performance, pay flexibility, privatization, and the contingent workforce – a workforce that is hired only if the market forces dictate a need.

Clearly, both external and internal labour markets of firms are facing dramatic adjustment challenges. But new problems may require new solutions, and there is legitimate debate as to whether policies designed for a full-employment, industrial-based, expanding and protected economy are appropriate for today's information age and global economy, where flexibility and adaptability are key. Decentralized, cooperative solutions that involve active adjustment assistance (and prevention) as opposed to passive income maintenance have taken on increased importance. It is in this broader context that sector councils should be evaluated as an adjustment mechanism.

Sector Councils in Canada

Historical Development

The emergence of sector councils in the 1980s should be seen as a response to the overall restructuring of economic activity. The particular histories of these sectoral initiatives illustrate well the interplay between the forces restructuring the economy and the emergence of new institutional frameworks adapted to the changing economic environment.

The first sectoral initiative in Canada which resulted in the formation of a joint business-labour council or organization was the Centre for Aerospace Manpower Activities in Quebec (CAMAQ), established in 1983 by employers belonging to the Aerospace Industries Association of Canada and the unions in the sector, as well as by the federal and provincial government. CAMAQ was established to promote joint action in the human resource area by employers, unions, educational institutions, and government agencies involved in planning for and training specialized workers for the aerospace industry in Quebec. The strong interest shown by the Quebec government in business-labour consultations in the second half of the 1970s and early 1980s, particularly at the sectoral level (seventeen sectoral mini-summits were held between 1977 and 1982), may explain why the first initiative emerged in this province (Fournier, 1986).

At the national level, the first sectoral initiative oriented towards joint action by business and labour took place in the early 1980s in the steel industry. The Canadian steel industry at the time was facing serious problems of access into the important American market. Business was interested in mobilizing the support of labour in view of their common interest in combating American protectionism. Labour agreed to support business on trade issues on condition that labour adjustment issues were also addressed. A particularly important concern to labour was adequate assistance for workers who lost their jobs because of layoffs and plant closures (downside adjustment).

The Canadian Steel Trade Conference was established in 1985, with equal participation of the major steel companies and the union representing steelworkers, the United Steelworkers of America. The initiative had come directly from business and labour themselves, with government playing the role of observer (Crookell, 1986) and providing financial support. In 1987 the name was changed to the Canadian Steel Trade and Employment Congress (CSTEC) to reflect the dual nature of the concerns of the organization.

In the second half of the 1980s important sectoral initiatives developed in the electrical/electronics industry and in the automotive services and repair industry. The federal Department of Employment and Immigration was closely involved in these initiatives.[2] Steering committees with labour and business representation from both sectors were formed to provide input into studies of the human resource needs. Both studies recommended that institutional structures be established to deal with the joint labour market concerns of business and labour in the two sectors. This recommendation was accepted by all parties and actions undertaken to make it a reality.

In the electrical/electronics industry a Joint Human Resource Committee of the Canadian Electrical and Electronics Manufacturing Industries was formed in 1987. The Electrical and Electronic Manufacturing Association of Canada, representing two hundred companies in the industry, and three unions participated. In 1989 the name of the committee was changed to the Sectoral Skills

Council (SSC). The Council's concerns have been primarily in the human resource area (see Joint Human Resource Committee, 1989), with particular attention to retraining of the current workforce to meet the rising skill demands of the industry and to ensuring that young people entering the sector are appropriately prepared. But the concerns have also included issues which go beyond a narrow definition of human resources, such as the implementation of technological change. In contrast to the steel industry, the electrical/electronics sector enjoyed significant employment growth in the 1980s, making the retraining of employed workers, or upside adjustment, the dominant concern.

In the automotive service and repair industry a joint human resource committee called the Canadian Automotive Repair and Service Council (CARS Council) was established in 1988, with financial support from the Department of Employment and Immigration. The committee was composed of representatives from five national automotive associations, community colleges, and training institutes represented through the Canadian Transportation Institute, and employees. As workers in this sector are largely unorganized, labour representation is not through unions; employee representatives are appointed by firms or other organizations. Like the electrical/electronics sector, employment opportunities have been strong in automotive service and repair in the 1980s. The major human resources concerns have thus been those of upside adjustment, in particular the retraining of the current workforce to meet the rising skill requirements from the ever-changing technology and the assurance of an adequate supply of well-qualified entrants into the sector. The issue of national industry standards in the area of apprenticeship training and certification has also been important.

The sectoral human resource studies initiated by the federal Department of Employment and Immigration have resulted in additional initiatives. For example, a study on the changing skill needs of the automotive parts industry called for the establishment of a joint training council and training delivery program. This recommendation was favourably received by both the Automotive Parts Manufacturers' Association and the Canadian Auto Workers. These two organizations in 1991 established the Automotive Parts Sectoral Training Council (APSTC). The automotive parts industry has been relatively healthy in the 1980s so the major concern of APSTC has been one of upside adjustment. In 1996 APSTC was disbanded, the only sector council to have so far suffered this fate.

Current Status of Councils

According to Human Resources Development Canada (HRDC, 1996: ix), a sector council is defined as 'a joint employer-employee organization that provides a neutral decision-making forum to determine human resource issues within the sector and to develop and implement a sectoral human resource strategy.'

In mid-1997 there were twenty-two operational councils funded or associated with HRDC. There are also a number of councils in the exploratory or developmental stages (biotechnology, plastics, telecommunications). A list of the operational councils is found at the beginning of this volume. There is great diversity in both the characteristics and the operations of sector councils in this country. This diversity manifests itself in a number of ways, including: form of employee representation (both unions and employee associations); focus (sectoral versus cross-sectoral or occupational); and types of activities (upside and downside adjustment programs, curriculum development, certification, establishment of training standards). It is thus difficult to speak of a typical sector council.

Sector councils are a recent phenomenon, with only four of the current councils (women in technology, CARS, CSTEC, and SSC) established before 1992. Six councils became operational in 1992, three in 1993, two in 1994, four in 1995, and three in 1996. The rapid growth in the number of sector councils in recent years is a direct result of the 1992 federal Sectoral Partnerships Initiative (SPI) which allocated $250 million for sectoral initiatives over a five-year period.[3]

Table 1 shows that out of twenty-two operational councils, eighteen have an industry orientation and fifteen are covered by the current Standard Industrial Classification (SIC) system. The four occupationally oriented councils are equally divided between those covered by the current Standard Occupation Classification (SOC) system and occupations that have not yet been captured by the occupational classification system. The major problem for a council in not being covered by a SIC or SOC is the greater difficulty in obtaining data, as official statistics are gathered on a SIC and SOC basis.

An overall industry or sectoral orientation does not necessarily mean that councils focus on all occupations within the sector. For example, the auto parts councils focused on the training needs of production workers.

One might be tempted to classify councils in sectors covered by the SIC as traditional and councils in non-SIC sectors as non-traditional or emerging. Based on this definition, most industry-based (i.e., non-cross-industry or occupation-based) councils would classify as traditional. But this is a problematic definition of traditional, as a number of councils currently covered by the SIC are in emerging industries (aquaculture) or rapidly growing industries (e.g., auto parts, culture, trucking, appliance repair). Equally, at least one of the councils not covered by the SIC (tourism) is actually an older, traditional industry.[4]

There appears to be no particular pattern to the formation of sector councils. They have been established in both mature and emerging industries; in high

TABLE 1   Classification of Sector Councils by Industry and Occupations

	Industry Sector	
	Councils with a SIC	Councils without a SIC
Primary industries	mining aquaculture horticulture fish harvesters seafood processors	
Manufacturing	steel auto parts electrical/electronics printing textiles	
Services	culture aviation maintenance trucking appliance repair auto repair	tourism environment software
	Occupations	
	Councils with a SOC	Councils without a SOC
	technologists women in trades	logistics international trade

tech and low tech industries; in the primary, manufacturing, and service sectors; in small sectors and large; in unionized and non-unionized sectors; and in sectors dominated by a small number of large firms and by a large number of small firms. The only part of the economy where the councils have not gained a foothold is the public sector, including public administration, education, and health. This feature of course reflects the deliberate private-sector orientation of the councils.

The vast majority of sector councils (sixteen out of twenty-two) have their head office in Ottawa. This concentration in the national capital may be explained by the need for proximity to HRDC headquarters; the presence in Ottawa of the head office of many business associations and labour unions and federations, and the existence in the national capital region of a large pool of qualified individuals to staff the councils.

The councils have been designed as national institutions serving all Canadians, and indeed the vast majority of them (seventeen) are national in scope, with activities in all regions of the country. However, the regional nature of certain sectors means that there are exceptions to this. For example, the absence of large-scale fishing in Ontario and the prairie provinces means that both the fish harvesters' and the fish producers' councils do not operate in those provinces. Equally, the concentration of the auto parts manufacturing in Ontario means that the activities of this council have been confined to this province. The Sectoral Skills Council is also confined to Ontario because its training trust funds are provincially regulated and funded, and have so far only been agreed to in Ontario.

While most councils undertake activities in all regions, only three, CSTEC and the horticulture and tourism councils, have set up regional or provincial offices or operate in a decentralized manner. Two factors may account for this lack of regional/provincial presence. First, since sector councils are trying to develop a national orientation to human resource issues, regional offices, unless set up for economies in the delivery of services, could dilute this focus. Second, the limited financial resources of the councils may mean that they cannot afford to maintain more than one office.

The human resource issues most commonly addressed by the councils are those of skills upgrading of the employed workforce and the recruitment of well-qualified new entrants into the sector to prevent skill shortages. Associated with these concerns are occupational standards and accreditation issues. Only three councils (steel, mining, and seafood processors) address downsize adjustment, as the SPI excludes this activity from funding.

A key objective of sector councils is to foster business-labour partnerships, and the union movement has played a key role in the development of sector councils. Indeed, unions participate in seventeen of the twenty-two operational councils. Of the five where unions have no presence, two are industry councils in non-unionized sectors (auto repair and aquaculture), and three are occupational councils where there is no union representation of workers (logistics, software, and technologists and technicians).

In principle, the councils should have employer/employee parity in decision-making, but only about half the councils conform to this model. The absence or weakness of union representation largely account for this deviation (although in one case – fish harvesters – it is the absence of employer representation). In one non-unionized sector (auto repairs) a mechanism for employee representation (the CARS council) has been developed to permit employer/employee parity in decision-making.

The HRDC model for sector council development requires the completion of a human resource study of the sector before the establishment of the council. It is believed that business and labour working together on the study fosters the development of a shared vision necessary for the success of the council. Sixteen of the operational councils were preceded by such a study. The exceptions included steel, women in trades, international trade, fish harvesters, and aquaculture.

Synthesis of the Papers in the Volume

Historical and Economic Perspectives on Sector Councils

Organizational Innovation by Serendipity

The Department of Employment and Immigration (now called the Department of Human Resources Development) has played a key role in nurturing the development of sector councils in Canada. In his paper Gary Fletcher, former director of the Sector Studies Division at the Department of Employment and Immigration, gives an insider account on the historical development of the federally funded sector councils. As is often the case in the development of new institutions, serendipity played a major role. The Department of Employment and Immigration never consciously set out to establish a network of sector councils; their emergence was the unpredictable outcome of a series of other developments.

Fletcher begins the story by noting that several government reports published in the early 1980s pointed to a need for better labour market information to resolve labour shortages. The minister of employment and immigration responded in 1982 by establishing the Canadian Occupational Projection System (COPS), which was to produce information to guide the department's labour market programs. COPS at first used mechanistic input-output models to project demand by industry and occupation. But the reality of rapid technological change led to the realization that these techniques were inadequate and had to be complemented with sector-specific information obtained through sector studies.

It was found that the usefulness of the sector studies was directly related to the degree of industry participation in the study. This was because employer and union involvement facilitated data gathering and provided first-hand insights on industry trends. Consequently, steering committees composed of senior business and labour officials were established to guide sector studies.

With the first sector studies, the involvement of business and labour ended once the study was completed. But it was increasingly realized that there was much to be gained by keeping the group together to guide the implementation of solutions to the problems identified. The department's Industrial Adjustment Service (IAS) provided financing for the establishment of a number of the pioneering councils, including CSTEC and Sector Skills Council. The sector council approach received a further boost in 1992 with the announcement of the Sectoral Partnership Initiative, which set the goal of establishing fifty-five councils within five years, although this overly ambitious goal has since been scaled down.

Economic Rationale for Sector Councils

Sector councils largely deal with human resource issues, which can be approached from both firm and sector perspectives. In the second paper, Douglas A. Smith of Carleton University examines the economic rationale for sector councils, with particular emphasis on the rationale for their promotion by government and the forces that would leave the private sector to establish councils without government assistance.

Smith believes that sector councils can be seen as 'association-like' organizations for which both firms and workers have a latent demand. If this is the case, a key question is why councils have taken so long to develop and why this development has required government assistance. Smith argues that the existence of externalities, or differences in social and private costs, can account for the lack of attention given issues that are most effectively handled on a sectoral basis. Since firms cannot be forced to join, they gain the benefits arising from the sector council without incurring the costs.

Smith focuses on four types of externalities or market failure: underprovision of labour market information; the inability of the private sector to establish standards; non-innovators in labour-management relations free-riding on innovators; and undersupply of employer training due to poaching. He argues that the most important way sector councils can promote private sector training is through the design of effective training programs.

Labour and Business Approaches to Sector Councils

An appreciation of the dynamics of sector councils requires an understanding of the different approaches business and labour bring to the table. Part two of the volume contains three articles on this topic.

The CLC Perspective

Kevin Hayes, senior economist at the Canadian Labour Congress (CLC), presents his organization's views on sector councils. The CLC sees labour participation in the councils as a way to advance its policy and union principles in the areas of labour adjustment, unemployment insurance, full employment, training, and policies targeting equity groups. In 1992 the CLC, adopted guidelines to assist its members participate in sector councils.

The CLC strongly believes sector councils must not be advisory in nature, but must have authority to determine program priorities and spend any allocations. When government funding is used, sector councils should ensure that public educational institutions are used for skills training. To ensure the accountability of sector councils, the CLC recommends that councils be established only on the joint initiative of the union and employer, that federally funded councils only be established on the recommendation of the Canadian Labour Force Development Board in consultation with provincial boards where appropriate, that councils become accountable to the stakeholders who name the representatives to the council, that the accountability of labour members is to the participating unions, and that labour representatives receive a labour-sponsored orientation program. CLC policy is that the training of the employed workforce is the responsibility of employers, and the training of youth and the unemployed is the responsibility of government. Income support for training of the unemployed should come from unemployment insurance, while the cost of training programs should come out of general revenue.

Many of the CLC guidelines on sector councils have been closely adhered to by union affiliates. Others, such as the joint business/labour determination of what sectors form councils and the use of UI funds only for income support, for a variety of reasons have not been respected.

Hayes points that recent changes in federal labour market policies may jeopardize labour's commitment to sector councils. The concept of a sectoral adjustment and training strategy emerged when the vast majority of workers in a sector were covered by unemployment insurance. This is no longer so, and under the new regime, it may no longer be workable. Equally, recent attempts by the federal government to off-load the cost of training onto the provinces and workers is a development which labour believes has negative implications for the future of sector councils. Monies for training initiatives, including sector councils, will increasingly come from the UI account, not general revenues.

Business Perspectives on Sector Councils

The Canadian business community has not issued a position paper comparable to the CLC guidelines on sector councils. This reflects the fact that no one business association determines the overall business perspective to the degree that the CLC determines the labour perspective. In addition, individual employers tend to be individualistic and feel little obligation to adhere to positions adopted by business associations, particularly if they perceive their interests not furthered by the collective position. Consequently, it is much more difficult to speak of a business perspective on sector councils than a labour perspective.

Jock Finlayson, vice president of the Business Council of British Columbia, offers a business perspective based on personal observations and experience, a review of the literature, and interviews with business representatives involved in the establishment of sector councils. He identifies six major reasons for business involvement in sectoral initiatives:

1/The single most important factor has been the desire on the part of business to improve employee skills in response to the rapidly changing external environment. Business representatives agree that industry must do more (or more effective) training, that skill requirements for entry-level employees are rising, that a substantial fraction of the workforce needs skills upgrading, and that raising skills can be usefully addressed at the sectoral level.
2/The development of national standards has been an important goal for business in a number of councils, including those in the aviation maintenance, auto repair, tourism, and environment sectors.
3/Councils are seen as a way to design and implement programs to attract qualified workers into the sector to overcome actual or projected shortages of skilled workers.
4/A number of businesses have perceived benefits from sectoral management-labour bodies in addressing issues associated with downside adjustment.
5/Certain firms and industry associations, as in the steel and textile sectors, see councils as a way to improve relations with unions.
6/Councils can facilitate access to government training funds.

Nevertheless, not all members of the business community see a need for sectoral councils. Finlayson identifies several factors that have contributed to industry opposition or lack of interest.

• Many businesses see no overriding human resources issues facing them, or at least no issues that can be dealt with at the sectoral level. Since human resource issues are the bread and butter of the councils, businesses with this perspective will obviously not be interested in participating.
• Industry structure and location can play a role in the development of sector councils. Business support comes easier when the industry is concentrated both geographically and in terms of the market share of the top firms. A high preponderance of small firms in a sector and lack of regional concentration constitute a barrier to the establishment of a council in a sector.
• Several features militate against broad industry participation in national sector councils. These include the large number of associations, which makes it more difficult to develop a robust business viewpoint, and differences in perspectives between national and provincial-based associations. Sector councils may risk losing support among industry associations if they offer services that compete with those produced by the associations. This reality

may be a limiting factor on the ability of sector councils to become financially self-sufficient.
- Business support for sector councils is sometimes undercut by the perception that the process is driven more by government preferences than by the real priorities of business. Dependency on federal government funding does little to allay this perception and explains why business strongly support the objective of council financial self-sufficiency.
- Certain non-unionized employers may be reluctant to participate in sector councils because of union dominance of the employee side. They fear involvement could be inimical to their interests of maintaining a union-free workplace. These views are particularly strongly felt when unions represent employees on councils in sectors with low rates of unionization.

Finlayson concludes that while business has given continuous and strong support to a handful of the older and well-established councils and some support to a number of the newer ones, widespread industry support for sector councils has not been demonstrated. This suggests that self-sustaining permanent sector councils are unlikely to be established in most of the industries identified by the federal government under its sectoral partnership initiative.

Leveraging the Employer Training Effort: A Union Perspective on the Sectoral Skills Council

The Sectoral Skills Council of the electrical/electronics industry has been one of the pioneering sector councils and is regarded as a model by many of the newer councils. In the third paper in this section, David A. Wolfe and D'Arcy Martin examine the experience of unions in the SSC's development in Ontario over the past decade. While certainly not a panacea to economic restructuring, Wolfe and Martin argue that the SSC has been very successful in increasing the resources devoted to training in the industry.

Wolfe and Martin note that the sectoral model emerged in the 1980s as an innovative way for management and unions to transcend their traditional roles. Collective bargaining was to be complemented by social bargaining, where adversarial styles of operation give way to consensual ones. The focus on training as a key component of the sectoral model reflected the importance placed on training by both unions and employers as a means to deal with the challenges thrown up by economic restructuring. The sectoral level was felt to be a more effective forum for dealing with training-related issues than the narrower firm or plant-based approach because it is easier to overcome free rider problems at this level.

The SSC originated out of the Joint Human Resources Committee established in the late 1980s by union officials and employers in the sector. Assisted by Employment and Immigration Canada, the committee sponsored a human resources study of the sector. This study identified a potential human resource problem facing the sector arising from the need to upgrade skills, and both labour and management agreed that an increased emphasis had to be placed on retraining the existing workforce and that the establishment of a sector-wide training fund would be the most effective means to increase the sector's training effort. The SSC was created in 1990 to administer this fund.

Both management and labour have benefited from participation in the SSC. For employers, the council remains part of the tool-box of competitiveness, enabling firms to gain access to government subsidized training funds and allowing them to shape training programs jointly with workers in a decentralized way that responds to the needs of the workplace. For labour, the SSC gives workers greater input into workplace change and aligns the process of economic restructuring more closely with labour's goals. Wolfe and Martin see the SSC increasing the scope for joint action in the workplace by focusing on issues outside the routine collective bargaining process. They argue that this may have positive spin-offs for the economy in general as research suggests increased trust and shared responsibility improve economic performance.

As of December 1995, the SSC had established training funds in 170 firms in Ontario covering 50,000 workers. The overall funding level is set at 1 per cent of the wage bill, with the cost shared equally between the private and public sectors. The federal government and the Ontario government each contribute one quarter. Originally, employers were to contribute one quarter and employees another quarter. This was a contentious point with certain unions who believe that training is the financial responsibility of the employer. In most workplaces, employees now negotiate that their share be paid by the employer.

A joint workplace training committee (JWTC) is established in each workplace to administer the training fund according to the guidelines set by the SSC. One of the tasks of the JWTC is to balance training expenditure between three type of training. Type I training, by far the most important, consists of job/skill upgrading, Type II consists of general education and training, and Type III is employee group-directed training. Wolfe and Martin conclude that by the objective criteria of number of workers and workplaces covered and level of expenditure, the SSC has been successful in facilitating the training effort in the electrical/electronics sector.

Sectoral Initiatives in Quebec and Ontario

In addition to the federal government's interest in sector councils, a number of provinces have also emphasized sectoral initiatives as a component of their human resource development strategies. The two most important have been Quebec and Ontario.

Sectoral Human Resource Initiatives in Quebec

While a number of the federally funded sector councils operated in Quebec in the late 1980s and early 1990s, almost no provincial sector councils were established during this period. This situation has changed dramatically, in the last several years, as the provincial government appears to have discovered the virtues of sectoral initiatives in general and sector councils in particular. In the first paper in this section, Jean Charest, provides a comprehensive overview of developments concerning sectoral human resource initiatives in Quebec in the 1990s.

Charest begins by pointing out that it has been at the firm level through decentralized collective bargaining that the business-labour relations have been most intense in Quebec in recent decades. Nevertheless, in the 1970s and 1980s there were a number of attempts at concerted action by the provincial government to foster business-labour cooperation at meso- and macro-economic levels, including socio-economic conferences and the Round Table on Employment.

In the early 1990s the groundwork for sectoral initiatives was prepared by a number of developments, including the launch of an industrial strategy based on industrial clusters and the release of a labour market policy paper that stressed business-labour partnerships and established the bipartite Société québécoise de développement de la main-d'oeuvre (SQDM). Considerable financial and organizational resources have been put at the disposal of employers and unions, who have a positive attitude towards sectoral initiatives. Conditions are thus ripe for the emergence of sectoral partnerships in the human resource area. Time will tell if this potential is realized.

It is instructive to compare the SQDM committees to the sectoral councils sponsored by HRDC. Both new organizational structures have the general objective of bringing employers and unions together to address human resource issues and share a number of characteristics. But there are some important differences. In general, the SQDM committees appear to be more closely controlled by government. The definitions of what are considered appropriate sectoral groupings for committees are set by the SQDM, while stakeholders are free to develop their own definitions of what represents an appropriate grouping in the HRDC model. The SQDM committees operate under the aegis of the SQDM while HDRC councils are established as independent entities. There is no expectation that the SQDM committees attain financial self-sufficiency, even in the long run, while HRDC sector councils are expected to become financially self-sufficient within three years of establishment.

Charest argues that the environment for the success of the SQDM sectoral committees is now propitious, due to the less central role of the state in the decision-making and operations of the committees and to the greater predisposition towards cooperation on the part of both employers and unions. Nevertheless, he believes that it is much too early to pronounce sectoral initiatives a success. Charest believes the potentially most valuable role for the sectoral level is as a transmission mechanism between public policy, particularly labour market policy, and the workplace, although he cautions sectoral initiatives must not be regarded as a panacea.

Sectoral Initiatives in Ontario

Ontario, like Quebec, has experienced considerable experimentation and innovation in the area of labour market policy over the last decade. In the second paper in this section, Neil Bradford provides a through examination of these developments, with particular attention to the Ontario Training and Adjustment Board (OTAB) and its objective of consolidating and extending sectoral training and adjustment councils.

Bradford argues that with the election of the Liberals in 1985, the Ontario government adopted a strategic framework that called for a transition to 'high value-added production' through corporatist institutions directly involving organized interests in public policy development and implementation. An obstacle to this transition was the limited history of social partnership in policy-making in the province as well as the adversarial nature of the industrial relations system.

Bradford stresses the key role of the Ontario Premier's Council in providing the intellectual foundations for the new policy. Its 1990 report identified a number of advantages of the sectoral approach: more relevant programming rooted in the expressed needs of the workplace parties; the potential for leveraging private sector training expenditures with public funds; and the sharing of the costs and benefits of training among firms thereby reducing the incentive to poach while increasing provisions of portable skills training. To obtain these advantages, the Premier's Council report recommended the creation of OTAB, which was announced in November 1989.

OTAB was formerly established in 1993. It was to be an independent provincial agency with decision-making authority led by interest group representatives to oversee the design, delivery, and funding of workplace adjustment and training. During an initial period of negotiation, the Ontario government remained active on the sectoral training front, by supporting (with HDRC) various units: sector councils in the steel, auto parts and electrical/electronics sectors; training trust funds in the construction industry; and sectoral centres of specialization in the community colleges.

OTAB's Sectoral and Workplace Training Council (SWTC) was to provide a new 'single window' on provincial sectoral labour market programming. It would be responsible for encouraging the development of sectoral agreements in a number of ways, including the allocation of funding, supervising the formation of sectoral committees to guide training practices, and ensuring that the design of sectoral initiatives took into account labour adjustment issues and needs. Principles were developed to guide the allocation of funds to sectoral initiatives. These included: equal labour-management partnership; significant financial contribution by industry; promotion of under-represented groups; and support for higher skill training. But the election of the Harris government in June 1995 and the subsequent closure of OTAB in April 1996 appear to have effectively ended Ontario's experiment with sectoral initiatives.

Bradford characterizes the recent history of sectoral initiatives in Ontario as 'one of considerable up-front intellectual investment to conceptualize them within a coherent high value-added provincial policy framework, followed by modest implementation success in industrial policy and little progress in labour market policy.' He argues that OTAB's difficulties can be traced to broader problems related to establishing corporatist arrangements in Ontario due to the absence of the structural, cultural, and organizational pre-conditions for corporatism. In addition, the innovative features of OTAB made success even more difficult to achieve. Its multipartite structure gave voice to a range of actors with little or no history of working together.

Sector Councils and Joint Governance

The emergence of sector councils is having an impact on the way business and labour relate at the workplace level. In this section, the dynamics of joint governance are explored and the experience of several of the pioneering sector councils with joint governance is examined.

The Dynamics of Joint Governance: Historical and Institutional
Implications for Sector Councils

Sector councils are not the first institutional framework for business-labour cooperation that has emerged in North America and many of the business-labour dynamics found in sector councils have been at play in other contexts. Joel Cutcher-Gershenfeld provides this historical and institutional context by looking at different initiatives for business-labour cooperation that have developed in the United States and at the issues surrounding this organizational form.

He begins by noting that the history of labour-management initiatives during the past century has revealed an enduring tension between the importance of joint activity and pressures arising out of separate labour or management issues. He identifies a number of labour-management initiatives in the United States that have certain similarities with Canadian sector councils. These include: plant or firm level labour-management committees in the railway, textile, garment, steel, and west coast longshoring industries; area labour-management committees (ALMC); and quality of working life, socio-technical systems and quality initiatives.

He considers the ALMCs in particular a precursor to sector councils. These bodies bring together business and union representatives on a geographical basis to deal with issues of interest to both parties. The effectiveness of ALMCs has depended critically on funding. Unfortunately, the committees are currently considerably underfunded and hence have limited capabilities. The role of non-unionized firms in the ALMCs has posed a serious dilemma in recent years. Exclusion of this group reduces relevance and legitimacy while inclusion unbalances the traditional bipartite governance process. Sector councils also must deal with these issues of funding, focus, and treatment of non-union employers.

Sector councils represent a transfer of decision-making authority from individual stakeholders to the group. Placing issues under joint governance brings both opportunities and costs. Cutcher-Gershenfeld identifies four dynamics at play in these circumstances: the complexities of joint decision-making when participants have different perspectives on decision-making; the management of internal union and employer pressures; the coordination of issues across levels; and institutional security.

The key characteristic of business decision-making is its hierarchical nature, while union decision-making is much more political. Without mutual respect and understanding, the combination of these two backgrounds can lead to impasse. Cutcher-Gershenfeld argues that a consensus decision process offers the best way to overcome these differences in decision-making cultures.

Many sector councils administer training programs and maintain committees at the plant level, resulting in the classic dilemma of the optimal degree of centralization. Greater central control can increase consistency and coordination; greater decentralization can foster innovation and adaptation to distinctive local circumstances. A dynamic balance between these two forces is needed.

Cutcher-Gershenfeld concludes by noting that ultimately, the primary criterion by which to judge sector councils is whether they produce accomplishments that would not otherwise happen or at least be more costly to achieve. An example would be if sectoral retraining programs resulted in a greater reduction in the length of unemployment for displaced workers compared to government training programs.

Although it is obviously hard to predict the future of sector councils, Cutcher-Gershenfeld concludes on a positive note. He believes sector councils will work from an evolving agenda, appropriately grounded in the interests of labour, management, and government. He sees sector councils developing skills in coordinating initiatives with government agencies and at the plant level. He believes sector council leaders will learn from experience and will protect the councils from unfavourable political winds. Finally, he sees sector councils adding value by creating mutual gains and at the same time constructively surfacing and addressing points of conflict.

Sector Councils as Models of Shared Governance

In the second paper in this section, Carol Joyce Haddad examines the experience of shared governance in training and adjustment in three key sector councils: the Canadian Steel Trade and Employment Congress (CSTEC), the Sectoral Skills Council (SSC), and the Automotive Parts Sectoral Training Council (APSTC). Her research findings are based on thirty-one interviews she conducted with key sector council officials in 1994. The study addresses three questions. How do business and labour members reconcile their different perspectives to reach agreement on council objectives and priorities? How do council members resolve disagreements and reach consensus? Finally, does the bipartite nature of councils contribute to their effectiveness in improving training design and delivery?

Haddad found that the perceived goal consensus between labour and management was quite high, ranging from 57 per cent for CSTEC to 88 per cent for the APSTC. In addition, labour-management differences had more to do with perceptions of rank order than actual goal divergence. The degree of intra-union goal consensus was found to be much higher than that of management.

Despite the high level of goal consensus, conflict exists. Philosophical differences generally lie behind disputes. For example, in CSTEC, disagreements have arisen over NAFTA, the role of labour in the design of training programs and course eligibility for accreditation, and the content of curriculum and the criteria for funding of 'upside' training proposals. Disputes in the SSC have centred on the rate of training fund contribution, employee contributions to the fund, apprenticeship, and the purpose of job training. Within the APSTC, the most contentious issues have been curriculum content, the use of peer trainers, and the hiring and roles of co-managing directors.

Haddad's interviews found that sector councils had developed mechanisms to make bipartite governance function. In particular, equal representation at all levels of decision-making facilitated the development of consensus decisions. In addition, strategic posturing and government funding give unions an independent source of leverage despite their inability to match company contributions to training funds. The two sides thus come from relatively equal positions of strength, which fosters agreement through compromise.

An innovative feature of sector training councils is the focus on training program design as well as delivery. Haddad points out that a major reason for the innovativeness and cost-effectiveness of sectoral council training in CSTEC and SSC is the decentralized system of training program administration through joint workplace training committees. Sector councils such as CSTEC also have developed innovative adjustment programs, including peer counselling, small business start-up, training referral, and job search/placement assistance, carried out by local adjustment committees and supported by teams called Helping Employees Adjust Together (HEAT).

Haddad concludes that sector councils have advanced the practice of joint governance in a number of ways. The bipartite structures by definition assure a co-deterministic approach to all issues. A relative equitable balance of power between business and labour, assured in part through government support to unions, fosters cooperation. Union participation in sector councils improves the design and administration of training and adjustment programs and expands unions' influence into areas traditionally the purview of management.

Joint Governance at CSTEC

In the final paper in this section, Anil Verma, Kai Lamertz, and Peter Warrian address the issue of whether CSTEC represents 'old-fashioned' labour-management cooperation or an innovation in joint governance.

They see joint governance as a flexible forum for decision-making that augments labour-management relations while operating within the traditional collective bargaining framework. According to Verma et al., the characteristics of joint governance include: shared executive decision-making by business and labour; formalization of the process through codification in the collective agreement; the voluntary nature of the agreement; continued interaction between labour and management and the use of procedural rules. They argue that the sharing of power in a joint governance situation introduces equalitarian and communal elements into the traditional hierarchical and adversarial relations between the two parties, creating new roles for decision-makers. This has important implications for the social structure of organizations.

Verma et al. put forward seven propositions concerning joint governance that they test with the CSTEC experience. They are: joint governance decision makers will experience less inter-group conflict and realize a significant proportion of their overlapping interests without jeopardizing independence; workplace decision-making in joint governance relations is characterized by a mixture of bargaining and joint problem solving; labour decision makers will learn new administrative skills while management decision makers will acquire more political competencies; trust will develop between joint governance decision makers through continual interaction and balanced social relations; shared beliefs and norms about decision-making interaction will develop among joint governance decision makers; social networks of decision makers with other organizational members will be characterized by large size, high reachability, high fluidity, and extensive heterogeneity; and organization members will perceive enhanced procedural justice after the implementation of a joint governance arrangement.

To test these propositions, the authors relied on interviews from seven focus groups of members of CSTEC joint training committees conducted by Ekos Research Associates and interviews with JTC members conducted in three plants by one of the authors. The data supported the view that joint decision-making is characterized by non-competitive relations among decision makers. Other findings included a close relation between the overall quality of relations before and after implementation of joint governance; positive spillovers from JTC roles to other areas, reinforcing the cooperative nature of overall labour-management relations; and important skill transfer and development effects.

Verma et al. conclude that good labour-management relations are a necessary foundation for effective JTC decision-making so that at the point of inception joint governance is an extension of what labour and management were previously doing. But where existing relations are already good, the establishment of joint governance mechanisms enables the parties to develop new roles and learn new skills. The authors argue that voluntary joint governance is intrinsically superior to mandated joint governance, which exists in European work councils. When joint governance is legislated, the parties are compelled to engage in a minimal level of cooperation and do not have the option of abandoning it. With voluntary joint governance, there is no safety net to fall on, agreement is paramount, and the partners try harder to achieve it.

Verma et al. argue that joint governance is a North American innovation which promotes high-quality decisions in a manner similar to the bottom-up system used by Japanese organizations. They also argue that despite the government assistance given CSTEC, government monetary incentives are not a necessary condition for joint governance, as shown by the development of joint governance arrangements in the United States. But government assistance can act as a catalyst and hence generate significant leverage.

Evaluation of Sector Councils

Program evaluations constitute an important component in any analysis of the overall impact of the sector councils. Human Resources Development Canada has conducted evaluations of CSTEC and the Sector Skills Council and is currently conducting long-term evaluations of more recently established sector councils. A series of reports on these councils have been released, as well as an overview report. But evaluating sector councils is extremely difficult because of their multiplicity of objectives and forms and their early stage of development. In our article in this section, we apply a set of generic program evaluation criteria to sector councils and evaluate them as an adjustment mechanism.

We develop a checklist of eight program evaluation criteria in order to separate the issue of criteria or objectives from the evaluation of the effectiveness of programs in meeting those objectives. This highlights the difficult trade-offs inherent in any attempt to meet a wide range of conflicting objectives.

1 / Target efficiency, which we define as the ability of a program to assist persons in the target group without benefits spilling over to persons in non-target groups.

2 / Allocative efficiency refers to the degree to which a program promotes the efficient allocation of resources, which usually means in the direction of, and not against, market forces.

3 / Distributive equity refers to the extent a program distributes disproportionately to those most in need (known as vertical equity or the unequal treatment of unequals) and to the extent a program treats persons in comparable circumstances in a similar manner (known as horizontal equity or equal treatment of equals).

4 / Administrative efficiency refers to the degree to which a program can minimize administrative costs in the delivery of services.

5 / Flexibility refers to the degree programs are adaptable to changing circumstances and can even reverse direction and self-destruct should their needs dissipate.

6 / The involvement of stakeholders, means that programs work better when there is greater commitment of those directly affected.

7 / Political acceptability refers to the extent programs garner wide political support, a factor in success.

8/A final criterion is the extent to which programs give attention to design and implementation detail.

We conclude that sector councils meet many of the program criteria outlined for a successful adjustment strategy and that governments should consider supporting sector councils as an option in the elaboration of labour adjustment strategies.

Sector Councils, Corporatism, and the Industrial Relations System

Can sector councils be considered a form of labour market corporatism? What effects has the innovation of sector councils had on Canada's industrial relations system? In this section, these two questions are addressed.

Sector Councils and the Corporatist Model

In the first paper in this section, Michael Atkinson and Cassandra Pervin ask whether sector councils constitute a form of neo-corporatism. This they define as a policy network, first, where the state recognizes the principle of equality in the representation of partners in the network and the partners agree to respect this equality principle; second, where business and labour organizatons are relatively centralized, enjoy a monopoly in interest representation, and exert a measure of control over their members; and third, where the involvement of social partners in the policy process is characterized by an element of participation, not simply advocacy. Based on case studies of CSTEC, the Sectoral Skills Council, and the APSTC, they find a number of the requirements for corporatism present and conclude that sector councils do represent neo-corporatist structures, if only in embryo.

Atkinson and Pervin then address the issue of whether sector councils represent a viable institutional stucture. While acknowledging the traditional barriers to macro-corporatism in Canada (such as a federal, parliamentary system, and the decentralized organization of business and labour), they argue that meso or sectoral corporatism may be viable under certain conditions – if it is attempted in areas with large potential gains to cooperation not requiring major concessions from either party; if labour and business are not internally divided; if the parties perceive a need for cooperation and this cooperation is not state-imposed; and where there is broad scope for the corporatist contact, which expands the opportunity for participation.

Finally, Atkinson and Pervin look at whether sector councils are desirable and answer in the affirmative. They believe sector councils represent an improvement over bureaucratic solutions to training and can have a positive effect on productivity. They also feel sector councils can reset the political balance by providing an equal representation for historically under-represented groups such as labour and can lead to the replacement of a bargaining mentality with the more socially beneficial one of joint problem-solving, leading to shared belief and understanding.

Role of Sectorial Initiatives in Industrial Relations

Sector councils represent a major innovation in Canada's industrial relations system. In the second paper in this section, Richard Chaykowski analyses the impact of the emergence of sector councils on our system of industrial relations. He points out that although sector councils are macro-level institutional arrangements, they provide a forum for union-management consultation and cooperation and their activities are aimed at the same outcomes that are generated through the conduct of industrial relations at the establishment level. While not directly involved in labour relations per se, as sector councils evolve, their activities increasingly influence and interact with the more established components of the industrial relations system.

Chaykowski finds that the formation of sector councils is not directly linked to the extent of unionization in an industry. Rather, the need is to reconcile the perspectives of unionized and nonunionized workers on the councils. Chaykowski also finds that, not surprisingly, cooperative union-management relations at the firm level foster the development of sector councils. Chaykowski points out that in the United States joint union-management programs in the human resource area have focused on the firm level, where they have been the outcome of collective bargaining. In Canada, comparable programs have been developed at the sectoral level. As an explanation of this difference, Chaykowski points to the much greater level of government support for sectoral initiatives in Canada and to the greater strength of the Canadian union movement.

While developed at the sectoral level, sector council programs are implemented at the establishment level where they interface directly with the established industrial relations system. Chaykowski argues that, from a strategic choice perspective, the participation of unions and employers in sector councils constitutes a major departure from traditional industrial relations activities and decision-making. Sector councils expand industrial relations and human resources strategies of employers and unions beyond a narrow focus on the workplace and collective bargaining at the establishment level towards a broader approach that includes inter-firm and inter-union cooperation. Government support for sector councils also is important as it legitimizes the notion of labour-management partnerships and enlarges the scope of cooperative industrial relations to the industry level.

Notes

1 For discussion of the positive role sectoral initiatives can play in economic restructuring and adjustment, see Ontario Premier's Council (1990), Ontario Training and Adjustment Board (1991), Warrian (1989a), O'Grady (1992), United Steelworkers of America (1991), Pomeroy (1992), Kochan (1992), and Haddad (1995).

2 For a discussion of the government initiatives that contributed to the emergence of sector councils, see Sharpe (1997).

3 The objectives of sector council development, as formulated in the SPI were to:
   1 / establish permanent private sector organizations that will lever long term private sector training investments in strategic human resource planning and development;
   2 / develop a training and learning culture in Canadian industry;
   3 / ensure leadership by the private sector in orienting the education and training system to better meet industry skill needs;
   4 / ensure an improved supply of highly skilled workers needed for growth;
   5 / create national occupational or skill training standards covering key occupations or skills clusters, which contribute to greater mobility of Canadian workers; and
   6 / increase private sector influence on all levels of government, leading to improving government actions and decisions affecting the sector.

   HRDC criteria for support of the operational phase of sector councils included requirements that the council be national in scope; that the sector have completed a human resource study; that the council be directed by employer/employee participants representing the major stakeholders in the sector; and that councils take employment equity principles into consideration in their strategic plans.

   The SPI was targeted to upside adjustment, with no provision for support of ownside adjustment. Upside adjustment activities, which directly improve the skills of employed workers, were considered to have greater potential to contribute to the government's competitiveness agenda. In addition, based on the CSTEC experience, the cost effectiveness of downside adjustment activities was considered problematic.

4 Tourism does not have its own SIC because it has been considered more a type of expenditure than an industry, although it is closely associated with the food and accommodation industry.

References

Canadian Labour Congress. 1992. 'CLC Guidelines on Sectoral Partnerships.' 13 April, draft.

Chaykowski, Richard and Anil Verma, eds. 1992. *Industrial Relations in Canadian Industry*. Toronto: Holt, Rinehart and Winston.

Crookell, H. 1986. Case Study of the Canadian Steel Trade Conference, University of Western Ontario. Mimeo.

Ekos Research Associates Inc. 1991. *Program Evaluation Study of the Canadian Steel Trade and Employment Congress: Final Report (Phase I)*. Prepared for Employment and Immigration Canada.

Fournier, P. 1986. 'Consensus Building in Canada: Case Studies and Prospects,' in Keith Banting, research coordinator, *The State and Economic Interests*. Volume 32 of the Royal Commission on the Economic Union and Development Prospects for Canada (Macdonald Commission). University of Toronto Press.

Gunderson, M. 1986. 'Alternative Mechanisms for Dealing with Permanent Layoffs, Dismissals and Plant Closing,' in C. Riddell, research coordinator. *Adapting to Change: Labour Market Adjustment in Canada*. Research volume 16, Macdonald Commission. University of Toronto Press.

– 1992. 'A Review of Evaluation Criteria Applied to CSTEC.' Appendix E in *Program Evaluation Study of the Canadian Steel Trade and Employment Congress: Final Report (Phase I)*. Ekos Research Associates Inc.

Haddad, Carol. 1995. *Sectoral Training Partnerships in Canada: Building Consensus Through Policy and Practice*. Final report to the Government of Canada, Canadian Studies Faculty Research Award, 17 February.

Human Resources Development Canada. 1996. *Sectoral Activities: Update Report* Spring.

Joint Human Resources Committee of the Canadian Electrical and Electronics Manufacturing Industry. 1989. *Connections for the Future: A Human Resources Strategy for the Canadian Electrical and Electronics Manufacturing Industry*. January.

Kochan, T. 1992. *Transforming Industrial Relations: A Blueprint for Change*. Don Wood Lecture in Industrial Relations, Industrial Relations Centre, Queen's University.

O'Grady, J. 1992. 'Integrating Sustainable Development into Workplace Governance.' Discussion paper prepared for the Environmental Round Table, 20 January.

Ontario Premier's Council 1990. *People and Skills in the New Global Economy*.

Ontario Training and Adjustment Board. 1991. *Skills to Meet the Challenge: A Training Partnership for Ontario*.

Piore, Michael. 1995. *Beyond Individualism*. Cambridge: Harvard University Press.

Pomeroy, F. 1992. 'Introducing Change in the Workplace,' *Business Quarterly* (Winter), pp.127–31.

Porter, M. 1991. *Canada at the Crossroads: The Reality of a New Competitive Environment*. Study prepared for the Business Council on National Issues and the Government of Canada, October.

Sharpe, Andrew. 1992. 'The Role of Business-Labour Sectoral Initiatives in Economic Restructuring,' *Quarterly Labour Market and Productivity Review*, nos. 1–2, Canadian Labour Market and Productivity Centre.

– 1997. *Sector Councils in Canada: Future Challenges*. Research Paper R-97-6E, Applied Research Branch, Human Resources Development Canada. (Ottawa).

United Steelworkers of America. 1992. *Empowering Workers in the Global Economy: A Labour Agenda for the 1990s*. Background and Conference Proceedings, 22–3 October, 1991. Toronto.

Waldie, K. 1986. 'The Evolution of Labour-Government Consultation on Economic Policy,' in Craig Riddell, research coordinator, *Labour-Management Cooperation in Canada*. Volume 15 of the Royal Commission on the Economic Union and Development Prospects for Canada (Macdonald Commission). University of Toronto Press.

Warrian, P. 1989a. 'Trade Union and Labour Market Planning: The Case for Sectoral Regulation.' Paper presented to a seminar on the Future of Social Democracy, University College, 17 March.

– 1989b. 'Industrial Restructuring, Occupational Shifts and Skills: the Steel and Electronic Manufacturing Cases.' Background paper prepared for Study Tier Two, Colleges and the Changing Economy, Vision 2000. Ontario Council of Regents.

PART I
HISTORICAL AND ECONOMIC PERSPECTIVES ON
SECTOR COUNCILS

1

A Historical Perspective on Sector Councils

GARY FLETCHER

In writing about sector councils from a historical perspective I was reminded of a passage I read about historians and history when I was a student many years ago. It was written by Alan Bullock (1959) in an anthology entitled *The Philosophy of History in Our Time*: 'the moment the historian begins to explain, he is bound to make use of general propositions of all kinds – about human behaviour, about the effect of economic factors and the influence of ideas and a hundred other things ... He cannot begin to think or explain events without the help of the preconceptions, the assumptions, the generalization of experience which he brings with him.'

Although I am not a historian, the reader should keep Bullock's thoughts in mind in reading this account of the development of sector councils. I have endeavoured to keep an unbiased view of the activities that led up to sector councils. But I was very involved in the early development of the program and my interpretation of events may differ from others who were not as involved to the same extent.

Although it will become evident in reading this chapter, I will point out now that the sector council program evolved in a rather serendipitous fashion. In developing a solution to a previously identified labour market issue, some analysts within the Labour Market Outlook and Structural Analysis Branch of Employment and Immigration Canada had developed a methodology and process to gather sound and reliable labour market information for occupational forecasting purposes. In employing this methodology and process, however, it was discovered that a number of other labour market issues were being identified within specific industry contexts. Because the identification, framing, and promotion of issues is one of the most important elements of the policy process, the analysts had inadvertently moved from collectors of information to an involvement in policy and program development. The development of an implementation stage through the establishment of collaborative labour-management bodies, completed the process.

From Occupational Forecasting to Sector Studies

The 1960s and 1970s were periods of steady and substantial growth in Canada. From 1961 to 1979 real GDP advanced at an average rate of 5 per cent a year. It is not surprising then that after twenty years of this kind of growth, weaknesses began to appear in the performance of the Canadian labour market. In 1976 the Economic Council of Canada noted in their report, *People and Jobs: A Study of the Canadian Labour Market*, that there was strong and growing possibility of labour shortages in certain occupations. Other labour market concerns being expressed at this time led to the establishment of two government-sponsored task forces. The minister of the Employment and Immigration Commission (EIC) established a Labour Market Development Task Force to study the problems, and a Parliamentary Task Force on Employment Opportunities for the 1980s was also set up.

Each task force published reports, and both were released in late 1981 and early 1982 (see EIC, 1981, and Government of Canada, 1982), ironically at a time when the country plunged into its first serious recession of the postwar period. Public interest began to shift to a growing unemployment problem rather than focus on labour shortages. Nevertheless both reports, as well as the earlier Economic Council report, pointed to a need for more and better labour market information to allow for a more efficient operation of the labour market. The response of the minister of EIC was to establish the Canadian Occupational Projection System (COPS) in 1982. COPS was mandated to generate and provide timely labour market information that would guide the department's training programs and certain aspects of its immigration program. It was also to provide career counselling material to federal employment centres and school guidance counsellors, as well as to private sector companies to help in human resource planning.

One of the first tasks undertaken by COPS was to develop models for making occupational demand projections. The Labour Market Development Task Force had argued that in certain circumstances there is potential for market failure in labour markets. If demand is changing at relatively stable rates, markets should be in balance. There would be appropriate feedback on vacancies, wages, etcetera, and the information would enable timely choices to be made regarding training, migration, and so on. The market would perform. But where dramatic shifts can occur in the demand for labour because of rapid adoption of new technologies, for example, sudden changes can simultaneously create and destroy the demand for certain occupations or for certain skills. Under this scenario it was argued that the market cannot supply the information quickly enough to make efficient choices with respect to training. In other words, with any rapid market change there will be a lag to the response time of training institutions to the changing circumstances and the time it takes to train in some occupations. It was believed that these adjustment lags resulted in substantial economic costs, and therefore potential gains could be obtained from improved projections that could reduce the reaction time.

There were to be two major aspects of COPS. On the demand side, occupational projections were to be made using methods similar to those employed by the US Bureau of Labor Statistics (BLS). There was also some work planned on estimating attrition rates so that some early warning could be given if higher than normal attrition was expected in certain occupations. Therefore, estimates were to be made of future job openings as well as occupational employment growth. But work was also to be undertaken on supply side considerations. It was planned to gather data on enrolments in apprenticeship programs, school enrolments, and numbers graduating from different university and community college programs.

There are some technical problems in using the BLS/COPS type models to forecast occupational demand, and attempts to overcome some of these problems, strangely enough, eventually led to sector councils. Both the BLS and COPS begin by using a macro-model to forecast aggregate economic output. Projected GDP is then disaggregated into its major demand categories, each of which are then further distributed among the various producing industries. An input-output table is then used to distribute the intermediate products and services. The resulting industry output projections are then translated into industry employment demand. An industry-occupational matrix, which provides the occupational structure or composition for each industry, is used to derive occupational employment projections for each industry. Occupational employment across industries are aggregated to obtain employment by occupation within the economy.

Although this is a sophisticated method for making occupational projections, there is also much room for developing forecasting errors. If errors are large, then it is likely better not to do any forecasting at all. Work at the BLS showed that major forecasting errors occurred both in the industry employment forecasts and in the occupational structures of various industries that were being used in the model. It was thought that not being able to account for relatively rapid technological change was a major source of error in both the industry output and employment forecasts, and it could also result in significant shifts in the occupational structure of various industries. These changes were difficult to anticipate and incorporate into the model in a timely way. Adoptions of new technologies could result in different requirements in an industry – for example, more plastics and less steel in automotive production. If circumstances could be anticipated, then changes could be made to the coefficients in the input-output matrix in order to incorporate their impacts on industry output and employment projections. In 1983 Leontief and Duchin published a paper on this problem and their methodology was used to make adjustments to the I-O coefficients. But the problem with changing occupational composition within different industries still remained.

The occupational structure used in the COPS model is derived from the five-year census. By the time these results are received, which is normally two years after the census has been taken, the industry-occupational coefficients are already out of date for industries which are undergoing rapid change. Major forecasting errors could arise from using an inappropriate occupational structure, especially if it continued to change over the next five to ten years, which was the projection period used by COPS. It was therefore believed that more credible forecasts could be developed by undertaking a program of industry studies. Industries undergoing rapid change would be identified and studies would be conducted to determine impacts of the changes. It was intended to determine the kind of technologies being adopted, the rate of adoption, the impact on the occupational composition of the industry, and the impact on skills. It was believed, perhaps naïvely, that such information could then be incorporated into the model and better forecasts would be obtained.

Five industry studies had been conducted for the Labour Market Development Task Force, with mixed results. In reviewing these studies, it appeared that there were two areas where changes could be made that would give an improved product. First, if the studies were to be successful industry participation would be needed to obtain the information required. Second, the studies should be conducted using a coherent study framework or structure.

We at EIC wanted to employ an approach that would provide us with information on the current occupational composition of an industry, but also one that would give some insight as to how production techniques were changing and how these changes affected the occupational structure. We also needed to know how skills were being impacted by the adoption of new technologies. Surveys had not worked in the past. Statistics Canada had tried establishment surveys to obtain data on occupational structure that would be more current than census data, but concluded that the survey data collected were too unreliable for publication. In any case, a survey would not give us the qualitative kind of information we needed in order to make some judgments on how and why occupational structures would be changing in the future, or how skills were changing.

It was at this time that Michael Porter had recently completed his work on corporate strategy, and Ira Magaziner and Robert Reich's 1982 book, *Minding America's Business*, was published. It was thought that an approach similar to that outlined in these works could be used to provide some insight and understanding of the dynamics of change within an industry, along with its implications for employment, occupational structure, and skills.

There are some definite advantages in using a strategic management framework for human resource studies at an industry level. It allows the study participants to develop a good understanding of the current business environment and shows how that environment is changing, and how industry is reacting to these changes. It is an approach that helps one understand the dynamics of the industry – the manner in which businesses combine their resources, the outcomes of particular configurations of work, or the uses of strategic alliances with customers or suppliers. These are all factors that affect the occupational structure and the skills needed by the workforce. The process becomes an exploration of the dynamics of workplace change, and when labour and management are involved in the study, both views of workplace developments are obtained. One can begin to distinguish between potential and actual developments and identify emerging trends, all of which were important.

There are also certain disadvantages, and as the studies proceeded these became the focus of some criticism. The information obtained from these studies was often impressionistic. Although it was obtained directly from plant visits, it was judged by some as being too qualitative, too 'soft,' too vague, imprecise, and the work was often dismissed because of its 'subjectivity.'

Problems arise because the approach is analyst-centred. Although the analyst begins to discover the facts and then develops tentative generalizations which are tested throughout the course of the study, at some point 'informed judgments' are made. But in using a strategic management framework, the analyst begins to develop an understanding of 'how things work and why.' The chain between the business environment, business strategies, and business performance can be logically analysed. The approach may have appeared to lack the methodological rigour of scientific research, but it is not haphazard and it is not careless. As for lack of precision, I believe it was John Maynard Keynes who said that 'It is better to be approximately right, than precisely wrong.'

From Sector Studies to Sector Councils

The human resource studies of particular industries were called sector studies. Magaziner and Reich had pointed out that 'one of the mistakes often made by corporate officials, economists and government policymakers is to confuse the definition of "businesses and industries".' They argued that there is a need to understand the competitive process before describing remedies. Businesses in the same industry, will have different markets, technologies, production methods, cost structures, and human resource requirements. Various business strategies and impacts on human resources will differ, as will occupational structures, skill requirements, and human resource problems. For these reasons it seemed appropriate to undertake human resource studies at this 'business' level.

Instead of using the term business studies, however, we used the term sector, defining sectors as a group of companies or workers sharing some common elements, which results in their having common human resource concerns. It was also believed that defining a sector in this way would make it easier to bring industry participants together to work on a problem than if we focused on more broadly defined industries where participants may not have a common problem. In some cases, however, the business connotation of the term sector became more of an ideal to aim for rather than an actuality in practice.

Our first three studies were initiated in 1982 and 1983 and were not very successful. In some cases analysts had problems in applying the strategic management framework, and in all cases we had great difficulty in trying to incorporate the information on occupational structure into the COPS model. Companies maintained their files in the form of 'job titles' which in many cases differed considerably from the Canadian Classification Dictionary of Occupations (CCDO) or the occupational titles and codes used by COPS. It took a monumental effort on the part of the sector studies analysts and the private sector participants to translate job titles into the CCDO codes and vice versa. It was finally concluded that this process, which in some cases was not possible at all, was so error prone that the effort was abandoned. But by that time sector studies had taken on a different focus.

Although we were not coming up with the results we had hoped for, the studies were certainly providing information that gave us an enhanced understanding of the impacts of particular technologies on employment and skills, and we felt that it would be worthwhile to continue to work on overcoming the difficulties encountered in the first three studies. The next few studies undertaken were a great improvement not only in terms of methodology but also in process. We had set up steering committees for the earlier studies but now both senior levels of labour and management were actually at the table. The consultants who were conducting the studies worked closely with the steering committee and consensus began to be reached on a number of human resource issues that had been identified through the study process. But it ended there. A considerable amount of labour market information had been generated and everyone had developed a better understanding of the issues, but we had no mechanism or mandate to keep the group together to work out and implement solutions to the problems that had been identified. Industry was left on its own to solve its problems.

This is where another strand to the story enters. Within EIC there was a program that had existed since 1963 called the Industrial Adjustment Service (IAS). The IAS was used to bring labour and management together to help workers find employment after major layoffs or plant closures. It had recently been used to fund some labour adjustment studies for the steel industry and then assisted in the establishment of a joint labour-management body called the Canadian Steel Trade and Employment Congress. This organization began to develop programs to help unemployed steel workers find employment. Although the IAS was being used in downside adjustment situations, there was nothing in the program specifications that prevented it from being used in upside adjustment situations. The Sector Studies Directorate used the IAS program for the first time in 1988 to assist in the establishment of the Joint Human Resources Committee of the Electrical and Electronic Manufacturing Industries.

A sector study of the electrical and electronic manufacturing industries had identified the human resource issues, consensus had been reached, and there was commitment and resolve on the part of the steering committee members to continue on and work towards solving the human resource development problems within the industry. A conference was held to bring in many more industry representatives, both labour and management, to discuss the study's findings and recommendations and sufficient interest was engendered for senior management and labour to attempt to work together to develop solutions and implementation plans. The EIC provided resources and staff to support a joint human resources committee. It was this committee which would emerge in 1990 as the Sectoral Skills Council.

With the setting up of the Joint Human Resources Committee in the electrical and electronic manufacturing industry the focus of sector studies began to shift. This was especially so in the study of the auto repair and service sector. In this case the Sector Studies Division within EIC had been approached by the Motor Vehicle Manufacturing Association (MVMA) to determine if they would be interested in working with industry representatives in trying to sort out the problems in the auto repair and service sector. The MVMA had been a major participant of an earlier automotive study and thought that the process could be used to advantage to bring participants together, identify issues, and obtain consensus. A study was completed and led to the establishment of another sector council, the Canadian Automotive Repair and Services Council, or CARS.

The emphasis of sector studies now became less of an occupational projection exercise (this was still done), and more of a problem-solving process which included a collaborative effort from the different parties that had a stake in the issues. Problems are often ill-defined, and different perspectives often lead to adversarial relationships. The sector study allowed for a better appreciation of the complexity of a problem and a joint search for information, understanding, and consensus. Establishing a sector council allowed for the development of mutually agreed upon solutions and implementation plans.

Developments in the 1990s

It has been said that timing is everything for successful policy development, and that advice is only effective when circumstances are such that new policies are needed. The perceived lack of training of potential employees in the private sector was becoming more of an issue in the late 1980s. The few sector councils that had been set up showed good potential for increasing training programs. They were being looked upon as an instrument that was promoting a 'training culture' in Canada. The timing was right.

The Labour Force Development Strategy, which was announced in 1989, recognized government-private sector cooperation as one means to increase the level of commitment of the private sector to training. Financial support was provided for conducting more sector studies, and for setting up sector councils. Funding was also provided for the development of occupational standards and for co-funding new training programs. In December 1992 the program was expanded once more through the Sectoral Partnership Initiative. With this program it appeared that sector councils were being viewed not only to ways to promote more training but also as vehicles to develop a better skilled workforce to encourage economic opportunity. In other words, councils and what they were doing could also be used to enhance the competitiveness of Canadian industries.

Ambitious goals were set and fifty-five sectors were to be covered over the next five years. Since then, of course, government cutbacks have resulted in a less ambitious program. In my view this is probably a good thing. The process of creating partnerships is not an easy one; indeed, with a large number of stakeholders, it can be difficult and time-consuming. Once formed cooperation can be very fragile and the participants must keep working at it. The success of the councils will always reside in the commitment, hard work, and leadership of the participants and the executive directors of the councils. This was especially the case with the early councils which were breaking new ground and had few precedents to guide them.

At some point, however, participants must see a payoff. Some industries that were approached decided not to participate; others requested a study but decided not to form a council after the study was completed. But these cases are in the minority. Twenty councils have been established to date and there are other sectors that, having gone through the study process, are now developing their mandate, working out a council structure, and preparing a business plan and budget. Five councils have also been established since the program was announced in 1989 without going through the sector study process sponsored by Human Resources Development Canada. These have been in sectors where stakeholders had a history of working together and had conducted their own studies of their industries.

It is interesting to speculate as to how sector councils will evolve in the future. I believe there is a recognition that labour-management collaboration on human resource issues is useful, and that councils are looked upon as one way of promoting more harmonious labour-management relations. This in turn often leads to greater productivity in a sector. There is often conflict in daily business life resulting in substantial financial and economic transaction costs to the firm. Developing better labour-management relations and better internal communications help reduce these costs, and this can be very important to the competitive advantage of companies. Industries also have different problems, or in some cases the same problems that should be tackled in different ways or employ different implementation approaches. Councils are well situated to undertake activities that fit their own industry and there may be substantial gains from such a flexible approach compared to a 'one-size-fits-all' approach.

As sector councils have become established, government has seen them in additional roles. For example, they can be used as a means of providing private sector leadership in the development and delivery of other government priorities. The youth internship program is an example. This can be a very valuable role for those councils well enough established to be able to participate. This also raises the question as to whether the idea of councils can be extended. In the same way that sector councils are tackling human resource issues, a council's mandate could be broadened to tackle other issues. The sector study–sector council model provides for a business-government collaboration in which the efficiency of the market is combined with the strategic role of government in providing the environment and infrastructure for growth. The development of the sector study joint process, along with the establishment of collaborative bodies, may be the approach to industrial policy that is needed in today's competitive world. As long as there is an incentive for parties to work together, many good things can be done. This is not to say that sector councils can be used to solve all of our problems, but there are certainly areas where they can make a major contribution.

The government itself must determine how sector councils fit into its overall economic policy framework. At present there appears to be a jumble of sector-based initiatives at both federal and provincial government departments. This raises a question as to how all these initiatives fit together to form an effective whole, or whether they fit together at all? In today's business climate, there is a need for better harmonization and coordination of federal sectoral programs as well as improved federal-provincial harmonization. Sector councils could have an important role to play in this area.

References

Bullock, Alan. 1959. 'The Historian's Purpose: History and Metahistory,' in Hans Meyerhoff, ed., *The Philosophy of History in Our Time*. Anchor Books.

Economic Council of Canada. 1976. *People and Jobs: A Study of the Canadian Labour Market*. Ottawa.

Employment and Immigration Canada. 1981. *Labour Market Development in the 1980s*. Report of the Task Force on Labour Market Development. Ottawa, July.

Government of Canada. 1981. *Work for Tomorrow – Employment Opportunities for the 80s*. Report of the Task Force on Employment Opportunities for the 80's. Ottawa.

Leontief, Wassily, and Faye Duchin. 1983. 'The Impacts of Automation on Employment, 1963–2000,' Institute for Economic Analysis. New York. Mimeo.

Magaziner, Ira C., and Robert B. Reich. 1982. *Minding America's Business*. New York: Harcourt Brace Jovanovich.

Porter, Michael. 1980. *Competitive Strategy*. New York: Free Press.

2

The Development of Sector Councils in Canada: An Economic Perspective

DOUGLAS A. SMITH

This chapter provides an economic perspective on the development of Canadian sector councils. Sector councils in Canada contain elements of uniqueness, although elements of the approach are either being used in other jurisdictions or were used at an earlier time, both in the United States and Canada. Joint committees, in particular, have been used in a variety of sectoral contexts in the North American industrial relations system.

The current Canadian initiatives have their roots in the work of the Task Force on Labour Market Development in 1981. However, support for the concept can also be found in the report of the Task Force on Employment Opportunities the same year, and in the Economic Council's publication, *In Short Supply*, in 1982. All of these reports pointed out the need for more training and more labour market information. The Economic Council devoted the most attention to the failure of market forces alone to provide adequate training and labour market information.

The underlying public policy was seen initially as purely informational. The intent in the early 1980s was to expand Canada's labour market information system within an entirely quantitative framework. The existing Canadian Occupational Projection System (COPS) was the intended vehicle for establishing an integrated system of demand and supply projections by sector. The real origins of what later became the Sectoral Partnership Initiative (SPI) can be found in early attempts to use industry-based data to fine-tune the COPS estimates.

The process of linking COPS and information from industry sectors did not proceed smoothly. The COPS data were occupationally disaggregated, but firms and their sectoral organizations generally did not maintain their statistics in comparable formats. Firms maintain data on employment levels at all of their locations but not in terms of the standard occupational categories used by Statistics Canada and in COPS. It soon became clear that firms approached the collection of data differently to government, and that their overall information on labour market issues was incomplete. The key thrust of the sector studies process emerged as a response to this problem.

Sector studies and then sector councils emerged as a method to assist firms in integrating their overall corporate planning with their human resource planning. Kochan, Katz, and McKersie (1986) describe related developments at the level of the firm rather than the sector. One of the issues raised in this chapter is the question of the appropriate level for some of these initiatives. Which types of issues are best handled sectorally and which types are best viewed as firm-based? When are sector councils necessary to spur initiatives by member firms? If these activities make firms more competitive and profitable, why were they not developed sooner by firms themselves?

Against this background, this chapter assesses the sector council experience in terms of the economic rationale for sector councils, previous Canadian experience, including the Industrial Adjustment Service, and related experience in the United States. The concluding section relates a number of the ideas and hypotheses that are raised to the experience of the sector studies process and of the activities of the sector councils.

The Economic Rationale for Sectoral Initiatives

Overview

There are a number of possible approaches to the assessment of the economic rationale for the development of sectoral initiatives. The focus here is on the rationale for public sector promotion of these efforts and on the forces that might lead the parties to develop joint sectoral initiatives in the absence of government support. Barriers to purely private sector initiatives are also reviewed in relation to the rationale for public support.

One limitation of any general treatment of sector councils is their diversity. Sector councils have been engaged in a wide range of activities, which include the following:

- carrying out sectoral assessments of training needs
- establishing a system to accredit training institutions used by the sector
- developing standards for training
- developing curriculum or adapting it to meet sectoral needs better
- testing of worker competencies
- sharing of training information among firms in the sector
- developing occupational standards

- evaluating the effectiveness of training efforts for workers in the sector
- providing information to potential new workers for the sector on employment opportunities
- developing entry standards for admission to apprenticeship and promoting the interprovincial portability of apprenticeship skills
- promoting training for supervisors in addition to producing training material for production workers.

This list does not include all of the activities of sector councils; it is selective in terms of the training and labour market information impacts that are the focus of this chapter.

Private Sector Incentives

Sector councils can be seen as association-like organizations for which firms and their workers have a latent demand. If firms and workers can potentially benefit from sector councils, why have they taken so long to develop and why have they required government support, at least at the outset? What are the advantages of sector-wide initiatives compared with related initiatives by individual firms and their workers? How do sector-wide initiatives relate to cross-sectoral initiatives which have characterized the way that many firms have dealt with related issues such as total quality management? Firms have shown their willingness to pay for services of this kind through industry association dues and through payments to belong to cross-industry organizations such as the Conference Board of Canada.

Continuing with the association analogy, there will be issues of common interest that are best handled on a multi-firm or sectoral basis. Purely private associations are a method of dealing with benefits that can be produced most effectively on a collective basis for a number of firms. This will be an issue of economies of scale but, as in the case of many associations, there will be important free-rider problems. The existence of such problems may be the explanation for why apparently profitable activities can be carried out on a sectoral basis only with support from government. Association activities, obviously, are carried out in a wide range of areas of common interest, but if free riding is important, these activities will be under-provided relative to the optimum.

The Role of Government

Overview

The standard economic efficiency rationale for government programs of this kind relates to externalities that lead private markets to misallocate resources relative to the social optimum. In the case of sector councils, this chapter investigates the efficiency rationale primarily in terms of training issues and labour market information. The training question builds on the work of Becker (1965), Gunderson (1974), and Davies (1986). The information issue is more straightforward. Information as a commodity, in the labour market and elsewhere, has important problems of appropriability that generally imply that there may be scope for government intervention to promote efficiency in its provision.

These externality-related issues provide the rationale for a wide range of government activities in the labour market extending well beyond sector councils. The related issues that will be pursued here are:

- *The innovation or R&D analogy.* Successful labour market innovations can produce social benefits in excess of the social costs of the resources required to generate them. This is, in fact, another example of the appropriability problem. Elements of this issue have already been raised by Adams (1986) and Riddell (1986). Gherson (1992), in fact, cites the Canadian Automotive and Service Council (CARS) as an example of a workplace innovation that initiated the development of a standards-based federal-provincial training system.
- *The competitiveness rationale.* This rationale is associated with the work of Michael Porter (1991). The competitiveness rationale cannot always be related easily to the standard microeconomic efficiency issues described above. Porter's work focuses on the four primary factors affecting competitive advantage: demand conditions; related and supporting industries; firm strategy and rivalry; and factor conditions. Factor conditions relate directly to the labour market and from there to sectoral initiatives. It is likely that most sectoral participants would identify competitiveness as the dominant rationale for the core elements of sector councils.
- *The income distribution or equity rationale.* Governments pursue a wide range of activities for reasons that extend beyond allocative efficiency. Recent research by Harris (1993) and others suggests that with continuing globalization, there may be downward pressure on the wages of the least-skilled members of the Canadian labour force. To the extent that sector initiatives can offset such developments, there may also be an equity rationale in addition to the efficiency rationale for these activities.

In the case of the activities of sector councils, markets may fail to provide the best outcome, relative to the ideal, in a number of areas. This paper focuses on the economic rationale for these activities, particularly with regard to the following:

- Provision of labour market information that is potentially of value to many firms. The public good aspect of information means that individual firms will have insufficient incentive to produce such information even if the benefits exceed the costs of production for the sector as a whole.
- Analysis of apprenticeship and related standards that affect all firms in the sector. Although there are private sector standards organizations, this is an area in which the government is frequently involved.
- Innovations in labour-management relations. This is a standard R&D externality in which non-innovating firms attempt to free-ride on the work of innovators.
- The potential externality associated with training. This appears to be the central rationale issue. Sector councils clearly undertake many activities that go beyond training and have rationales unrelated to training. However, they would not have attracted the attention or the resources that they have if training concerns were not paramount.

The following subsections deal with each of these rationale issues.

Innovation and Information

Information as a commodity is likely to be under-provided relative to the theoretical optimum, as Arrow (1962) and others have argued. The literature on innovations, including the work of Nordhaus (1969), also suggests potential problems of markets failing to achieve the social optimum. In the case of both information issues and innovation, the literature on market failure suggests that, in such cases, there may be a potential for public sector intervention to promote improvements in economic welfare.

Note that the literature on under-provision implies that there is a potential gain in economic efficiency. The actual result will depend on how effectively the public sector is able to deal with the issue that has led markets to fail. The rationale for government intervention lies in market failure, but it is an open question as to whether government is able to improve on the private optimum. The market failure that prompts government action can deal either with the production of knowledge or its diffusion. This section considers these related issues in the context of the activities of sector councils.

Research activities are intended to produce knowledge or information. In the case of industrial R&D labs, that knowledge can produce new products or processes. However, innovations can extend beyond the production level to include the process of production and how it is organized or operated. Such innovations are referred to as workplace innovations and many sector councils support activities that may generate useful workplace innovations.

In a market economy, firms will fund activities to generate workplace innovations only when the return from doing so is competitive with other investments. That is, they will invest in such activities only up to the point at which the marginal private benefits equal the marginal private costs. Some research on improved workplace practices may be profitable if all users who benefit can be made to pay but will be unattractive if these users cannot be made to cover their share of the development costs.

It is also the case that society has an interest in the widespread diffusion of new knowledge about effective workplace practices. Unlike the case of private goods, the use of knowledge by one firm does not reduce the amount available for other users. From a social perspective, the marginal cost of using knowledge that is already produced is zero. This creates an obvious dilemma for private production because development costs can never be recouped. This provides a rationale for public support of activities to disseminate information on innovative workplace practices.

Comparable issues of the rationale for government support are also faced in the area of R&D. The federal government and some provinces provide a variety of support programs, including both direct grants and tax credits, for industrial R&D. In spite of intellectual property laws, the benefits of R&D appear to spill over to non-performers. These spillovers represent the appropriability problem and are widely recognized as the main source of the economic rationale for government intervention.

In the case of workplace innovations, spillovers may be even more important than in the case of industrial R&D. Patents, copyright, or protection through the use of trade secrecy laws may work imperfectly in the area of industrial R&D, but these forms of protection are used on a widespread basis. Workplace innovations, on the other hand, appear more difficult to protect. This implies that imitation of successful innovations is more likely so that the government support rationale, which depends on the magnitude of the spillovers, is stronger.

Training

The major federal government commitment to sector councils has been through the 1992 budget allocation to the five-year Sectoral Partnership Initiative. This funding has been reduced since the initial announcement but continues to assist sector initiatives to develop human resource management efforts in the private sector. One of the difficulties in trying to pin down the activities of sector councils is that human resource development activities can take different forms in different sectors. The interpretation of this chapter is that sector councils were intended to play a central role in developing a greater training capacity in

Canada. As a result, the long-run success of the councils as a group will be judged in terms of the benefits that are ultimately determined to flow from the incremental training in both quantity and quality dimensions that can be attributed to them. To the extent that sector councils are involved in the development of agreements to accredit or certify private training, to establish standards, or to develop components of a curriculum, this can have impacts on both the quantity and the quality of the training that is provided.

The recently reported evidence of Bassi (1994) on private sector training in the United States is directly related to the theoretical rationale for sector councils developed in this section. The focus of the Bassi study is on education programs within firms. This is instructive because these programs typically provide the most general forms of training, the most portable, and the ones that are most likely to be under-provided through the market. Bassi determines that within her sample of seventy-two firms:

- Most of the training programs of the firms within this sample were relatively new.
- There is no simple pattern that explains why different firms develop different kinds of educational initiatives.
- None of the firms in the sample had developed quantitative measures of training impacts. Associated studies showed that managers were able to identify impacts in terms of the ability to use new technology, product quality, and worker communication ability. The area of measuring returns remains somewhat of a puzzle since we have evidence that many firms are devoting more resources to training and development without requiring quantitative assessments.
- From the point of view of sector councils, the most interesting result is that firms considered the most important public sector policy for promoting private sector training was the provision of information on the design of training programs.

The primary barrier to training that was identified by Bassi related to the high fixed costs of developing the content and methods of instruction for training programs. She argues that the public goods properties of the front-end components of training programs mean that they will be under-provided without public support, presumably because they are easily imitated and difficult to protect through copyright. Responding firms identified employer networks as the best vehicle to share and spread fixed costs in the development of these front-end components of training.

The general framework for assessing labour market training externalities is provided by Gunderson (1974) and has been extended by Davies (1986). The starting point for these models of training is the work of Becker (1964) who developed and formalized the distinction between general and specific training. In the absence of a variety of market imperfections, market forces alone should deal with training activities optimally. General training, which appears most problematic for markets, can be provided optimally through wage adjustments in which workers finance portable training. This removes the so-called poaching externality that characterizes much of the popular discussion in this area. Specific training is then paid for either by the firm or through different sharing arrangements between firms and workers that generate incentive effects that have been widely analysed in the literature.

There are many real-world problems that may influence the provision of training through private markets. Imperfections in both labour and product markets are always a potential issue and likely an important one in this case. The most important imperfections are likely accounted for by problems with capital markets. In the simplest Becker model, workers pay for training that is portable but should be able to borrow against future incomes to do so. Capital market barriers can be an important impediment in this regard.

Building on the work of Boskin (1975), Davies (1986) also pursues the issues of distortions in the amount of training provided through markets that may be related to capital markets and to the tax system. Specifically, progressive income taxes reduce the returns to training and inconsistent tax treatment of physical and human capital may bias investment between the two. The tax system may also bias the mix of general and specific training provided by firms. This results from the firm's ability to deduct the costs of providing specific training as a business expense, whereas there is no comparable tax incentive to provide general training which is financed through reduced output and lower wages while training.

Gunderson and Thirsk (1994) also review the potential biases of the tax system against human capital. They argue that there are potential gains from ensuring that investments in human capital are taxed on the same footing as investments in physical capital. Some of the externality arguments raised here may, in fact, argue in favour of more favourable tax treatment for human than for physical capital.

Davies (1986) also discusses the transfer externality associated with the existence of a tax-supported system of unemployment insurance. Individuals invest in training based on expected private gains. However, if better-trained individuals also experience lower rates of unemployment, taxpayers will gain. Davies suggests that public support for training can be viewed as adding taxpayer demands to those of trainees.

Globalization and Competitiveness

The focus of sector councils on training is a reflection of the important structural changes in the world economy that continue to influence developments in the Canadian labour market. Harris (1993) and other economists have noted that globalization reflects continuing world-wide increases in the share of exports in GDP. Firms invest in production facilities around the world and will obtain different products or components from the most cost-effective locations. The result, in Canada, has been a reduction in opportunities and a lower wages for workers in the less-skilled categories.

Documenting the labour market effects of globalization requires data that are often difficult to acquire, but some US figures are relevant here. Murphy and Welch (1992) show large recent earnings gains for college graduates relative to high-school graduates, but the more detailed analysis of Katz and Murphy (1992) may be more relevant in terms of training implications. These authors show that earnings inequality has increased significantly *within* educational levels since 1970.

This increased inequality of earnings within education categories is partly explained by different firm and industry training approaches to globalization. As described by Harris (1993), the reaction of some firms to increased competitive pressures is to economize by contracting out and to lay off their least-skilled workers. In other cases, however, the reaction has been for firms to adopt new technologies and to train their workers to use them. Bartel and Lichtenberg (1987) document the importance of trained workers for the successful transfer of new technologies. More recently, Bartel (1995) provides firm-level evidence linking training, wage growth, and worker performance on the job. In such cases, sector councils that promote such initiatives may be the source of both better and more jobs in Canada than would exist without training.

Equity Issues

Governments are elected to provide programs desired by voters and there is a case to be made that developing mechanisms to provide greater training opportunities for Canadians is such a priority. The rationale could be on market failure grounds alone, but equity or income distribution issues may also be important. Gunderson (1974) discusses the training externality in the context of merit goods, which can include an income distribution concern. In the context of changes that are occurring in low-skill labour markets, training efforts, depending on how they are targeted, may have an income distribution rationale. This appears to be a difficult issue to disentangle empirically in the case of sector councils.

How Unique Is the Canadian Sector Council Experience?

Historical Antecedents

There is an extensive North American historical background that points in the direction of the sector council approach to workplace problems. Some related historical work is described in Shultz and Weber (1966) and in Kruger (1968), and for even earlier time periods in Jacoby (1983). The Basic Steel Human Relations Research Committee (HRC) which operated in the United States in the 1950s and 1960s is probably the best example of a joint labour-management sectoral initiative. Some elements of the Canadian Steel Trade and Employment Congress (CSTEC) bear a direct relationship to the HRC. Other sector approaches were also developed in the 1960s in the meat-packing, automobile assembly, and longshoring industries.

Many of the structural changes that have reshaped the steel industry in the United States began in the 1950s. At that time, the US Steel Company and the three other leading firms accounted for roughly 60 per cent of domestic production. Imports were beginning to penetrate the market, although mini-mills and subsequent industry changes had not yet emerged. Substitutes for steel were developed in a number of applications and employment levels started to decline. A lengthy strike in 1959 contributed to the decision to initiate the HRC. The committee was constituted as a supplement to the normal process of bargaining. Its rationale was that some issues cut across firms, to the level of the sector, and that some planning and related issues were handled better when separated from the pressures of the negotiation process. The committee dealt with a variety of issues similar to some that have been addressed recently by sector councils in Canada. Job security provisions, general approaches to structural and technological change, and early retirement plans as well as job training were all on the agenda of the HRC at one time.

The HRC approach continued on an informal basis following the formal winding up of the Committee in the late 1960s. The Experimental Negotiating Agreement (ENA) approach which led to a number of no-strike agreements in the US steel industry in the early 1970s was developed on the basis of initiatives that can be traced back to the HRC. Similarly, the sector-based Employment and Income Security program that was established in the 1977 contract between the Steelworkers Union and the industry reflects the operation of the HRC.

There is also a link to earlier Canadian efforts that have received substantial international recognition. The Industrial Adjustment Service (IAS) is part of the overall set of programs provided by Human Resources Development Canada for dealing with labour market adjustment issues. In particular, the IAS deals with actual or potential workforce adjustment situations. Both IAS and sector councils reflect partnership approaches to dealing with adjustment and related issues. The CSTEC, for example, but for its scale could have been an IAS initiative. Sector councils depart from the IAS approach in that they are ongoing and are intended, ultimately, to be independent of government.

Recent Experience in the United States

More recently, cooperative arrangements in the United States have been promoted by the Consortium of State Labor-Management Initiatives with the assistance of the Bureau of Labor-Management Relations in the Department of Labor. These programs, which differ somewhat from state to state, have a common purpose of developing joint programs to promote competitiveness. Most involve training and human resource planning initiatives. In this sense, they parallel Canadian initiatives in that there is public sector support and they focus on training. A number of states, primarily in the northeast, have developed labour-management programs that are described in Howitt et al. (1989). An important difference that characterizes this experience and several others in the United States is that these initiatives have been more focused on firms than on sectors.

Programs involving cooperation between labour and management have existed in a variety of formats since the 1960s, but the recent efforts of the Labor Department were developed in response to labour market adjustment problems resulting from the 1981–83 recession. Although these efforts were less sectorally focused, they were primarily restricted to firms in the mining and manufacturing sectors, where workers were subject to the greatest degree of exposure to international competition.

Some of the states in the consortium, particularly West Virginia, Iowa, New York, and Illinois, provided support to regional and industry labour-management committees. These committees carried out many activities that are comparable to those of Canadian sector councils. Howitt et al. indicate that approximately half supported research towards identifying common problems and that most supported state-wide labour-management conferences. The central focus of these state programs was on the development of joint programs to promote competitiveness. Training and related human resource planning activities were an important component of most of these programs. There has not been an overall evaluation of the effectiveness of these programs at the state level, although Ferman et al. (1991) have reviewed positively some elements of the joint training programs developed through these state initiatives.

An important difference between the Canadian sector councils and the American experience with the consortium relates to the scale of public expenditure. Howitt et al. estimate that the largest of the programs operated by any of the twelve states in the consortium spent approximately $2 million in 1988 and that the total expenditure for all twelve states was in the vicinity of $10 million. This is in sharp contrast to the initial allocation of $250 million to Canadian initiatives.

Future Directions for Sectoral Initiatives

Overview

Sector councils are intended to support human resource development in the private sector. Primarily a new initiative, elements of sector councils can be found in earlier policies and programs, particularly in the activities of the Industrial Adjustment Service. Sector councils are diverse; some have narrower objectives than others and no two can be described as essentially the same in structure and function.

In reviewing the problems that led to the development of sector councils, some common concerns emerge. These include: the need for more training; improvements in training quality, often in community colleges and in apprenticeship; more sectoral initiatives to deal with recruiting and retaining workers in the sector; and the image of the sector that may make recruitment more difficult.

Beyond these common concerns, experience differs across sectors. The sector studies process requires agreement among participants that the problem has been identified accurately and that it is truly sectoral. Consensus is important, but many participants emphasize that it applies only to certain sectoral initiatives and is not deemed binding for traditional union bargaining relationships. Bargaining is often described as a combination of conflict and compromise and this applies also to any agreement to participate in sector councils.

The specific focus of councils also differs substantially, partly based on the initial reason for establishing them. In the case of CSTEC, for example, much of the initial focus was on downside adjustments reflecting the major transitions that have taken place in the Canadian steel industry. Other sector councils, however, have concentrated on upside adjustments. More detailed human resource planning, anticipating future demands and skill needs, and developing forward-looking training initiatives are all elements of the upside approach.

The Role of the Federal Government

The sector councils that have developed have in most cases evolved from an initial sector study process initiated and supported by Human Resources Development Canada. The rationale for beginning with a sector study is to provide an agenda around which sector councils can be developed and to promote an initial consensus about possible solutions to the problems on the agenda. The public sector role is primarily that of a catalyst. There appears to be some indication that there is a larger public sector role in the formative stages when the sector consists primarily of smaller firms. Sector studies have provided the necessary background information to encourage private sector firms and worker organizations to devote the time and resources needed to make the councils work. The willingness of the partners to continue to fund sectoral organizations will depend on the extent to which these organizations are delivering benefits that cover the costs incurred.

There is also an interesting intergovernmental element to the way that the federal government, through Human Resources Development Canada, has used the sector studies process. Through the sector councils, it has been able to influence a wide range of initiatives that are within the jurisdiction of the provinces. Changes in the area of labour standards, apprenticeship training, and industrial training provided through provincial community colleges have all been affected by sector councils. This might not, at first glance, be the best way to deal with such issues but, in fact, this may have been the only way for the federal government to contribute to such efforts.

Evaluating Sectoral Councils

This chapter has focused on rationale issues, but it would have been useful to contrast stated rationales and activities with the actual activities and outcomes of the sectoral councils. Unfortunately data are not yet available to do this. In related work in the United States, Mavrinac and Jones (1995) review much of the literature on financial and non-financial returns to workplace innovations. These returns are measured at the level of the firm, and the overall conclusion is that workplace innovations do have measurable returns. In the case of sector councils, however, there is a serious attribution problem. The ultimate impacts of sector councils will be observed at the level of firms and their workers. However, it is hard to disentangle independent firm initiatives in a sector from changes that can be traced back to the councils.

More generally, how do firm and sector initiatives relate to profit-maximization and measured profits? If all firms adopt the results of sector initiatives, the results will not be found in excess returns – these will have been competed away. What are the implications if excess returns go only to early adopters, and is this likely when we are assessing sectoral initiatives? Mavrinac and Jones argue that much of the profit impact depends on the capabilities of the firm in which the organizational change has occurred to improve worker and product quality in a cost-effective way that does not compromise competitiveness.

There may be selection bias in evaluating the results of the introduction of training and other workplace innovations related to the operation of sector councils. Case studies in particular may focus on firms that have done well financially for other reasons. Strong financial performance may be a requirement of investments in various activities promoted by sector councils rather than the cause of the performance.

From the perspective of firms, it seems somewhat unusual that there is not more tracking of the returns to investments in human capital, whether the initiative is one that is pursued independently by firms or is sectoral. Mavrinac and Jones, for example, argue for more corporate experimentation and record-keeping in this area. Surveys of training activity in the private sector regularly reveal that firms find it difficult to answer questions about their training activities that they are able to answer about, for example, their R&D activities.

A number of factors will affect the way specific workplace practices, introduced as a result of the activities of sector councils, will have an impact on the financial returns. These will include competitive circumstances, technology conditions, firm-specific factors such as the current workplace environment, and existing education and training levels of workers.

Training clearly plays an important role in the rationale for sector councils and is at the same time very difficult to evaluate empirically. New evidence such as that of Bartel (1995) provides important information on the returns to training. However, the central analytical issue in assessing the costs and returns of sector councils is to evaluate training that can be attributed to their activities. This is not only a key analytical issue but is also fundamental for the long-run success of sector councils. These organizations are likely to continue to receive public and private sector funding only if meaningful links between their activities and financial returns for firms and workers can be established.

As a policy process, sector studies and the resulting sector councils are a hybrid. Many features have been borrowed from earlier initiatives but the sector council approach has gone farther than was possible before in Canada. Most earlier experience, in Canada and elsewhere, focused more on firms than on sectors. Sector councils are completely voluntary and will succeed, in the long run, only if both parties see their interests being advanced. As indicated above, demonstrating the net benefits of incremental training attributable to sectoral initiatives will likely be very important. However, this remains as an analytical problem because the methodologies to measure the impacts of private sector training are not well advanced.

References

Adams, R.J. 1986. 'Two Policy Approaches to Labour-Management Decision-Making at the Level of the Enterprise,' in W.C. Riddell, ed., *Labour-Management Cooperation in Canada*. Toronto: University of Toronto Press.

Arrow, Kenneth J. 1962. 'Economic Welfare and the Allocation of Resources for Invention,' in Richard R. Nelson, ed., *The Rate and Direction of Inventive Activity*. Princeton: Princeton University Press.

Bartel, Ann P. 1995. 'Training, Wage Growth and Job Performance; Evidence from a Company Database,' *Journal of Labor Economics* 13, no. 3, pp. 401–25.

Bartel, Ann P., and F. Lichtenberg. 1987. 'The Comparative Advantage of Educated Workers in Implementing New Technologies,' *Review of Economics and Statistics*, 69, no. 1, pp. 1–17.

Bassi, L.J. 1994. 'Workplace Education for Hourly Workers,' *Journal of Policy Analysis and Management* 13, pp. 55–74.

Becker, G. 1964. *Human Capital*. New York: Columbia University Press.

Betcherman, G. 1992. 'Are Canadian Firms Under-Investing in Training,' *Canadian Business Economics* 1, no.1, pp. 25–33.

Boskin, M. 1975. 'Notes on the Tax Treatment of Human Capital,' in *Conference on Tax Research*. Washington, DC: Department of the Treasury.

Davies, J. 1986. 'Training and Skill Development,' in W.C. Riddell, ed., *Labour Market Adjustment in Canada*. Toronto: University of Toronto Press.

Economic Council of Canada. 1982. *In Short Supply: Jobs and Skills in the 1980s*. Ottawa: Supply and Services Canada.

Ferman, L.,M. Hoyman, J. Cutcher-Gershenfeld, and E. Savoie, eds. 1991. *Joint Training Programs*. Ithaca, NY: Industrial and Labor Relations Press.

Gherson, Gilles 1992. 'Where the Jobs Are,' *Financial Times of Canada*. 28 September.

Government of Canada. 1981. *Work for Tomorrow – Employment Opportunities for the 80's*. Report of the Task Force on Employment Opportunities for the 80's. Ottawa.

Grossman, Gene. 1992. 'Promoting New Industrial Activity: A Survey of Recent Arguments and Evidence.' *OECD Economic Studies*, Paris.

Gunderson, Morley. 1974. 'The Case for Government-Supported Training Programs,' *Industrial Relations/Relations Industrielles* 29, no. 4, pp. 709–25.

Gunderson, Morley, and Wayne Thirsk. 1994. 'Tax Treatment of Human Capital,' in A. Maslove, ed., *Taxes as Instruments of Economic Policy*. Toronto: University of Toronto Press, pp. 39–92.

Harris, R. 1993. 'Globalization, Trade and Income,' *Canadian Journal of Economics* 26, no. 4, pp. 755–76.

Howitt, A., J. Wells, and S. Marx. 1989. 'A National Overview of State Labor-Management Cooperation Programs,' *IRRA Annual Proceedings*. Madison, Wisconsin.

58   Douglas A. Smith

Jacoby, S.M. 1983. 'Union-Management Cooperation: Lessons from the 1920s,' *Industrial and Labour Relations Review* 37, no.1, pp. 18–33.

Katz, L., and K. Murphy. 1992. 'Changes in Relative Wages, 1963–1987: Supply and Demand Factors,' *Quarterly Journal of Economics* 106, no. 2, pp. 35–78.

Kochan, T., H. Katz, and R. McKersie. 1986. *The Transformation of American Industrial Relations.* New York: Basic Books.

Kruger, A.M. 1968. *Human Adjustment to Industrial Conversion*, Research Study No. 45. Ottawa: Task Force on Labour Relations.

Mavrinac, S.C., and N.R. Jones. 1995. *The Financial and Non-Financial Returns to Innovative Workplace Practices.* Cambridge: Harvard Graduate School of Business Administration.

Murphy K., and F. Welch. 1992. 'The Structure of Wages,' *Quarterly Journal of Economics* 107, pp. 285–326.

Nordhaus, W. 1969. *Invention,Growth and Welfare.* Cambridge: MIT Press.

Parsons, Donald M. 1990. 'The Firm's Decision to Train,' *Research in Labor Economics* 11, pp. 53–75.

Porter, M. 1991. *Canada at the Crossroads.* Ottawa: Supply and Services Canada.

Rogers, J. 1995. 'The Wisconsin Regional Training Partnership,' *IRRA Annual Proceedings.* Madison, Wisconsin.

Riddell, W.C. 1986. 'Labour Management Cooperation in Canada: An Overview' in W.C. Riddell, ed., *Labour Management Cooperation in Canada.* Toronto: University of Toronto Press.

Shultz G.P., and A. Weber. 1966. *Strategies for Displaced Workers.* New York: Harper and Row.

Task Force on Labour Market Development. 1981. *Labour Market Development in the 1980s.* Ottawa: Department of Supply and Services.

PART II
LABOUR AND BUSINESS APPROACHES TO
SECTOR COUNCILS

3

A Labour Perspective on Sector Councils

KEVIN HAYES

Over the past ten years almost every private sector union in Canada has explored a sectoral training strategy. It has been seen as a way of increasing the employer's investment in training and representing the membership in adjustment and training issues.

In exploring a sectoral strategy, unions have been guided by a number of principles that have grown out of their long experience in labour-management relations and the particular experience of several unions in initiating sectoral councils. Working with individual companies and employer associations, unions have faced the question of how councils should be governed and how they would operate. Unions and employers wanted to keep their collective bargaining agenda separate from sectoral activities. A consensus on some key principles emerged among the unions of the Canadian Labour Congress (CLC) and were published as the CLC sectoral guidelines. There was also a common position on public policy as it related to training and adjustment. These questions, however, were not part of the guidelines.

The purpose of this paper is to explain the CLC guidelines and to comment on what progress has been made in applying them to union involvement in sectoral initiatives. The paper also examines the concerns that labour has about the future of sectoral training initiatives following federal withdrawal from training and labour-market programming under the Employment Insurance Act.

Background Issues

As pointed out by Wolfe and Martin in their paper in this volume, sector councils arose not as part of a grand design but rather as a direct response to the impact of economic restructuring. The federal government, through the provision of initial funding, also played an important role in supporting this innovation. These bipartite initiatives all have a different history. Labour's strategy or perspective was formulated by labour's role in the steel, electrical/electronic, and auto parts initiatives. The emergence of the initiatives reflected a growing awareness by unions of two key training and adjustment issues in sectoral arrangements: the necessity for unionized employers to involve their unions in dealing with training and adjustment; and the fact that it is easier to overcome concerns about the free-rider problem and other competitive issues when the focus of negotiation shifts from the plant to the sectoral level.

Labour's interest in a sectoral approach to training and adjustment may be recent, but the trade union movement in Canada has a long history with training and in programs that help workers adjust to industrial change. That history included the long struggle to have government, particularly the federal government, play a major role in supporting training and adjustment. At the turn of the century, our founding federation, the Trades and Labour Congress of Canada, pressed the federal government to become more involved in vocational training. The first step towards a federal role in training came in 1910 with the naming of a federal Royal Commission on Industrial Training and Technical Education, which reported in 1913. A year later business, labour, women's groups, and others organized a national convention which passed resolutions calling on provincial and federal governments to become more involved in vocational education.

But federal support for industrial and technical training programs only emerged in 1919 after the First World War with a federally financed national network of provincial employment offices and the passage of the country's first non-agricultural training legislation, the Technical Education Act. Even these tentative steps were only taken after labour and business organizations sent a joint memorandum to the federal cabinet on the need for federal involvement in technical education. It urged the government to work with other levels in ways 'that will bring technical education within easy reach of all classes.'[1]

Education and training policy, and how they are shaped and controlled, have enormous implications for the economic and social security of every worker. The sectoral level is but one level for labour to shape economic and social strategies in response to economic restructuring. In shaping these strategies, labour starts from the position that training is a universal right. It must be available without barriers to all employed workers, the unemployed, and those wanting to enter or re-enter the labour force, and it must be entrenched in employment law. As a basic employment or labour standard we believe that every worker should be entitled to a minimum of forty hours of training each year during normal working hours without a loss of pay.

Whether we are talking about a sectoral strategy or community college training, labour believes the content of training must be geared to workers' needs as they see them and must be developmental. This means that whatever is learned provides a basis for further learning and knowledge. Skills must be taught in a way that goes beyond a particular job and leaves trainees better able to take on different tasks in the future. In other words, training must go beyond the narrow requirements of a particular employer. The skills must be portable and be applicable to other employers and work situations. This is one of the virtues of a sectoral strategy.

In our view, a sectoral strategy must be seen in the wider context of an adult learning system. From a worker's perspective, a good training system should equip workers to have more control over technology, their jobs, and their work lives, by building on workers' existing capabilities and preparing them for the future. Every worker's skills apply to a broad range of occupational requirements. Good adult learning and training systems must build on those skills. None of this is incompatible with training and adjustment programs designed and delivered at a sectoral level.

In 1991 when the affiliated unions of the CLC began preparatory work on training and adjustment issues for the 1992 CLC convention, sector initiatives were a key concern. In part our concern was heightened by the contradictory actions of the federal government. While it was aggressively pushing a sectoral strategy, it was cutting Unemployment Insurance benefits and reducing its funding for training from the Consolidated Revenue Fund. Labour feared that the federal government's enthusiasm for devolving responsibility for program delivery to sectoral organizations was in fact part of a larger strategy of cutting Unemployment Insurance and shifting the cost of training and job programs from general revenues to the UI fund. There also was a real fear that the federal government planned to withdraw totally from training and labour market programs. The early drafts of the Charlottetown Accord included a provision to give the provinces exclusive jurisdiction over these programs. In addition to the concerns about devolution and cuts to UI and training, some unions saw the federal sectoral strategy as a piece in an even larger scheme of labour market deregulation.

When unions such as the Steelworkers and the Communication Workers were pioneering and fostering the development of sector organizations in the 1980s, federal labour market policy was relatively stable and predictable. Even in 1989 when the Conservative government launched its UI reforms and the labour force development strategy, the thrust of the policy was to increase federal investment in training and human resource development. But in the 1990s, as the federal government looked to UI as part of the solution to its deficit problems and its constitutional problem, labour market strategies became less and less predictable. The failure of the Meech Lake Accord and the rejection of the

Charlottetown Accord with its provision to devolve training to the provinces did not restore policy stability. There was a brief period following the election of the Liberals in 1993 where the emphasis was again on training and human resource development. A larger federal role in training, however, was scrapped following the 1995 Quebec referendum. The provincialization of training ended up as a central piece in the new Employment Insurance Act.

When the CLC sector guidelines were adopted in 1992, they were not intended to deal with the policy issues of training program delivery and constitutional change. A policy paper on unemployment insurance and training, 'Restore Unemployment Insurance and Invest in Training,' passed by the CLC convention in 1992 addressed labour's view on the changes in federal policy. The guideline simply warns that labour participation in sectoral councils should support and not undermine CLC policy and trade union principles in the key policy areas such as full employment, unemployment insurance, training, national employment services, and the removal of labour force barriers to women, Aboriginal Canadians, persons with disabilities and visible minorities.

The guidelines therefore attempt to address several questions specific to a bipartite relationship in a sector council or in a committee conducting a human resource study of a sector. They deal with the union relationship with management; the composition of sector councils and committees; powers of the committee or council; the accountability of sector councils; and the financing of council programs. Central to all these questions is what general principles should define the relationship with management or the employers. Training and adjustment, like everything else in worker and management relationships, is not neutral terrain, no matter how much we may share common goals. Our perspective is different. Collective bargaining illustrates this.

In our guidelines we say that sectoral councils or committees must be a joint union-employer initiative. A key objective is to increase employer's investment in training and represent the membership on adjustment and training issues. The council must be a cooperative relationship where labour and employers are equal and where the decisions and operations of the council or committee are co-determined and co-managed. In other words, the working relationship between labour and management must be based on the legitimate and independent interests of each.

Where there is no clear union involvement in a particular sector but where the program is funded by government, there should be representation from a central labour body such as the CLC or provincial labour federations. We believe a sectoral initiative can only be sustained if workers have an independent voice on the council. If the councils are properly constituted along industry lines as opposed to narrow occupational classifications, there will be large numbers of unionized workers.

Composition of Councils

Four of the fourteen guidelines outline the features of the composition of a council needed to achieve true equality of partnership:

1/parity of labour-employer representatives;
2/sectoral/councils/committees to be co-chaired;
3/nominations and appointments of labour members to be made by labour; and
4/if there are non-labour and non-employer representatives on the council or committee they will have voice but no vote.

Representative boards where employers and labour are equal in number is not a particularly new notion. Co-chairing is a more radical idea, and it has worked. It is essential to an organization where decisions and operations are co-determined and co-managed, particularly where labour and management recognize that each have legitimate and independent interests.

If workers are to have a legitimate voice, it is essential to ensure that labour nominate and appoint worker representatives. It stretches credulity to believe that employers can select worker representatives and expect them to enjoy genuine independence. Worker representatives chosen by employers can be intimidated and have neither the resources nor the legal and moral obligation to represent worker interests. Some of the principles on parity were formalized in 1989 when the federal government invited labour, business, education, and other key stakeholders to look at new relationships for decision-making regarding labour force development. This consultation process led to the development and application of labour-business parity in the establishment of the Canadian Labour Force Development Board in 1991. Labour also insisted on parity in the subsequent creation of provincial and local boards. Parity meant not only that business and labour would have an equal number of members, but also that the board or council would be co-chaired and co-managed.

Labour argued that the parity principle has been an accepted feature of public policy for over fifty years beginning with the establishment of the Unemployment Insurance Commission in 1940. The former Canada Employment and Immigration Advisory Council followed the same principle in the make-up of the council. This was the model recommended by the Canadian Labour Force Development Board (CLFDB), and endorsed by the federal and Ontario governments in the creation of local boards in that province.

These principles of equality were not applied in the appointments to the several hundred federal committees and councils at the local and sectoral level prior to the establishment of the CLFDB. Labour had virtually no representation on the former local advisory councils and community futures committees under the Canadian Jobs Strategy introduced in 1985. Workers had only token representatives on many sectoral committees that were funded by the federal government to study sectoral human resource issues. These committees were often the first step in the creation of a council.

Any progress made in establishing labour-employer equality in the governance of provincial labour force development boards was however short-lived. The Harris government has dismantled the Ontario Training and Adjustment Board, and boards in Newfoundland and Nova Scotia are also being disbanded. Only New Brunswick and Saskatchewan will be left with a provincial labour force development board. British Columbia has a new Industry, Training and Apprenticeship Commission, a government agency with eight business representatives, eight labour representatives, four public post-secondary and training representatives, and four government representatives. The commission replaces the B.C. Labour Force Development Board. The parity principle was weakened at the CLFDB in its restructuring following massive cuts in its budget; it is still co-chaired but not now co-managed. Furthermore, the new Employment Insurance Act provides no protection for the parity principle. It does refer to sectoral partnerships but provides no legislative base for sectoral initiatives as to its structure or its role in training. Sectoral initiatives, in so much as they are established to provide training, will be subject to provincial criteria as prescribed in the act.

Powers of Council

Unions exist to represent the interests of workers. Sector councils are not mere advisory bodies. With respect to the power of the councils, the CLC guidelines state that:

5 / Sectoral councils/committees will have the authority to determine program priorities and spend any money allocated to the council.
6 / Where government funding is used, sectoral councils/committees should incorporate into their terms of reference or mandate the commitment to use public educational institutions for skills training.

The union movement has fought for many years for an educational system that is open to everyone so that they can gain the skills and knowledge to function fully in their lives at work, at home, and in the community. Training programs must be carried out in conjunction with public education institutions. This does not mean, however, that the sector council is bound to use public institutions regardless of cost or appropriateness of the course available. Clearly some of these institutions may have to modify their own structures and approaches, but they are an invaluable resource to channel training in a broader direction, sensitive to the needs of workers as clients and offering accountability to the public. In fact, we want to see the governance of community colleges and vocational institutions turned over to boards that genuinely represent the diverse interest of labour, business, and other groups within the community including teachers, support staff, and students.

Accountability

We see sector councils exercising real power. They can make a difference in the economic prospects of the industry. But more importantly, they can have a significant impact on the individual worker's security and adaptation to changing technology and other changes in the workplace.

Unions are concerned about accountability in any decision-making process; and it is not just regarding accountability to our own members that we advocate union representing workers. We see unions representing the interests of workers. It is a moral, political and legal responsibility. It is the reason for unions representing workers in national and international organizations such as the ILO and OECD.

Is there any other way to assure an independent voice for workers without fear of reprisal or without intimidation? Five of our guidelines on sector councils deal with accountability:

7/ Sectoral councils/committees must be established only on the joint initiative of the union and employer.

8/ Where federal government funding is used a council can be established, only on the recommendation of the Canadian Labour Force Development Board in consultation with provincial training boards where appropriate.

9/ Once established, sectoral councils are accountable to the specific employer and labour stakeholders who name the representatives to the council.

10/ Accountability of labour members will be to the individual participating unions.

11/ Labour representatives on sector councils and committees should receive a labour-sponsored orientation program.

A concern of labour has been 'hot-house' sectoral organizations initiated by program brokers. The definition of what constitutes a sector, we believe, is extremely narrow as it has been applied in the funding and creation of some sector councils. They have no union participation or independent worker representation. In some cases the employer's role is at best marginal or passive. Some of the councils that fit all or part of this description include the Canadian Professional Logistics Institute and the Software Human Resource Council.

Labour argues that councils and even committees should be established on the joint initiative of the union and employer. This certainly would give substance to claim that sectoral initiatives are partnerships of employers and workers. Moreover, it makes sense that no council be established without a recommendation from the CLFDB. Our concern is the absence of any oversight by the stakeholders in the formative stages of a council. With this requirement in place, councils that have no legitimate worker representation could not arise.

For adequate accountability we also want a labour-sponsored orientation program for worker representatives and a similar program for employer representatives delivered by employers. Since it is a social bargaining process, workers are not well served if their rights are undermined by council decisions that are contrary to trade union principles on worker rights.

Financing Sector Council Activities

Labour has always viewed the training of the employed workforce as a financial responsibility of employers. Providing training for youth and those who have not been in the paid labour force is clearly a responsibility of government. Similarly the cost of retraining the unemployed should be borne by unemployment insurance funds for income support and by government for non-income support training programs.

We see training trust funds as an important instrument for financing sectoral training programs. In our guidelines we state:

12/ Unemployment Insurance funds should be used only for earnings replacement for UI claimants on training programs.
13/ The funding of sectoral councils/committees activities (e.g., consultant studies, travel) should be financed by employers and/or CEIC.
14/ Labour contributions should be 'in kind,' not cash.

The principle of limiting UI funds to income support is shared by business and other stakeholders. This position was a prominent part of the 1990 CLMPC recommendations on the federal government's labour force development strategy.[2] In fact it was the number one recommendation of each of the CLMPC task forces. The CLFDB echoed the same recommendation in its report to government on developmental uses of UI. Both the former and the current government have ignored this advice.

Conclusion

The question that this paper asks and attempts to answer is: Have the CLC Sectoral Guidelines accomplished what they were designed for? The guidelines attempt to articulate the principles that should shape the bipartite relationship of a sectoral organization. Training and adjustment, like everything else in worker and management relationships, is not neutral terrain no matter how much we may share common goals. The guidelines are based on the general principle that the working relationship must be based on the legitimate and independent interests of each party. Unions such as the Canadian Auto Workers would argue that a sectoral partnership for training does not mean that it is joining a coalition to promote industry competitiveness, or even supporting workplace change. They view sectoral partnerships simply as a means of providing effective training.

The guidelines were developed in the early 1990s when almost every union in Canada was exploring a sectoral strategy to provide skill upgrading and training. The ground-breaking work done by the Steelworkers in developing the governing structure for the Canadian Steel Trade and Employment Congress firmly established the parity of employer and employee representation as a principle for union participation. By 1996, half of the twenty-two sectoral councils had union-employer parity.

The organization of the Sectoral Skills Council of the Canadian Electrical and Electronics Manufacturers in 1990 triggered a discussion on the roles of government, employers, and unions in the financing of sectoral programs. The CLC guidelines suggest that the union contribution should be 'in kind,' not in cash, and that UI money not be used for non-income support. Councils have in the main supported this position. Most councils with large training programs like CSTEC and the Sectoral Skills Council use public educational institutions. In fact, sector councils have become very successful in developing a close working relationship in the design and redesign of training delivered in conjunction with community colleges, CEGEPs, and technical institutes across the country.

The area of greatest disappointment with the guidelines has been in getting government to agree to a more deliberative process for the creation of a sectoral partnership. Labour suggested that a sector council be created only on the joint initiative of the union and employer and, if federal funding is used, the council be established in the recommendation of the CLFDB. But councils have been created without union participation and the CLFDB's role is still too limited.

In so much as the guidelines were primarily concerned with the principles that should define the relationship of the employers and unions in a sectoral organization, they have ensured that workers' interests have been well represented. These principles have also served workers well in sectoral human resource studies; the first step in the creation of a council. The guidelines were not intended to provide specific guidance in large public policy issues that directly affect the very purpose of sectoral strategy. The withdrawal from training and the huge changes to Unemployment Insurance are just two examples of public policy with enormous consequences for a sectoral strategy. The guidelines simply warn unions that a sectoral arrangement should not contribute to undermining labour policy in these key areas.

The provincialization of training and employment programs under the Employment Insurance Act means that sectoral councils will be severely hobbled in developing national training programs. Provincialization is not a mere inconvenience forcing sectoral organizations to shop around for support with each province; it fundamentally changes the focus of sectoral partnership from training to the nebulous residual role that the federal government has under the Employment Insurance Act.

Labour certainly had no quarrel with the declared objectives of the original federal sectoral partnership policy, which were to increase private sector training funds that might otherwise *not* have been committed; to foster cooperation between labour and management on training and human resources issues; to develop a commitment to high-quality portable training; and to ensure that training is accessible to all equity groups. The residual federal role, however, leaves the federal government and sectoral organizations with precious little to work with. Ironically, federal withdrawal from training will increase overlap and duplication as provinces and territories establish their own training priorities. Yet the elimination of overlap and duplication is the rationale for much of the new policy.

It could be argued that federal labour market policy through the Employment Insurance Act has been transformed almost overnight from a human resource development strategy to one of labour market deregulation. The question remains: Is the new Sectoral Partnership Initiative a vehicle for deregulating the labour market? Regardless of what the federal government may have in mind for sectoral initiatives, the provinces will be setting the priorities for training and have a large role in other labour market programs. Deregulation is what some provinces want and the federal government appears willing to accommodate them.

The cuts in UI benefits for laid-off workers may have an even greater impact on sectoral organization than the provincialization of training. The CLC esti-

mates that only one-third of the unemployed will receive unemployment benefits under the new act. Even for those who do qualify, benefits will be for a
much shorter period. The new rules for unemployment benefits as well as
employment benefits under the act leaves sectoral organizations with much
fewer options, particularly in helping laid-off workers. The prospects for creating and maintaining a viable sectoral strategy with national standards are
extremely bleak.

In many ways as we move into the next century, Canadian workers and
industry are back to where we were at the beginning of the twentieth century. At
the very time when there should be a larger federal role in developing a national
strategy for labour force development, it is withdrawing. Nobody knows if a
sectoral strategy can survive in this environment.

Notes

1 Luella Gettys, *The Administration of Canadian Conditional Grants: A Study in
Dominion-Provincial Relationships* (Chicago: Public Administration Service 1938),
p.80.
2 Report of the CLMPC Task Force on the Labour Force Development Strategy, the
Canadian Labour Market and Productivity Centre (Ottawa: 24 March 1990); 1992
Unemployment Insurance Development Uses, Expenditure Plan, Canadian Labour
Force Development Board (Ottawa: October 1991).

4

A Canadian Business Perspective on Sectoral Human Resource Councils

JOCK A. FINLAYSON

By early 1997, more than twenty national sector councils (NSCs) were operating in Canada. All of these institutions devote much if not all of their attention to human resource issues. All receive some level of financial support from the federal government to cover administrative and operating costs, and/or to fund various programs. Apart from these sector councils, the federal government is also engaged in sponsoring human resource studies and other types of activity in about thirty other sectors, often under the auspices of Human Resources Development Canada's Industrial Adjustment Service. Whether full-fledged sectoral institutions will eventually emerge in these latter industries is uncertain.

Since 1992 the federal government has heavily promoted joint, business-labour sectoral initiatives as a means to promote human resource planning and establish a stronger training culture in Canadian industry. Underlying this policy is a presumption that business is systematically underinvesting in human resource development (Betcherman, 1992), and that improving the quality and quantity of human capital is critical to maintaining Canada's high standard of living (Riddell, 1995). Ottawa defines a sector council as a 'joint employer-employee organization that provides a neutral decision-making forum to determine human resource issues within the sector and to develop and implement a sectoral human resource strategy' (HRDC, 1996a: 2). The types of initiatives pursued by these bodies may include training funds, sector-specific skill development programs, the generation of improved sectoral labour market information, or the development of industry-wide occupational and training standards.

Existing Canadian sector councils are diverse. Most are organized around traditional and generally well-defined industries. Examples include the (now-defunct) Automotive Parts Sectoral Training Council, the Textiles Human Resources Council, the Mining Industry Training and Adjustment Council, and the Canadian Steel Trade and Employment Congress. Others represent newer, emerging or difficult-to-define sectors (e.g., the Cultural Human Resources Council, the Software Human Resource Council). Still others are not really sectors at all, but instead are best described as 'cross-sectoral' in nature, grouping together certain occupations or skill sets. The Forum for International Trade Training, the Canadian Professional Logistics Institute, and the Women in Trades and Technology National Network all fall in this category (Larratt-Smith, 1994; Sharpe, 1992).

A majority of Canadian sector councils embody the principle of an equal partnership between employers and employees, with the latter usually represented by trade unions. But here too there are differences. Employee organizations play a significant role in most councils, but not always through unions. Unions have no identifiable place within the governance structures of the Canadian Professional Logistics Institute, the Software Human Resource Council, or the Canadian Automotive Repair and Service Council. The Canadian Council for Human Resources in the Environment Industry has some union involvement but does not provide for equal employer-employee representation. Sometimes constituencies other than business and labour are part of the governing bodies of sector councils; the educational community, for example, is represented on the boards of the automotive repair and environment councils.

These differences can make it difficult to generalize about sector councils. They also complicate efforts to analyse and draw useful insights from the experiences of the companies and industry associations involved in councils. Yet few analysts or participants would disagree that the views of employers, and especially their willingness to participate in and lend financial backing to these institutions, will be critical to the effectiveness and longevity of sector councils.

This chapter offers a business perspective on sectoral training and human resource councils. It is based on the personal observations and experiences of the author, a review of some relevant primary and secondary literature, and confidential interviews conducted with eighteen private sector and two government representatives knowledgeable about efforts to establish and, in some cases, to operate sector councils in Canada. While the main focus is on sectors where NSCs exist (or are planned), some attention is also paid to the views of industries that have either eschewed or exhibited a high degree of scepticism about involvement in joint sectoral institutions.

It should be stressed at the outset that the diversity evident among sector councils also exists within the business community. This is hardly surprising. There are more than one million firms in Canada with paid employees (Government of Canada, 1994a: 3). They span most sectors of the economy and vary enormously along a host of dimensions, including size, nature of industry, level of workforce skills, ownership structure, stage of development, presence of unions, average job tenure, and market orientation. Industry associations – there are more than 450 in Canada – are similarly diverse. Understandably, then, business is not necessarily of one mind in its approach to sector councils. Still, some general lessons may be learned by probing attitudes towards sectoral initiatives expressed by business representatives from a cross-section of industries.

Reasons for Business Involvement in Sectoral Initiatives

Participation in sector councils that concern themselves with training and other aspects of human resource development may offer several potential benefits from the perspective of employers.

Increased Skills

Most scholars and business analysts agree that improving employee skills (upside adjustment) is a priority for a growing number of Canadian firms. This unquestionably has been the single most important factor prompting business to become involved in sectoral institutions. Virtually all areas of business operations, including those touching on employee development and industrial relations, have been profoundly affected by the rapidly changing external environment.[1] Such external changes have certainly influenced the operation of internal labour markets at the firm level.

According to a major survey of companies undertaken as part of the Queen's University Human Resource Management project, the four features of the external environment most often cited as affecting firm-level human resource management practices and decisions were increased competition, regulatory requirements (workers' compensation, employment standards, pay equity, labour law, and so on), changing technology, and growing foreign market orientation (Betcherman, McMullen, Leckie, and Caron, 1994: 13). The same survey found that in 72 per cent of the establishments surveyed, new technologies had triggered changes in work processes and resulted in higher skill requirements in the past five years. Approximately three-quarters of the respondent firms indicated that raising employee skill levels was an element of their business strategy.

Most business representatives active in existing as well as proposed sector councils appear to be in broad agreement that industry must do more – or at least more effective – training; that skill requirements for entry-level employees are rising; that a substantial fraction of the present workforce will need skill upgrading; and that these and related 'upskilling' issues can usefully be addressed at the sectoral level (Larratt-Smith, 1994; HRDC, 1995a-g, 1996b-e).

In several recent sectoral initiatives, increasing workforce skills has been the principal concern of industry participants. A few examples:

- Apart from dealing with standards/accreditation issues (see below), the Canadian Automotive Repair and Service Council (CARS) is working to upgrade the skills of – and raise the amount of structured training provided to – automotive repair technicians and other workers in the industry, primarily through its Investment in People program. Human Resources Development Canada contributed $8 million to this program over a three-year period ending in September 1996; this amount was matched by the industry. To date, more than ten thousand employees have received training under this CARS program (HRDC, 1995b).
- The main activity of the now-disbanded Automotive Parts Sectoral Training Council (APSTC) focused on mounting a structured training program designed to improve workers' knowledge of the industry. To this end, the council developed the Auto Parts Certificate (APC), a three-part training program aimed at production workers. The skills taught, however, were more contextual and generic than technical in nature – a fact that attracted criticism from some firms, and contributed to the erosion of business support for the initiative. The council's stated aim was to have the APC recognized as the industry standard (Larratt-Smith, 1994: 22; Haddad, 1995: 80–2).
- The electrical/electronics industry's Sectoral Skills Council (SSC) has succeeded in increasing the amount of training in this industry, thereby helping companies and employees alike to meet the challenges posed by rising skill demands. The SSC's innovative training fund, under which companies and the federal and Ontario governments together contribute an amount equal to 1 per cent of each participating firm's wage bill to a workplace-specific fund, has provided resources to pay for incremental training (Haddad, 1995).
- Since the early 1990s the Canadian Steel Trade and Employment Congress (CSTEC) has put more emphasis on upside adjustment and on increasing the amount of training provided to production workers in the industry. This came after the success of its initial downside adjustment programs had been demonstrated. Implementation of downside adjustment projects revealed that many remaining workers lacked the skills needed to use new technologies. Accordingly, a skill upgrading program, funded in part by the federal government, was developed over 1992 and became operational in 1993 (Haddad, 1995).

Training at the management level has been an area of interest for some sector councils, particularly where small firms account for a major share of output of the industries concerned. Progress has been slow, however. The senior staff of several councils have voiced frustration over failed attempts to implement programs for managers (Larratt-Smith, 1994: 27). It is questionable whether management skills ought to be a primary focus of joint sector councils. Generic management-type training in marketing, finance, technology, personnel, and other fields is already widely available at colleges and other educational institutions. Industry associations are also increasingly active in this area.

Standards Definition/Certification

Encouraging the development of national standards has been a central goal of the federal government's sectoral policy. This has included promotion of interprovincial standards for apprenticeable trades through the Red Seal program, assessment of the need for standards as part of sectoral human resource studies, and inclusion of standards issues in the work programs of sector councils (assuming at least some industry support exists for this). Federal policy makers believe that 'occupational/skills standards are important in ensuring that employers have the workers they need to meet the changing needs of the workplace.' Employees, for their part, should gain because 'widespread acceptance of occupational standards can provide career ladders ... and ease the process of changing employment in the event of layoffs' (HRDC, 1994: 19).

It is useful to distinguish between different types of standards. Occupational standards define core skill sets for occupations in an industry. Curriculum or training standards might include a defined set of training modules or a prescribed content and sequencing of instruction at a college. Certification standards identify a process for assessment and acceptance of certification for certain occupations within or across industries (Warrian, 1992).

In some industries, there appears to be an emerging consensus that national occupational and skill standards would be beneficial to employers by raising workforce skill levels, facilitating mobility, and focusing training efforts on well-defined skill sets (CLFDB, 1994a: 8–11). In a few sectors business may see value in moving beyond the articulation of occupational or skill standards by establishing formalized accreditation and certification programs. For example, largely at the behest of business, the Canadian Council for Human Resources in the Environment Industry has set the ambitious goal of establishing a fully-developed national system for accrediting and certifying environmental practitioners.

Standards development, however, has not been a priority for most of the national sector councils now operating (Larratt-Smith, 1994: 22–3). Lack of interest by business is certainly part of the explanation. Employers do not always see a need for occupational standards. Sometimes, there is concern that setting standards could introduce rigidities and impede firms' efforts to respond to changes in technologies, markets, and the organization of work. In certain cases, common standards may hold no appeal for leading companies that have based their competitive strategies on achieving superior training and service levels; this reportedly has reduced interest in sectoral institutions on the part of influential firms in the auto parts, software, and retail and restaurant\food services industries, among others (confidential interviews, January 1996). In at least one council (software), tackling standards has been a sensitive issue because doing so would intrude on the turf of their sponsoring industry associations (Larratt-Smith, 1994: 22).

More generally, many business representatives are suspicious of government's role in this whole area, with some even fearing that accepting voluntary standards at the industry level could be a prelude to government regulation. Nor does it help that traditional apprenticeship programs – the best example of formal occupational standards (coupled with certification) – suffer from a poor reputation in much of the Canadian business community, mainly because of concerns that they are inflexible, narrowly focused on specific occupations, and too lengthy in duration. Negative attitudes toward apprenticeship are especially prevalent in most service and advanced technology industries – industries which do not normally employ apprenticeable trades, and where unions are traditionally weak.

Even when there is agreement that standards would be beneficial, barriers may stand in the way. Building consensus on the content of occupational (and training) standards is a complicated and time-consuming endeavour that can tax the limited financial and human capabilities of both councils and industry participants. The need to deal with multiple provincial jurisdictions can add to the complexity. Nevertheless, standards development has been an important goal for business in a number of existing sector councils:

- A 1991 human resource study of the aviation maintenance industry found that, apart from aircraft maintenance engineers, most skilled occupations are non-licensed, do not follow a defined career path, and are not provided with a common body of structured training (Employment and Immigration Canada, 1991b). It recommended that the proposed sector council work to define occupational standards for the industry. The Canadian Aviation Maintenance Council, established in 1991, has set a goal of developing national standards for thirteen skilled non-licensed trades as well as core curricula indicating how the skills and knowledge associated with the occupational standards are to be taught. The curricula will apply to both the workplace and classroom components of training. The council is working with colleges and technology institutes to ensure that its curricula are appropriately delivered (HRDC, 1995c).

- In mining, national standards for operations/production occupations do not exist. The 1993 human resources study prepared for a joint business-labour steering committee recommended that a new sector council work to develop and implement such standards (Employment and Immigration Canada, 1993a: 11). Once it becomes operational in 1997, the Mining Industry Training and Adjustment Council is expected to devote some attention to standards development issues.
- Since its inception in 1988, industry participants in the Canadian Automotive Repair and Service Council (CARS) have made a concerted effort to develop up-to-date apprenticeship training and certification standards.[2] Driving the need for new standards is the rapid pace of change in automotive technologies. Working closely with provincial apprenticeship officials, CARS coordinated the writing of a new nation-wide occupational standard for automotive service technician, which included the development of national curriculum and entry-level standards. It is currently updating existing occupational analyses for five other occupations in the automotive repair industry (service manager, service advisor, parts person, heavy truck technician, and collision technician). Revised training standards for entry-level workers have been described as CARS' most impressive accomplishment to date (HRDC, 1995b: 39–40).
- Coordination of efforts to develop national occupational standards and certification programs is a main task of the Canadian Tourism Human Resource Council (CTHRC), which was established in 1993. Despite the fragmented nature of the tourism industry and the presence of a plethora of separate sub-industry and provincial associations (in addition to a national industry body), considerable progress has been made. Development of standards actually began several years before the formation of the CTHRC. A key goal of employers active in the council is to spur and coordinate these ongoing efforts and facilitate the adoption of standards on a nation-wide basis. By 1994 more than fifty sets of occupational standards had been developed, twenty of which were national. The council's governing body has agreed to work towards a national credentialling system for selected occupations in the sector (CLFDB, 1994a: 10; HRDC, 1996e).
- The Canadian Council for Human Resources in the Environment Industry (CCHREI) has created a mechanism that could eventually lead to national certification and accreditation for selected occupations in the environmental sector (HRDC, 1995a: 21).

* The principal stated objective of the Canadian Professional Logistics Institute is to establish a new profession by setting standards for individuals working in the field of logistics. The institute has established standards in the core logistics disciplines of materials management, distribution management, and integrated logistics management. It is also responsible for assessing and certifying the competence of individuals aspiring to obtain the designation 'professional logistician.' By the end of 1995 approximately one hundred people had acquired this designation (HRDC, 1996b).

A final point: if government decides – whether prodded by employers or not – to make certification compulsory in more occupations, the role of sector councils in this area could expand significantly. For its part, the federal government insists that standards development be industry-driven and have genuine buy-in from the private sector (HRDC, 1994: 21–2). This certainly accords with the preferences of business. However, it should not be forgotten that the provinces have jurisdiction over both education and close to 90 per cent of the labour force. As a result, they are and will remain the main policy makers with respect to determining which occupations will be subject to compulsory certification.

Recruitment/Skill Shortages

A third reason why employers in some industries have shown interest in forming a national sector council is concern over actual or predicted shortages of appropriately qualified workers. In these cases, companies have hoped that sector councils would design and mount programs to attract more qualified individuals into specific occupations. Recruiting adequate numbers of skilled workers has been of concern to business participants in the Canadian Aviation Maintenance Council, the electrical/electronics industry's Sectoral Skills Council, the Software Human Resource Council, and the Canadian Council for Human Resources in the Environment Industry, among others.

Industry players in CARS have been particularly exercised about recruitment. Anticipating shortages of technically oriented employees, they have been anxious to attract more women and young people into the sector. In cooperation with HRDC and various community colleges, CARS has implemented a youth internship program. Designed to offer job experience coupled with some classroom training, the program aims to give a period of apprenticeship training (about one year) on an up-front basis to potential recruits to the industry. The companies pay a modest wage to interns during work terms; HRDC pays tuition for classroom instruction as well as certain administration costs (HRDC, 1995b: 26–31).

While industry forecasts of future labour shortages are quite common, sometimes they turn out to be wide of the mark. For example, while the aviation maintenance industry identified this as its most pressing human resource problem in the late 1980s, subsequent downsizing led to significant layoffs of skilled technicians in the early 1990s, with the result that a 1995 report found that 'no major personnel shortages exist at present' (HRDC, 1995c: 5). Canada's poor record of output and employment growth in the 1990s, and the prospect of continued modest growth over the next few years, should serve to allay widespread concerns about labour shortages, although the problem will no doubt continue to plague a few industries, such as software.

Downside Adjustment

Downside adjustment has figured prominently in the work of numerous federal government-sponsored Industrial Adjustment Service (IAS) business-labour committees since the mid-1980s. It was also mentioned in several of the human resource studies of various industries completed under the auspices of Employment and Immigration Canada in the late 1980s and early 1990s. Overall, however, downside adjustment has not been a priority for NSCs, in part because the federal government's 1992 Sectoral Partnership Initiative did not provide funding for this purpose. A 1994 study of nineteen councils reported that only six saw downside adjustment as relevant to their mandates (Larratt-Smith, 1994: 25).

In certain industries, however, business participants have concluded it would be advantageous to address downsizing and adjustment problems through a joint employer-employee body.

- The best-known example is the Canadian Steel Trade and Employment Congress (CSTEC). Funded generously by government, CSTEC was established several years before Ottawa unveiled its Sectoral Partnership Initiative in 1992. Its Worker Adjustment Program was launched in 1988 to aid steel workers faced with layoff or plant shutdowns. Between 1988 and 1994, more than eleven thousand displaced workers were assisted, with excellent overall results but at a high cost per worker. By 1992, CSTEC's mandate had been extended beyond downside adjustment to include training activities for employed workers (Haddad, 1995: 11–16; HRDC 1995g; Sharpe, 1992).
- In considering possible roles for a sector council, mining industry representatives concluded that some attention should be paid to workforce dislocation and adjustment. With employment levels down by almost 30 per cent since the early 1980s and numerous mines slated to close within the next decade,

many employees face the prospect of job loss (Employment and Immigration Canada, 1993a: 11–12). Once it is up and running in 1997, the Mining Industry Training and Adjustment plans to establish a jointly (business-labour) administered adjustment program.

- The past several years have brought rising unemployment and numerous plant shutdowns in the printing industry, mainly through technological change and increased competition. Pre-press occupations have been most seriously affected. Industry participants in the Impression 2000 Graphic Arts Training Council recognized a need to retrain unemployed workers, either for other jobs in the printing industry, or for other lines of work. However, because the federal government's Sectoral Partnership Initiative precluded the use of funds to develop programs for workers who lost their jobs in a particular industry, the council has not pursued any initiatives in this area (HRDC, 1995d).

Improved Relations with Unions

Sector councils are a vehicle for management and labour to discuss workplace-related issues of mutual interest outside the often adversarial context of collective bargaining. Some analysts have suggested that the mandate of sectoral organizations could be widened to encompass topics such as work reorganization, reward systems, and workplace governance, in addition to training and skill development (Kumar, 1995: 147). To date, there is little evidence of this happening. Few appear keen to expand the reach of sector councils into areas touching on collective bargaining or firm-specific human resource policies. However, in a number of cases companies and industry associations have been encouraged to take part in discussions around sector councils because they judged that doing so could assist in building a better rapport and understanding with trade unions in their sector over the longer term (Larratt-Smith, 1994: 30).[3]

Better relations with labour has certainly been an objective pursued by steel company executives involved in CSTEC. But steel is not the only example. Textile industry leaders believed that labour-management relations in the sector would benefit from the work of the Textiles Human Resources Council. In her study of three sector councils, Haddad reported business representatives on the Automotive Parts Sectoral Training Council expressing the hope that working within the council might eventually lead to increased cooperation and a greater willingness on the part of unions to promote a joint work culture in the industry (Haddad, 1995: 85–6). The same theme was sounded in the 1993 human resources study done for the pulp and paper industry, and has continued to resonate with some company representatives since then (Employment and Immigration Canada, 1994; confidential interview, industry representative, December 1995). Some mining company executives involved in discussions on creating a joint sector council evidently viewed the primary purpose of the whole exercise as 'improving the overall climate of labour relations in the industry' (confidential interview, mining industry representative, December 1995).

Lobbying Government and Accessing Public Funds

The opportunity to *lobby government(s) on training/human resource matters* can also be an important reason for business to be part of sectoral institutions. Such lobbying might be aimed at securing public funds to assist in defraying the cost of training existing workers, or the goal might be to win government support for other human resource–related programs (e.g. recruitment, standards development).[4]

As Ottawa developed its sectoral policy in the early 1990s, it became clear to many in the business community that the federal government had concluded there was a legitimate role for it – and hence public money – in supporting industry-level training and adjustment programs. That the federal government had generously funded the Canadian Steel Trade and Employment Congress since the mid-1980s, and that both the federal and Ontario governments had agreed to contribute resources to assist in training the employed workforce in the electrical/electronics industry through the Sectoral Skills Council, reinforced this impression. When the five-year, $250 million federal Sectoral Partnership Initiative was unveiled in 1992,[5] various industry associations began to assess whether government funding might be tapped to help pay for training and other human resource activities in their sectors; among those showing interest at this time were the tourism, software, textile, plastics, and trucking industries (interviews, December 1995 to January 1996). Accompanying these expressions of interest in new sectoral organizations, however, was some rather obvious resentment over the scale of government funding provided to a handful of existing sectoral bodies, particularly CSTEC. Within the larger business community, CSTEC's success was partly attributed to the steel companies' and unions' highly effective lobbying efforts in Ottawa.

It became apparent over time that a deficit-plagued federal government would not be opening its wallet to fund industry skill training and upgrading programs, although modest amounts would continue to be available. With this realization came some diminution in interest in creating new sector councils on the part of several of the industries consulted in the course of researching this study. As Ottawa's enthusiasm for expensive sectoral initiatives flagged, that of the NDP-led Ontario government increased, as evidenced by its support for the

Automotive Parts Sectoral Training Council (which was almost entirely financed by government). What must be emphasized here is not the experience of specific industries or councils, but the more general point that if government is prepared to use tax dollars to assist (selected) companies in training and developing their human resources, at least some parts of the business community will always have incentives to behave in ways designed to facilitate their access to these scarce resources. In the 1990s, participation in building joint sector councils has been a visible means by which business could demonstrate to federal policy makers its interest in human capital development.

Other Reasons

The above discussion does not exhaust the list of reasons why companies and industry associations have agreed to participate in and lend support to the work of sector councils.

* *Improving a sector's image* – in the eyes of policy makers, current and potential employees, and/or the public at large – has been an objective of business in a number of sector discussions. Correcting the allegedly poor image of auto repair occupations remains an issue for CARS. Worries over the supposedly unflattering reputation of skilled occupations in the aviation maintenance industry bolstered private sector support for the Canadian Aviation Maintenance Council. Enhancing the image of the textile industry, and differentiating it from the more labour-intensive apparel industry, has been a goal of business participants in the Textiles Human Resources Council. One of the initiatives proposed by the Canadian Tourism Human Resource Council was a 'career image' project designed to alert young people to career opportunities in the industry. Doubts about an industry's image often feed concerns over recruitment, and are cited with surprising regularity in the documentation issued by or pertaining to sector councils. Yet it is legitimate to ask whether the image and reputation of an industry are really appropriate issues for joint sector councils. Business associations may be more logical candidates to tackle these problems, although the fact they do not represent unions or employees may limit their capacity to address industry image and the recruitment of skilled workers.
* Many companies are keen on *forging closer ties with educational institutions*, particularly at the post-secondary level, and this has been a concern of industry in several national sector councils. Educational partnerships can be essential to the tasks of upskilling, recruitment, and developing standards. This has been a priority for the Software Human Resource Council and the

Canadian Council for Human Resources in the Environment Industry, among other NSCs. A 1993 agreement between the Software Council and HRDC mentioned the following specific objective: create more than 150 partnerships between business and educators to build an infrastructure for continuous learning (HRDC, 1996c). CARS is another example. Part of its work in standard-setting and accreditation has entailed strengthening linkages with and providing support to the colleges that deliver automotive training. To help address the problem of outdated college equipment, CARS has obtained equipment donations from the industry to training institutions. It also contributes to upgrading the knowledge of automotive instructors through professional development workshops The organization representing college automotive educators is represented on the CARS board – an arrangement that enjoys the formal backing of the Association of Canadian Community Colleges (HRDC, 1995b).
* Finally, in two Canadian sectoral initiatives, CSTEC, and the Western Wood Products Forum (which, however, was never a national institution), business representatives were motivated by a desire to address *market access and trade issues* that were affecting the outlook for their respective industries. For business, these sectoral bodies provided a useful forum for this purpose, in that they brought management and labour together to lobby government on trade issues. These cases are somewhat unusual, however.

Factors Limiting Business Support for Sector Councils

The evidence indicates that, for various reasons, business has sometimes been unable or unwilling to take part in joint sectoral institutions, or else has approached the prospect with considerable trepidation. A number of factors have contributed to industry opposition or lack of interest.

Is There an Overriding Human Resources Issue?

First, business participants in sector-level discussions may not feel that their industry has a major or overriding human resource issue, or at least, not one that can or should be dealt with on an industry-wide basis. In these circumstances, broad business support for any proposed permanent joint sector council is highly improbable.

Human resource management in North American business tends to be a decentralized, largely firm-level sphere of activity (MacDuffie and Kochan, 1995). Companies are confronted daily with the challenge of developing and managing their human resources, including recruitment, retention, and the provision of appropriate training to new and existing workers. This is a normal part of operating a business; it does not necessitate any kind of sector-based strategy or the establishment of a formal sectoral institution. While interest in addressing human resource issues on a sectoral-basis may be growing among some employers, the diversity and individualism that characterize Canadian business can be a potent obstacle to generating sustained industry support for sectoral initiatives. Nor should the impact of the usual competitive dynamic at work in a largely market-based economy be overlooked. The reality is that firms in most industries in Canada are in competition for customers, capital, and skilled employees. It is not surprising that this may dampen interest in fashioning industry-level human resource strategies or programs.

A recent summary of federally supported sectoral initiatives lists about fifty sectors where various activities are under way (HRDC, 1996a).[6] While most employers in these industries may share an interest in human resource issues and welcome the prospect of a government-funded human resource study, this does not necessarily mean that a shared business position in favour of forming a sector council is likely to develop. Still less does it signal a disposition on the part of business to establish new institutions that will be wholly or largely dependent on the private sector for funding.

Industry Composition and Structure

The number of enterprises in an industry, the role of small business, and the geographic dispersion of firms are all relevant considerations when analysing the prospects for business participation in new sectoral institutions.

More firms implies more fragmentation, increased diversity of opinions and perceived interests, bigger logistical challenges, and more difficulty in articulating a coherent industry viewpoint or achieving a workable consensus. Plainly, business support for joint sector councils comes easier when industries are relatively concentrated – and especially when there are a limited number of leading firms (Warrian, 1992). Yet, including the self-employed, 99 per cent of all businesses in Canada are small, defined as fewer than one hundred employees in manufacturing and fifty in services. The number of small firms with paid workers has jumped by more than half since 1981. By the mid-1990s approximately 55 per cent of all private sector workers in Canada were either self-employed or worked for small enterprises (Government of Canada, 1994a: 3). And the evidence suggests that small business's role in influencing overall labour market conditions will continue to grow in the years ahead.

When small business constitutes a major part of an industry, the challenge of building a national sector council is magnified. For many small firms, a simple inability to participate often limits their interest in such initiatives. Time, and financial and human resource constraints, can be formidable obstacles to private sector buy-in and involvement, and are particularly important for small firms. Experience suggests that even when a council is actually up and running, securing the support and participation of small firms can be problematic. This has been identified as an issue in a number of existing sector councils (see, for example, Larratt-Smith, 1994: 26; and Haddad, 1995: 95–6). Yet small companies, at least potentially, are also likely to be the principal beneficiaries of the types of services and programs that NSCs might offer. Larger firms, endowed with extensive in-house human resource capabilities and other resources, have less to gain from the programs or knowledge available through joint sectoral organizations.

A relatively high degree of economic concentration has facilitated industry support for several national sector councils, including those in the steel, textiles, aviation maintenance, and mining industries. Strong backing from the major Ontario-based auto manufacturers was critical in solidifying industry support for CARS. A fragmented industry structure, an absence of readily identifiable industry leaders, and the presence of many smaller firms have slowed progress in building viable sector councils in printing, logistics, horticulture, the environment, and culture, among other industries. These same factors may have impeded efforts to launch sectoral initiatives in several other industries, including retail and construction (although other factors are also relevant in these cases).

Diversity among firms and the presence of numerous small firms are not insurmountable obstacles, however. The electrical/electronics industry's SSC 'represents a broad range of firms' in the industry, with some from telecommunications joining as well in recent years. It has a mix of unionized and non-union, large and small, and Canadian and foreign-owned companies. Notwithstanding this, there is reportedly 'a remarkably high level of agreement' about its purposes and priorities (Haddad, 1995: 45). Despite having thirty-five thousand service outlets, a mix of large and small businesses, and several distinct industry segments, CARS has been successful in marshalling effective business support. Tourism, another fragmented industry in which smaller firms are plentiful, has been able to come together under a national umbrella group to make progress on occupational standards and other issues.

Geographical dispersion is another aspect of industry structure that bears on the success of councils, as well as on the likelihood they will be created in the first place. A high degree of dispersion makes it more difficult to develop a common industry position. It also presents logistical barriers, especially when the focus of activity is national, and the industry is populated by many small firms. That several of the more solidly entrenched sector councils are in industries concentrated in particular provinces or regions is probably no coincidence. Examples include those in textiles, electrical/electronics, and, to a lesser extent, steel. Establishment of the auto parts sector council was facilitated by the dominant role played by Ontario-based firms, although its recent demise suggests that this factor alone is no guarantee of a council's survival or success. The human resource council that exists in Quebec's aerospace industry, the Centre for Aerospace Manpower Activities in Quebec, CAMAQ, is another example. Creation of the new Canadian Grocery Producers Council was dependent on the support of a handful of major firms based in Ontario and Quebec.[7] This raises the question of whether provincial or regional sector councils might be a more workable model than full-fledged national councils for building business-labour consensus on how to deal with training and human resource issues. As part of its advocacy of an 'industry-led workforce development strategy,' the now defunct B.C. Labour Force Development Board recommended that business and labour explore the potential for new provincially-based industry training models (BCLFDB, 1995). The re-elected NDP government in British Columbia appears keen to follow up on this advice. Sectoral human resource and industrial policy already has a strongly provincial flavour in Quebec (see the chapter by Charest in this volume); increasingly, this is likely to be the case in other large provinces as well, as the federal government scales back its training and labour market programming activity and policy initiative shifts to the provincial level.

Role of Industry Associations

Another, related consideration is the role and impact of industry associations. Canada has more than 450 national business and industry associations, and together they form a rather heterogeneous group. The vast majority are small, with budgets in the range of $1–2 million. Many are national in scope, linking companies across the country into a single interest aggregation and advocacy structure. However, the provinces' predominant role in many policy fields affecting the private sector, together with Ottawa's continuing loss of financial clout, means that provincially-oriented business associations are now assuming greater importance.

Most associations are firmly rooted in specific industries or sub-industries, and it is this type of association which has been the focus of federal and provincial sectoral human resource initiatives. A few are horizontal, seeking to represent businesses across diverse industries. While not numerous, these horizontal associations can be powerful business voices on some public policy issues (Stanbury, 1993: 30–2). Because their members are drawn from diverse industries, however, such associations are not well positioned to deliver targetted human resource services or programs to their members, and they are not involved directly in the vast majority of the sectoral organizations of interest here.

Canada is noted for an absence of powerful 'peak' business associations with a mandate to facilitate cooperation and consensus-building among sectoral and sub-sectoral associations.[8] Academic analysts suggest that Canadian business associations on the whole are rather poorly financed, and have in most cases a limited capacity to provide services to their members. Associations are often preoccupied with lobbying and public policy advocacy, and not infrequently they fall prey to turf battles (Coleman, 1985 and 1988; Industry Canada, 1994). Owing to their limited authority over members, associations in Canada can find it difficult to bind their companies to any particular policy position. Except in rare cases, joining a business association is a voluntary decision, in contrast to the situation in several European countries. Adams, in a recent analysis of Germany's experience with labour-management cooperation, highlights the significant influence exercised by industry associations over their members in areas such as industrial relations and in-company training (Adams, 1995: 30–4). This is far removed from the typical Canadian experience.

Despite these limitations, there is no shortage of respected and influential Canadian industry associations which enjoy a widely accepted legitimacy to speak on behalf of their constituents on a range of subjects, including training, labour, and other human resources issues. On balance, the existence of an effective and representative industry association, particularly at the national level, has been helpful in generating private sector support for NSCs. Numerous examples can be cited. The Electrical and Electronics Manufacturers' Association of Canada (EEMAC) favoured establishing the Sectoral Skills Council and Training Fund and initially provided office space for the nascent council's first executive director. The Canadian Textiles Institute backed the creation of the Textiles Human Resources Council. The national association representing grocery product manufacturers – one of Canada's strongest industry groups – mobilized business support for the recently formed Canadian Grocery Producers Council. Both the Motor Vehicle Manufacturers Association of Canada and the Automotive Industries Association were instrumental in building private sector enthusiasm for CARS. Similarly, without the active involvement of the Air Transport Association and the Aerospace Industry Association, the Canadian Aviation Maintenance Council would never have been created. Further confirmation that industry associations can be critical to the success of sector councils is provided by the case of auto parts. The Automotive Parts Manufacturers' Association (APMA) was divided internally on creating a new joint sector council, but it went along with the idea because of support from some of its member firms. As time passed, the association grew increasingly disenchanted and it eventually withdrew from the institution, effectively signalling the end of the Automotive Parts Sectoral Training Council (confidential interview, federal government official, January 1997).

Several characteristics of the overall business association network in Canada may militate against broad industry participation in NSCs. The sheer number of associations with a stake in a particular sector may frustrate efforts to produce a robust business viewpoint (e.g., software). Tension between national and provincially-based associations is another fact of life in some industries. Winning the support of provincial mining associations for a national human resource sector council has been difficult. Most provincial mining bodies see training, education, and labour-related issues as falling naturally within provincial jurisdiction. A few even question whether the Mining Association of Canada – the Ottawa-based association that has spearheaded the industry's involvement with the national sectoral initiative – has a legitimate role to play in this area (confidential interview, mining industry representative, December 1995). Tourism shows that problems stemming from federal-provincial fragmentation can be overcome, although here too the presence of multiple associations has served to slow progress while increasing the administrative and logistical burden on those involved in sector-level activity. Tourism also suggests that the lure of government money potentially available for industry human resource programs can spur the development of common positions in a fragmented sector.

Of course, the mere presence of strong business associations is certainly no guarantee that a joint sector council will develop. First and foremost, industry leaders must conclude that it is in their firms' interest to address training and other human resources issues on a sectoral basis, and secondly that the best way to proceed is via some form of new institution. At present, for various reasons, a significant number of Canada's most effective and best-funded industry associations do not appear particularly interested in the national joint sectoral model promoted by HRDC. They include national associations in banking, insurance, brokerage, restaurants and foodservices, retail, construction, plastics, chemicals, telecommunications, oil and gas, and pharmaceuticals, among many others. Despite previous interest in the idea of a new national sectoral institution, key members of the Canadian Pulp and Paper Association have recently moved away from this position – in part because the association itself has done considerable work on training and standards issues (confidential interviews, industry representatives, January 1996). It is always possible, of course, that a few of the sceptics may change their minds and come to see benefits in a joint sectoral approach to training and human resource development.

Finally, a look ahead leads to a prediction that Canadian business associations increasingly will be seeking to diversify their revenue base and expand their product mix through a proliferation of fee-for-service type programs. Indeed, a significant number of business associations are already moving in this direction. This trend raises the prospect that some industry associations could eventually come to view NSCs as competitors in offering services – training courses, updated standards, and so on – to their (shared) members. To survive, joint sector councils will have to be careful to avoid competing with and duplicating the services of their core industry stakeholders. Yet the managers and private sector supporters of councils face the dilemma that, as government funding dwindles, they may have little choice but to search out products and services that offer the promise of generating a stream of revenues. The potential for tension between NSCs and industry associations in this area is obvious, and is one of the factors that casts doubt on the likelihood that large numbers of financially self-sufficient sector councils will emerge in the foreseeable future.

Perceived Government-driven Agenda

A frequently cited business worry is that sectoral initiatives are being driven more by government objectives than the real needs of industry. Interviews with several private sector representatives suggest that as federally-supported sectoral activities multiplied in the first half of the 1990s, the perception grew in business circles that government policy was characterized by a top-down rather than a bottom-up dynamic. This perception helped to weaken business support for some existing councils (e.g., the Impression 2000 Graphic Arts Training Council). To the extent that it becomes more widespread, the odds of creating successful councils in other industries will diminish. By definition, dependence on public funds fosters the impression that a sectoral body is likely to be highly responsive to government's agenda. This is one reason why the issue of self-sufficiency is important to the long-term viability and legitimacy of sector councils.

Concerns over Union Influence

In contrast to the United States, unions in Canada have held their position in the labour market. Despite continued economic restructuring and falling employment in many industries where unions traditionally have been strong, union density ratios have remained stable, at approximately 37 to 38 per cent of the non-agricultural workforce, during the first half of the 1990s, compared to roughly 16 per cent in the United States (Conseil du Patronat du Québec, February 1996: 8). However, union density is markedly lower in the Canadian private sector (slightly more than one-fifth). With virtually all job growth now concentrated in small firms and service industries, private sector union density ratios seem destined to decline. Over time, unions may become a less significant force in many of the industries where sectoral initiatives are under way. Having said this, the fact remains that unions have been important participants in most of the sectoral organizations created with federal government support to date.

In training and other areas of human resource management, the objectives and concerns of union leaders will often differ from those espoused by business. As one leading Canadian scholar has written: 'Management is interested primarily in improvements in productivity, quality and flexibility. Unions are interested in more fundamental organizational change to strengthen the union's role in workplace governance, increase worker responsibility and control over work processes, [and] expand opportunities for advancement and development' (Kumar, 1995: 136). The same author adds that, 'because distrust between employers and unions often has deep roots, many joint [workplace] programs are only experiments.' While these particular observations relate to workplace change, they are also apposite to sectoral initiatives.

Several commentators contend that joint sectoral institutions are unlikely to succeed without a strong, representative employee voice, usually through unions (Warrian, 1992; Sharpe, 1992). The federal government's sectoral policy rests on essentially the same presumption, positing a model based on partnership and bipartite equality. (Because of government's role and, in some cases, the presence of stakeholders other than business or labour, many sector councils are perhaps better described as embodying a tri- or multi-partite structure.) In highly unionized sectors, a model based on an equal partnership between employers and union representatives will not normally be a barrier to business participation – indeed, as suggested earlier, it can be a positive factor. But the same is not true in all sectors.

Based on the evidence gathered for this study, a common worry of non-unionized employers is that union dominance of the 'employee side' of sectoral institutions may result in the promotion of a union policy agenda that is inimical to their own objectives. Union goals may include increased union penetration into unorganized segments of the industry, or the promotion of apprenticeship or other certification requirements which some leading firms in the industry view as likely to raise costs or constrain flexibility. Perhaps most problematic for the establishment of viable sector councils is a situation where a sizable fraction of an industry is comprised of non-unionized firms, but unions are well-entrenched elsewhere in the sector.

Business participation in the Impression 2000 Graphic Arts Training Council has been affected by the split between union/non-union firms in the industry, which is comprised of more than forty-five hundred mostly small companies. Two-thirds of the sector is non-unionized, and smaller non-union firms have been unreceptive to the council. HRDC's 1995 evaluation report observed that many companies see the council as dominated by unions and government (HRDC, 1995d: 12). They believe that unions cannot properly represent all workers in what is a largely non-unionized sector. Business associations in the industry reportedly worried that even providing mailing lists to aid in distributing the council's newsletter could 'promote union activities' (ibid.: 14).

Less than enthusiastic participation by the non-unionized segment of the auto parts industry – a significant portion of the total – in the Automotive Parts Sectoral Training Council has been ascribed to their 'fear of unionization' and of the Canadian Auto Workers (CAW) especially (Haddad, 1995: 95). For a time, labour and management in the council were able to work together on the board of directors, but both the council itself and its flagship training program won at best a mixed reception from the industry at large. 'Non-union plants, in particular, are suspicious of CAW influence in the course material' used for the APC program (HRDC, 1995f: 16). These problems helped to unravel the organization as employer support gradually eroded.

In the fish-processing sector, both the presence of multiple-industry associations and negative attitudes towards unions on the part of small east coast operators slowed progress in getting a national council up and running. Many smaller companies in Atlantic Canada reportedly were reluctant to participate (confidential interview, fish-processing association official, January 1996). Within the IAS committee that preceded the National Seafood Sector Council, employees were represented solely by unions; this is not expected to change in the new NSC.

Interviews with industry association officials reveal that concerns over the objectives and influence of unions have also dampened business interest in forming joint sectoral institutions in a variety of industries where NSCs do not presently exist, including retail, financial services, restaurants/foodservices, plastics, biotechnology, furniture, and some segments of construction, to name a few. But the impact of the union factor should not be exaggerated. Sector councils have been created, and a few have demonstrated at least some success, despite the presence of large numbers of non-unionized enterprises in the industries concerned. Tourism is one example. The electrical/electronics industry's Sectoral Skills Council (SSC) is another. Its membership has grown to the point where upwards of 70 per cent of the firms involved are now non-union, with representatives of non-unionized companies also sitting on its board (confidential interview, former SSC staff member, December 1995).

Finally, the fact that there seems to be a degree of flexibility in how the governing bodies of sectoral councils are structured also warrants mention. Unions do not seem to have an identifiable role in the software and logistics councils, and have limited representation in the Forum for International Trade Training (HRDC, 1996a). In some councils, ways have been found to represent employees other than through unions (e.g., CARS and the Canadian Council for Human Resources in the Environment Industry). In still other cases, where the industry has a substantial non-unionized component (tourism, horticulture), union representatives occupy less than half of the positions on councils' governing bodies.

Conclusion: Business Interests, National Sector Councils, and Public Policy

Overall, the Canadian business community has displayed modest interest in joint sectoral approaches to training and human resource development. In most of the industries examined, however, this has been accompanied by doubts and a degree of scepticism about the 'value-added' and long-term viability of establishing new sectoral institutions.

Referring to existing councils, one commentator has written that 'to a considerable extent, it would appear that the councils are still looking to HRDC as the source of innovative ideas' (Larratt-Smith, 1994: 19). Another analyst has suggested that, while sector councils may not be 'government-mandated,' whatever success they have enjoyed so far 'is due in large part to government support.' She also identifies the impermanence of government funding as the biggest obstacle to their future success (Haddad, 1995: 114, 26); this point is also made in a number of the evaluation studies prepared for the federal government in 1995–6. These observations are revealing. They nurture a suspicion that a significant portion of federally-sponsored sectoral activities in the 1990s has not rested on a sturdy foundation of private sector support.

Business attitudes towards national sector councils have been shaped by a sometimes complex interplay among different forces: government policy preferences, the key human resources issues facing the industry, the extent of unionization, the existence and effectiveness of industry associations, and the mix of small and large and organized and unorganized workplaces in the sector. Based on the experiences of existing councils, it is clear that business has given fairly strong backing to a handful – CSTEC, the SSC, and CARS come to mind – and some support to several newer councils, including those in the aviation maintenance, tourism, textiles, software and environment industries, among others. However, in many other instances, widespread industry support has not been forthcoming. One principal conclusion of this paper, then, is that self-sustaining, permanent sector councils are unlikely to be established in most of the industries identified by the federal government under its Sectoral Partnerships Initiative.

The role of government has been critical in the evolution of national-level sector organizations. Many analysts argue that government should be pro-active in seeking to encourage firm-level innovation, strengthen partnerships, and promote a 'training culture' in industry. Current public policies, it is sometimes argued, 'do not provide the support or incentives to encourage high-performance workplaces' (Betcherman, McMullen, Leckie, and Caron, 1994: 101). This provides one rationale for a continuing government role in sponsoring joint sectoral initiatives. But it does not shed much light on what form this role should take, or how extensive taxpayer support for sector councils ought to be.

The question of government funding and organizational self-sufficiency is central to the outlook for sector councils. Admittedly, this raises some complex issues. To the extent that they are considered public goods which provide benefits to society that would not be produced by individual firms and workplaces operating outside of the structure of sector councils, a case may exist for continuing government support for these labour market institutions. In a position paper published in 1994, the Canadian Labour Force Development Board offered the following advice: 'The role of government is to "kick-start" or facilitate the establishment of sector initiatives. Long-term sustainability must be the responsibility of the workplace parties ... There should be a broad expectation that successful sectoral organizations will move steadily toward increased self-sufficiency' (CLFDB, 1994b: 3–4).

Business associations and company representatives interviewed for this chapter generally subscribe to the principle of council self-sufficiency, albeit some question whether government will actually adhere to its stated policy in this area. The recent evaluation reports prepared for HRDC also suggest that, in most of the operational sector councils, business participants believe the organizations should be planning for self-sufficiency.[9] Self-sufficiency means covering basic operating and administrative costs. It does not necessarily preclude a role for public funding to assist sectors in mounting training or other programs – for example, youth internships – that government, for its own reasons, may wish to see implemented within the private sector. But it does imply that industry itself rather than taxpayers will meet the lion's share of the cost of training and other workplace-oriented human resource development programs, as well as the (modest) administrative cost of operating a council.

A related issue is the time period over which council self-sufficiency is to be attained. Officially, HRDC has set a three-year time frame; in practice, some existing sector councils have received government support beyond this. Business participants in many existing councils doubt whether an adequate level of industry funding can be achieved within three (or even four or five) years to cover both basic operating costs and a meaningful level of program activity.

Federal policy-makers, faced with declining departmental budgets and anxious that sector councils be seen as credible in the eyes of their constituents, might well consider a two-pronged approach. First, they should refrain from establishing councils in the absence of clear support from a significant fraction of the key industry players and segments. And second, they should be prepared to discontinue government funding in cases where the private sector is not willing, over a reasonable period, to provide sufficient financial (and other) resources to cover councils' administrative budgets, and to sustain their own identifiable workplace-based training or other human resources programs. Applying these disciplines is likely to shrink the number of existing sector councils, and it will certainly reduce the odds of creating a host of new ones. But at least those that endure will have demonstrated that they are truly valued by their industry constituents.

Notes

The views expressed in this chapter are the author's and do not necessarily reflect those of the Business Council of British Columbia. The author wishes to thank Andrew Sharpe for his helpful comments on an earlier draft.

1 See Kumar, 1995: chap. 2; Kochan and Osterman, 1994; Locke, 1995; BC Labour Force Development Board, 1995.
2 These industry participants include associations representing motor vehicle manufacturers, importers, dealers, and parts and equipment wholesalers and retailers.
3 This has also been a reason why some associations and companies have participated in federal Industrial Adjustment Service (IAS) committees.
4 CARS went a step further. It lobbied the federal government in an unsuccessful effort to obtain a tax rule change that would allow automotive technicians to deduct the cost of their tools (HRDC, 1995b: 10).
5 The amount was later reduced to $135 million over five years.
6 Some of these sectors are really industry segments of groups of linked occupations.
7 See Alan Toulin, 'Food Firms Start Council to Train Workers,' *Financial Post*, 19 October 1995: 13. The industry-led Canadian Grocery Producers Forum laid the groundwork for the creation of this sector council.
8 The Conseil du Patronat du Québec is an exception, as it includes both large companies

and most of the sectoral and sub-sectoral industry associations active in the province of Quebec. The Business Council of British Columbia, which includes approximately a dozen industry associations, also seeks to act as a peak association on some issues.

9 Auto parts was an exception. Even before it collapsed, many firms in the industry apparently believed that without substantial ongoing government funding directed at both the council's training program and its operating costs, the organization would not endure (Haddad, 1995; HRDC, 1995f). Because a large and influential segment of the industry placed such a low value on the actual work and output of the council, the eventual loss of business support is not surprising.

References

Adams, Roy. 1995. 'From Adversarialism to Social Partnership: Lessons from the Experience of Germany, Japan, Sweden and the United States,' in Adams et al., *Good Jobs, Bad Jobs, No Jobs*. Toronto: C.D. Howe Institute.

Betcherman, Gordon. 1992. 'Are Canadian Firms Underinvesting in Training?' *Canadian Business Economics* 1, no. 1. Fall.

Bercherman, Gordon, Norm Leckie, and Anil Verma. 1994. *HRM Innovations in Canada: Evidence from Establishment Surveys*. Kingston: Industrial Relations Centre, Queen's University.

Bercherman, Gordon, Kathryn McMullen, Norm Leckie, and Christina Caron. 1994. *The Canadian Workplace in Transition*. Kingston: Industrial Relations Centre, Queen's University.

British Columbia Labour Force Development Board. 1995. *Training for What?* November.

Canadian Labour Force Development Board. 1993. *First National Industry Sectors Conference*. 16–17 November, 1992, Toronto.

– 1994a. *Second National Industry Sectors Conference*. 8–9 November, 1993, Toronto.

– 1994b. *CLFDB Position Paper on Sectoral Initiatives*, 18 April.

– 1995. 'Third National Industry Sectors Conference.' 14–15 November, 1995, Aylmer, Quebec (unpublished).

Chaykowski, Richard, and Anil Verma. 1992. 'Adjustment and Restructuring in Canadian Industrial Relations: Challenges to the Traditional System,' in Chaykowski and Verma, eds., *Industrial Relations in Canadian Industry*. Toronto: Holt, Rinehart and Winston.

Coleman, William. 1985. 'Analyzing the Associative Action of Business: Policy Advocacy and Policy Participation.' *Canadian Public Administration*, 28, no. 3: 413–33.

– 1988. *Business and Politics: A Study of Collective Action*. Kingston and Montreal: McGill-Queen's University Press.

Conseil du Patronat du Québec. 1996. *Bulletin Relations du travail* (February).
Employment and Immigration Canada. 1988. *Canadian Textiles Industries: Human Resources Study*, November.
- 1991a. *Software and National Competitiveness: Human Resource Issues and Opportunities*. Prepared by the Software Human Resources Steering Committee. December.
- 1991b. *Human Resources in the Canadian Aircraft Maintenance Industry*. December.
- 1992. *Human Resources in the British Columbia Wood Products Industry*. Prepared for the Western Wood Products Forum.
- 1993a. *Breaking New Ground: Human Resource Challenges and Opportunities in the Canadian Mining Industry*. Prepared for the Steering Committee of the Human Resources Study of the Mining Industry. Summer.
- 1993b. *Human Resources in the Environment Industry*. Prepared for the Steering Committee of the Environment Industry, March.
- 1994. *The Canadian Pulp and Paper Industry: A Focus on Human Resources*.
Government of Canada. 1994a. *Growing Small Businesses*. February.
- 1994b. *Building a More Innovative Economy*. November.
Haddad, Carol. 1995. *Sectoral Training Partnerships in Canada: Building Consensus Through Policy and Practice*. Report to Government of Canada. February.
Human Resources Development Canada. 1994. *Sectoral Partnership Initiative: Program Policy*. 1 June.
- 1995a. *Case Study Report on the Canadian Council for Human Resources in the Environment Industry*. Evaluation and Data Development, Strategic Policy. December.
- 1995b. *Case Study Report on the Canadian Automotive Repair and Service Council*. Evaluation and Data Development, Strategic Policy. December.
- 1995c. *Case Study Report on the Canadian Aviation Maintenance Council*. Evaluation and Data Development, Strategic Policy. December.
- 1995d. *Case Study Report on Impression 2000: Graphic Arts Training Council*. Evaluation and Data Development, Strategic Policy. December.
- 1995e. *Case Study Report on the Forum for International Trade Training*. Evaluation and Data Development, Strategic Policy. December.
- 1995f. *Case Study Report on the Automotive Parts Sectoral Training Council*. Evaluation and Data Development, Strategic Policy. December.
- 1995g. *Case Study Report on the Canadian Steel Trade and Employment Congress*. Evaluation and Data Development, Strategic Policy. December.
- 1996a. *Sectoral Activities: Update Report*. Spring.
- 1996b. *Case Study Report on the Canadian Professional Logistics Institute*. Evaluation and Data Development, Strategic Policy. January.
- 1996c. *Case Study Report on the Software Human Resource Council*. Evaluation and Data Development, Strategic Policy. March.

- 1996d. *Case Study Report on the Horticultural Human Resource Council (HHRC)*. Evaluation and Data Development, Strategic Policy. March.
- 1996e. *Case Study Report on the Canadian Tourism Human Resource Council (CTHRC)*. Evaluation and Data Development, Strategic Policy. March.
- 1996f. *Formative Evaluation of the Sectoral Partnership Initiative*. Evaluation and Data Development, Strategic Policy. January.
Industry Canada. 1994. 'Industry Associations in Canada.' Unpublished draft manuscript distributed to selected industry associations.
Kapsalis, Costa. 1993. 'Employee Training in Canada: Reassessing the Evidence.' *Canadian Business Economics* 2 (Summer), pp. 3–11.
Kochan, Thomas, and Paul Osterman. 1994. *The Mutual Gains Enterprise: Forging a Winning Partnership Among Labor, Management and Government*. Boston: Harvard Business School Press.
Kumar, Pradeep. 1995. *Unions and Workplace Change in Canada*. Kingston: Industrial Relations Centre, Queen's University.
Larratt-Smith, Mark. 1994. *National Sectoral Human Resource Councils as Agents of Economic Growth and Job Creation*. Report prepared for Human Resources Development Canada. November.
Locke, Richard. 1995. 'The Transformation of Industrial Relations? A Cross-National Review,' in Kirsten S. Wever and Lowell Turner, eds., *The Comparative Political Economy of Industrial Relations*. Madison, Wisconsin: Industrial Relations Research Association.
MacDuffie, John P., and Thomas Kochan. 1995. 'Do U.S. Firms Invest Less in Human Resources: Training in the World Auto Industry.' *Industrial Relations* 34 (April), pp. 147–68.
Riddell, Craig. 1995. 'Human Capital Formation in Canada: Recent Developments and Policy Responses,' in Keith Banting and Charles Beach, eds., *Labour Market Polarization and Social Policy Reform*. Kingston: School of Policy Studies, Queen's University.
Sharpe, Andrew. 1992. 'The Role of Business-Labour Sectoral Initiatives in Economic Restructuring.' *Quarterly Labour Market and Productivity Review* 1–2. Ottawa: Canadian Labour Market and Productivity Centre.
Stanbury, William. 1993. *Business-Government Relations in Canada*, 2nd ed. Scarborough: Nelson.
Warrian, Peter. 1992. 'Are We Ready for a Quantum Leap in Labour Market Policy,' in Canadian Labour Force Development Board, *First National Industry Sectors Conference*. 16–17 November, 1992, Toronto (published in 1993).

5

Human Resources Think for Themselves: The Experience of Unions in the Sectoral Skills Council

DAVID A. WOLFE and D'ARCY MARTIN

Since the early 1980s, the Canadian economy has experienced an unprecedented degree of economic change. Workers and firms have coped with the effects of two major recessions, as well as a period of deep structural adjustment. This structural adjustment arises from the same global forces of integration and technological change affecting the other industrial economies; but it is compounded by the introduction of the Canada–US Free Trade Agreement in 1989 and the North American Free Trade Agreement of 1991. The FTA and NAFTA accelerated the restructuring of the manufacturing sector in the Canadian economy, as US-based multinational firms began to rationalize their production in the low-wage, low value-added segments limited to serving the domestic market. Many of these plants were not as technologically sophisticated as their American counterparts, nor could they realize similar economies of scale because of shorter production runs (O'Grady, 1994: 257).

The combination of two recessions and the underlying structural adjustment has created an unprecedented degree of turnover in the labour market. Workers in industrial jobs considered secure for decades suddenly face the daunting prospect of unemployment or adjusting to the introduction of new technologies and new forms of work organization. The challenge for them is how best to adapt to these dramatic changes. While business leaders and many politicians present these changes as the product of impersonal and irresistible global forces, workers and their unions insist that these forces can be shaped by progressive and intelligently crafted policy.

Unions have tried at several levels to promote such policy. In collective bargaining at the workplace level, they have proposed clauses to govern technological change, training, and severance. In provincial and federal government discussions, they have proposed legislation in these same areas. Yet in the 1990s, in English Canada, the greatest success of unions has been at the sectoral level. In structures such as the Sectoral Skills Council, and counterparts in other industries, unions have refined their thinking about the governance, methodology, and content of vocational training. While there remain significant differences among unions in each of these areas, they blur the closer one comes to the workplace. Gradually, a consensus concerning co-determination of decisions, participatory methods, and broadened curriculum has emerged. It is this 'worker-driven training' model which has developed during the several years of union participation in sectoral structures, and has been asserted in response to the radical changes in the labour market.

Technological change is a dynamic process that brings with it both gains and losses. Historically, it has created new skills and new kinds of jobs while it replaced traditional skills and jobs. Over the long term, it has resulted in higher levels of employment and increased incomes, but this process has not occurred quickly or efficiently (Freeman and Soete, 1994). The prospect of long-term employment and productivity gains provides little consolation for those whose jobs are placed in jeopardy by the current wave of restructuring. The adoption of new technologies and the consequent demand for skill upgrading and new forms of work organization are profoundly unsettling. All training and technological development depends upon the willingness of people to adjust to change. The challenge is how to adapt to the skill requirements and organizational dynamics of the new technologies without sacrificing the benefits that workers have struggled long and hard to gain under the existing production system. In effect, workers are often asked to abandon the security and protection of the system they know for a new approach fraught with uncertainty.

New technological systems with their attendant changes can be structured to include a recognition of workers' needs, assuming the political strength and organizational resources exist to promote such an outcome. For labour, decisions about how skills are developed and training occurs within the firm, or what forms of work organization are adopted, must be viewed within the context of the prevailing balance of power in the industrial relations system. In settings governed by collective bargaining relationships, policy towards training and technological change develops as part of that system. Decisions to get involved in new training initiatives or new forms of work organization are also linked to the organizational dynamics and existing practices of the system. In the context of the recent restructuring, managers, industrial associations, and unions all perceived the need for new forms of cooperation to meet the challenge of emerging training needs. In the training area, they realized real partnerships are possible when there is a shared stake in the outcome and real expertise is brought to bear on the problem by both sides. In this environment, some employers have accepted that they can succeed by providing an effective collective voice for their employees. And unions have begun to see cooperation over skills development as one path to achieve greater employment security for their members.

One development in the training arena over the past decade has been the negotiation of sectoral agreements between employers' associations, labour unions, and the federal and provincial governments. These agreements have been hailed as a uniquely Canadian solution to the traditional problem of under-investment in workplace-based training. The sectoral model emerged in the 1980s as an innovative way for management and unions to transcend their tradi-tional roles in the collective bargaining process. This chapter explores the potential of the sectoral approach to training in the context of a specific place and time: the electrical and electronics manufacturing industry in Ontario between 1986 and 1996. The structure created to promote workplace-based training is the Sectoral Skills Council. The paper explores the reasons for the emergence of the sectoral approach in the electronics industry and documents the experience to date. It considers some of the lessons learned in implementing the model and concludes with a brief analysis of the relevance of the model for the broader challenges that unions currently face.

Competing Perspectives on Training

Faced with the dramatic economic restructuring described above, employers and governments have looked to skills training as a way out of the quandary. They view training as a way to facilitate labour adjustment, as well as to increase the productivity and competitiveness of industry. According to Robert Reich, the former US Secretary of Labor, the great fault line in the United States today is between those with higher educational qualifications and train-ing and those without: 'The right education and skills don't guarantee a good job in the new economy, but they are a prerequisite' (Wartzman, 1995). For its part, the government of Canada recently declared that, 'as the pace of global competition quickens and technological complexity intensifies, the fortunes of individuals and of nations turn increasingly on the skills they already possess or are prepared to acquire. The right skills are the key to building the smarter, more productive economy on which job and income growth depend. Skilled and adaptable workers are needed to master, and re-master, the increasingly sophisticated technology and work methods that are making virtually every occupation, in some sense, high tech' (Government of Canada, 1994: 39).

For employers and governments, such formulations are common sense, so obvious as to hardly require justification. As a result of the rapid pace of tech-nological change and the increased pressures of global competition, employers have attempted to alter workplace practices to encourage greater flexibility and increased productivity. Training is seen by employers as part of this realignment of production processes. New training initiatives are often an attempt to keep pace with international competitors. In a business culture more prone to regard training as a current expenditure than a long-term investment, overall cost has been a critical factor in determining employers' level of commitment. This concern about the cost effectiveness of training has often overridden other indicators of success, such as the quality, portability, or equity of the training being provided.

Within the labour community, this close identification of higher skill levels with improved productivity and competitiveness is a source of great concern. Labour analysts emphasize that training on its own cannot reverse industrial decline. The labour movement maintains that training can be part of a full employment strategy, but is not, and should not be, the only part. Its primary labour market role should be to sustain higher wages and replace some of the high-wage/low-skill jobs lost to economic restructuring of the past two decades. Labour regards training as a social right, an extension of the right to public schooling for children. Hence priority should be given to those adult workers with limited formal education, those least well served in the first round of access to educational capital. As well as remedying past inequities, good training should extend to working class people some of the experience of 'self-directed learning' generally associated with professional education, thus restoring an element of worker control in the design of jobs. Similarly, priority should be given to choice in the hands of the learner, with counselling support through the union, and adequate funding for lost time of work financed through a payroll tax on employers. This has generally been resisted by firms as too expensive or too constraining on their operations.

The unions involved with the sectoral initiatives of the 1980s tried to negotiate their conception of worker-driven training, in contrast to the competency-based approach preferred by management. From their perspective, competency-based training leads to fragmented, rigid jobs and discourages critical, creative thinking by workers. It also undermines their ability to act collectively in the workplace. In contrast, worker-driven training 'aim(s) at maximizing the amount of control in the hands of the workers by deepening, not fragmenting, their understanding of the workplace processes. It (is) defined by workers and encourage(s) them to exercise, sharpen and act on their judgments.' The goal of the training is to help workers build secure futures for themselves and their communities by placing greater control over their choices about lifelong learning in their own hands (Martin, 1995: 104).

Several of the union staff who participated in the initial design and structure of some of the sectoral initiatives developed their conception of worker-driven training through the training subcommittee which met at the Ontario Federation of Labour from 1988 to 1993. They contributed directly to a policy statement on education and training approved at the thirty-third annual convention of the labour federation in November 1989. The policy statement established eight guidelines for good training, which were accepted in the labour movement as the basis for negotiations with both employers' associations and governments in sectoral training initiatives:

1. Skills training must be developmental. Every training program must teach skills in a way that goes beyond a particular job and leaves the trainee better able to take on different tasks in the future.
2. Skills training programs must be open to all, not just the youngest or fittest. Special efforts must be made to use training as a vehicle for equality for women, visible minorities and others who have been discriminated against in the education system and the workplace.
3. Skills training must be designed to raise the level of skill of the entire workforce, not just selected occupations or selected areas.
4. Skills training must flow from a worker-based identification of skill needs and not be restricted to narrowly-defined job performance factors identified by employers or consultants.
5. Skills training must support the development of good job design and technology that enhance the skills of workers.
6. Skills training should enable workers to have more control over their jobs.
7. Skills training should incorporate the practices of good adult education, starting with an understanding of what participants already know and what they want to know. It must respect the ability individuals bring to their training and should encourage questioning, discussion and participation.
8. Skills training should help people work more safely, and learn about individual and collective rights. It must equip the participant to put that knowledge and experience into action (OFL, 1989: 92–3).

While these principles were widely supported, it proved difficult to implement them in a uniform fashion in the sectoral agreements. The decentralized nature of Ontario's collective bargaining system meant that the benefits of training were diffused widely. Yet without a universal payroll tax, the costs of training were being born at work sites. Hence in some workplaces extensive training programs were operating, while at other locations little or no training was happening. The subordinate position of unions within the workplace, especially with regard to the future plans of the firm, impeded the efforts of labour representatives to design training programs that anticipated skills needs, and to provide the support and counselling needed for members to shape their learning process. Despite these obstacles, the process of social bargaining that gave rise to the sectoral agreements afforded the labour movement a rare opportunity to overcome some of their disadvantages and to have 'the clout, skills, and information flow needed to work as genuine equals with management and educational institutions in structuring training opportunities' (Martin, 1992: 74).

The Sectoral Approach to Training

The emergence of the sectoral training initiatives was not part of a grand policy design; rather, it arose as a direct response to the impact of economic restructuring. Several of the sectoral organizations were supported by the federal Department of Employment and Immigration through the provision of initial funding to undertake human resource studies. Bipartite initiatives at differing stages of development and human resources studies are currently under way in dozens of sectors across the country.[1] The three most formalized initiatives were found in the steel industry, in electrical/electronic manufacturing, and in automotive parts; each received some degree of their continuing funding from both the federal and provincial governments.[2] The emergence of these initiatives reflected a growing awareness of several key issues: the necessity for unionized employers to involve their unions in dealing with training and adjustment; the need to deal with these issues outside of the limiting framework of the two-interval model of collective bargaining; and the fact that it is easier to overcome concerns about the free-rider problem and other competitive issues when the locus of negotiation shifts from the plant to the sectoral level (O'Grady, 1994: 271–2).

The growth of this awareness during the 1980s supported the perception that the sectoral level was a more effective forum for dealing with training-related issues than the narrower firm or plant-based approach. This was the level where most of the restructuring, training, and adjustment issues were confronted; it was also where both management and labour had 'knowledge of the problems facing the industry, the backing of their own organizational resources and a vested interest in solving the problems' (Warrian: 1989). For the labour movement, the sectoral level was an arena within which its perspective could shape economic and social strategies around restructuring. It also represented a way to gain access to increased educational and training opportunities for workers in the sector. Management, for its part, could tap into increased training resources, gain a chance to work with labour, and an opportunity to help shape sectoral institutions according to their specifications. For governments, sectoral initiatives acted as pilot programs for the devolution of training delivery to the labour market partners. As such, they corresponded to the federal government's desire to devolve responsibility for program delivery to those most directly affected. Sectoral agreements also provided an opportunity to promote better workplace relations through increased interaction between unions and employers and joint responses to industrial adjustment (Warrian, 1989).

These concerns guided some of the key leaders who participated in the discussions that created the Sectoral Skills Council (SSC) in the electrical and electronic manufacturing industries. The industry comprises a crucial component of Canada's industrial structure, representing some 10 per cent of employment in manufacturing, and a disproportionately high percentage of industrial research and development expenditures and earnings from manufactured exports. The sector is also a major site for both production and consumption of microelectronic technology. In 1988 the industry association and the relevant unions formed the Joint Human Resources Committee to address the sector-wide issues of training, retraining, technological change and adjustment. With funding support from Employment and Immigration Canada, they launched a human resources study to identify the impact that economic restructuring was having on the labour demands of the industry and the training needs of their workforce.

The result of that study, *Connections for the Future*, revealed that the industry suffered significant job losses during the first recession of the 1980s, but subsequently grew at twice the rate of general manufacturing in Canada (Canadian Electrical and Electronics Manufacturing Industry, 1989). By 1987 employment levels had surpassed their previous peak. However, the net result of the restructuring was a significant change in the occupational and skill mix of the workforce. At the root of the change was a dramatic shift between the proportion of production jobs and the number of white-collar, salaried ones. The job categories that grew the fastest were those with higher professional and technical qualifications. At the same time, a new configuration of skill requirements was emerging within the smaller production workforce, resulting from the general shift towards those occupations with higher skill levels. The effect of these changes was compounded by the declining pool of new labour market entrants for the industry to draw upon. The human resource study also suggested that the existing post-secondary educational system was not providing sufficient graduates to meet the skill requirements of the industry. For its part, the union was concerned that without access to better training opportunities, its members were going to lose their chance at the higher skill jobs in the industry. Through their involvement with the study, key segments of both management and labour came to the view that they must retrain and redeploy the existing workforce in order to meet future skill needs.

For both management and labour, this required a major shift in thinking. The culture of the high-tech industries, particularly in the electronic segment, emphasized youth and the highly educated managerial and engineering staffs. The protective ethos of the Canadian labour movement, particularly in the defensive political climate created by free trade agreements with the less unionized United States and Mexico, discouraged joint initiatives with employers. It took determined leadership by the co-chairs of the process, Ted Priestner, chief executive officer of Westinghouse Canada, and Glenn Pattinson, vice-president of the Communications and Electrical Workers of Canada, to bring all parties to the table.

The participants in the Joint Human Resources Committee initiated discussions concerning the establishment of a sector-wide training fund to address the need for vocational training and upgrading, paid educational leave, and union education programming for education delegates and technology stewards. The union participants in this process were familiar with their role in shutdowns and cutbacks; but their involvement in the sectoral, bipartite negotiations leading to the creation of the training fund posed new challenges. The creation of the Sectoral Skills Council encompassed a process of social bargaining, as opposed to the traditional forms of collective bargaining with which union leaders were familiar. The social bargaining involved business leaders, labour representatives, government officials and educators. The term social bargaining implies a method for reconciling diverse interests through a process that requires both consensual and adversarial styles of operation. Internally, shared responsibility in the bipartite negotiations raises the real problem for unions and their leaders of co-option; union representatives took some time to adjust their perspective to this new type of bargaining, without abandoning their identity. Although the process created major strains for those who participated, it also afforded them an opportunity to place their issues squarely on the bargaining table (Martin, 1995: 102–4). At the end of the process, the report of the Joint Human Resource Committee called for the establishment of a permanent joint council to act on human resource issues and the creation of a new sectoral training fund.

The Industrial Setting of the Sectoral Skills Council

The electrical and electronic manufacturing sector is diverse and dynamic. Its strength lies in manufacturing custom-made and/or specialty products for specific market niches. Firms in the industry have responded to new competitive pressures in North American and abroad, as well as technological developments occurring across the industry. Despite the two recessions and economic restructuring of the past decade, the sector has enjoyed one of the highest rates of

TABLE 1   Employment in Manufacturing and Electrical and Electronic Products in Canada, 1983–1995

	Manufacturing		Electrical and electronic products		% Share of mnfg
	Employment (000)	% Change	Employment (000)	% Change	
Year					
1983	1717.0		126.8		7.38
1984	1757.8	2.4	133.9	5.6	7.61
1985	1798.1	2.3	138.8	3.7	7.72
1986	1860.3	3.5	144.1	3.8	7.75
1987	1944.6	4.5	150.7	4.6	7.75
1988	1992.3	2.5	157.0	4.2	7.88
1989	2030.8	1.9	160.2	2.0	7.89
1990	1910.5	−5.9	146.7	8.4	7.68
1991	1713.6	−10.3	125.8	−14.2	7.34
1992	1620.4	−5.4	119.7	−4.8	7.39
1993	1617.2	0.2	115.6	−3.4	7.15
1994	1654.8	2.3	113.6	−1.7	6.86
1995*	1697.2	2.6	118.8	4.6	7.00

Source: Statistics Canada, Annual Estimates of Employment, Earnings and Hours, 1983–95, 1996 Cat. 72-F002XDE, various years.

growth in Canadian industry. In Ontario, the industrial heartland of the country, the industry accounts for 15 per cent of manufacturing GDP; it is even more remarkable for its relative contribution to the total increase in manufacturing GDP in Ontario in the past decade. The electrical and electronics products industry (including telecommunications) outrivals automotive products as the engine powering the growth of manufacturing. Between 1984 and 1995 it was the only industry which both grew at a faster rate (169 per cent) and accounted for a larger share of increase in total manufacturing GDP (56 per cent) than the auto sector. This result is not completely surprising given the critical role of electrical products as the core enabling technology in the emerging information technology paradigm (Freeman and Soete, 1994).

However, the substantial growth of the industry over the past decade did not translated into a commensurate growth of employment. The data in Table 1 indicate that the industry recovered rapidly from the recession of the early 1980s and added new jobs at a faster rate than the manufacturing industries as a whole. Just as the Sectoral Skills Council came into existence in the early 1990s, the sector was devastated by the combined impact of the Free Trade Agreement and the second recession. Employment levels plummeted and remained well below the peak that was reached in 1989. Canadian firms, both

TABLE 2   Employment Distribution in the Fabricating, Assembling, Installing, and Repairing Occupations of Electrical, Electronic and Related Equipment, 1971–1991

SOC	Occupations classifications	1971	1981	1986	1991
853	Group Totals	82,740	125,175	135,160	122,840
8530	Foremen/women: fabricating, assembling and repairing occupations: electrical electronic and related equipment	7,930	9,990	8,685	5,290
8531	Electrical and related equipment fabricating and assembling occupations	18,585	22,575	21,040	15,575
8533	Electronic and related equipment installing and repairing occupations	21,175	39,740	43,030	43,100
8534	Electronic and related equipment fabricating and assembling occupations	8,960	15,040	15,195	13,380
8535	Electronic and related equipment installing and repairing occupations	5,930	13,715	17,630	21,310
8536	Inspecting, testing, grading and sampling occupations: fabricating, assembling, installing and repairing electrical, electronic and related equipment	5,450	9,025	8,685	5,490
8537	Radio and television repairers	9,810	9,695	9,150	9,190
8538	Occupations in labouring and other elemental work: fabricating, assembling, installing and repairing electrical electronic and related equipment	2,185	2,895	3,930	3,010
8539	Fabricating, assembling, installing and repairing electrical, electronic and related equipment	2,720	2,505	2,665	1,525

Source: Statistics Canada, Census 1991, The Nation: Occupations, Cat. No. 93-327 and Census 1986, Occupational Trends, 1961–1986.

domestic ones and branches of multinationals, are under pressure to expand the scope of their market operations. Their production lines are being integrated into an overall North American market, where they face competition not only from their domestic and international rivals, but even internal competition from other plants for limited company resources.

The combination of substantial increases in output with dramatically falling employment indicates the extent of workplace restructuring that occurred over the past decade. Many firms attempted to adjust workplace practices to achieve greater flexibility and productivity with lower levels of staffing. The impact of restructuring was especially severe for non-skilled secondary labour, most frequently in the positions occupied by women. The occupations in the industry that grew most rapidly were those involving installing and repairing, while those involving assembling and fabricating declined. Not coincidentally, the occupations which grew the most were those with proportionately more employees with some post-secondary education, while those that declined were those with fewer employees with post-secondary education (Table 2). Although the presence or absence of post-secondary certificates is only a crude proxy for the changing level of demand for skills, it suggests that those employees with the lowest skill levels are most vulnerable in the present period of rapid economic and technological change sweeping the industry.

The Sectoral Skills Council in Operation

The agreement signed in July 1990 by the key players in the human resource study – the Electrical and Electronic Manufacturers' Association of Canada (EEMAC), the Communication and Electrical Workers of Canada (CWC), the International Brotherhood of Electrical Workers (IBEW), and the United Steel Workers of America (USWA) – marked the official beginning of the council. The Sectoral Skills Council signed separate agreements with the Ontario Ministry of Skills Development and with Employment and Immigration Canada. The sector-wide agreement includes provision for vocational training and upgrading, paid educational leave, and union education programming for delegates and technology stewards. While it is one of a number of sectoral initiatives launched in the past decade, it has grown rapidly to offer training to the largest number of eligible workers, through the largest number of participating workplaces.

The experience of the SSC suggests that the differences between labour and management over the training question are not insurmountable. Employers in electrical and electronics manufacturing have joined the fund because it meets their interests directly. For them, the council remains part of a tool-box of competitiveness. It gives firms in the industry access to government-subsidized training funds, while at the same time offering them an opportunity to shape their training programs jointly with their workers in a way that responds to immediate workplace needs. Increased skill levels in the industry will have positive effects in their own right, but the structure of the council also gives firms the opportunity to share authority with their workers in a non-hostile environment. This sharing of authority on questions concerning training could, over time, increase understanding, and possibly, the level of trust between employers and employees. For those employers interested in developing a culture of cooperation with the union on other issues, such as job design, participation in the SSC can be worthwhile even when direct benefits are minimal.

In theory, cooperative training programs also allow labour a greater say in the way change is introduced in the workplace, and aligns the process of economic restructuring more closely with labour's goals. Highly skilled and less fragmented jobs can release workers from the tyranny of Taylorist time-and-motion-oriented systems of production. A key issue for the unions involved with the SSC was the commitment they won that training would be funded only if it provided portable skills in an equitable manner that was incremental to training the companies were already funding. In the end, the council was able to accommodate the different perspectives of both management and labour: first, by providing the opportunity for firms to raise skill levels to increase flexibility and productivity; and, secondly, by providing workers with the opportunity to further their personal education goals.

In practice, many frictions from other spheres of management-labour relations affected the operations of the council. In some workplaces, management was flexible in releasing the union representatives on joint workplace training committees (JWTCs) from their regular work, so that they could promote training, do their share of the administration, and counsel co-workers encountering difficulties in a more high-commitment environment. In other locations, the prerogatives of management rights were exercised more traditionally. In those locations, committee participants incurred the resentment of co-workers because no replacement was provided for them when they undertook training work. Even worse, sometimes the participants in training programs themselves had no replacement, with the result that both front-line supervisors and co-workers had to pick up the slack and resisted the 'training culture' as a barely disguised form of speed-up.

The SSC, with its focused effort on issues outside the routine collective bargaining process, increases the scope and possibilities for joint action in the workplace. Given the difficulties of the present economic climate, this understanding may have positive spin-offs for the economy in general. Current industrial relations theory stresses the importance of increased trust and shared responsibility in workplace relations. Cooperation in the provision of training for employed workers is seen by some as a key to the adoption of a more innovative workplace model (Kochan and Osterman, 1994). Both employers and employees must be involved in determining the conduct of training at the level of the firm. Where there are unions, they should be the body recognized as representing workers. Where there is no union, employers need to establish a representative body of employees to participate in decision-making on the training contract. From this perspective, the experience of workers and their employers in working together to solve joint problems in the workplace through the Sectoral Skills Council may contribute to the adoption of this model.

Although it represents a major commitment on the part of all parties to expand their training efforts, the SSC should not be regarded as a comprehensive response to the challenges of economic restructuring. It was designed to complement other private and public efforts to promote the development of the electrical and electronic manufacturing industry during a period of expansion. Labour and management cooperation is limited to the specific area of training, whereas other sectoral initiatives, such as that in the steel industry, were driven more by trade and adjustment concerns. Such training efforts are viewed by the labour movement as an important contributor to worker education and development, but they cannot, by themselves, be regarded as a substitute for a broader economic and industrial strategy.

Under the terms of the 1990 agreement, a sectoral training council was established to set broad policy guidelines to administer the Sectoral Training Fund, through a secretariat, on a daily basis. The role of the council is:

- to provide business and labour with a forum for discussion of the major human resource issues facing the industry, outside of the collective bargaining process;
- to identify, and set overall direction for, human resource areas in which joint sectoral action would be appropriate and effective;
- to guide the work of individual, issue-specific subcommittees, to review, amend and approve their proposals/recommendations, and to act on them;
- to represent business and labour on human resource issues of joint concern, and to communicate the industry's views on such concerns to others, e.g. education, government.

The Sectoral Skills Council is comprised of twelve members, six each from management and labour. The management representatives are senior-level executives nominated by the industry association and the union members are senior-level representatives nominated by their respective unions. In addition to the three initial signatories to the agreement, participation now includes five other unions: the International Association of Machinists and Aerospace Workers, the International Federation of Professional and Technical Employees, the Canadian Auto Workers Union, the Laborer's International Union, and the United Food and Commercial Workers. A key aspect of the council's organization is its parity structure. Although the electrical and electronic manufacturing sector is largely non-union, the insistence of the unions that the committee consist of equal union and management representation established the principle that non-union employees are represented by unions in the decision-making process.

The council meets four times a year and its activities are coordinated by a professional secretariat, consisting of an executive director and two associates, one each from management and labour. There are also three subcommittees: the training subcommittee administers the use of the sectoral training fund and provides support to the Joint Workplace Training Committees; the education subcommittee works to ensure that education providers in the colleges, universities, and school system are responsive to the needs of the industry; and the sectoral change committee functions as an apprenticeship subcommittee and is working on a new certificate program for skilled trades that will facilitate skills upgrading and greater portability (Haddad, 1995: 40–1).

In the past two years, the SSC has become involved in a number of important projects in areas concerning work reorganization and human skills training, such as the school-to-work transition project. In 1994 the council began work with a local school board and the community college system in Ontario to design, develop, field test, and evaluate a prototype curriculum in manufacturing technology for secondary schools and community colleges. It was designed to improve the school-to-work transition by creating a more integrated curriculum from secondary school to the college level. It has expanded to include boards of education and colleges in all ten provinces and the number of test sites has grown to twenty-one schools (Sectoral Skills Council, 1995c: 13).

The SSC does not replace collective bargaining. In fact, in unionized plants, a decision to join the council must be written into the collective agreement. Despite the fact that half of the funding for sectoral training is provided by the federal and provincial levels of government, only management and labour have decision-making authority in the running of the council. Meetings are conducted on the basis of consensus, with no neutral chair, which means a mutual veto on all major decisions, both at the sectoral and the workplace level. Hence people are forced to listen to each other and to decide which issues really matter. This generates a powerful external discipline that says neither management nor labour can afford a stalemate. In one study of the council's operation, a key accomplishment identified by some of the longest-serving participants is its ability to establish a joint process for making decisions about training priorities within the industry (Haddad, 1995: 48).

The Sectoral Skills Council is responsible for setting training guidelines and ensuring that they are followed in each workplace which joins. These guidelines are contained in the Operating Handbook for the Sectoral Training Fund (1993), which establishes broad policies on specific training questions. The council receives contributions to the fund from workplaces and governments, and distributes funding in response to proposals. It also resolves disputes referred to it by individual workplaces and monitors expenditures under the fund for auditing and evaluation purposes.

The overall funding level for the fund is set at 1 per cent of the wage bill for each of the participating workplaces. The cost of the fund is shared between the private sector and the two participating governments: the federal government and the government of Ontario.[3] Both the overall level of funding and the source for the private sector contribution were critical points of controversy in the establishment of the council. The unions originally sought a funding level of 2.5 per cent of payroll, and some even demanded that management pay the entire private-sector share of the cost. Other unions were prepared to accept the principle that employers and employees would share the private sector contribution on the understanding that the issue of the employee contribution could be a subject of negotiations. In the end, the unions that signed the agreement settled for the 1 per cent contribution and those that would not accept the principle of any employee contribution withdrew. In practice, all unionized firms that participate in the training fund have negotiated that the employee contribution is paid by the employer. The wording of the agreement was subsequently amended to state that the total private-sector contribution constitutes half of the fund without specifying there must be an employee contribution. The unions that objected to the idea of an employee contribution have subsequently rejoined the fund. In non-unionized firms, the employer consults with the employees to determine various mechanisms for making the contribution.

Joint Workplace Training Committees

In addition to the broad industry-wide structure, management and workers form JWTCs which are responsible for the fund at the local level. In large part, these committees are responsible for the fund's training activities. Each workplace fund is self-contained and consists of the contributions from the employer and the participating workers at that workplace, plus the matching government funds leveraged by their contributions. Membership in the fund is voluntary, open to both unionized and non-unionized firms. To join, both employer and employee groups within a firm must agree to participate. All employees in participating workplaces are eligible to join the fund and receive training benefits. This includes management, production, office, technical, professional, sales, and maintenance employees. Each worker in the fund has money set aside at the SSC for training, equivalent to 1 per cent of his/her wages while within the fund. The financial system of accounting and fund disbursement has worked well. Training funds have been received quickly and allocated efficiently in the committees. In fact, the administrative costs of running the fund have been held down to 8 per cent of total operating expenditures.

The Sectoral Skills Council's unique decentralized structure offers an opportunity for working people to participate in the development of training programs.

The fund's success depends on two things: the ability of workers and management within the joint workplace training committees to work together in shaping training programs; and the committee's ability to arouse interest among workers in training in the workplace. The Sectoral Skills Council currently (as of January 1997) makes training available to 54,500 workers in Ontario in 208 firms, through the agency of 218 JWTCs. The launching of the fund at the onset of the 1990s recession clearly slowed its rate of growth and diffusion throughout the industry, but in the past two years the size of the fund has grown and the number of participating workplaces expanded. There has also been a noticeable increase in the number of small and medium-sized firms joining. A greater proportion of these firms are non-unionized and this has shifted the balance between union and non-union workplaces; there are now seventy per cent non-unionized firms as opposed to thirty per cent unionized.

Local union officers are developing confidence and sensitivity to their members as they assess and meet the full range of learning needs. Without dropping the adversarial commitment to defend their members' rights, the unions are also developing a different experience in working with managers. The members now see their union as a vehicle for learning and for protecting their health, as well as negotiating wages and benefits. The majority who have never had individual disputes with management now have ongoing contact with their union representatives in ways that increase their range of interests and job choices.

Membership and Responsibilities

The real core of the training initiative resides in the operation of the joint workplace training committees. These committees are responsible for calling and chairing meetings, and their decisions are taken by majority vote. The committees ensure that fund contributions on behalf of the firm and its workers accurately reflect the number of employees covered, and that they are made on a regular basis to the SSC. They are responsible for monitoring that the training financed through the fund is incremental to the training that firms would have otherwise undertaken, and also make sure that the training provided for employees fits the broad eligibility criteria established for each of the fund's four types of training. They select the local training proposals to recommend to the Sectoral Skills Council for funding under each of the types of training and ascertain that the training is of acceptable quality, cost, and flexibility. A critical role performed by the committees is encouraging workers to learn about how and where to exercise their training rights and responsibilities.

An effective JWTC is one where decision-making truly involves both parties and where divergent parts of the workplace come together to work out a joint training program. To receive funding, all requests must include the signatories of the employee and employer representative of the committee. These requests are then sent to the SSC for final approval. It is often difficult for divergent parties with a history of conflict within the workplace to begin the process of joint decision-making. Labour and management representatives must engage in a honest dialogue about the respectives needs of the firm and its workers, and they must seek a consensus. In the eyes of some union staff involved with the fund, a worst-case scenario is one in which the JWTC is completely driven by the union, with the management representatives merely acquiescing to the process. They fear that this type of process is not sustainable and that management may simply withdraw from participating at some future point. Conversely, JWTCs completely driven by the management agenda are equally worrisome.

Startup Process

Virtually all participants agree that a key to the success of the process is the initial recruitment of members for the joint workplace training committees. According to the evaluation of the SSC conducted for the federal and provincial governments, more than half of the JWTCs surveyed relied on a process of handpicking members or appointing people especially for the key roles on the committee. In some of the unionized workplaces labour representatives are either elected to the committees or membership is assumed by elected officers of the plant local. In all cases, the employers pay for their employees time to participate in the committees (Canadian Facts and ABT Associates of Canada, 1994: 23).

Two-thirds of the committees undertook some kind of formal analysis of their firms' training needs. It was common, however, for labour and management to each come to the JWTC with a prepared list of training priorities. Using these prepared lists, the committees developed a training priority list and worked down it. These prepared lists were usually fashioned among labour or management representatives in consultation with employees in the workplace (Canadian Facts and ABT Associates of Canada, 1994: 25).

Of the JWTCs surveyed for the evaluation, nineteen out of twenty-four encountered problems in starting up operations and offering training (Canadian Facts and ABT Associates of Canada, 1994: 26). These teething difficulties were related to the extensive reliance placed on the committees and the large number of responsibilities each committee had. Over one-third of the committees stated that a significant effort was required to determine the training needs of the firm, to ascertain the training programs available, and to develop a joint decision-making process. Since committee membership is part-time and limited, the resources of the members were heavily taxed. On average, members spent eight hours a week on committee activities. According to some participants in the council, it has taken longer, typically, for the JWTCs to start in unionized workplaces due to the more formalized approaches used to establish them. However, these committees have proved better able to withstand changes in management personnel within their workplaces. In non-unionized workplaces, the establishment of the JWTCs has depended to a great extent on the degree of support from senior management (Canadian Facts and ABT Associates of Canada, 1994: 23–7; Haddad, 1995: 65).

Training designed and provided by the SSC has helped to facilitate the start-up process. It has developed training programs to inform committee members about the fund in particular, and training in general. These programs are open to all members and both union and management are represented. Moreover, extensive training courses are offered through the group training section of the fund and experienced members of JWTCs as well as staff at the SSC, are used to train new members.

The joint workplace training committee process has had mixed results. According to the program evaluation, as well as a number of additional interviews, in workplaces with good relations, the SSC may have enhanced the relationship. However, in workplaces with poor relations, there were reports of initial scepticism on both sides. Some firms have been more forthcoming with information about the firm's future plans. Accordingly, union members in the JWTC have had an opportunity to help shape new production designs and work patterns and to anticipate future demands. Management has also commented on improved employee morale and self-esteem (Canadian Facts and ABT Associates of Canada, 1994: 27).

Union Activities

The unions involved in the SSC have made a concerted effort to provide orientation for their members participating in the JWTCs. The Communications, Energy and Paperworkers Union (CEP), for instance, has developed a Facing Training Program with financing from the Sectoral Training Fund to prepare their members with the skills necessary to influence the development of training programs within the committees. The program is designed to inform union participants in committees of union policies and experience about job training, to encourage union participants to see themselves as education delegates, and to equip union participants with skills to analyse the learning needs of their fellow workers and to use the range of supports provided by the SSC. The goal of the unions is that their participants be advocates and counsellors among the membership, rather than training administrators. Given the highly decentralized nature of the fund and the emphasis placed on local determination of needs, union-provided training is deemed essential to ensure that the labour perspective on training is reflected in the individual workplaces involved.

Among the participating unions, cooperation in such activities has run against the grain. Raids have occurred, and ideological and political differences among the unions remain. Yet the first Facing Training Program was instructed jointly by staff from the Steelworkers and the CWC; in 1994, Steelworker staff participated in a CEP session; and in mid-1995, the Canadian Auto Workers sent participants and resource people to a joint session with the Steelworkers and CEP. A further session in late 1996 involved more of the unions, and in the interim periodic caucuses were held to resolve differences. Such caucuses are particularly important since a minority of the workplaces in the SSC are unionized; further, the expanding electronics segment of the sector is overwhelmingly non-union, while the electrical segment, with its strong union presence, is steadily losing ground through partial and complete plant closures.

Access to Training

Consistent with the original objectives of the training fund, most training programs are open to all workers. Generally, JWTC members have taken it upon themselves to act as salespeople for the training initiatives. Newsletters have been prepared. In workplaces with significant literacy problems, a telephone help line has been established. In workplaces with minorities with limited English-language skills, contacts with linguistic facilities have also been established. For the most part, training is freely available for all willing participants. In a few instances, there has been a need for limits on enrolment. In two work sites, for example, enrolment is limited to those who can be spared from their work or allocated on a needs-must-wants basis (people with needs are given training first, followed by people who must have training, and finally, those who want training). In a well-developed, unionized workplace, individual workers can be assured that the training programs offered will have met union approval. Moreover, in a unionized workplace, the union itself can direct the attention of workers to training opportunities.

There is also some evidence that participating in the Sectoral Training Fund is generating a more positive attitude on the part of some firms to their own approach to training. In one instance reported by Haddad, after joining the fund and establishing its own JWTC, one medium-sized, non-unionized firm then hired its own training director and developed a strategic training plan for the entire firm, using the resources of the JWTC. Eventually, the head of the firm decided to assign responsibility for the company's entire training budget, some

3–4 per cent of payroll, to the JWTC (Haddad, 1995: 64). This case indicates that the fund can play an important role in diffusing a training culture more widely among firms in the sector. The relative absence of such a culture has frequently been cited as a major deficiency in the approach to training exhibited by many Canadian firms (Premier's Council, 1990).

Training Types

The actual training supported by the fund is distributed among three different categories:

- Type I training, which consists of job/skill updating/upgrading, constitutes 62 per cent of fund expenditures;
- Type II, which consists of general education/training, constitutes 20 per cent of fund expenditures; and
- Type III, which consists of employee group–directed training, constitutes 10 per cent of fund expenditures.

Type IV was originally designed to provide employee assistance and counselling in a plant closure situation. However, only a small proportion of the funds reserved for Type IV were used and in 1992, the remaining funds were rolled over into Type I training, which makes the fund more flexible. The remaining 8 per cent of the fund is set aside to cover administrative costs. The actual training costs covered by the fund include tuition, trainee's lost time, travel and accommodation, books and supplies, teachers' salaries, curriculum development, and the rental of office facilities.

Type I

Type I training is intended to encompass training 'over and above what the firm is already doing. It should provide basic or technical skills directly relevant to trainees' jobs in that workplace and "portable" skills.' Portable skills should have direct application in other firms in the industry. Such training must upgrade, update, maintain, or broaden existing skills (Sectoral Skills Council, 1993: 21). It can involve trade apprenticeships; trades upgrading, technician/ technologist training, or professional upgrading or updating. Type I funding is not intended to support training which would otherwise be paid for by the firms themselves (Sectoral Skills Council, 1993: 22).

Three main kinds of Type I training have been performed: technical upgrading, basic skills courses, and interpersonal skills. Technical training courses included design for manufacturing, analog design, aluminum welding, metrology, machine shop, metallurgy, and ISO 9000 standards. Basic skills courses were designed to improve literacy in computers, English, math, and technical illustration. Group or team skills were enhanced through stress management, interpersonal skills, time management, and supervisory training courses. In fact, over 30 per cent of all training was related to computer training. On average the training programs last one week (or thirty-seven hours), with slightly less time for office workers than plant workers. They cost about $357 per worker per course (Canadian Facts and ABT Associates of Canada, 1994: 33).

The distribution of the locations for Type I training opportunities is important. Thirty-five per cent of the training is performed at community colleges, 31 per cent on the job, 20 per cent in an outside training facility, and 4 per cent and 3 per cent in high schools and universities, respectively. A major issue for the unions over the past decade has been maintaining a central role for public institutions in the provision of publicly funded or subsidized training. The high percentage of sectoral training performed by public institutions suggests that this objective has been achieved in the case of the Sectoral Training Fund. In participating non-union firms, the ratio of private to public training is higher (Canadian Facts and ABT Associates of Canada, 1994: 28).

Management has been concerned that training provided by the community college system is often outmoded or inadequate to meet their needs. According to union representatives on the council, the involvement of the colleges with the fund affords them a valuable opportunity to link their capabilities to the needs of industry. In some instances, the colleges have come into the workplace to provide the necessary training, employing both their own staff and additional personnel recruited for the purpose. This makes the training more accessible for employees, and also ensures that the colleges are carrying out the training on the types of equipment and instruments actually used in the workplace. In addition, the SSC has been working with the Ontario Council of Regents, the governing body of the Ontario Community Colleges, in the area of prior learning assessment and recognition (PLAR). This enables individuals to receive college credit for non-college learning, thereby providing opportunities for non-traditional learners and to ensuring that work experience will be recognized in a college environment. Through the program, individuals can earn up to a 75 per cent credit for a course by preparing a portfolio which documents their skills and expertise (Ontario Council of Regents, 1994).

The Sectoral Skills Council has also used the Ontario government's union-designed basic education skills training (BEST) program for literacy training. The BEST program offers a Grade 12 update and is designed to meet the needs of workers shut out of the educational system or those who have had difficulties

TABLE 3   Sample of Training Activities under the Sectoral Training Fund

Courses completed, under way, or planned:

Type I training:
1 Technical upgrading/updating courses:
   Design for manufacturability
   Extrusion technology and skills
   Analog design
   Lotus 1-2-3
   Sales techniques
   Electrical products education course
   Electrical training course (principles)
   Advanced computer packages
   The nature of vibration
   The theory of power measurement
   Aluminum welding
   Steel welding
   Blueprint reading
   Motor fundamentals
   Wiring/schematics
   Basic electrical safety theory
   Metrology
   Machince shop
   Fortran programming
   Numberically controlled machining
   Metallurgy
   Materials handling
   Programable logic control
   ISO 9000 standards
   CSA N285 standards
   Arc welding
   Supercalc
   HP graphics gallery
   Boiler & pressure vessel codes
   Material handling (chrome & forklift truck)
   Implanter process interface
   M16 ferroelectric thin films
   Competitive marketing strategies for high tech products
   Data modelling
   Introduction to oracle
   QA auditor training course
   How to better organize files & records
   CTI cryogenics cryopump
   Autocad intermediate
   Understanding photolith & process control
   Hazardous chemicals safety

TABLE 3 (*Continued*)

Courses completed, under way, or planned:

Project management
Advanced trouble shooting
Waste elimination now/picos training
Understanding data communication
Principles of quality assurance
Strategic management of R & D
Behavioural interviewing
Compensation training
Sheet metal practical & safety training
Quantitative analyses
Strategic selling
Oracle manufacturing modules
Production and inventory management
Payroll for supervisors
Facilitation skills
Power electronics circuits
Power switchgear equipment
Robotics packaging
2 Basic skills courses:
Basic skills in the workplace
Computer literacy courses (introduction to computers)
Basic English
Basic math skills
Trigonometry refresher
Keyboard skills
Hard disk DOS
WordPerfect – Level I
Programming methodolgy
Technical illustration
3 Group/team/personal skills:
Stress management
Interpersonal skills
Time management – supervisory training
Spanish

Type II training:
1 Lotus 1-2-3
2 Writing for business
3 Introduction to computers
4 English grammar (English as a second language)
5 Records management
6 Communication skills for women
7 Effective speaking and human relations

TABLE 3 (*Concluded*)

Courses completed, under way, or planned:

Type III training:
1 Facing training (for union JWTC members)
2 Analog design
3 Time management
4 Stress management
5 Image & communicaiton skills
6 Cultural diversity awareness
7 Teambuilding workshop
8 Understanding NAFTA regulations
9 Competitive benchmarking

Type IV training:
PLANT CLOSURE SITUATIONS:
1 Employee assistance and counselling program

---

in formal educational institutions. It enables working people without a high school education to begin the process of lifelong learning. As it is a union-led program, these workers can be taught in an supportive environment.

The importance of basic literacy training should not be underestimated. In many instances, electrical and electronic manufacturing workers have been outside of the formal education system for a long period. Furthermore, many workers entered the workforce decades ago when the skills needed were radically different. The number of literacy-related courses requested in the first few years of the program suggests that the formal education of some workers in the sector are relatively low. Basic remedial education is required before the JWTCs can engage in more advanced training programs.

The effectiveness of Type I training depends on two main criteria: the extent to which funding has increased the amount of training within the industry as a whole; and the ability of the fund to sponsor training which is truly portable. A small survey of participating members in the fall of 1993 indicated that firms participating in the program have increased training and broadened the areas of training. A number of other indicators suggest increased training activity or, at least, increased interest in training activities. The rapid growth of the SSC over the past five years indicates that firms have begun to take the program more seriously. The number of firms participating in the fund and the amount of training activity has increased dramatically in each of the past two years as the industry pulled out of the recession. The rate of annual expenditure from the fund has grown from $2.2 million in 1993–4 to $6.6 million in 1994–5, just over $8 million in 1995–6 and an estimated $11.5 million in 1996–7.[4]

Anecdotal evidence from individual workers indicated that the fund provided the first training available to them in their workplace. In other, more advanced workplaces, the evidence suggests that training programs have become more open and available as a result of the fund. Active recruitment campaigns by JWTC members of their fellow workers into training programs shows that the existence of the fund is contributing to a heightened awareness of the importance of training among the participating workplaces. Taken together these indicators do suggest increased training activity. In some JWTCs, benchmarks for portability have been established, which include: the ability of the learner to use the skills at a later date; and whether or not the training course offers a certificate or credit which can be used to gain access to more advanced training courses or to improve the learners' qualifications.

Type II

Type II training covers general education, and was intended to enable participants to pursue training and education opportunities that are career-related. The program does not have to be related to a job; it may also include training the employee to a better position the employee Fund member to take advantage of future employment opportunities, either inside or outside the industry (Sectoral Skills Council, 1993: 23). Assistance from the Type II training fund covers the cost of tuition, books and supplies, and teachers' salaries. It may also be used to reimburse the trainee's salary in full.

Type II training activities must be initiated by the worker. In the original structure of the fund, workers were required to accumulate training credits based on a complex formula to gain access to the funds. In practice, the system proved too cumbersome, the calculations were excessively difficult to keep track of, and it created additional administrative problems for the fund. After extensive consultations with JWTC members, in the fall of 1994 the SSC decided to eliminate the system of accumulating credits. Under the new system, each employee is entitled to a maximum of $3,000 once every three years, and if circumstances warrant, the maximum can go up to $5,000. The JWTCs are to decide what constitutes these special circumstances.

As expected, Type II funding was not widely used in the first few years of the fund's operation. Programs often have substantial costs, such as tuition and books, and the short time the fund had been operating had not enabled participants to build up sufficient credits to support a long-term program. Furthermore, neither the purpose and nor the availability of Type II was readily apparent to workers. Individuals did not realize the extensive benefits available to them under the fund, and the programs demanded a considerable commitment of time on the part of the participants. During 1994–5, a major controversy developed between management and labour representatives on the SSC concerning Type II Funds. Management urged that the allocation simply be folded into Type I, and that workplace committees have the discretion to allow individuals to draw on Type I funds for personal development. The unions insisted that the original agreement be respected, and that additional resources and publicity be provided to encourage individual workers to exercise their entitlement. This classic debate between training for employment needs and training as a social right was resolved in favour of the unions. Yet the tension between 'competency-based' and 'worker-driven' perspectives on training simply moved onto other terrains.

Since the revisions to the Type II funding in 1994, there has been a noticeable increase in this category of training and education. In conversations with union members participating in the fund, Type II funding was seen to have important symbolic value far beyond its actual use to date. For working people, Type II funding provides an opportunity to pursue lifelong learning opportunities. For these workers, who have been shut out of the formal education system for a long time, Type II funding is a prized opportunity.

Type III

Type III training is group-directed training designed to give groups of employees workplace or process skills. Process skills refer to union-sponsored and management-led development courses and a variety of group-based soft skills. Funding is available for groups to develop an understanding of the environment in which their firms and unions operate. Type III funding is used to sponsor union classes on subjects such as international affairs, the structure and finance of Canadian industry, human rights, racism in the workplace, and labour actions for the environment. Type III funds provide unions with the opportunity to perform new and greater labour-led training exercises. For management, it has been used to sponsor image and communication skills, team-building workshops, stress management, and time management. Again, participation in these programs is strictly voluntary and approvals of all funding must be made in JWTCs and receive the approval of both management and employee representatives (Canadian Facts and ABT Associates of Canada, 1994: 27).

Conclusion

By the objective measures of size, rate of growth, the number of workers and workplaces involved, and its overall level of expenditures, the Sectoral Skills

Council is clearly a success. It has enabled large numbers of working people to gain better access to training opportunities. It has also helped improve the competitive position of the electrical and electronic manufacturing industry by allowing firms to obtain government-subsidized training dollars. The decentralized structure of the Sectoral Training Fund has allowed each participating workplace great latitude in designing and preparing workplace training programs, and the joint decision-making process within the committees has enabled labour and management to take concrete actions to deal with the problems of labour force adjustment.

The measures of effectiveness for initiatives such as the SSC are still differently constructed by business, labour, education providers, and the governments involved. While improving labour relations within the sector has been acknowledged as a goal of council participants, progress in this area has not been monitored in a systematic manner. Similarly, the three criteria applied to all training proposals are that they be portable, incremental, and equitable. Yet there are no longitudinal studies on the degree to which learners in SSC programs have carried on their studies elsewhere. There is pressure from the business side to discard the incremental element in favour of the essentially meaningless term 'value-added.' And the record-keeping capacity needed to track equity of access and outcome in training has yet to be put in place. The lack of central monitoring is in part a conscious decision to under-manage council activities, to avoid burdening local workplace committees. In part it is a consequence of rapid growth, whereby systems such as computerized record management have not kept pace with the scale of the operation. And in part, it may reflect a deliberate ambiguity among the council participants, a tacit view that 'what we don't know can't divide us.'

The degree to which different actors have different perceptions was dramatized in a recent study prepared for the council by Stuart Ross and John Nyman. They found, for example, that workers thought advanced computer skills were essential for some jobs in the sector, while frontline management considered them of secondary importance. On other issues union and management were in agreement, while college educators saw the needs very differently. Between industry and education, between management and labour, different views of the council's role continue to interact, as part of an ongoing process of social bargaining – a process with more diverse participants and a wider range of issues than traditional collective bargaining (Ross and Nymen, 1996).

The external pressures on the SSC are also considerable. Since it now involves almost 55,000 employees across the province, and is relatively harmonious in a very polarized labour relations climate, its profile has increased steadily. Given that the federal and Ontario governments were contributing nearly $4 million each annually in core operations, with other projects adding significantly to the total, this had become a significant fiscal matter for both levels of government. However, the shift in policy at both levels away from providing direct funding for in-firm training has placed a cloud over the future of the council. At the time of writing, the federal share of the council's income was secure only to the end of 1997, while the provincial contribution was being wound down as part of a general policy by the Ontario Conservatives to terminate all subsidies to business.

In their spring budget of 1996, the provincial Conservatives withdrew their support for the Ontario Training and Adjustment Board, as well as several other sectoral initiatives.[5] Responsibility for training programs was restored to the Ministry of Education and Training. At the same time, the federal government has systematically narrowed the role and mandate of the Canadian Labour Force Development Board. The elimination of OTAB and the attenuation of the CLFDB have removed the protective umbrella, the shelter under which unions could balance sectoral and regional needs for training; while the loss of funding for sectoral initiatives has isolated the electrical and electronic manufacturing sector, imposing greater stress on the will and skill of the union side to navigate these hazards to sustain a worthwhile initiative until the broader balance of political forces shifts more towards labour interests.

From the labour perspective, the experience with the SSC has offered the participating unions an opportunity to put into practice many of the principles of good training that they developed in the previous decade. None of the unions regard the council and its training programs in an uncritical light, although there remain some significant differences over the best principles for the design of sectoral training initiatives. Further, the capacity of the unions to support and guide representatives in the JWTCs has been limited. During the rapid expansion of the fund, the staff time needed to monitor the nature and quality of the training being approved at the local workplaces has been in short supply.

Despite these limitations, and the uncertainty created by the withdrawal of government support for its future funding, involvement in the council has offered the unions the opportunity to expand the participation of a large number of their members in the determination of their own training and education options. In so doing, it has both increased the presence and relevance of the union for their members and provided an opportunity for those members to gain greater experience in influencing key decisions in their own workplaces. In an era when unions are subjected to increasing pressures and strain, activities such as these enhance the bond between the union and its membership and help its members deal more effectively with the rapidly changing workplace.

Notes

The research for this paper was supported by SSHRCC grant number 884-91-0034. The authors are indebted to Ammon Salter for his invaluable research assistance.

1 See Sharpe, 1992, for a fuller account of the various sectoral studies supported by Employment and Immigration Canada. As of September 1996, twenty-two national HRDC-funded sector councils were operating across the country.
2 Although these initiatives were national in scope, they all received support from both the federal government and the government of Ontario. A substantial portion of the training undertaken was also located in Ontario. However, by January 1997, the auto parts council was no longer in existence and government funding for the other two was being wound down.
3 Although the council is designed to be national in scope and discussions have been held with the provincial governments of Alberta and New Brunswick, to date the fund operates exclusively in Ontario and all of the participating workplaces are located in that province.
4 These figures are supplied by the Sectoral Skills Council.
5 For a more detailed account of the troubled existence and untimely demise of the Ontario Training and Adjustment Board, see Wolfe, 1997.

References

Canadian Electrical and Electronics Manufacturing Industry, Joint Human Resources Committee. 1989. *Connections for the Future*. Toronto.
Canadian Facts and ABT Associates of Canada. 1994. *Evaluation of the Canadian Electrical and Electronic Manufacturing Industry (CEEMI) Sectoral Training Fund*. Ottawa: Program Evaluation Branch, Human Resources Development Canada, and Toronto: Policy Branch, Ontario Training and Adjustment Board.
Freeman, Chris, and Luc Soete. 1994. *Work for All or Mass Unemployment? Computerised Technical Change in the 21st Century*. London and New York: Pinter Publishers.
Government of Canada. 1994. *A New Framework for Economic Policy: Agenda Jobs and Growth*. Ottawa: Department of Finance.
Haddad, Carol J. 1995. *Sectoral Training Partnerships in Canada: Building Consensus through Policy and Practice*. A Report to the Government of Canada. Eastern Michigan University, Ypsilanti, Michigan.
Kochan, Thomas A., and Paul Osterman. 1994. *The Mutual Gains Enterprise: Forging a Winning Partnership among Labor, Management and Government*. Boston: Harvard Business School Press.
Martin, D'Arcy. 1992. 'Unions and Training in Ontario,' in Nancy Jackson, ed., *Training*

for What? Labour Perspectives on Job Training, pp. 66–75. Toronto: Our Schools/Our Selves Education Foundation.

– 1995. *Thinking Union: Activism and Education in Canada's Labour Movement.* Toronto: Between the Lines.

O'Grady, John. 1994. 'Case 2: Province of Ontario, Canada: Removing the Obstacles to Negotiated Adjustment,' in Werner Sengenberger and Duncan Campbell, eds., *Creating Economic Opportunities: The Role of Labour Standards in Industrial Restructuring*, pp. 255–78. Geneva: International Institute for Labour Studies.

Ontario Council of Regents. 1994. *Prior Learning Assessment Program.* Toronto.

Ontario Federation of Labour. 1992. 'Education and Training. A Policy Adopted at the 33rd Annual Convention,' in Nancy Jackson, ed., *Training for What? Labour Perspectives on Job Training*, pp. 87–103. Toronto: Our Schools/Our Selves Education Foundation.

Premier's Council. 1990. *People and Skills in the New Global Economy.* Toronto: Queen's Printer for Ontario.

Ross, Stuart, and James Nyman. 1996. 'Occupational Standards for Members of the Manufacturing Workforces of the Electrical and Electronics Industry.' Ottawa: Sectoral Skills Council.

Sectoral Skills Council. 1993. *The Operating Handbook of the Sectoral Training Fund.* Ottawa.

– 1995a. *The Sectoral Skills Council: A Joint Human Resources Development Initiative in the Canadian Electrical/Electronics Industry.* Ottawa.

– 1995b. *The Ten Essentials for an Effective JWTC.* Ottawa.

– 1995c. *Year-in-Review, 1994–1995.* Ottawa.

Sharpe, Andrew. 1992. 'The Role of Business-Labour Sectoral Initiatives in Economic Restructuring.' *Quarterly Labour Market and Productivity Review* 1, no. 2, pp. 26–35.

Warrian, Peter. 1989. 'Trade Unions and Labour Market Planning: The Case for Sectoral Regulation.' Paper presented to the Seminar on Social Democracy, University College, University of Toronto.

Wartzman, Rick. 1995. 'A Clinton Potion to Restore Middle Class's Love, Brewed by Labor Secretary, Stresses Job Training.' *Wall Street Journal.* 11 January.

Wolfe, David A. 1997. 'Institutional Limits to Labour Market Reform in Ontario: The Short Life and Rapid Demise of the Ontario Training and Adjustment Board,' in Andrew Sharpe and Rodney Haddow, eds., *The Emergence of Labour Force Development Boards in Canada.* Ottawa and Kingston: Caledon Institute for Social Policy and School of Policy Studies, Queen's University.

PART III
SECTOR INITIATIVES IN QUEBEC AND ONTARIO

6

The Configuration of Sectoral Human Resource Initiatives in Quebec in the 1990s

JEAN CHAREST

The aim of this chapter is to present the overall configuration of sectoral human resource initiatives in Quebec in the 1990s.[1] Although some of the initiatives referred to in this chapter date back to the 1980s, sectoral initiatives have only truly emerged in Quebec since the beginning of the present decade. Despite their recent nature, they represent a significant innovation in the field of industrial relations and, as such, unquestionably constitute an important subject of research.

The chapter first reviews some of the milestones in the recent history of Quebec labour market policies and of concertation practices between the actors in the industrial relations system. This historical overview is important to the understanding of both the conditions that have led to the emergence of recent initiatives and their differences from earlier experiences. Attention will also be drawn to the dual origins of recent sectoral initiatives in Quebec – that is, their links to labour market policy and to industrial policy.

Next, the general configuration of sectoral initiatives in Quebec will be outlined by first presenting their 'topography,' that is, the coverage of these initiatives in various economic sectors and in relation to the labour force concerned. The principal characteristics of sectoral initiatives related to human resources will then be highlighted. These two elements – topography and characteristics – will provide the basis for both the overview and a discussion of their potential.

In the conclusion, a number of issues for the actors and for the industrial relations system raised by sectoral-level participation will be examined. The conclusion also identifies a number of potential avenues of future research that could increase our knowledge of sectoral initiatives, a phenomenon that is still largely uncharted in the field of industrial relations.

Finally, it should be noted that this chapter deals with sectoral initiatives and labour force development initiatives from a strictly Quebec perspective. Thus, the analysis is limited to the policies of the Quebec government and to labour-management sectoral initiatives that are rooted in the Quebec economic context. Federal government policies and national sectoral initiatives operating in Quebec supported by Human Resource Development Canada (HRDC) will therefore not be dealt with.[2]

Concertation, Confrontation, and Sectoral Initiatives in Quebec

Sectoral initiatives in the area of human resources are a recent phenomenon in Quebec labour relations. They represent something of an anomaly in a relatively decentralized system of industrial relations in which the microeconomic level and collective bargaining have been at the forefront of labour-management relations for several decades. However, it should be noted that these initiatives build on a number of efforts at concerted action over the past twenty years. Indeed, in some ways these earlier experiences laid the groundwork for the more recent initiatives. Yet these recent initiatives signal a break with the neoliberal policies pursued during the earlier period. It is within this historical context that the recent emergence of a sectoral approach must be situated.

Milestones in Labour Market Concertation in Quebec

The last twenty years have seen a number of concertation efforts in Quebec. Most were the result of government initiatives aimed at fostering collaboration between employers and unions at the meso- and macro-economic levels.[3] In particular, during the first two mandates of the Parti Québécois government (1976–85), thirty-seven socioeconomic conferences were held, including three national summits, in addition to some twenty sectoral mini summits and regional conferences. As Fournier points out, the PQ government's strategy of concertation between the actors was ambitious:

The long-term objective of the Quebec government was to develop 'a new social contract,' based on a joint tripartite approach in a number of sectors. In exchange for 'social peace,' the partners would be invited to engage in economic planning and to participate in all basic economic decisions. This cooperative initiative would eventually be formalized in the establishment of a tripartite economic and social council, in which the government would assume an arbitral role. (1986a: 308)

Although the sectoral summits resulted in a number of innovative initiatives (e.g., Corvée-Habitation, a joint initiative which was successful in revitalizing the residential construction industry), the overall result of these concertation processes fell far short of the government's initial objective. These efforts, which amounted neither to a 'new social contract' nor to 'tripartism,' were characterized by state domination of the process and a cautious attitude on the part of employers and unions. The deep recession of 1981–2, the confrontation between public and parapublic sector unions and the government in the early 1980s, as well as the strong ideological differences between the union movement and business in Quebec, contributed largely to the collapse of this effort.

At the very end of its mandate, the PQ government launched another ambitious concertation experiment, this time explicitly focused on employment. In 1985 the government created the Round Table on Employment (Table Nationale de l'Emploi), with a mandate to develop a full employment policy with employers and unions. However, this effort did not survive the change in government that took place later in the year.

Indeed, the Liberal party's return to power in the fall of 1985 marked a clear break with the previous government's efforts at national concertation. At the time, the unemployment rate in Quebec was 11.8 per cent, only two percentage points lower than during the 1982 recession, and the new government's strategy, which was largely supported by the business community, embraced the rising neoliberalism of the time. The solution to the employment crisis was not to be found in cooperation between the actors, still less in institutional mechanisms such as the Round Table on Employment. On the contrary, it was deemed necessary to free the private sector from the governmental, regulatory, and institutional constraints which were stifling its potential expansion. The second half of the 1980s was to see a liberation of 'market forces' in Quebec. This strategy was bitterly denounced by the union movement, which opposed the state and employers over every aspect of the neoliberal agenda, from privatization to fiscal reform. This was not, to say the least, a climate conducive to tripartite concertation.

Swimming against the current of neoliberal discourse, and peripheral to the Quebec state, two economists, Lise Poulin Simon and Diane Bellemare, initiated the Forum for Employment (Forum pour l'emploi) in 1988. The aim of this multipartite concertation body was job development with a view to achieving full employment. The importance of the forum lies in the fact that it revived the idea of concertation around the issue of employment and defended the necessity of developing an 'active' labour market policy.

Beginning in the early 1990s, a number of departures from the government's neoliberal approach can be identified, which would prepare the ground for sectoral initiatives in the area of human resources. First of all, it should be recalled that, despite strong economic growth between 1984 and 1990, the unemployment rate in Quebec did not fall below 9.3 per cent (1989), which signalled, even to the government, that unemployment would continue to be a tough nut to crack.[4] Subsequently, the recession of the early 1990s drove the unemployment rate back up sharply. Structural changes in the Quebec economy, chronic under-investment in labour market training, economic globalization, and the deterioration of public finances all added to the worrying portrait of the Quebec economy. Taken together, these factors combined to foster the idea that profound changes were taking place and, more particularly, that a new strategy of labour force development was needed.

It is within this context that two government policies marking a departure from strict neoliberal thinking and reviving the idea that social concertation could be a strategic variable in the 'new race for world competitiveness' can be situated. In 1991 the Ministry of Manpower, Income Security and Skills Development published a policy statement on labour force development (MMSRFP, 1991). Just a few months later, the Ministry of Industry, Trade and Technology launched its industrial strategy, based on the concept of 'industrial clusters' (MICT, 1991). The two initiatives made sectoral-level concertation the basis for improving the competitiveness of the Quebec economy and for expanding employment. In both cases, the government's proposals met with a favourable response from employers and unions.

Labour Force Development and Concertation

The Liberal government's policy statement, *Partners for a Skilled and Competitive Québec*, marked a change in direction in the area of labour force development, including partnership between business and labour leaders. Indeed, tripartite partnerships were said to be 'common to all successful economies.' Acknowledging that since the 1969 Manpower Vocational Training and Qualification Act successive governments had never succeeded in developing a coherent, overall labour market policy, the new policy statement proposed to fill this gap. In order to succeed in the race for competitiveness, henceforth Quebec's 'number one resource,' its labour force, had to be relied on (MMSRFP, 1991: 8–9).

The following key elements of the government's new labour force development strategy sum up the approach outlined in the document:

• gradually refocus labour force development measures, moving away from measures of a 'passive' nature towards more 'active' measures;
• have the actors themselves take responsibility for labour force development;
• decentralize and regionalize labour force development policy;
• establish a permanent structure of concertation between business, union, and

government through the creation of the Société québécoise de développement de la main-d'oeuvre (SQDM);
- bring about unified management of all labour force programs by repatriating to Quebec all federal monies devoted to the labour force; and
- rely on the sectoral approach involving the actors for questions relating to the labour force.

This policy statement marked a significant departure from the neoliberal approach of the second half of the 1980s. The idea of leaving labour force development in the hands of market forces and private initiatives clearly seemed inadequate; instead, market forces needed to be guided. Moreover, in some respects the government was still counting on the goodwill of employers to invest in human resources since, other than the creation of a forum for concertation, the only other concrete measure was a training tax credit instituted some time earlier. Employers were satisfied with this type of incentive-based approach, which would supposedly lead to the gradual development of a training culture in private enterprises. The union movement, however, had long been demanding more stronger measures, notably a requirement that firms devote a certain percentage of their total wage bill to training, failing which they would be forced to pay an equivalent levy.

In particular, this policy statement established the sectoral approach as a strength to be exploited in labour force development. Although there had been efforts at sectoral concertation in the 1980s, in the form of sectoral labour force adjustment committees (CAMOs), these were essentially responses to major crises in particular sectors (e.g., textiles, railway), were often aimed at a specific objective (e.g., the creation of a training centre or labour force retraining) and had a life span limited to the attainment of the objective in question. The singular exception was the Centre for Aerospace Manpower Activities in Quebec (Centre d'adaptation de la main-d'oeuvre aérospatiale au Québec, or CAMAQ).

The new policy statement, although inspired by these earlier experiences, recast the sectoral approach in another perspective, that of creating 'prime forums for joint action' (MMSRFP, 1991: 41) for labour force and economic development. The government was thus proposing to make them part of a proactive strategy of adjustment in the context of economic restructuring, as the following quotation illustrates: 'Changes in the economy are apparent first and foremost by economic or industrial sector. The government and its partners are thus relying increasingly on a sector-based approach to labour force development, because the reality of employment and skills development varies from one industrial sector to another.' (MMSRFP, 1991: 39)

Thus, with a focus on the distinctiveness of individual sectors, the government planned to establish committees in a great number of sectors under the responsibility of the SQDM. These committees would also be given the task of forging links with the regional development process and with the new industrial development strategy of the Ministry of Industry, Trade and Technology. As it turned out, it was not until 1995 that the SQDM fully elaborated its sectoral strategy.

Industrial Development and Concertation

In December 1991 the Liberal government took another strategic turn when it launched the industrial cluster strategy. In the presence of several dozen industrial, financial, and union leaders, the minister of industry, trade and technology, Gerald Tremblay, made public the document *Vers une société à valeur ajoutée* ('Moving Toward a Value-Added Society') (MICT, 1991) which signalled a shift away from the neoliberal strategy of the previous years. Inspired by the work of Michael Porter (1990),[5] the minister proposed a strategy focused on the development of synergy among the parties at the sectoral level to move from a mass-production economy to a value-added economy.

On the one hand, in terms of general directions, the MICT policy stressed the importance of the quality of production, the mobilization of human resources, the development of medium- and long-term strategies, a new partnership between the public and private sectors, and even a new social contract. The statement concluded: 'The strategy of industrial clusters is based on the following premise: in an increasingly competitive world, success is no longer the product of individual efforts aimed at short-term goals. From now on, success will be the result of a pooling of our efforts.' (MICT, 1991: 7, our translation). On the other hand, in structural terms, the MICT policy advanced the idea of bringing together the main employer and union actors on a sectoral basis within 'decision-making committees' (tables de décideurs).

Apart from activating the process, the government's role in this strategy was to support the other actors. It also had a fairly precise idea about the possible role of these committees:

From the beginning the Government of Quebec has made its mission to act as a catalyst, facilitating processes and initiatives which would be determined by decision makers within sectoral round tables. Without claiming that these round tables would become formal representatives or spokespersons for their sector, nevertheless they could adopt a common vision of development of their sector, evaluate the state of their industry, advise the Government on measures to be taken and, possibly, take measures likely to improve competitive conditions within their operating environment. (MICT, 1994: 1, our translation)

At the outset, the MICT identified thirteen clusters: five competitive clusters which were already internationally competitive and possessed substantial networks and partnerships; and eight strategic clusters that were important for regional development and had good growth potential.

Although this was first and foremost an industrial development strategy, the issue of human resources was part of the mandate of the decision-making committees. It was in relation to these sectoral committees that the MMSRFP policy statement on labour force development proposed a linkage of sectoral processes. Although the sectoral approach thus received a double stamp of approval from the government (as well as from business and labour), this also meant a certain duplication in mandates concerning human resources, at least for a while.

Bill 90: A Further Step towards a Labour Market Policy

The election of the Parti Québécois government in September 1994 ushered in a new stage in the development of an active labour market policy. For present purposes, what needs to be emphasized is the adoption of the Act to Foster the Development of Manpower Training (Government of Quebec, 1995). This law requires that, beginning 1 January 1996, employers devote at least 1 per cent of their wage bill to training their workforce or pay a penalty in the form of a levy of up to that amount. The tax would be deposited in a new national manpower training fund administered by the SQDM. The law applies initially to firms with a wage bill of $1 million or more. Firms with a wage bill of $500,000 or more were included as of 1 January 1997, and those with a wage bill of $250,000 or more will be brought under the law on 1 January 1998. Smaller firms will still have access to the training tax credit instituted by the previous government.

This measure sought to accelerate the development of a training culture in firms that have not been responding quickly enough to the incentive provided by the tax credit or to the exhortation to invest in human resources. While reinforcing the role of the SQDM and promoting concerted action by the parties, the government thus decided to force the hands of more employers with regard to investment in training. Although well received by the unions, the policy was opposed by employers. Nevertheless, it has not led to a cooling off of participation in the SQDM's concertation structures, at least not so far. In view of the fact that the SQDM will play an important role in the implementation of the policy, and considering the government's support for the sectoral approach, it might even be thought that the law will accelerate the development of the SQDM's sectoral committees.

The SQDM's New Policy of Sectoral Intervention

The final component of the sectoral approach was put in place in October 1995 when the SQDM's board of directors adopted a policy of sectoral intervention. In its new policy, the SQDM enlarged the mandate of sectoral committees in order to 'support the development of sectoral partnership structures that can deal with the structural and cyclical causes of labour market imbalances and promote the development and implementation of strategies to expand industry areas of excellence and reduce the effects of industrial restructuring on employment' (SQDM, 1995: v).

This clearly involves going beyond the ad hoc and limited character of the earlier sectoral CAMOs in order to establish permanent structures which will fit within a perspective of sectoral regulation of the labour market and even of industrial development. The SQDM policy stipulates, among other things, that sectoral committees will be introduced in 'as many economic sectors as possible' (p. 2). In cases where the establishment of sectoral committees would be difficult, particularly because of the internal organization of a sector or lack of commitment by the actors to working together, the SQDM provides for other, more flexible forms of sectoral intervention involving, for example, more specific mandates of shorter duration.

The sectoral approach thus constitutes, for the SQDM, the preferred form of labour market intervention. Indeed, its hopes are pinned firmly to this strategy. More precisely, the new policy states that:

SQDM's sectoral approach encourages private and public partners to work in concert towards a common employment and skills development objective ...

The sectoral approach has a multiplier effect on SQDM's initiatives. Its actions are taken up, repeated and distributed by the partners so that, through sectoral communication networks, they spread throughout a sector to reach its businesses and labour force ...

The sectoral approach sheds light on short- and medium-term economic, technological, social and organizational changes ...

The sectoral approach promotes the control of labour and job market initiatives ...

The sectoral approach helps improve the interface between business, labour and government in particular by designating sectoral committees to represent an economic sector on employment and skills development issues when working with government departments and organizations.

The sectoral approach encourages the inclusion of businesses' particular regional and provincial features by ensuring that the necessary coordination and harmonization of provincial and regional initiatives and analyses occurs ...

Finally, the sectoral approach helps provide the regions with follow-up means for their economic development to the extent that the economic sectors are of strategic importance to them. (SQDM, 1995: 1–2)

Thus, we are currently witnessing in Quebec what could be called an intensive phase with regard to the development of the sectoral approach in the area of human resources: the government's political support for the approach has never been as clear and firm; financial and organizational resources have been put at the disposal of employers and unions; and the parties' reaction to the new approach is certainly positive. In this regard, over the last few years both the official pronouncements of employers and unions regarding concertation on employment, and their positive reactions to the government's sectoral initiatives (both MMSRFP and MICT), attest to a commitment which is unprecedented in the history of Quebec labour relations. Conditions therefore seem ripe for the emergence of sectoral partnerships in the area of human resources and certain experiences in the area during recent years indicate that there is a potential for achieving concrete results. It remains to be seen to what extent employers and unions grab the ball and run with it.

Profile of Quebec Sectoral Initiatives in the Area of Human Resources

A Transition Period

Sectoral initiatives in the area of human resources in Quebec are presently in a period of transition as well as constant development. The experiences of the 1980s at the sectoral level were a continuation of the enterprise CAMOs (labour force adjustment committees) which aimed generally at developing joint solutions in a context of crisis within firms (e.g., a market decline, a financial crisis, or a technological lag). This model was copied on the sectoral level when the principal actors in the sector requested it. Essentially, this allowed unions and employers to conduct an evaluation of their sector and to develop revitalization plans. This process, funded by the provincial and federal governments, was carried out within a committee with the help of an external resource person. Thus, the mandate was framed narrowly in terms of a sectoral crisis and a reaction to exogenous shocks already harming the industry and employment. Concertation of actors had an ad hoc character, so to speak, and a limited duration.

The configuration of the sector in question did not necessarily correspond to a very precise definition. Thus in some cases a sectoral initiative might have come from a major group[6] (e.g., the rubber products industry) as defined by Statistics Canada's Standard Industrial Classification (SIC); yet in other cases the initiative might have been limited to an industrial class[7] (e.g., plate work industry). It should be remembered that when major groups are used to define sectors, seventy-six economic sectors can be identified. If industrial classes are used instead, there are 862 economic sectors (Statistics Canada, 1989). Experience thus seems to indicate that in granting funds to a sectoral concertation initiative, governments in Quebec and Ottawa were certainly flexible about how employers and unions chose to define their sectors.

The current profile of sectoral initiatives in Quebec reflects this transition between older sectoral CAMOs and the more recently established sectoral committees. Some of the former sectoral CAMOs will be merged or restructured in order to better correspond to the configuration (comprising some thirty-five sectors) that the SQDM wishes to introduce. The mandates of the older sectoral CAMOs will also be redefined so as to correspond to the new objectives of the SQDM's sectoral policy.

Moreover, given the mandates of the SQDM and the MICT's decision-making committees, there was a degree of duplication of sectoral initiatives related to human resources. All of these initiatives must therefore be included in the present analysis in order to develop a portrait of sectoral practices related to the question of human resources. However, the new SQDM sectoral policy provides that its sectoral committees will become responsible for human resources matters. Gradually, then, the picture of sectoral initiatives in this area is likely to change as the SQDM committees move to the foreground.

Even though they are not the subject of this chapter, it should be emphasized that Quebec employers and unions participate in the federal sectoral initiatives sponsored by HRDC (generally called 'human resource development sectoral councils'). Here too, then, there is a risk of duplicating activities related to labour force development in Quebec. However, the SQDM and HRDC have agreed that the Quebec representatives on the federal sectoral councils will be chosen by the SQDM sectoral labour force committees covering the sectors concerned. This is aimed at ensuring the best possible linkages while minimizing duplication by the Quebec (SQDM) and federal (HRDC) committees in a given sector.

Topography of SQDM and MICT Sectoral Initiatives

The SQDM's sectoral committees are similar in many respects to HRDC's sectoral councils. Each brings together employer and worker representatives from

TABLE 1   List of Sectoral Labour Force Committees in Quebec and Date Established, October 1995

Quebec Centre for Aerospace Labour Force Adjustment (1983)*
Sectoral Labour Force Committee of the Quebec Road Transport Industry (Apr. 1990)
Sectoral Labour Force Committee of the Quebec Rubber Industry (Nov. 1992)
Sectoral Labour Force Committee of the Industrial Metal Products Industry (Feb. 1993)
Sectoral Labour Force Committee of the Travel Industry (Sept. 1992)
Sectoral Labour Force Committee of the Plastics Products Industry (Apr. 1993)
Sectoral Labour Force Committee of the Sawn Timber Industry (July 1993)
Sectoral Labour Force Committee of the Hotel and Restaurant Industry (Jan. 1994)
Sectoral Labour Force Committee of the Crafts Industry (Sept. 1994)
Professional Committee for Writers, Creative Artists and Performers of the Quebec
    Cultural Sector (Jan. 1995)
Joint Sectoral Labour Force Committee of the Doors and Windows, Kitchen Cabinets
    and Woodwork Industry of Quebec (Nov. 1994)
Sectoral Labour Force Committee of the Quebec Steel Industry (May 1995)
Sectoral Labour Force Committee in Museology (Mar. 1995)
Sectoral Labour Force Committee of the Quebec Chemical, Petrochemical and Refining
    Industry (May 1995)
Quebec Council on the Development of Human Resources in Tourism (June 1995)
Sectoral Labour Force Committee on Dance, Music and Theatre (Oct. 1995)
Sectoral Labour Force Committee of the Hunting and Fishing Supplies and Services
    Industry (Oct. 1995)
Sectoral Labour Force Committee of the Agriculture Industry (Oct. 1995)
Sectoral Labour Force Committee of the Quebec Textile Industry (Sept. 1995)
Sectoral Committee for Industrial Electrical Equipment (GRAPÉLEC) (Sept. 1995)

---

*Although CAMAQ was officially established in 1983, activities had been taking place since 1978.

a particular sector in order to analyse issues relating to labour force adaptation and to identify concrete courses of action with regard to this adaptation. The SQDM and HRDC play an important role in this process by, among other things, providing most of the funding for committee operations and providing resource people.

In November 1995 the SQDM set the number of committees at around twenty. Table 1 provides a list of the committees as well as the date on which each was established. In addition to these committees, in November 1995 the SQDM indicated that sectoral committees were being organized in the pulp and paper, environment, retail trade, computers, clothing, printing, automobile sales and repairs sectors. It should be added that the SQDM is also responsible for regional interventions and those targeted at specific client groups (e.g., persons with disabilities, immigrants, and so on).

TABLE 2   Sectoral Industrial Clusters of the Quebec Ministry of
Industry, Trade and Technology, March 1994

Competitive Clusters
Aerospace
Pharmaceutical products
Information technology products and the media sub-cluster
Metal and mineral processing industries
    – Chemical and chemical products industry sub-cluster
    – Metallurgical industry sub-cluster
    – Mining industry sub-cluster
Electrical power generation, transmission and distribution equipment

Strategic Clusters
Surface transportation equipment
Petrochemical and plastics processing industry
    – Petrochemical sub-cluster
    – Plastics processing sub-cluster
Agrifood products
Habitat and construction and the building automation sub-cluster
    – Habitat sub-cluster
    – Construction sub-cluster
    – Building automation sub-cluster
Fashion and textiles
Forest products
Environment
Cultural industries

As for the industrial cluster strategy, Table 2 provides a list of these sectors, which gave rise to the creation of decision-making committees.

In the area of agrifood products, the Quebec Ministry of Agriculture, Fisheries and Food (MAPAQ) is responsible for implementing the industrial cluster strategy. Several months after the MICT strategy was announced, MAPAQ organized the Quebec Agricultural Summit at which the partners agreed, to 'set up sectoral concertation groups, commonly referred to as 'networks', in which producers, processors and distributors are represented, as well as other groups such as unions, financial institutions, universities, corporations and professional associations, with the common objective of improving their business relationships with each other from the perspective of winning markets' (MICT, 1994: 91, our translation).

The definition of the word 'partners' is particularly important here, in view of the place given to trade union organizations. In the case of the agrifood networks, it appears that trade unions (as distinct from 'unions' of agricultural producers) were generally introduced late (and then only timidly) into the process of concertation (Poulin, 1995: 124).

In August 1994, there were eleven sectoral networks[8] mandated to develop a strategic plan and to adopt the necessary means to achieve it (Comité de suivi, 1994). Two years after the strategy was launched, an MICT document (1994) and a Monitoring Committee document from the Quebec Agricultural Summit (Comité de suivi, 1994) reported strong participation in the various clusters and networks. Indeed, at the time there were some nine hundred decision-makers involved in the clusters and some three hundred in the networks.

Table 3 indicates the sectors covered in whole or in part by sectoral initiatives. The economic sectors and sectoral initiatives do not match up perfectly, since the underlying definitions of these fields are not identical. The table therefore provides only a general idea of the economic sectors in which there exist sectoral initiatives in Quebec. Sectors that are not yet involved in these activities are also identified.

For the purposes of this comparison, the eighteen industrial divisions of the Standard Industrial Classification were used (Statistics Canada, 1989), to which were added the twenty-two major groups of the Manufacturing Industries Division in order to provide a more detailed picture of this particularly important division.[9] In addition, for each of the sectors identified in the first column, the table shows its relative share of employment (expressed as a proportion of the total number of jobs in August 1995 according to Statistics Canada). Given that in many cases sectoral initiatives involve only a part of industrial activities in Standard Industrial Classification sectors, the total number or the total percentage of jobs affected by SQDM or MICT sectoral activities cannot be determined precisely, at least not by using the employment data that appear in Table 3. Nevertheless, these indicators of sectoral employment provide an idea of the degree of coverage of sectoral activities in Quebec as well as the importance, in terms of employment, of the sectors not covered by sectoral activities.

It should be noted that three of the thirty-eight economic sectors identified in the first column are not covered by the SQDM sectoral committees because they comprise the public and parapublic sectors (government, educational, health and social services). Of the thirty-five private industry sectors: fifteen are covered in whole or in part by SQDM labour force sectoral committees, committees were being organized (as of November 1995) in a further five sectors; and the furniture sector had a CAMO from 1989 to 1995. Thus, almost half of these sectors were covered in whole or in part at the time (or nearly two-thirds if the committees being organized are taken into account).

As regards the number of jobs potentially affected, it can be seen that the

TABLE 3 Economic Sectors in Quebec, Distribution of Jobs, SQDM Sectoral Committees, MICT Cluster and MAPAQ Network Committees*

Economic sectors and percentage distribution of jobs†		SQDM sectoral labour force committees	MICT and MAPAQ clusters and sub-groups
Primary sector	1.3		
Agriculture	Not Avail.	Yes (agricultural products; horticulture)	Yes (networks)
Fishing and trapping	Not Avail.	Yes (hunting and fishing supplies and services)	No
Logging and Forestry	0.7	No	Yes (forest products)
Mining, quarrying and oil wells	0.6	No	Yes (mining)
Manufacturing sector	18.2		
Food	1.6	No	Yes (networks)
Beverage	0.4	No	No
Tobacco products	Not Avail.	No	No
Rubber products	Not Avail.	Yes (rubber products)	No
Plastic products	0.5	Yes (plastic products)	Yes (plastic processing)
Leather	0.3	No	Yes (fashion and textiles)
Textiles	0.5	Yes (textiles)	Yes (fashion and textiles)
Clothing	2.0	In preparation (clothing)	Yes (fashion and textiles)
Wood	1.2	Yes (sawn timber, doors windows)	Yes (forest products)
Furniture	0.6	No	No
Paper	1.2	In preparation (pulp and paper)	Yes (forest products)
Printing	1.5	In preparation (printing)	No
Primary metal	0.9	Yes (steel)	Yes (metallurgical industry)
Fabricated metal products	1.3	Yes (industrial metal products)	No
Machinery	0.7	No	No
Transportation equipment	1.4	Yes (aerospace)	Yes (aerospace; surface transportation)
Electrical and electronic products	1.3	Yes (grapélec)	Yes (Elec. power. gen. trans. and dist.)
Non-metallic mineral products	0.4	No	No
Petroleum and coal products	Not Avail.	Yes (chemicals, petrochem. and refining)	No
Chemical and chemical products	0.8	Yes (chemicals, petrochem. and refining)	Yes (chemical ind.; pharmaceutical ind.)
Other manufacturing industries	0.8	No	No

TABLE 3 (Concluded)

Economic sectors and percentage distribution of jobs†		SQDM sectoral labour force committees	MICT and MAPAQ clusters and sub-groups
Construction	4.3	No	
Services	75.5		
Transportation and storage	4.1	Yes (road transport)	Yes (surface transportation equipment)
Communication and other utilities	3.8	No	Yes (information technology)
Wholesale trade	6.4	No	NA
Retail trade	12.7	In prep. (retail trade; auto sales and repairs)	NA
Finance and insurance	4.0	No	NA
Real estate operators	1.5	No	NA
Business services	5.2	In preparation (computer services)	Yes (information technology)
Government services	6.3	NA‡	NA
Educational services	7.0	NA	NA
Health and social services	11.9	NA	NA
Accomodation, food and bev. services	7.1	Yes (hotel and restaurant; tourism)	NA
Other services	5.5	Yes (travel; crafts; writers, museums; dance music, theatre; environment)	Yes (culture; environment)

*Data on SQDM committees are from November 1995; data on clusters are from March 1994; and data on networks are from August 1994.
†According to the 1980 Standard Industrial Classification, Cat. 12–501 E.
The percentage distribution of employment was calculated using data from Statistics Canada's *Employment, Earnings and Hours* for the month of August, 1995, Cat. 72–002. The total number of jobs for that month was 2,593,600.
‡NA: Not applicable

SQDM sectoral committees are operating in sectors covering approximately two-thirds of jobs in the manufacturing sector. In the service sector, the retail trade, accommodation, and food services are the most significant in terms of the number of jobs concerned, accounting for approximately 19 per cent of the total number of jobs in Quebec. However, at least as of November 1995, a number of fairly large industries are still not covered by SQDM committees (e.g., food services, construction, communication, wholesale trade, finance and insurance), or are no longer covered (i.e., furniture).

As for the industrial clusters committees and the agrifood networks, as one might have expected given the nature of the ministries responsible for these committees, the sectors covered are essentially in the primary and manufacturing sectors, although some cluster committees do exist in the service sector.

Two observations flow from this mapping of the SQDM, MICT, and MAPAQ committees. The first is that, even leaving aside the sectors to which the committees do not apply in the first place, there are certain sectors of activity that are not covered by any of the three types. This is the case for the following sectors: beverages, tobacco products, furniture, machinery, non-metallic mineral products, other manufacturing industries, wholesale trade, finance and insurance, and real estate services. Together, these sectors account for 14.8 per cent of total employment in Quebec. If public and parapublic employment, which represents 25.2 per cent of total employment in Quebec, is excluded, then 74.8 per cent of jobs in Quebec could in principle be covered by SQDM, MICT, and MAPAQ sectoral committees. Of this percentage, the 14.8 per cent of jobs in sectors not covered by a sectoral committee in November 1995 accounted for 20 per cent. In other words, at that time, at least one in five private sector jobs was not yet (or was no longer) covered by any of the Quebec sectoral committees. However, it cannot therefore be inferred that four out of five jobs were covered by a sectoral committees since, as was seen earlier, in certain cases the sectoral committees only partially cover the sectors and jobs defined by the Standard Industrial Classification. Nonetheless, it is reasonable to conclude that the majority of jobs are certainly covered by one or another of the Quebec sectoral committees.

The second observation concerns the duplication of sectoral initiatives. In fact, in several economic sectors there is an overlap between the SQDM committees and those of the MICT and MAPAQ. However, in the near future, the SQDM committees will take over sectoral concertation in the field of human resources, leaving to MICT and MAPAQ the field of industrial development strategies. Thus, we now turn to a closer examination of the characteristics of the SQDM's sectoral committees.

TABLE 4   Criteria for Characterizing
SQDM Sectoral Labour Force Committees

1. Mission of the Committees
2. Composition:
   – actors involved
   – criteria of participation
   – size of committee
3. Definition of the Sectors
4. Committee Powers
5. Structure
6. Decision-making Process
7. Principal achievements and projects
8. Intensity of participation
9. Length of existence and permanence
10. Funding

Characteristics of the SQDM's Sectoral Committees

In order to establish the principal characteristics of the SQDM's sectoral committees, a schema of ten criteria was developed, inspired particularly by the features suggested by Murray and Verge (1994) related to union representation
beyond the firm level, as well as by the observations made by Sharpe (1995)
regarding federal sectoral councils (HRDC). Information on the criteria was
gathered from official SQDM documentation (1994a) as well as from an interview with an official of the SQDM[10] (see Table 4).

1. Mission of the committees: 'Promote and consolidate partnership on a sectoral basis in cooperation with regional corporations and government departments and agencies and other organizations concerned (MICST, MEQ, HRDC,
etc.). The aim is to enable local control over development of key factors for the
competitiveness of a sector's businesses and work force' (SQDM, 1995: 3).
    More precisely, sectoral committees are responsible for:

– developing continuous training ...;
– identifying the specific needs of a sector regarding human resources management and
  organization of work and developing methods and approaches to deal with the problems identified;
– developing effective measures regarding labour, business or job creation that will help
  stabilize employment and reduce the sector's unemployment rate;

– taking the problems of target client groups into account and suggesting possible solutions to businesses in their sector ...;
– in keeping with their mission, provide information among businesses and workers in the sector concerned in Quebec. (SQDM, 1995: 3)

Thus, in line with the government's new philosophy of intervention, the mission aims to foster partnership and local responsibility. From this perspective, the government sees itself more as a catalyst than as a director of labour-management concertation, as was the case during the era of socioeconomic summits of the 1970s and 1980s. The government is placing resources and a structure at the disposal of employers and unions, indicating to them that they should take the dynamic of sectoral intervention into their own hands.

Furthermore, it is certainly the case that the committees' mission is ambitious. The mandate includes 'the development of key factors for the competitiveness of a sector's businesses,' which opens the door to work on aspects other than human resources that concern the development of firms, notably the 'organization of work.' The mission also fits within a wider employment policy, considering the mandate of stabilizing employment and reducing the rate of unemployment in the sector concerned. Finally, the mandate focuses on the links to be established between the sectoral committee and the firms and workers in the sector. In other words, the SQDM does not want the committees to work in isolation, but instead to develop communication between the sectoral and microeconomic levels. This represents a tall order for several economic sectors in which there is little in the way of internal organization or in which there are numerous actors at the microeconomic level.

2. *Composition*: The committees consist of representatives of employers and workers, including trade unions or professional associations. The number of representatives is not limited and there is no requirement that there be the same number of employer and employee representatives. The committees also include SQDM and HRDC resource persons, as well as other government partners as needed. The committees are therefore fundamentally bipartite in nature since the government representatives attend as resource persons.

Representation within the committee must reflect the reality of the sector as regards the existence of employer associations and unions, professional associations, self-employed workers, and so on. Moreover, when nominating their representatives, organizations are asked to take into account the representation of the regions in which the sector is concentrated. It is therefore the organizations, not the government, which are responsible for nominating their representatives.

Only representatives of associations are permitted to sit on sectoral committees. An employer or a worker cannot sit as an individual or for the sole purpose of representing a particular firm. Moreover, representation is limited to employers' and labour organizations. Special interest groups such as the unemployed, women, the low-paid or ecologists, are not represented.

In principle, the size of a sectoral committee is not prescribed. Nonetheless, based on a sample of eleven sectoral committees, it was possible to establish that the average size is fourteen members, and generally includes some four or five resource persons from government or other bodies. In most cases, the number of employee and worker representatives are quite evenly balanced.

3. Definition of the sectors: The practice established in the 1980s was not based on a very precise definition of the economic sectors. To assure a more coherent approach within the framework of its new policy, as well as to avoid the creation of a multitude of sectoral committees, the configuration of economic sectors, which number approximately thirty-five, has been established by the board of directors of the SQDM in 1996. However, certain sectors which are too large may be sub-divided into sectoral sub-committees.

4. Committee powers: The powers of the committees include the specification of its mandate and its operationalization, the composition of the committee itself, as well as certain operating details (e.g., the choice of the chairperson, the selection of personnel if applicable, and the frequency of meetings). As regards the operating details, however, the SQDM (1995: 4) asks that 'organizational flexibility and versatility' be given priority. Thus, within the framework of the overall mission and the mandates laid down by the SQDM, the committee defines the elements that it wishes to establish in the sectoral appraisal; it can define the occupational standards for the labour force; and can establish a training program. In fact, the committee has a large degree of autonomy as regards its objectives, means, and strategies, to the extent that this fits within the framework of labour force development in its own sector. However, each committee must submit its annual action plan to the board of directors of the SQDM for approval. The board therefore retains a supervisory role over the committees.

Furthermore, the sectoral committee has the power to define the nature of the linkages with the regional branches of the SQDM and regional partners as regards the objectives and means more specific to the regions.

5. Structure: The sectoral committee's structure is generally simple, comprising little more than a committee and a chairperson. A committee can be chaired by a representative of the parties or by an external resource person. However, the SQDM encourages the parties to assume this role themselves, which can be done by alternating between a union and an employer chairperson. Furthermore, the committees have the power to develop structures of their own choosing to facilitate their operation (for example, the election of an executive committee which ensures a degree of administrative and organizational follow-up between meetings of the whole committee, or the creation of a sub-committee to deal with a particular question). The committees also have the power to hire their own staff, chosen from outside the resource personnel already provided by the government.

6. *Decision-making process*: The committees work on the basis of a consensus between the employer and worker representatives rather than on the basis of a majority vote. The decision-making procedure is in keeping with the idea of bringing the two parties along together on questions concerning labour force development. With such a procedure, as was seen above, the number of representatives of each side need not be exactly equal.

7. *Principal achievements and projects*: Given the recent nature of the SQDM's new sectoral policy, few specific results have been produced within the framework of the new approach. Essentially, the achievements of the committees are those already attained within the framework of the mandates of the sectoral CAMOs. For the new committees, therefore, it is more appropriate to talk about projects under way or to be accomplished. However, it may be said that, both for the earlier CAMOs and the new committees, there are three main axes around which action is organized:

- diagnosis of the sector's labour force[11] (profile of the sector and of the labour force, analysis of training needs, analysis of actual and future labour force requirements, analysis of the environment, strengths and weaknesses of the industry, recommendations);
- development of an action plan comprising short-, medium- and long-term objectives, as well as the measures chosen by the committee – in short, the committee's intervention strategy to follow up on the recommendations of the diagnosis; and
- implementation and follow-up of the action plan (e.g., defining occupational standards for various jobs in the sector, establishing training programs for the current and future labour force, creating training centres or institutes, producing information tools concerning employee training for firms, conducting

specific studies related to the labour force in the industry, other special activities such as conferences, and promotion linked to the labour force).

The CAMOs with the most experience, such as CAMAQ (aerospace) and CAMO-Route (road transport) already have many of these achievements to their credit.

8. Intensity of participation: There are no exhaustive data currently available on the pace of work in the committees or the participation of union and employer representatives. Nevertheless, a cursory analysis indicates that there has been a considerable variation between the CAMOs. The pace of work, for example, can vary from one meeting per month to a few each year.

9. Length of existence and permanence: According to the list of committees published by the SQDM in November 1995, the twenty sectoral committees can be divided according to their length of existence into the following groups: two committees have been established for more than five years, five from two to three years, three from one to two years, and ten for less than a year. In general, the lifespan of the CAMOs used to be predetermined (usually about three years). This will no longer be the case under the SQDM's new policy, which includes provision 'allowing the dissolution of a sectoral committee if concrete results are not achieved' (SQDM, 1995: 4).

10. Funding: The sectoral committees have always been largely financed by the two levels of government. In fact, the contribution of employer and worker representatives was generally no more than 20 to 25 per cent of the total budget. This annual budget varied according to the committee's activities but was no more than $250,000. Moreover, the previous funding formula involved a progressive reduction of the combined contribution of the two levels of government (equal shares) from 80 per cent of the total in the first year, to 70 per cent in the second year, 60 per cent in the third, and then to 40 per cent thereafter.

Following a round of consultations with the different employer and union representatives in Quebec in 1995, the purpose of which was to sound them out on sectoral committee funding, the board of directors of the SQDM decided to eliminate this policy of diminishing funding and to stop requiring the parties to make a financial contribution. In fact, the contributions of the SQDM and HRDC now serve to fund 'the production and updating of the sector appraisal and the development and monitoring of the action plan, the salary of a coordinator, secretarial expenses, travel expenses of consultants and the expenses of providing businesses and workers in the sector with information' (SQDM, 1995: 4). The annual budget is determined jointly by the SQDM, HRDC, and the parties represented on the sectoral committee. The contribution of these parties to the activities of the committee may take the form of cash or services in kind (the chairmanship of the committee, the loan of physical space, the salaries and travel expenses of their representatives, active contribution to the work of the committee, and so on). The $250,000 maximum annual financial contribution of the two levels of government will stay in place, and any costs above this threshold will be assumed by the parties themselves.

This new funding rule is very important, for it makes it easier for the committees to develop a perspective that goes beyond the short-term. By fully financing the work of the committees (so long as the committees meet their objectives), the SQDM is providing committees with the assurance that they will be able to operate on a permanent basis in line with their mandates and new objectives. On the other hand, the parties' lack of financial input in the work of the committee might translate into a lack of real involvement or responsibility on their part. Nevertheless, it remains the case that the time spent on sectoral committee activities and the attainment of its specific objectives remains the essential criteria for judging the extent to which employers and unions have taken responsibility for labour force development. Thus, although it has retained the right to approve the annual funding of the committees, the SQDM has shifted the responsibility for taking charge of their sector to the parties by concentrating their energies on the development of a dynamic of concertation.

A Favourable Context for the Development of Sectoral Initiatives

Compared to previous experiences with concertation in Quebec, it would appear that several aspects of the current context are favourable to the development of sectoral initiatives. The first of these elements are the ongoing economic transformations and the pressures they are exerting on unions and employers, notably in the sectors more closely linked to international trade. The current drive towards liberalization and globalization of trade are leading firms to seek ways to improve their competitiveness. Product quality, increased productivity, and market instability are all factors that put pressures on enterprises in a wide range of economic sectors. In this respect, the importance of human resources for the firm has come to be widely acknowledged the last few years, at least in official pronouncements. Data on spending on company-level training in Canada show that the need to invest in human resource development cannot be ignored. In short, the overall economic situation and identification of issues linked to labour force development seem as clear to employers as they do to unions.

In addition, the labour relations climate in Quebec has been characterized for several years by a muting of conflict as well as the introduction of a range of innovations by the actors, especially in enterprise-level practices (such as new forms of work organization, compensation, collective bargaining and dispute settlement, as well as long-term contracts). Beyond the enterprise, the last several years have also witnessed signs of a more general rapprochement between the parties compared to previous periods of confrontation. In this respect, the Forum for Employment has certainly played an important role in propagating the discourse of concertation. The various sectoral committees created during the 1980s and 1990s, as well as the diverse instances of joint participation in regional development efforts, have also provided unions and employers with experience in concertation. In short, the context seems favourable to the development of concertation.

For its part, the state is playing a different role in relation to unions and employers than it often has in the past. In particular, during the concertation efforts of the late 1970s and early 1980s, the Quebec government played a major role and was indeed accused by employers and unions of being too directive. Moreover, while the union movement has often demanded that the state play a greater role in the management of the economy, business has always been very critical of state intervention and thus welcomed the government's adoption of a neoliberal approach between the mid-1980s and early 1990s. What could be termed a new philosophy of state intervention, considering the changes of direction in labour market policy and industrial policy at the beginning of the 1990s, is now expressed by a government that is shifting responsibility to unions and employers. While publicly favouring voluntary participation by the social actors in the elaboration of development strategies, the state assures a legislative and organizational framework which places employers and unions at the centre of the decision-making processes.[12]

Conclusion

Sectoral initiatives in Quebec in the area of human resources are taking place in a context of relatively recent experience with concerted action, a context which was moreover broken by a period of considerable confrontation among the actors, notably with regard to neoliberal policies. It would seem that the policies of labour force and industrial development initiated at the beginning of the 1990s mark something of turning point in favour of the development of concertation. More particularly, sectoral level concertation began to develop in the 1980s and it is now benefiting from the support of unions, management, and the Quebec government. The overall environment also seems rather favourable to these initiatives.

In comparison with the still recent historical context of the late 1970s to the beginning of the 1990s, two particular changes have taken place that have influenced the introduction of sectoral initiatives in labour force development. First, the role of the state is less central in the decision-making and operations of the sectoral committees, even if its political support and the organizational resources it provides to employers and unions remain fundamental. Secondly, the ideological postures of unions and business towards concertation over labour force development also appear to have changed markedly since the 1970s and 1980s. The social actors seem more disposed than ever to work together jointly in developing the labour force, despite their differences over certain aspects of the legal framework of the process.

Nonetheless, it remains the case that in general, sectoral initiatives are still relatively recent and that the new sectoral policy of the SQDM has only just become well known. At this stage of the process, we believe that the actors in the Quebec industrial relations system face a particular challenge, that of gradually determining the place of an intermediate (or mesoeconomic) level of labour-management relations within a system in which the microeconomic level remains the cornerstone of industrial relations. In our view, this raises the specific question of the articulation of the levels of representation and bargaining in a socio-economic environment that is undergoing deep-seated transformations.

While there is little doubt, at least at the moment, that collective bargaining will continue to be conducted at the microeconomic level, it is also the case that the sectoral level appears more and more as a level of regulation of certain aspects of work and even of industrial development. It has come to occupy part of the space of representation and negotiation between the actors. What is more, it also appears to be an intermediate level between the macroeconomic level of public policies and the microeconomic level of collective bargaining. In this sense, the sectoral level functions as a transmission mechanism between public policy and the workplace. A specific role and place for the sectoral level will therefore need to be found within the overall system of representation and bargaining in the Quebec industrial relations system; failing this, it may lose its meaning and usefulness. Although it might be thought that the sectoral level represents the 'missing link' in the overall configuration of relations between the actors, we must be cautious about viewing it as a panacea for labour force and employment development. The enthusiasm for launching sectoral initiatives all over the place is bound to come up against the reality of sectors that are very different and unequal in terms of the social partners' response and willingness.

Notes

1 This chapter is based on one of the chapters of the author's Ph.D. thesis entitled *Restructuration économique et transformations des relations du travail: configuration, émergence et impacts des initiatives sectorielles dans les contextes québécois et canadien* (Economic Restructuring and the Transformation of Labour Relations: The Configuration, Emergence and Impact of Sectoral Initiatives in the Quebec and Canadian Contexts). The thesis research was being supervised by Professor Gregor Murray, Département des relations industrielles, Université Laval. Nonetheless, the study is the sole responsibility of the present author.

2 The relationship between federal and Quebec initiatives are dealt with in SQDM (1995) and Charest (1997).

3 The brief overview of concertation efforts in Quebec found in the text provides no discussion of the Conseil consultatif du travail et de la main-d'oeuvre created in 1968 or of the Conférence permanente sur la main-d'oeuvre established in the early 1990s. For more detailed treatments of concertation efforts, see Bellemare and Poulin Simon (1986), Fournier (1986b), and Murray and Verge (1994).

4 This is clearly acknowledged in the *Policy Statement on Labour Force Development* which was released in 1991.

5 Porter also wrote the preface to *L'Atlas industriel du Québec* (Gagné and Lefèvre, 1993) which deals with the MICT's industrial clusters.

6 Also known as the two-digit classification.

7 Also known as the four-digit classification.

8 In May 1995 the eleven original networks were subdivided into twenty-four new networks.

9 Because the two major groups covering the textile industry have been combined, Table 3 actually reports on twenty-one major groups.

10 Réal Gauvin, researcher, *Direction de l'intervention sectorielle et territoriale*, SQDM. The author wishes to thank Mr Gauvin for his generous cooperation. However, the interpretation of the data that is presented in this chapter is the author's sole responsibility.

11 The SQDM provides the sectoral committees with a detailed guide on how to conduct a sector appraisal and how to develop an action plan (SQDM, 1994b).

12 Note that the replacement of the SQDM by a new institution, the Commission des partenaires du marché du travail, by the end of 1997 does not invalidate this state-

ment. The new commission still confirms the role of employers and unions as decision-makers and still confirms the sectoral approach.

References

Bellemare, Diane, and Lise Poulin Simon. 1986. *Le défi du plein-emploi: Un nouveau regard économique*. Montreal: Éditions Saint-Martin.

Charest, Jean. 1997. 'Restructuration économique et transformations des relations du travail: configuration, émergence et impacts des initiatives sectorielles dans les contextes québécois et canadien.' Ph.D. diss., Département des relations industrielles, Université Laval.

Comité de suivi du sommet sur l'agriculture québécoise. 1994. *Bilan annuel des retombées du sommet – An 2*. Québec: Secrétariat du Sommet sur l'agriculture québécoise.

Fournier, Pierre. 1986a. 'Consensus Building in Canada: Case Studies and Prospects,' in Keith Banting, ed., *The State and Economic Interests*. Royal Commission on the Economic Union and Development Prospects for Canada. Volume 32. Toronto: University of Toronto Press, pp. 291–335.

– 1986b. *La concertation au Québec*. Québec: Direction générale des Publications gouvernementales.

Gagné, Pierrette, and Michel Lefèvre, eds. 1993. *L'Atlas industriel du Québec*. Montréal: Publi-Relais.

Gouvernement du Québec. 1995. *Loi favorisant le développement de la formation de la main-d'oeuvre*. Éditeur officiel du Québec.

Ministère de la Main-d'oeuvre, de la Sécurité du revenu et de la Formation professionnelle. 1991. *Partners for a Skilled and Competitive Québec. Policy Statement on Labour Force Development*. Québec: MMSRFP.

Ministère de l'Industrie, du Commerce et de la Technologie. 1991. *Vers une société à valeur ajoutée*. Québec: MICT.

– 1994. *La stratégie industrielle du Québec 'Le point.'* Québec: MICT.

Murray, Gregor, and Pierre Verge. 1994. 'La représentation syndicale au-delà de l'entreprise.' *Les Cahiers de droit* 35, no. 3.

Porter, Michael E. 1990. *The Competitive Advantage of Nations*. New York: Free Press.

Poulin, Lise. 1995. 'L'approche filière et les tables de concertation.' *Les actes du 1er Colloque syndical sur l'industrie québécoise de l'agro-alimentaire*. St-Hyacinthe: Fédération du commerce inc. (CSN), pp. 123–6.

Sharpe, Andrew. 1995. 'Sectoral Councils in Canada: Overview and Directions for Research.' Paper presented to the 32nd annual conference of the Canadian Industrial Relations Association. Montreal, Université du Québec à Montréal.

Société québécoise de développement de la main-d'oeuvre. 1994a. *Interventions sectorielles, territoriales et clientèles-cibles en matière de main-d'oeuvre au 1er avril 1994*. Québec: SQDM.

– 1994b. *Le diagnostic sectoriel et le plan d'action.* Québec: SQDM.
– 1995. *Taking Charge: Sectoral Policy Initiatives.* Québec: SQDM.
Statistics Canada. 1989. *Standard Industrial Classification.* Catalogue 12–501 E. Ottawa: Supply and Services Canada.
– 1995. *Employment, Earnings and Hours.* Catalogue 72–002. Ottawa: Supply and Services Canada.

7

Ontario's Experiment with Sectoral Initiatives: Labour Market and Industrial Policy, 1985–1996

NEIL BRADFORD

The decade between 1985 and 1995 in Ontario politics was one of considerable policy experimentation and institutional innovation.[1] In these years, successive Liberal and New Democratic Party governments pieced together a new provincial economic development strategy emphasizing productivity-enhancing investments in knowledge, skills, and technology. The aim was to mount a higher value-added, higher-wage job creation response to the challenges of the new global competition. Critical to the economic strategy's realization were 'social partnerships' forged in new institutions located between state and market, granting private sector representatives leadership roles in the design and delivery of public policy. Priority was placed on developing such partnerships and institutions at the sectoral level in two policy fields: labour market adjustment and training, and industrial development. In the early 1990s the Ontario Training and Adjustment Board (OTAB) and the Sector Partnership Fund (SPF) became the focal points for a concerted provincial effort at sectoral policy-making in Canada's industrial heartland.

This chapter analyses Ontario's ten-year policy experiment with sectoral approaches in labour market and industrial policy, including recent decisions taken by the Progressive Conservative government elected in June 1995 to abolish both OTAB and the SPF. The Ontario experience is relevant to wider debates about the emergence and viability of sectoral councils in Canada, since in this province a systematic effort to conceptualize sectoral initiatives within a new economic development strategy was followed by an ambitious attempt at implementation through novel structures in both labour market and industrial policies. The chapter reveals the complexities of such innovations in Ontario, and explores some of the broader implications of this experience for viable sector-based policy partnerships.

The chapter is organized into three parts. The first part tracks the emergence of the concept of sectoral strategies in Ontario in three key locales of policy deliberation in late 1980s and early 1990s. The second part examines sectoral policy-making in action through case studies of OTAB and the SPF. The brief histories of OTAB and the SPF reveal significant differences in outcomes, at least as measured by the degree and range of new sectoral activity actually generated. Simply put, Ontario's attempt to develop training and adjustment councils beyond those already existing in the steel, automotive parts, and electrical/ electronics sectors, foundered on the difficulties encountered in establishing OTAB. In the face of OTAB's protracted start-up problems, Ontario's sectoral focus shifted to industrial policy where the SPF managed to facilitate considerable sector strategic planning leading to implementation of some concrete initiatives. The final section of the chapter interprets this finding, arguing that OTAB and SPF each represented distinct forms of corporatist policy-making, and further, that their respective performances were shaped by the interplay of three factors influencing the viability of such arrangements in Ontario: the level at which the corporatist structure was launched; the scope of the policy agenda that was subject to negotiation among the social partners; and the state's role in facilitating and steering the process.

The Emergence of Sectoral Approaches in Ontario

In the years from 1985 to 1995 Liberal and NDP governments departed from Ontario's long-established public policy orientations and intergovernmental positions. The pillars of postwar governance in Ontario have been aptly described as a market-driven approach to economic management and a nation-building approach to dealings with the federal government and other provinces (Haddow, 1994: 485). Indeed, Ontario had been Ottawa's most important ally across the range of constitutional disputes that shaped Canadian politics from the mid-1960s to the early 1980s. At the same time, decades of uninterrupted prosperity combined with pragmatic Progressive Conservative rule had limited the state's economic role, and dampened official interest in social policy experimentation.

After 1985 political and economic forces converged to discredit this policy passivity and benevolent nation-builder stance. The end of the forty-year reign of the Progressive Conservatives coincided with the acceleration of structural transformations in the global economy, and in information and communications technologies, that placed intense competitive pressures on Ontario's manufacturing base. In this environment, Liberal and New Democratic Party governments faced the challenge of directing a rapid restructuring of the province's economy and workforce. For this daunting task, both governments sought new policy ideas, and enhanced administrative and fiscal capacities. Within the institutions of federalism, Ontario ministers and officials became aggressive claimants for their 'fair share' of federal financial transfers in social and labour market programming (Government of Ontario, 1995; Informetrica Ltd., 1993). Meanwhile Premiers Peterson and Rae emerged as vocal critics of federal monetary, fiscal, and trade policies which they argued magnified external pressures on the Ontario economy and constrained the province's ability to make change.[2] Within their own borders, considerable public policy resources were dedicated to the formulation and implementation of a new provincial development strategy that would feature a far more active role for the state than that countenanced by either previous Ontario administrations or the incumbent federal Progressive Conservative government.

There were three key contexts or processes that expressed Ontario's interest in a new provincial development strategy. Deliberations were officially launched through the Premier's Council created in 1986 by David Peterson. Two substantial reports were released by the council, the first in 1988 focusing primarily on industrial restructuring, and the second in 1990 looking in detail at labour force development. These reports became intellectual reference points for further discussion among political parties, policy experts, civil servants, and interest organizations about provincial economic renewal. Of particular significance here was the Economic Policy Review undertaken by the New Democratic Party in the months prior to assuming office in September 1990 (Roberts and Ehring, 1993: 208–9; Walkom, 1994: 92–7; Ernst, 1995: 4–11). This review involved a number of prominent social democratic thinkers debating the strengths and weaknesses of the Premier's Council work. Its themes influenced how the council's path-breaking work was eventually translated into public policy. The third and final expression of the new development strategy came in the major policy statement of the NDP government in 1991, known as Budget Paper E, accompanying its first budget (Ontario Ministry of Treasury and Economics, 1991). The progression of policy thought across these three locales of idea generation is crucial for understanding the emergence and operation of Ontario's sectoral initiatives in labour market and industrial policy in the 1990s.

The Premier's Council was created as a multi-partite, twenty-eight-member advisory body led by business, labour, educational representatives, and selected cabinet ministers, mandated to 'steer Ontario into the forefront of economic leadership and technological innovation.' Its creation reflected the new government's concern that the regular bureaucracy was neither prepared nor inclined to embark on a major reformulation of provincial economic policy. Given control over a sizable economic development budget, the council was expected to map long-term expenditure priorities for the government. Its first report,

Competing in the New Global Economy, issued in 1988, concentrated on industrial restructuring policies for moving corporate strategy toward higher value-added activities. The report's departure point was that Ontario's continued prosperity in the global economy demanded improved productivity. It marked the official introduction in Ontario of the policy argument that competitive advantage could be restored and maintained through adding value in production, not by cutting costs, shedding labour, or reducing social entitlements.

From this perspective, the report described weaknesses in the province's manufacturing base, such as comparatively poor performance in technological innovation and exports. It also revealed gaps in the public infrastructure to help firms upgrade their operations in internationally traded core industries that the council viewed 'as the fundamental drivers of our future wealth and prosperity.' It criticized ill-conceived public policies that too often substituted regional and social concerns for competitiveness goals, resulting in industrial assistance that did not 'benefit high-growth industries in need of more strategic investment in R&D and marketing.' The report recommended that public policy target support to 'indigenous threshold firms' in new high-growth, high-technology products and services, while also working to 'encourage all industries to move to competitive higher value-added per employee activities' (Ontario Premier's Council, 1988: 11–34).

To this end, the council proposed a range of government expenditures on firms striving to compete globally on the basis of world-class performance in high value-added activities such as technological research, product development, process innovation, and international marketing. The list of relevant inducements was lengthy: tax incentives for capital investment in high-growth industries for research and development, and in mature industries to help reorganize production and product lines; government procurement opportunities in strategic technologies; risk-sharing loans to threshold firms to help finance product development and marketing; venture capital assistance for start-up support for high technology firms. The aim was to create a provincial manufacturing base populated by indigenous multinational corporations, not necessarily domestically owned but in all cases capable of succeeding internationally through quality and innovation. Given the breadth of the challenge and the time constraints forced by global competitors, the council made a strong case for the existence of significant market failures in high value-added restructuring, and the associated need for strategic policy intervention to assist the transition.

With its focus on industrial policy and corporate behaviour, *Competing in the New Global Economy* tended to downplay the role of labour market policy and workers in the transition to high value-added activity. Although general reference was made to the need to improve supports for workers coping with technological change, labour leaders expressed concerns about the marginalization of their agenda. In response, the council decided to produce a second report that would balance, and hopefully complement, the initial business-centred analysis. In 1990 *People and Skills in the New Global Economy* was published. The main premise underlying this report was that the productivity of labour was no less important than that of capital for the province's economic renewal. Reforms to education, training, and worker adjustment programs were critical components of an 'aggressive labour market policy' that could 'play a significant role in assisting Ontario's companies and workers to move to higher value-added products and markets.'

The council scrutinized existing skills development policies and institutions, both federal and provincial, and found them lacking in significant ways. It chided the federal government for designing labour market policy through a 'rear-view mirror.' This led to an excessive preoccupation with short-term stabilization and with the needs of the long-term unemployed or new entrants to the labour market, which the council said deflected attention from the urgent competitiveness challenge of upgrading the skills of employed workers in traded sectors. It was further suggested that these programs to assist the unemployed and employment-disadvantaged often failed to ensure that target groups were provided with the resources and skills to avoid falling into insecure, low-wage employment. Against the provincial government, the council argued that Ontario's efforts to 'respond to the federal government's reduction in levels of funding for job training programs, as well as to the federal government's reactive approach to training policy' had largely 'exacerbated existing problems.' More generally, the council decried the proliferation of labour market programs and bodies that prevented formation of a transparent, coherent training system and policy. Duplication, overlap, and gaps in federal and provincial programming were both confusing and costly for clients (Ontario Premier's Council, 1990: 108–19).

Alongside this brief against existing government practice, the council highlighted the problem of market failure in adjustment and training. Through analysis of other jurisdictions, a training deficit in Ontario was identified in relation to the demands of high value-added production, traceable to inadequate private sector investment in workplace skills. From the council's perspective, Ontario employers relied too much on government, public education, and immigration to meet their training needs. The growing importance of generic technical and organizational skills increased the likelihood that a firm-centred, purely market-led approach to labour adjustment would not furnish adequate training for higher value-added activity.

The Premier's Council was drawn to institutional solutions between state and market. It referred frequently to lessons from sectoral initiatives under way through federal leadership across Canada to coordinate labour market programing and service delivery (Ontario Premier's Council, 1990: 137–9). These initiatives were spread across sectors where workplace representatives came together formally and in an ongoing way to manage either downside, exit problems, or upside, expansionary opportunities. Examining Ontario examples in the steel and electrical industries, the council identified a number of advantages in the sectoral approach. These included: more relevant programming rooted in the expressed needs of the workplace parties; the potential for levering private sector expenditures with public training funds; and the sharing of the costs and benefits of training among firms thereby reducing the incentive to poach while increasing provision of portable skills training encouraging efficient labour mobility.

Building on these potential benefits, the council's central recommendation in its second report was the creation of a provincial training board. OTAB was conceived as an independent provincial agency led by interest group representatives to oversee design, delivery, and funding of workplace adjustment and training. The agency would not simply be given advisory authority as in the case of federal labour market boards, but would exercise decision-making power, and be mandated to reform the system to prepare workers and managers for the challenges of high value-added activity. The agency's executive authority would be exercised within the broad policy direction and accountability structures of government.

With its explicit framing in relation to existing sector councils, the OTAB proposal tabled by the Premier's Council has been characterized as a vehicle 'to generalize the experience of the steel and electrical sectors across the rest of the economy' (Wolfe, 1997: 6). Claiming that implementation of OTAB would represent a 'fundamental change in Ontario's approach to training,' the council stated that 'rather than being a delivery system focused on the individual firm, the new approach will look to sectors and regions as the organizers of training delivery.' Accordingly, the central structural innovation in this OTAB model were sectoral training committees, composed of business and labour representatives who would 'create and administer a regime for training in their respective industry sectors' (Ontario Premier's Council, 1990: 143–5). OTAB's labour market representatives would be responsible for encouraging formation of such sectoral committees, providing official recognition, channelling provincial funds in line with appropriate matching criteria, and ensuring cooperation with the federal government in sectors where it was engaged. OTAB's sectoral training committees would be the key provincial instrument to increase private and public sector training. The council concluded that the main priority for the agency would be to undertake sectoral consultations 'to determine with each industry sector whether and what goal would be appropriate,' followed by annual public reviews of sectoral progress.

Beyond its clear sectoral thrust, there were a number of other noteworthy features in the Premier's Council conceptualization of OTAB. First, the governance structure was strongly bipartite, with an equal number of business and labour representatives. Provincial and federal governments officials would sit in ex-officio status. Second, priority was placed on competitiveness goals, understood in terms of meeting the needs of employed workers in sectors producing traded goods and services. As such, the government, not OTAB, would retain responsibility for social policy labour market concerns related to equity and access. Third, emphasis was placed on limiting the size of the OTAB bureaucracy. A small secretariat outside of government, staffed in part through rotating secondments from the labour market partners, was envisioned. Finally, consensus on the need to increase provincial investment in adjustment and training did not extend to business-labour agreement on precise means to achieve this goal (Ontario Premier's Council, 1990: preface).

At about the same time that the Premier's Council was mapping its vision of new industrial and labour market policy approaches, the opposition NDP began its own searching policy review. Overseen by the caucus's critic for economic affairs, Floyd Laughren, the economic policy review was organized around work from leftist policy analysts, some of whom had also contributed to the Premier's Council reports. More importantly, many of these analysts would soon join Floyd Laughren in taking up prominent positions in the NDP government. In many ways, the Premier's Council reports provided the departure point for the party's rethinking. In some cases, the critique was explicit, particularly in relation to the 1988 *Competing in the New Global Economy*. Here party thinkers welcomed what they saw as the council's break with traditional neoclassical thinking about competitiveness and the commitment to the high value-added as opposed to cost-cutting restructuring strategy. They also endorsed the general support for a positive government role in productivity growth and shaping corporate behaviour (Mackenzie, 1992: 10–11).

However, the economic policy review was critical of the council's limited view of policy instruments, confined as it was to various business subsidies. This theme was extended to emphasize rejection of the firm-centred policy analysis, fearing that such financial assistance would lead only to a 'few hundred "threshold" firms at the public trough.' Instead, policy should focus on linkages among firms for 'deepening and broadening our productive base' (Gindin and Robertson, 1992: 35–7). This line of argument led to a different approach to industrial policy. Eschewing reliance on tax incentives to individual firms, this approach conceptualized technological and organizational innovation as a social process. The innovative ability of firms depended on a larger web of institutions connecting scientists, engineers, managers, and workers. Experience in other jurisdictions suggested that cooperative relationships between producers, suppliers, and research communities underpinned the 'collective advance of technical knowledge' (Wolfe, 1992: 20–9).

Industrial policy needed to do more than subsidize individual firms. It had to 'create a new array of social and political institutions capable of supporting increased levels of social productivity and a higher standard of living' (Wolfe, 1992: 21–2). A central determinant of national or sub-national competitiveness was the institutional capacity to generate and diffuse innovations across the economy through networks sharing ideas and combining resources. In these terms, the NDP policy thinkers gave currency to the notion of a sector-based industrial policy. The goal, it was argued 'is to develop production networks rather than world class entrepreneurs' (Gindin and Robertson,1992: 37). Furthermore, such networks and sectors tended to cohere in clusters that were regionally defined, providing a provincial base for renewed community or local economic activity.

As regards labour market policy, the economic policy review also broke with the Premier's Council at certain key points. The timing of the 1990 election precluded any direct response to the council's second report, *People and Skills in the Global Economy*. Nonetheless, it was clear that the party thinkers rejected the equity-efficiency trade-off proposed in the OTAB model.

In question here were a number of the council's inter-connected themes and assumptions: the focus on internationally traded sectors and employed workers; the separation of economic and social policy goals in labour force development and the associated division of labour between OTAB and the government in adjustment and training programming; and the empirical data, glossed over in the Premier's Council report, showing a trend in high value-added production toward labour market polarization in terms of job quality and income levels. Party deliberations took full account of the rapid growth of non-standard or contingent work, questioning the relevance of the council's labour market strategy to these workers, and indeed its feasibility in an economy generating many low-wage, unstable employment ghettos outside the core traded sectors. Training and adjustment policies for employed workers in traded sectors required broadening to incorporate equity and access for all workers, employed and unemployed. Such policies also required flanking by other labour market measures in the areas of employment standards and labour relations (Myles, 1989; Ernst, 1995: 7).[3]

In sum, the New Democratic Party's industrial and labour market policy agenda, as it took shape in the months before the party took office, was more complex and ambitious than that presented by the Premier's Council. Whatever its shortcomings as a rigorous exercise in policy analysis and development, it responded in ways that the council exercise had not to the experience and claims of constituencies beyond business and labour, particularly equity groups such as women, visible minorities, and people with disabilities. These interests were not recognized as central actors in the council's high value-added policy discourse (Dehli, 1993: 100).

Of course, this economic policy review only acquired larger, province-wide significance after September 1990 with the surprise election of a majority New Democrat government. In attempting to find its bearings in power, the government drew on the intellectual capital vested at the Premier's Council, the reformulations generated through the party process, as well as further discussions with key party constituencies (Ontario Federation of Labour, 1990). The resulting synthesis was formally expressed in background material to the government's first budget in April 1991. This budget, most remembered for its mild Keynesianism, also contained a framework statement of the new government's economic and social policy direction. Seeking to develop a 'progressive competitiveness' alternative to what it saw as the federal government's neo-liberal agenda of deflation, downsizing, and privatization, Ontario's Budget Paper E stated:

Ontario cannot afford the rigidity induced by policies which focus on cutting wages and eroding public sector contributions to productivity. The alternative approach for government is to play a role as facilitator of structural change, not only to minimize the costs of transition and distribute them more fairly, but actively to promote the development of high-value-added, high-wage jobs through strategic partnerships. The approach of the Ontario Government is based on the conviction that sustainable prosperity is best achieved on the basis of increased equity and cooperation. (Ontario Ministry of Treasury and Economics, 1991: 87)

In effect, the government would aim to bridge the economic efficiency and social equity divide that separated the labour market policy visions of the Premier's Council and the party. In doing so, it would also reject the firm-specific industrial policy of the council in favour of the party's sectoral approach to coordinate 'a variety of practices involving firms or outside agencies, such as trade associations, apprenticeship programs, labour education facilities, joint marketing arrangements and regulatory commissions, each of which facilitates inter-firm cooperation' (Ontario Ministry of Treasury and Economics, 1991: 92).

The stage was thus set for Ontario to begin its experiment with sectorally based policy-making. Budget Paper E indicated that the showcase policy fields for this approach would be labour market policy and industrial policy, the former finding expression through a multipartite planning approach at the provincial level, and the latter taking the form of sectoral planning processes requiring extensive inter-firm and labour-management cooperation. The government looked to establish its own version of OTAB, and a new industrial strategy centred around the Sector Partnership Fund.

The Operation of Ontario's Sectoral Initiatives

The Ontario Training and Adjustment Board

Observers of the Liberal Peterson government have concluded that the ideas and recommendations of the Premier's Council were 'virtually ignored by both the Liberal Party and cabinet and by the Queen's Park bureaucracy for the life of that government' (Mackenzie, 1992: 13.). Indeed, beyond the creation of the Ontario Technology Fund to manage certain aspects of the industrial policy agenda, most of the work of the Premier's Council reports languished on the sidelines during the Peterson governments (Hall, 1996: 4–15). An announcement in 1989 of the formation of OTAB and the dismantling of the provincial training bureaucracy was not followed by any coherent implementation effort.

However, the election of the NDP government signalled significant new political commitment to practising more anticipatory economic development policy through institutional innovations. One of the new cabinet's first moves was to create an inter-ministerial working group to develop a framework for provincial training and adjustment policy that considered both the Premier's Council OTAB model and the ongoing provincial social assistance review (Wolfe, 1997: 9). This charge was significant since it affirmed the NDP government's view that labour market policy should merge economic efficiency and social equity goals. At about the same time that it created the inter-ministerial group, the new government signalled its interest in sectoral labour market approaches, signing a five-year agreement to contribute to a training program under way in the electrical/electronics industry. It further supported formation of a training centre in the plastics sector in cooperation with Humber College (Ontario Ministry of Treasury and Economics, 1992: 28). Other sectoral training initiatives were anticipated after the recommendations of the inter-ministerial committee and, most importantly, decisions on the proposed OTAB.

In November 1991 the government released a consultation document on its plans for provincial labour market policy. *Skills to Meet the Challenge: A Train-*

ing Partnership for Ontario established the outlines of the NDP's OTAB model. While rooted in the Premier's Council vision, this model reflected the influence of the earlier party policy review, and the new government's initial compromises reached with its labour market partners. As the minister of skills development later stated, 'What we did in terms of adjusting the models to our own purposes was to try to expand the partnership somewhat, in particular so that we would be assisting unemployed workers and people who want to re-enter the workforce as well as those with jobs in having a say in the development of policy around training and adjustment in Ontario' (Ontario, *Standing Committee*, 1993: 1348).

The NDP made four significant revisions to model that had been endorsed by the Liberal government. First, the range of programs to be transferred from government to the agency was extended to include those serving the employment disadvantaged. Second, programs were to be grouped under four separate councils – Workplace and Sectoral Training, Apprenticeship, Labour Force Adjustment, and Labour Force Entry and Re-entry – each with its own funding envelope and leadership structure mirroring the agency's executive board. Third, the composition of the executive board or governing body would be less bipartite and more multipartite in character. The composition was: eight business and labour representatives, four from social equity groups (specifically, women, visible minorities, persons with disabilities, and Aboriginal Canadians), two from the education and training sector, and one federal and one provincial ex-officio representative. Fourth, the OTAB secretariat would be staffed by public servants who would transfer along with their programs to the new agency without any loss of seniority, benefits, and existing collective agreement protections (Ontario Training and Adjustment Board, *Skills to Meet the Challenge*, 1991: 34).

With this model on the table, the government began public consultations on both the provincial body and a proposed network of local training boards designed jointly with the federal government (Government of Ontario, Canadian Labour Force Development Board, Employment and Immigration Canada, 1991). The ensuing process proved complex and drawn-out. It soon became clear that each of the private sector partners invited to sit on OTAB arrived with its own understanding of the basic purposes of training. It followed that each had rather different views of OTAB's policy focus, program priorities, and financing strategies (Bradford and Stevens, 1996).

Equally clear, however, was the government's commitment to devolving substantial policy responsibility to its partners. Much time and resources were devoted to helping the groups equip themselves for effective participation in the proposed agency. Indeed, almost all of 1992 was consumed with trying to establish the representational foundations for OTAB's operation. The social partners set up their own steering committees to consult their constituents on basic issues such as the agency's mandate. The government supported formation of permanent reference groups for OTAB's representatives to improve accountability in decision-making and institutional legitimacy. Public funds were made available to assist those groups, particularly in the equity and education communities, to develop structures to sustain their involvement in the board. Adding to the complexity of the initial consultations were unexpected demands for greater representativeness. A range of constituencies not contemplated in either the Premier's Council model or the government's, such as youth, construction employers and employees, and injured workers, asked for their own representatives. Some francophone groups wanted a separate, French-language OTAB while the provincial Building and Construction Trades Council initially called for a separate construction training and adjustment board. As this complex consultative exercise unfolded, the most senior civil servant involved remarked that the aim was to launch a 'round table of diversity' where 'participation will breed creativity' (Steed, 1993: 23). Yet there was a clear risk that this diversity, rooted in divergent labour market world views among the partners, would breed disputes of an order threatening to paralyse the process. In fact, the government faced an extraordinary challenge in steering debates among the social partners to the common ground necessary for institutional innovation. Below is a description of the divergent views of the social partners, tracking their manifestation at critical decision points in the establishment of OTAB (Bradford and Stevens, 1996: 156–61).

Business had accepted the original Premier's Council version of OTAB as an opportunity to use the discourse of competitiveness and skill development to orient publicly funded programs and services towards the type of competency-based and applied skills training it deemed most useful. Labour's vision of training reflected a long-standing desire among workers for self-determination, equality, respect, and genuine consultation on workplace issues. Many individual unions and the Ontario Federation of Labour (OFL) saw training as an increasingly important issue which they could not afford to leave as a unilateral business decision. For example, the Canadian Energy and Paperworkers (CEP) argued that 'the need for training is not just a question of productivity and/or profit for the company, although we may share some these concerns with management. As we see it, training is about the future of our role in society as working people. It is *our* issue' (CEP, 1993: 87). The worker-driven vision of training challenged business's focus on competitiveness and 'puts workers in a better position to shape the future and start to eliminate job discrimination based on gender, race and ethnicity.' In these terms, the union concluded that 'while OTAB has the potential to promote worker-driven training across the province, its direction is not set. We will have to fight to make sure that OTAB meets our needs' (CEP, 1993: 11).

Within business and labour there were also different views about the benefits of participating in joint planning structures, and the degree to which compromises should be made. On the labour side, the Canadian Auto Workers (CAW) was much more sceptical of joint labour-management cooperation in training decisions than either the CEP or United Steel Workers of America. For business, there remained basic questions of representation and whether there could be a reliable business voice to decide province-wide training issues. Organizations representing different sectors, particularly small business, were wary of decisions that might have an uneven and detrimental effect on their own membership.

Like business and labour, social equity groups had also developed particular understandings of training, reflecting their own workplace and community experience. In general, they all 'welcomed the integration of social and economic policy in the OTAB legislation,' and argued that 'employment equity must be linked to the entire labour adjustment and training system' (Ontario *Standing Committee*, 1993: 1711). In their view, 'good training' was a broad concept. In the words of the spokesperson for the Ontario Women's Action on Training Coalition: 'The new training boards must establish one integrated system that meets the needs of all individuals at all points in their lives. People don't only need skills for working; they need skills for living in healthy, economically vibrant communities. We want to ensure that social equity objectives are first established, then achieved and maintained within a training system that promotes social justice as well as economic objectives' (Ontario, *Standing Committee*, 1993: 1711).

Equity groups not only argued for greater access to state funded programs but a more basic reconceptualization of the training system. They noted that the dominant conception of skill acquisition and knowledge – viewed as a rational progression from elementary and secondary school to post-secondary education or apprenticeship and finally to firm- or workplace-specific skills – did not recognize either the different ways these groups might acquire skills or the barriers they faced in following the prescribed route. Women's groups maintained that training had to support gender equity, be learner-centred, and provide collateral supports such as income and child care to enable women to participate. Visible minority groups emphasized that an anti-racism focus should be at the basis of training policy formation and program design. Groups representing the disabled were concerned that a training system remove access barriers and provide accommodations to facilitate their participation. Francophone groups wanted the language and economic barriers faced by their community to be addressed.

As a spokesperson for a community-based training organization put it; 'People who are not job-ready have a set of barriers that is not so much related to the recession's lack of jobs as it is to personal or systemic barriers. Our concern is that the training needs of our target groups will not be considered by OTAB to be worthy of investing in, not 'the best returns on investment' (Ontario *Standing Committee*, 1993: 1578).

Social equity groups developed linkages across their concerns, 'using their participation in OTAB as a base from which to do grass-roots organizing, developing their consensus-building skills' (Steed, 1993: 23). The OTAB consultation process brought together groups which had previously not worked together, enabling them to develop common positions on labour market issues. They also developed ties with activists in the OFL and individual unions, providing the basis for connecting their agendas and advancing common positions.

The advancement of this social equity agenda was contested. Business, in particular, saw social equity concerns as diluting or overshadowing the role it (and the Premier's Council) assigned to competitiveness per se in Ontario's training system. Business spokespersons feared the proposed OTAB would have 'a more important social than economic focus' and that the achievement of a more competitive economy had been relegated to a 'secondary status' (Ontario, *Standing Committee*,1993: 1597). They criticized the government for producing an OTAB model that strayed from the original purposes of the Premier's Council.

These fundamental differences among the social partners crystallized in further disputes over the coverage of OTAB's mandate, the governing body's decision-making rules, and payroll training taxes (Bradford and Stevens, 1996: 159).[4] The question of whether OTAB's mandate should cover the public sector proved to be a major area of contention. Business groups did not want money for private sector training diverted to the broader public sector and took the position that adjustment measures for this restructuring should remain a government responsibility. They insisted that OTAB's mandate apply only to the private sector. The OFL and public sector unions, on the other hand, wanted the public and broader public sector included to guarantee training funds for members affected by widespread public sector restructuring. While the final wording of the mandate referred to OTAB's responsibility for both the private and public sectors, the business steering committee won assurances from the government that OTAB's focus would be the private sector. After OTAB was established, business continued to resist any shift away from private sector concerns. Significantly, business did not provide a slate of its members to sit on a proposed council to examine broader public sector training issues, suggesting a boycott of the council.

With its multipartite representation, OTAB's decision-making rules became another source of controversy. Business wanted to avoid being outvoted by a coalition of labour and equity representatives and indicated that it would not provide nominations to the board unless the issue was resolved to its satisfaction. The business steering committee proposed that in the absence of consensus a double majority model be adopted. This model would require the support of the majority of business and labour directors in addition to a simple majority vote. Equity groups proposed a triple majority model in which they would be dealt with collectively as a third partner. A majority of votes from business, labour, and equity groups would be required. Eventually a compromise between a double and triple majority model was devised. The decision-making model protected business from being outflanked by other groups, gave equity groups some influence where consensus could not be achieved, and maintained the dominance of both business and labour on the governing body.

Finally, the business steering committee rejected the OFL's demand that a 1 per cent payroll training tax be levied against employers to increase private sector funding for training. Business representatives argued that any investment in training should be voluntary and that a compulsory tax would act as a disincentive to the development of business-labour training trust funds. In other words, existing sector agreements on training could be imperilled if a tax was implemented. As one business spokesperson put it, 'Top-down directives will not move business people to train' (Ontario, *Standing Committee*, 1993: 1825). The issue was more or less resolved when the government informed business that it would not implement a training tax unless recommended by OTAB. Compulsory leveraging of employer investment in training would therefore not be done without the consent and approval of business.

In the midst of these disputes, and following a formal round table session intended to reach consensus, the minister of skills development introduced legislation in late 1992 to establish OTAB. Remarkably, some groups complained that things were moving too quickly. The Board of Trade of Metropolitan Toronto felt that the process had been 'a forced march,' and that government should devise 'a more carefully thought out plan' (*Canadian HR Reporter*, 1992: 15). In fact, once legislation was introduced the business community began to rethink the entire exercise, preferring to recast OTAB as a more conventional advisory body to government. The Ontario Chamber of Commerce stated that it was 'inappropriate to give OTAB spending authority for funds that should be accountable back through the legislature ... that means that the independent portions of OTAB, the various boards and councils relying on reference groups/interest groups nominees, should be advisory, not decision-making' (Ontario, *Standing Committee*, 1993: 1376). This revisionism was not confined to business interests. A key labour representative stated publicly that the eighteen months of policy work and consultation leading to the enabling legislation had been largely wasted and that the government's institutional experiment would not work. He suggested an alternative: 'We should obligate employers to train their workers, and focus public dollars on training the unemployed. The government should have put someone in charge to just do it' (Steed, 1993: 23).

Despite the controversies, the government finally passed the OTAB legislation and in July 1993 appointed the governing body, nearly three years into the government's mandate. A budget was approved of $442 million for the first year of operation. Through all these debates, the government still hoped that OTAB could be an effective vehicle for delivering more and better sectoral training. In the words of the minister, 'We have a history of successful initiatives in bringing bipartite sponsorship to training initiatives, and those are ongoing at this point in time in our province. There is no reason to imagine why we cannot, at the upper level of our training system, use a similar kind of partnership to govern the training and adjustment policy development and implementation in Ontario' (Ontario, *Standing Committee*, 1993: 1348).

Indeed, as the OTAB implementation process dragged on, the government pursued specific initiatives on the sectoral training front. It signed a three-year Sectoral Training Agreement in the auto parts sector, complementing its earlier support in the steel and electrical and electronics sector. As part of the social contract exercise for restraint and restructuring in the public sector and broader public sector, the government created a $300 million adjustment and training fund. This initiative involved formation of sectoral panels to operate a cross-sectoral job registry providing labour market matching services for workers and employers. It built on an existing broader public sector Transition Assistance Fund which had spawned a sectoral adjustment and training health care strategy, the Hospital Training and Adjustment Program, modelled after the private sector Canadian Steel Trades Employment Congress. Through training trust funds, the government initiated in the construction industry a number of inter-employer, bipartite umbrella trusts that allowed for some sectoral labour market planning. The JobsOntario Training Fund, while focused on subsidies for individual firms in hiring social assistance recipients, also aimed to 'encourage larger employers and sectoral associations to create jobs for eligible unemployed workers' (Ontario Ministry of Treasury and Economics, 1992). Finally, there continued development in the community college system of sectoral centres of specialization providing focused upgrading for workers. Such centres included the Canadian Plastics Training Centre at Humber College, the Canadian Automotive Institute at Georgian College, and the Woods Products Development at Conestoga College.

It was in relation to these various initiatives that OTAB's Sectoral and Workplace Training Council was to provide a new single window on provincial sectoral labour market programming. It would ease access for private sector clients and help rationalize programs, and focus public expenditures. The council would be responsible for encouraging the development of sectoral agreements in a variety of ways. It would channel provincial funds; require formation of sectoral committees to guide training practices; work with sectoral committees to establish mutually acceptable criteria to guide training activities; ensure that the design of sectoral initiatives took into account labour adjustment issues and needs; and promote training opportunities for individuals who face barriers to participation in training.

Yet before this single window could open, OTAB's newly appointed governing body and the government's training bureaucracy had to sort through further implementation issues. From late 1993 to early 1995, attention shifted to setting up the five new councils, deciding protocols for the bureaucracy comprising some 550 staff members, drafting OTAB's strategic plan, formalizing relationships with the twenty-five local boards, and negotiating the memorandum of understanding with government (OTAB, Co-Chairs' Report, 1994). These tasks required nearly a year of intensive work and were completed in June 1994. It was another six months before the councils began to meet to focus on central tasks in OTAB's mandate: program reform and new sectoral training agreements.

The implementation planning undertaken by OTAB's governing body was paralleled by inter-ministerial meetings within government to address unresolved issues. Prominent among these was finalizing a framework to allow the new agency to make progress on sectoral training initiatives. This was an obvious priority as the three existing sectoral agreements with provincial participation were funded on a time-limited basis through an approval process outside the initial OTAB budget. There was no specific mechanism for funding sectoral training and it was not clear whether provincial funding contributions for future agreements would be approved by OTAB through a predetermined funding allocation or by cabinet on a case-by-case basis. The fact that OTAB's budget was divided between the five councils also made it difficult to shift monies into new sectoral agreements.

However, the biggest increase in the government's labour market budget was not additional funds to OTAB or sectoral initiatives but to JobsOntario training which was aimed at getting social assistance recipients off the welfare rolls through wage and training subsidies for individual employers. Further, as part of its 1992 budget, the government launched the second major track of its sectoral policy approach – industrial policy. The next section reviews developments in this field.

The Sector Partnership Fund

OTAB's implementation process revealed fundamental areas of disagreement among Ontario's labour market partners. However, amid the disputes there was one point of fairly clear agreement: the high value-added strategy required integration between labour market and industrial policies. The minister of skills development underlined that the government's approach was to encourage 'industries to meet both their training needs, their research needs and so on, as clusters with related needs instead of remaining unlinked to each other and simply flying solo' (*Canadian HR Reporter*,1992: 17). Members of the professional training community itself urged the government not to establish OTAB in the 'absence of an overall industrial strategy for the province' (Ontario, *Standing Committee*, 1993: 1366). From the labour perspective, one union representative stated: 'The minister has stated that OTAB is part of a long-term industrial policy framework for Ontario. We agree. "Part of" are key words. It must be emphasized that training is not an industrial strategy. Training by itself cannot bring an end to economic dislocation and the resulting human misery that thousands and thousands of workers are currently experiencing' (Ontario, *Standing Committee*, 1993: 1507).

In its industrial policy proposals, the NDP again combined themes from the Premier's Council and its own economic policy review. The government did not want to target support to individual firms or to continue spending on mature, crisis-ridden companies in the steel and pulp and paper industries that became unexpected assistance priorities of the government in its first year in office. More generally, the government wanted to find an alternative to the traditional industrial policy dependence on direct expenditures and tax incentives designed and delivered by bureaucrats.[5] This approach was brought together in the industrial policy framework released in July 1992. Government expenditures would henceforth neither focus on individual firms nor take the form of general incentives, but would be channelled to enhancing the 'people and physical' infrastructure of the new economy, specifically worker skills and high technology. Knowledge, both scientific and organizational, was emphasized as the critical variable for successful high value-added production. Equally important for competitiveness, however, was the broader societal and institutional capacity to diffuse it across firms in the economy. Implicit was the notion that there was a common public and private interest in contributing to the economy's knowledge-generating infrastructure. In these terms, the framework announced the government's intent to begin joint planning with networks of firms and unions in specific sectors. The goals were threefold: to lever private sector resources for upgrading sectoral competitiveness; to tailor all government expenditures to the particular product, market, and organizational conditions prevailing in sectors; and to introduce a kind of market test into industrial policy supports by confining government's role to 'creating capabilities and promoting winning activities – the competitive fundamentals – rather than trying to pick the winning companies or sectors of the future.' The framework pointed to industry-wide training programs as a prime example of how firms could improve their competitiveness through cooperation at the sectoral level (Ontario Ministry of Industry, Trade and Technology, 1992: 12–18).

The centrepiece of the industrial policy framework was the Sector Partnership Fund, approved as a new initiative and announced in the 1992 budget with funding of $150 million over three years, later extended to six (Ontario Ministry of Economic Development and Trade, 1995). Under this program, the government would elicit from critical interests in the sector, cooperative competitiveness strategies, and fund concrete initiatives to make the shift to higher value-added activities. The sector strategies were to include diagnosis of sectoral strengths and weaknesses, identification of common challenges, and analysis of priority initiatives to meet such challenges. Such initiatives could address training requirements, research needs, marketing opportunities and so forth (Wolfe, 1996: 19).

Responsibility for the formulation of strategies was given to the sector partners themselves. The SPF defined a sector as a group of Ontario-based firms that produced similar goods or services, using similar processes and technologies, and that have identified themselves as a sector. Each sector required a forum or council for sector issue identification and consensus building, that included representation of business and trade unions and other relevant interests. The SPF was available to all sectors in the economy. The government did not predetermine inter-sectoral funding priorities, and provision was also made for cabinet to adjust provincial expenditures across sectors and activities on an annual basis. At the same time, however, the funding approval process decided by the government was rigorous.

The government specified a number of conditions that sector councils would have to meet to qualify for provincial money. Sector strategies had to reflect a consensus among all interests represented in the process. Specific initiatives proposed for funding had to constitute an incremental addition to the activities of the sector, and not substitute for activities that would have taken place regardless of the fund's existence. They could not overlap or duplicate other areas of government programming. Finally, once drafted, the sector strategies and proposed initiatives would be scrutinized by bureaucratic officials who would then carry the proposals forward to the Cabinet Committee on Economic Development for approval. Also proposed was an internal government sector council which would meet quarterly and be composed of representatives from sector ministries, Treasury Board, and Cabinet Office. The council's role would focus on coordination and facilitation of strategies, involving technical review of submissions and administration of the Fund.

In practice, the Ministry of Economic Development and Trade (MEDT) was responsible for coordinating the industrial policy framework and implementation of the SPF. Under its direction, line ministries with sectoral responsibilities such as Forestry, Health, and Agriculture and Food were assigned leadership roles in facilitating approval of strategies formulated by the sectoral partners. MEDT directly led strategy development only in those sectors where there was no established ministerial partner, such as aerospace, computing, and plastics. MEDT became a kind of industrial policy central agency supporting the various line ministries in their external work with the sectoral councils, and in their internal responsibilities for bringing forward proposals to the Cabinet Committee on Economic Development. This internal bureaucratic division of labour reflected a desire to break down the ministerial walls that characterized traditional industrial policy making and reinforced the government's desire for shared ownership of the SPF as an initiative relying for its momentum on joint planning in the private sector.

In recognition of Ontario's limited experience with this kind of cooperative planning, one of the fund's goals was to assist in developing new inter-firm relationships, analytic abilities, and program or service delivery capacities. To this end, a maximum $500,000 provincial contribution was available for helping sector partners to equip themselves to prepare their strategies. This money could be used for sector capacity building projects such as strengthening emerging industry associations, providing initial diagnosis of the sector's capabilities, and retaining consultants to assist in developing a sector strategy. A first step for many industries before undertaking planning and seeking approval for initiatives was to use the SPF to create a sectoral governance structure or council to forge new associational structures that would cultivate inter-firm cooperation and labour-management partnership.

Consistent with the philosophy of supporting winning activities rather than picking winners, the SPF gave priority to sectors that were independently organized and conveyed an interest in working with government. By letting the proposals develop externally, the government believed it would improve the quality of the submissions and their prospects for sustainability through increasing commitment of private not public resources (Ontario Ministry of Industry, Trade and Technology, 1992:24). Following approval of a strategy, the government was prepared to make a financial contribution for implementation of up to 50 per cent of funding secured from the sector partners themselves or other governments. The government's aim was clear enough: provide initial monies to engage firms and labour market partners in a planning process, lever sufficient private sector investments to implement sectoral programs, networks, and infrastructure, and over time allow market forces to determine their viability.

The SPF was in operation by 1993. Thus there is a basis for preliminary assessment of its performance or impact. According to David Wolfe, a key participant in the design of the initiative and a close observer of its subsequent operation, the SPF was a mixed success (Wolfe, 1996:21). On the one hand, it provided an opportunity for many firms, unions, members of the scientific research community and the like to come together for the first time to identify common challenges and potential solutions. These consultations produced an unexpectedly large number of sector strategies with broad buy-in from social partners. Between 1993 and 1995, only two sector strategies were rejected, one because it appeared the group wanted to use the process to lobby the government, and the second because the business representatives refused to cooperate with labour (Chamberlain, 1995). Overall, the content of the sector strategies conformed closely to the expectations of government, in part because the template created by government for the plans was clear and in part because individual ministries worked closely with their sector partners in their preparation.

On the other hand, the implementation of concrete initiatives, where financial contributions were required from the government's social partners, was not so successful. In fact, the SPF budget was consistently underspent, suggesting that many sector strategies did not contain proposals that could meet the conditions for funding (Wolfe, 1996: 25) The gap between the sector planning and initiative implementation raised concerns that millions of public dollars could be spent on a process that did not lead to meaningful results. It was possible that the matching fund formula was simply an insurmountable barrier for many small and medium-sized businesses that could most benefit from cooperation. Alternatively, the gap between planning and implementation could be seen as an indicator of success. The market test that demanded significant private sector investment in approved initiatives worked to guard against flawed or dubious projects from being funded. The incentive was for the social partners in the planning process to identify only those proposals that all could mobilize their own resources behind. Clarification of these matters awaits systematic evaluation of the SPF.[6]

Regardless, by the time of the June 1995 provincial election, the SPF process had engaged two thousand participants from twenty-eight sectors, involving twenty-two unions, ninety-three industry associations, and twenty-eight college and universities (Ontario Ministry of Economic Development and Trade, 1995) Despite some difficulties in the partnerships, particularly between the CAW and business representatives in the auto parts and aerospace sectors, the SPF process appeared to be evolving towards a functional form of government-facilitated, bipartite planning (Ernst, 1995: 21). The government committed about $75 million of the $150 million SPF budget and levered an additional $95 million from the private sector for joint projects. Sector strategies were approved in fifteen sectors, representing a broad cross-section of the provincial economy. These sectors included telecommunications, computing, aerospace, auto parts, food processing, environmental industries, health industries, plastics, furniture, and cultural industries. Many sector strategies identified training issues, ranging from raising skill levels for workers and managers, to equipping the workplace parties to undertake major work reorganizations. Other common areas of emphasis were improved access to capital, and support for expanded international marketing, and export development (Wolfe, 1996: 25).

However, the SPF's most significant impact in terms of concrete initiatives funded appears to have been support for sector-based technology and business resource centres. The aerospace sector strategy resulted in the creation of the Ontario Aerospace Council to help companies collaborate on pre-competitive research, establish an aerospace industry training certificate program, and bid on major national and international contracts. A similar sector-based technology centre was established for environmental industries to assist in commercialization of environmental technologies. In the food sector, new funding was provided to the existing Guelph Food Technology Centre to improve technology transfer. Further funding was provided to the Ontario Winery Adjustment Program, a sectoral arrangement established in the late 1980s in response to free trade. In computing, a sector resource facility was funded to provide technical support to small and medium-sized firms and improve their international marketing and export competitiveness. In auto parts, a sector strategy was approved, involving funding from the federal and Quebec governments, to establish a permanent sectoral council to coordinate initiatives in specific areas such as manufacturing practices, access to capital, work organization, apprenticeship training, and global marketing (Ontario Ministry of Economic Development and Trade, 1995; 1996). Beyond their specific activities, these centres were potentially significant value-adding innovations in a larger sense. They could institutionalize the cooperative sectoral relationships engendered through the initial planning stage of the SPF, providing a context for organizing further investments in collaborative services and programs. It seems reasonable to conclude that they constituted the logical first step in confirming the sectoral planning capacity that was fundamental to the long-term success of the SPF.

In the end, the achievements of the SPF seem to reside more in the process it engaged than in the products it delivered. The mere fact that constructive planning on sector-wide issues was occurring not only distinguished the SPF from OTAB, but suggested a potential shift in the provincial business culture, and to some extent the labour relations climate, away from narrow competition among firms and conflict between unions and management. The SPF was designed to realize the competitive advantages argued by authoritative analysts of the new economy to flow from such inter-firm cooperation (Best, 1990; Coleman, 1988: 260–85). Given the high number of sectors that participated in the SPF and the degree of consensus achieved on strategic plans, it was understandable that Ontario's sectoral focus moved from labour market policy to industrial policy. The SPF represented a more promising institutional framework than OTAB for implementing sectoral initiatives in Ontario.

Assessing Ontario's Sectoral Experience: Labour Market and Industrial Policy Compared

The above case studies describe a pattern of frustration and dashed expectations in Ontario's sectoral activity in labour market policy, and modest but comparatively impressive progress in industrial policy. In attempting to account for this outcome, it is helpful to consider the concept of corporatism and the factors that condition the viability of this form of policy-making (Atkinson and Pervin, this volume). Corporatism can be defined as a framework for political management of the economy that directly involves interest organizations in policy development and implementation. It requires that such groups combine interest representation, policy participation, and membership control roles (Cawson, 1986: 38; Goldthorpe, 1984: 324). Ideally, corporatism involves ongoing bargaining among highly centralized, comprehensive business and labour organizations possessing policy expertise, formally recognized by the state, and delegated significant control over the public policy outputs. Corporatist arrangements, it has been argued, can moderate political conflict by providing incentives for compromise on specific issues and an enduring context for finding common ground among different interests. They may also contribute to positive economic performance by providing better and faster policy intelligence on the critical needs of producer groups (Katzenstein, 1985: 191–211).

Indeed, comparative studies examining employment, inflation, and restructuring patterns in the 1970s and 1980s highlighted the relative success of corporatist jurisdictions. Almost all of these success stories were found in Western Europe, leading observers to hypothesize that there were identifiable preconditions – structural, cultural, and organizational – necessary to develop and sustain corporatism. Three factors have often been seen as critical: the organizational capacity of the social partners to define their policy interests and deliver constituency support or compliance around compromises negotiated with other representatives; an ideology of social partnership rooted in labour-management mutual respect in the workplace; and a government able to combine the roles of negotiation facilitator and policy participant.

To what extent should OTAB and the SPF be included in the corporatist family? In both cases, the state recognized certain interest groups and invited them to assume new responsibilities as participants in the making of policy. The principle of equal representation of business and labour interests in the decision-making process guided the state in its design of both OTAB and the SPF. Both involved substantial delegation of authority over the content of programs and public expenditures to the social partners who were expected to identify priorities through cooperative negotiation. The social partners were not simply information providers to bureaucrats or advisors to government. They were representatives of societal interests empowered by the state to direct and shape the course of provincial industrial and labour market policy. Indeed, the government's commitment to a substantive devolution of authority through both OTAB and the SPF was underscored in the considerable time and resources devoted to enhance the organizational capacities of the social partners to assume policy responsibilities.

Given the roles and responsibilities of government and organized interests in these policy bodies, it is fair to conclude that both OTAB and the SPF matched up reasonably well with defining features of the corporatist model. However, they did so in particular ways. Specifically, three factors capture important differences between the corporatism of OTAB on the one hand and the SPF on the other. The first factor concerns the level at which the corporatist arrangement was cast, that is, at the macro-societal, economy wide level or at the meso-sectoral, industry specific level. The second factor concerns the scope or range of issues that were open to negotiation among the social partners. The final factor involves the role played by the state, specifically the degree to which officials provided direction to the social partners, and clarified expectations about acceptable outcomes.

OTAB was an attempt at province-wide macro-corporatism. Its implementation revealed the relative absence of the key pre-conditions mentioned above for this corporatist form in Ontario, and the great complexity in attempting to create them. The organization of Ontario business and labour seems neither sufficiently centralized nor comprehensive enough to permit effective, sustained policy participation at the provincial level. Each community has significant lines of internal division that inhibit the ability to close ranks around positions, not to mention mobilize support for compromises on the kind of broad, cross-cutting policy questions framed at OTAB. In terms of the culture supporting social partnership, the labour relations climate in Ontario has always been more adversarial than collaborative, and perhaps never more so than in the period between 1990 and 1995. Business groups linked the government's major training and adjustment proposal to other policy initiatives they strongly opposed, such as labour relations reform and employment equity. As the Canadian Federation of Independent Business stated, 'OTAB and OLRA are so very linked. You're talking about training for jobs and killing jobs' (Khan, 1992: 7). On the other hand, labour was emboldened by the NDP victory and their pressures certainly reinforced the significant modifications made by the government to the Premier's Council OTAB model. Yet the introduction of the social contract in 1993 brought to the fore internal divisions in the labour movement and strengthened the position of those unions basically opposed to participation in corporatist policy structures (McBride, 1996: 87–8).

OTAB was also an innovative form of labour market corporatism in its multipartite governance structure which gave formal representation to numerous social actors with little or no history of working together. This novel departure from the familiar European tripartite corporatist template certainly reflected the diversity of Ontario's labour market and the full range of employment problems wrought by rapid economic restructuring. Yet it made consensus-building on both agency governance and policy priorities difficult in the extreme, and likely to require years of organizational learning from all partners. In sum, the government faced a highly unstable interest group alignment at the macro-societal level in seeking partners for OTAB's implementation.

Controversies about OTAB's structure and representation lead into consideration of the second key factor shaping the viability of Ontario's corporatist experiments: the scope of the issues subject to negotiation. OTAB's policy focus was wide-ranging, consistent with a macro-societal institution with diverse interest representation. It emphasized ensuring equitable access to basic skills acquisition for groups historically facing barriers, and integrating the long-term unemployed, social assistance recipients, and new entrants into the labour market. Here, business representatives raised concerns about the loss of focus on their core efficiency concerns through incorporation of the social equity agenda. Not surprisingly, consensus among business, labour, and social equity groups proved elusive. The social partners remained more advocates of their own training policy world views than participants in cooperative policy-making.

This all points to the importance of the final factor, the role of the state. The government was consultative and tentative throughout the process. At critical junctures in the implementation process, there was insufficient political will to reign in debates, and either make decisions or specify a range of acceptable outcomes for social partner negotiation. While this stance may be taken as evidence of the commitment to devolving authority, it seems clear in retrospect, particularly given the policy differences that persisted between the business community on the one hand, and the labour and social groups on the other, that much firmer government direction was required if this institution was to achieve an organizational identity and find a policy focus.

In sum, OTAB's macro-societal structure, diffuse mandate, and wide range of program responsibilities all conspired to reduce the likelihood of consolidating a viable sectoral policy structure. In such circumstances, a much stronger form of political leadership was required than actually materialized.[7] In the case of OTAB, key successes reported by the Premier's Council from the sectoral council experience of the 1980s were lost, principally that there must be a limited number of core issues, low expectations regarding the outcome of the initiative, a close linkage to workplaces, and leadership committed to finding areas of mutual self-interest (Ontario Premier's Council, 1990: 138).

In considering these three factors – the corporatist level, the issue scope, and the state's role – in relation to the SPF, a different picture emerges. Most importantly, the SPF was organized at the sectoral meso-corporatist level, and therefore, the task of meeting the pre-conditions for effective policy-making was less daunting (Atkinson and Coleman, 1989: 87–94). The SPF could rely on industry associations and individual unions to represent fairly cohesive interests in a joint planning process on a limited set of issues. So the prospects for constructive participation and identification of common ground among stakeholders were much greater.

Furthermore, questions about the mandate of the fund, or the larger nature and purposes of industrial policy, were simply not brought to the sectoral table for negotiation. The SPF channelled sectoral planning to five specific categories of activity, which in turn flowed from the competitive fundamentals enunciated in the industrial policy framework. While focused on the new goal of facilitating high-value added production, dialogue among the social partners was effectively confined by the government's funding criteria to areas of common ground. It followed that the partnerships forged at the sectoral level were limited to a more traditional set of interests, principally business associations, organized labour, and scientific researchers. Ideological conflict tended to be muted by the shared interest in securing some form of state assistance in meeting specific sectoral challenges.

Perhaps the most important factor contributing to sectoral activity generated under the auspices of the SPF was the role played by the state. The government defined the characteristics of an eligible sector and recognized the critical interests. It made available money and expertise to support emergence of sectoral council structures, set the terms for an acceptable planning process, and provided a template for the content of sector strategies and established clear criteria for funding of initiatives. With the SPF, significant policy responsibility was devolved to the social partners, but within explicit parameters and expectations. In short, the government's role was far more directive and authoritative than in the case of OTAB.

Assessing OTAB and SPF in light of these three factors, then, it seems that in the Ontario context, the prospects for viable sectoral partnership initiatives are best at the meso-level in corporatist arrangements where the state retains a significant measure of direction, and where the policy agenda is focused and fairly circumscribed. This configuration of factors allowed the SPF process to move forward, while its absence at OTAB left the social partners struggling to define a focus and a rationale for participation.

Conclusion

At the end of the day, Ontario's ten-year experiment with sectoral inititiatives was distinguished by considerable intellectual investment to conceptualize them within a coherent high value-added provincial development strategy, followed by modest implementation success in industrial policy and virtually no progress in labour market policy. Despite high expectations, the province managed only to sign labour market training agreements in the three industries where sectoral councils were already in operation through federal government leadership. In industrial policy, new planning agreements were concluded in fifteen sectors. Moreover, as OTAB struggled to emerge and the SPF moved forward, the province's two sectoral policy tracks existed largely in isolation of one another. As the NDP left office in June 1995, the important goal of integrating labour market and industrial policies through sectoral activity remained substantially unaddressed.

The election of the Progressive Conservative government in June 1995 marked the beginning of the end for Ontario's experiment with sectoral policy approaches. Two dynamics certain to damage prospects for cultivating already fragile corporatist arrangements were suddenly injected into the provincial mix. Most obviously, the government's economic thinking was antithetical to both the spirit and practice of corporatist policy-making. Rather than seeking partners to overcome market failures in providing adequate training and technology investments, the new government appears committed to privatizing responsibility for such matters to individual firms. The state's role in providing support for sectoral initiatives is effectively dismissed in a sweeping critique of micro-economic intervention and unproductive business subsidies. Instead, the government will concern itself with general policies of taxation, expenditure, and regulation, removing what it views as the impediments to private investment put in place from 1985 to 1995.

The second important change flowing from the election has been a shift in the strategic behaviour of the Ontario business community. Business representatives engaged in the corporatist processes established by the NDP were immediately presented with a far more direct political route to advance their own policy agenda. Traditional channels of influence were reopened to a cabinet sharing the business community's competitiveness priorities and the related criticisms of the view of economic development policy that crystallized in the late 1980s and early 1990s. These changes quickly reverberated through the corporatist boards and councils, most dramatically at OTAB, where the business representatives launched a unilateral offensive aimed at dramatically altering the structure and purposes of the institution. The thrust of the proposal was to eliminate equity representation and programming, and to dramatically downsize OTAB's staff and budget. Relations among the social partners, always difficult, deteriorated further.

Given the new political alignment in Ontario, it was hardly surprising that within the first year of their mandate, the Progressive Conservatives eliminated OTAB and the SPF, as well as related corporatist structures such as the Premier's Council and the Workplace Health and Safety Agency. In the case of the SPF, its budget was initially frozen in July 1995 and subsequently cancelled in November. In the May 1996 budget, the finance minister announced a new $50 million program, funded from savings from other cancelled programs, that appears to address some of the same objectives as the SPF, specifically, the need to 'strengthen Ontario's sectors' and 'bridge the training gap.' By the end of 1996 this program had not yet materialized. Ontario may continue with some version of sectoral industrial policy, but there is little reason to believe it will involve corporatist planning, or government-facilitated cooperative initiatives among groups of firms and unions. The finance minister introduced the program as a 'new private-sector-driven approach to business development' (Ontario Ministry of Finance, 1996: 21).[8]

OTAB's demise, like much else in its brief history, was more drawn-out than that of the SPF. Surviving the initial July and November 1995 cuts, it was effectively placed on a death watch. The reform councils, including the Workplace and Sectoral Training Council, were eliminated, and the governing body was directed by the government only to make recommendations on the future of Ontario's training system to an internal review led by the Ministry of Education and Training. OTAB's proposals to the ministry review included greater emphasis on sectoral training approaches. However, presentation of this advice proved to be the institution's last act. In April 1996 the Management Board of Cabinet announced the termination of OTAB. Training policy and program responsibilities would be returned to the Ministry of Education and Training, with a much reduced budget, and no mention of support for sectoral councils or training agreements (Government of Ontario, 1996: 71–85; Wolfe, 1997: 28,31).

OTAB and the SPF represented significant attempts at institutional innovation in Ontario. They responded to years of well-documented market and government failures in equipping workers and firms for economic restructuring challenges. Launched in a province with few of the organizational and cultural pre-conditions associated with viable corporatist policy making, both institutions clearly required years to mature. However, the OTAB and SPF experience underscores the obstacles to such complex innovations in Ontario, not the least of which is pronounced vulnerability to the vagaries of partisan politics. Still lacking a firm foundation of support among the social partners, these fledgling institutions became easy targets for a new government committed to radical retrenchment of the province's role in economic development.

Notes

1 The author was a member of the Ontario Public Service from 1992 to 1995. Much of the description of provincial policy-making presented in this chapter is based on personal observation and informal discussion with public servants. For helpful comments on an earlier version I would like to thank David Wolfe, Michael Mendelson, Andrew Sharpe, and Mark Rosenfeld. The author alone accepts full responsibility for any oversights or errors in interpretation.

2 There were two noteworthy exceptions to Ontario's critique of federal policies during this period. Premier Peterson and Premier Rae both supported Ottawa's attempts to accommodate Quebec in the constitution through the Meech Lake and Charlottetown Accords. As well, the federal government's efforts to create labour market institutions that involved business and labour more directly in policy formation was consistent with new policy thinking in Ontario.

3 For further discussion of the limits of the Premier's Council's labour market policy thought and recommendations, see Mahon, 1990: 93–5.

4 The establishment of local boards was also a source of conflict between OTAB's business and labour representatives. For details, see Bradford and Stevens, 1996: 160–1, and Wolfe, 1997: 15–18.

5 The fact that this kind of firm-specific assistance was increasingly constrained by continental trade agreements was another motivation for pursuing a non-targeted sectoral approach to industrial policy.

6 More broadly, the SPF could be criticized for eschewing use of stronger regulatory industrial policy instruments both to sustain social partnerships and mandate desirable

investment and employment performance. For this view of sectoral policy strategies, see Gindin and Robertson, 1992: 37, and Gindin, 1995: 263–4.

7 In this regard, it is noteworthy that Bob Rae's memoirs make no mention of OTAB. He identifies the Jobs Ontario program as his government's significant training policy achievement. Also revealing is his observation that his energies were consumed by national constitutional questions in 1991 and 1992, the critical start-up period for OTAB. He notes more generally about the NDP's governing style: 'We certainly consulted, both formally and informally, to the nth degree.' See Rae, 1996, 171–93, 227–38.

8 The May budget also announced a $20 million initiative (funded through reallocated monies from cuts to other programs) 'to work with entrepreneurs, sectors and communities to improve Ontario's competitiveness through advanced telecommunications applications and infrastructure.' The Telecommunications Access Partnerships (TAP) program indicates some continuity with the SPF, although the absence of any reference to the role of labour in the process suggests differences in program design and the meaning of partnership (Ontario Ministry of Finance, 1996: 24; Ontario Ministry of Economic Development, Trade and Tourism, 1996).

References

Atkinson, Michael M., and William D. Coleman. 1989. *State, Business, and Industrial Change in Canada*. Toronto: University of Toronto Press.

Best, Michael. 1990. *The New Competition: Institutions of Industrial Restructuring*. Cambridge: Polity.

Bradford, N., and M. Stevens. 1996. 'Whither Corporatism?: Political Struggles and Policy Formation in the Ontario Training and Adjustment Board,' in Thomas Dunk, Stephen McBride, and Randle W. Nelsen, eds., *The Training Trap: Ideology, Training and the Labour Market*. Winnipeg/Halifax: Society for Socialist Studies/ Fernwood Publishing, pp. 145–67.

Canadian HR Reporter. 'Going tit for tat with ... OTAB's top gun.' 13 August 1992.

Cawson, Alan. 1986. *Corporatism and Political Theory*. New York: Basil Blackwell.

Chamberlain, A. 1995. 'Bob Rae's New Friends.' *Toronto Star*. 1 May.

Coleman, William D. 1988. *Business and Politics*. Montreal: McGill-Queen's University Press.

Communications, Energy and Paperworkers Union of Canada. 1993. *Worker-Driven Training: A Research Report*. Toronto.

Dehli, Kari. 1993. 'Subject to the New Global Economy: Power and Positioning in Ontario Labour Market Policy Formation,' *Studies in Political Economy* 41 (Summer), pp. 83–110.

Drache, D., ed. 1992. *Getting on Track: Social Democratic Strategies for Ontario*. With the assistance of John O'Grady. Montreal and Kingston: McGill-Queen's University Press.

Employment and Immigration Canada. 1989. *Success in the Works: A Policy Paper*. Ottawa.

Ernst, Alan. 1995. 'Towards a Progressive Competitiveness? Economic Policy and the Ontario New Democrats 1988–1995.' Paper presented at the Canadian Political Science Association annual meetings, Université de Québec à Montréal.

Gindin, S. 1995. *The Canadian Autoworkers: The Birth and Transformation of a Union*. Toronto: James Lorimer.

Gindin, S., and D. Robertson. 1992. 'Alternatives to Competitiveness,' in D. Drache, ed., *Getting on Track*, 32–45.

Goldthorpe, J., 1984. 'The End of Convergence: Corporatist and Dualist Tendencies in Modern Western Societies,' in J. Goldthorpe, ed., *Order and Conflict in Contemporary Capitalism*. Oxford: Oxford University Press.

Government of Ontario, Canadian Labour Force Development Board, and Employment and Immigration Canada. 1991. *Local Boards: A Partnership for Training*.

Government of Ontario. 1995. *Ontarians Expect Fairness from the Federal Government*. Toronto: Queen's Printer for Ontario.

– 1996. *Doing Better for Less*. Toronto: Queen's Printer for Ontario.

Haddow, Rodney. 1994. 'Ontario Politics: "Plus Ça Change ..."?' in James P. Bickerton and Alain-G. Gagnon, eds., *Canadian Politics*, 2nd ed. Peterborough: Broadview Press, pp. 469–90.

Hall, Douglas J. 1996. 'Industrial Policy in Ontario, 1985–1995.' Paper presented at Canadian Political Science Association annual meetings, Brock University, St Catharines, Ontario.

Informetrica Ltd. 1993. 'Ontario and the Unemployment Insurance System.' Paper prepared for Ministry of Intergovernmental Affairs.

Katzenstein, Peter. 1985. *Small States in World Markets: Industrial Policy in Europe*. Ithaca: Cornell University Press.

Khan, Treena. 1992. 'Job-training agency grapples with mandate.' *Globe and Mail*. 25 July.

Mackenzie, H. 1992. 'Dealing with the New Global Economy: What the Premier's Council Overlooked,' in D. Drache, ed., *Getting on Track*, pp. 5–16.

Mahon, Rianne. 1990. 'Adjusting to Win? The New Training Initiative,' in K. Graham, ed., *How Ottawa Spends 1990–91*. Ottawa: Carleton University Press, pp. 73–112.

McBride, S. 1996. 'The Continuing Crisis of Social Democracy: Ontario's Social Contract in Perspective,' *Studies in Political Economy* 50 (Summer), pp. 65–95.

Myles, J. 1989. 'Post Industrialism and the Service Economy.' Paper prepared for Ontario NDP caucus, Economic Policy Review.

Ontario Federation of Labour. 1990. 'The Report of the Premier's Council on Education, Training and Adjustment: Comment and Review.' Toronto.

Ontario, *Hansard*. 1993. *Standing Committee on Resource Development.*

Ontario Ministry of Economic Development and Trade. 1995. *Ontario Sector Snapshots: A Progress Report on the Sector Development Approach.* Toronto: Queen's Printer for Ontario.

– 1996. *Annual Report 1994–1995.* Toronto: Queen's Printer for Ontario.

Ontario Ministry of Economic Development, Trade and Tourism. 1996. 'News Release: Ontario Launches $20–million Telecommunications Access Partnerships.'

Ontario Ministry of Finance. 1996. *1996 Ontario Budget.* Toronto: Queen's Printer for Ontario.

Ontario Ministry of Industry, Trade and Technology. 1992. *An Industrial Policy Framework for Ontario.* Toronto: Queen's Printer for Ontario.

Ontario Ministry of Treasury and Economics. 1991. *Budget Paper E: Ontario in the 1990s.* Toronto: Queen's Printer for Ontario.

– 1992 *Investing in Tomorrow's Jobs: Effective Investment and Economic Renewal.* Toronto: Queen's Printer for Ontario.

Ontario Premier's Council. 1988. *Competing in the New Global Economy.* Vol. 1. Toronto: Queen's Printer for Ontario.

– 1990. *People and Skills in the New Global Economy.* Toronto: Queen's Printer for Ontario.

Ontario Training and Adjustment Board. 1991. *Skills to Meet the Challenge: A Training Partnership for Ontario.* Toronto: Queen's Printer for Ontario.

– 1994. *Co-Chairs Report.*

Rae, Bob. 1996. *From Protest to Power: Personal Reflections on a Life in Politics.* Toronto: Viking.

Roberts, W., and G. Ehring. 1993. *Giving Away a Miracle.* Oakville: Mosaic Press.

Steed, J. 1993. 'No consensus on job-training scheme.' *Toronto Star,* 16 July.

Walkom, T. 1994. *Rae Days: The Rise and Follies of the NDP.* Toronto: Key Porter.

Wolfe, David. 1992. 'Technology and Trade: Finding the Right Mix,' in D. Drache, ed., *Getting on Track,* pp. 17–32.

– 1996. 'Negotiating Order: The Sectoral Approach to Industrial Policy in Ontario.' Paper presented at Canadian Political Science Association annual meetings, Brock University, St Catharines, Ontario.

– 1997. 'Institutional Limits to Labour Market Reform in Ontario: The Short Life and Rapid Demise of the Ontario Training and Adjustment Board,' in Andrew Sharpe and Rodney Haddow, eds., *Partnerships for Training: Canada's Experience with Labour Force Development Boards.* Kingston: School of Policy Studies, Centre for the Study of Living Standards, and Caledon Institute of Social Policy.

PART IV
SECTOR COUNCILS AND JOINT GOVERNANCE

8

The Dynamics of Joint Governance: Historical and Institutional Implications for Sector Councils

JOEL CUTCHER-GERSHENFELD

The rise of sector councils in Canada represents an important institutional development in North American industrial relations. These forums foster joint dialogue and action on training, worker participation, job creation, and other sector concerns. Without joint sector councils, these issues would be addressed on either a more piecemeal, micro basis or on a more diffuse, macro basis. If labour, management, and government leaders are to realize fully the potential of Canada's sector councils, however, it is important to understand their historical and institutional context.

Sector councils have historical antecedents in labour-management committees and councils that have been established throughout the past century – at plant, company, community, industry, and national levels in the United States and Canada. Institutionally, sector councils involve a form of joint governance which has unique dynamics, presenting both constraints and opportunities. This chapter builds on these historical and institutional dynamics and dilemmas in order to present elements of a future vision for Canada's sector councils.

A key assumption that underlies this chapter is that labour, management, and government bring to a sector council a mixture of common and competing interests. As such, the fundamental challenge facing such a council is twofold: the parties must be skilled in identifying and pursuing common concerns; and they must be effective in bringing forward and addressing points of conflict.

Historical Context

There is a long history of joint labour-management initiatives, both in North America and abroad. This analysis will highlight key developments in North America that have implications for Canada's sector councils. Overall, the history of labour-management initiatives during the past century reveals an enduring tension between the importance of joint activity and the pressures arising out of separate labour or management interests.

Early Labour-Management Initiatives

In the early 1900s the Protocol of Peace was developed by prominent American industrialists and politicians as an early framework for the voluntary mediation of labour disputes. The use of the protocol collapsed, however, due to the resistance by most employers to recognize and legitimize the unions representing their workers. Though Canada's unions today have a legal basis for legitimacy that reaches far beyond this turn-of-the-century experience, it is important to note that sector councils still must operate in a context where there is an underlying tension between the property rights of employers and employees' rights around collective action.

In the 1920s and 1930s, there were a variety of labour-management initiatives, especially in the railroad, textile, and garment industries. In railroads, for example, the Canadian National Railway and the Baltimore and Ohio (B&O) Railroad were both well known for the use of labour-management committees at multiple levels to address issues of safety, productivity, training, and other matters. In the garment sector, the joint activities at the men's suit manufacturer Hart, Schafner and Marx addressed strategic issues in the business, such as initiating the launch of a new line of lower-priced men's suits (Douglas, 1921).

Interestingly, many of the shop-floor committees in existence at this time were linked to the early Taylorist Society forums (Jacoby, 1983). Eventually, there was a split between the labour movement and the Taylorist Society, but there was an extended period in which common cause was found between the Taylorist emphasis on the principles of scientific management and the unions' opposition to the arbitrary rule of the foreman. A review of the minutes of these early meetings and shop-floor committees reveals agenda items that could be found in countless joint activities today – issues of people not being released for training, supervisors or workers sidestepping safe practices, and work redesign to improve operations. Thus, the process of jointly addressing issues of importance to labour and management quickly comes down to the details of daily activities, which is as true for worksite initiatives today as it was seventy-five years ago. An implication for sector councils involves the importance of parallel details at the sector level on issues such as training and job creation.

During the Second World War there was a variety of joint initiatives associated with the war effort. In the United States, for example, there were over five thousand of these labour-management committees. One study of the committees by Dorothea de Schweinitz found that only about one-third were successful as joint forums in improving operations (de Schweinitz, 1949; Gold, 1976), but this still represents a large-scale body of shared experience. In the immediate postwar years most of the committees were disbanded in a wave of union-management conflicts over the scope of bargaining and other matters. This experience reveals that joint activities (such as sector councils) are fragile in the face of conflicts between employers and unions over fundamental issues that are seen as threatening institutional or organizational survival.

The 1950s and the 1960s saw the rise of high-profile labour-management initiatives in two sectors – the steel industry and west coast longshoring. In steel the focus was on new technology and dispute resolution. In longshoring the Modernization and Mechanization agreement represented a direct trade-off of increased job security for the present workforce in exchange for support as the industry moved to containerization. Here the joint activities were able to assist in addressing a focused issue or challenge around the adjustment to new technology.

A study of these many early labour-management initiatives by William Gomberg concluded that they were viable only as long as they remained an adjunct to collective bargaining (Gomberg, 1967). Where the joint efforts were utilized as a substitute for collective bargaining, Gomberg found that one party or the other came to see the joint activity as contrary to its interests. In the absence of joint support, the initiative foundered. During the 1970s and 1980s a variety of labour-management committees emerged that are vulnerable to the same pressures that Gomberg found. Yet, as we will see shortly, some of these joint efforts have also proven more enduring than the committees Gomberg studied. Into which group will Canada's sector councils fall – the fragile initiatives that disappear, or the robust initiatives that have endured? The future vision at the end of this paper identifies key factors to consider if sector councils are to be robust initiatives.

Area Labor-Management Committees in the United States

An important precursor to Canada's sector councils can be found in the emergence of area labor-management committees (ALMCs) and construction industry committees in the United States (Cutcher-Gershenfeld, 1985). A handful of these committees were established in the quarter-century following the Second World War, most of which served as community-wide institutions for the mediation of labour disputes. Beginning in the early 1970s, however, community labour-management committees began to be established in the United States with a focus on economic development. As regions began to see an exodus of firms and jobs, many unions and employers would begin to meet and explore how to retain existing firms and even expand employment. The ALMC in Jamestown, New York, which was established in 1972, became the prototype for such committees.

A study of ALMCs, sponsored by the US Department of Labor, highlighted a number of experiences directly relevant to Canada's sector councils (Leone, Eleey, Watkins, and Gershenfeld, 1982). The study found that the effectiveness of an ALMC depended on its mission, staff, and funding. With respect to staff and funding, the findings of the study were unambiguous. Without a stable stream of funding it was not possible to maintain staff, and without staff it was not possible to effectively implement and administer programs. Based in part on this logic, the Labor-Management Cooperation Act of 1978 was passed, but it has never been funded at levels sufficient to provide ALMCs with more than partial start-up assistance. As a result, the approximately one hundred ALMCs in North America mostly operate with limited staff and, consequently, limited capabilities.

For Canada's sector councils, the ALMC experience in the United States raises questions as to whether present streams of funding are adequate to support current programs and whether this funding will remain stable over time. There are certainly cases where sector councils create public value through the attraction and retention of jobs, training in skills that are not firm specific, networking among firms and unions, and other such activities. To this extent, public funding could certainly be justified.

In the United States it was also found that long-standing ALMCs adjusted their focus over time, reflecting the shifting priorities of the member unions and employers. For example, the Jamestown ALMC began with a focus on retaining and attracting jobs. As the member employers and unions began to explore worker participation, however, the Committee began to offer seminars and technical assistance on these matters. Workplace training began as a relatively minor focus, but grew incrementally in partnership with the local community college to the point where many dozens of training courses came to be coordinated through the ALMC.

In contrast, consider the Lansing, Michigan, Capital Area Labor-Management (CALM) Council, which endured for more than a decade, but has deteriorated in recent years. This organization served as an effective forum on a variety of worker participation and joint labour-management issues, but found itself supplanted in recent years by a regional quality roundtable organization. One key feature of the new regional quality organization is its appeal to a wide range of non-union employers – a structural feature of CALM that may have been insurmountable.

The experience of ALMCs suggests that the present agenda for sector councils will have to evolve over time as the priorities and interests of the member organizations shift. Moreover, some topics may not be appropriate or sustainable within the councils' present structure. A particularly complex issue involves the role of non-union employers, who have a legitimate claim to services funded through tax dollars and who represent jobs in the sector, but who also bring imbalance to the governance process.

With respect to the mission and focus of ALMCs, one study by Robert Keidel found that innovative practices tended not to spread from one part of a firm to other parts of the same firm. Instead, a joint committee or team would be found in one firm and then, through the ALMC network, the innovation would next be found in another part of a different firm. Keidel used the term 'theme appreciation' to capture the way a particular theme or concept would take on a life of its own as it spread through that ALMC network of employers and unions. It will be interesting to follow the emergence and diffusion of themes within and across sector councils in the same way.

QWL, STS, and Quality Initiatives in Canada and the United States

At this same time that labour-management committees were being established in increasing numbers, there was the concurrent rise of the quality of work life (QWL) movement in North America and the socio-technical systems (STS) approach in England, Scandinavia, and North America (Trist, 1981; Gershenfeld, 1983). These initiatives highlighted the redesign of jobs in order to address issues of alienation and motivation at work. Some of the most far-reaching experiments along these lines were in continuous process industries, such as chemicals, food processing, or paper. For example, the Shell Sarnia plant (Rankin, 1990) and the Gains Pet Food plant (Walton, 1980) have been extensively documented. As well, regional organizations were established that, like ALMCs, stand as important precursors to sector councils. Examples include the Ontario Quality of Working Life Centre and the Michigan Quality of Work Life Council.

The QWL and STS initiatives were marked by ideological splits, both in the labour and management communities. In each case the participants in the joint initiatives were criticized by peers, who contended that the joint activity had compromised their separate interests. This disagreement was, in part, a factor in the split between the Canadian and American components of the United Autoworkers Union (UAW) which led to the formation of the CAW in 1985. A key element of the debates over the QWL and STS principles arose from the increased use of these principles in non-union settings and the degree to which the participatory processes served as a barrier to unionization.

For sector councils, the implications of these experiences are twofold. First, participants in sector councils will face criticism from within their ranks that their participation brings them too close to parties who (in part) have conflicting interests. Second, there will be tension when the work of sector councils benefits non-union firms. Both of these implications are more visible and more intense for unions, but they also can be found in the employer community.

By the early 1980s there was a wave of quality circle (QC) initiatives that were similar to the QWL and STS efforts, but with a focus on quality. One study estimated that, by 1984, over one-third of all US businesses featured some formal institutional arrangement for worker participation (New York Stock Exchange, 1982). While the limitations of the QC model became apparent with the demise of countless initiatives, a more comprehensive, systems approach to quality is proving more enduring. The vast majority of firms that are suppliers to others or that purchase from suppliers are using supplier certification audit procedures, with the ISO 9000 standard and industry-specific standards, such as QS 9000, currently in ascendancy. A close look at these procedures reveals a priority being given to in-station process control and other work processes that are most effective when joined with some form of worker participation. Further, the emphasis on just-in-time (JIT) delivery and reduced in-process inventory all mean that purchasers are concerned that unionized operations demonstrate constructive labour-management relations.

For sector councils the quality movement is relevant in a number of ways. Despite the many unionized workplaces with advanced quality initiatives, there is still a perception (and sometimes a reality) that worker involvement in quality issues can increase commitment to the employer and weaken commitment to the union. Consequently, these quality issues represent a potential agenda item within sector councils which may be very important to the employers but viewed with mixed feelings by many unions. At the core of the union ambivalence is the logic of systems thinking, which emphasizes treating the workplace as a system and having all stakeholders adopt the superordinate goal of 'optimizing the whole.' While most union members and leaders are proud to produce quality products and services, most are not willing to treat this as their superordinate goal. Further, other union goals of political action, job security, and safety can sometimes run counter to the inexorable logic of continuous improvement under quality initiatives – depending on how 'continuous improvement' is defined.

Thus, a brief review of the last century's experience with joint union-management initiatives reveals a number of clear implications for Canada's sector councils. The early history suggests that joint union-management institutional arrangements at industry or sector levels (as well as at the workplace level) are not new and that these initiatives are marked by an enduring tension around the degree to which they serve the interests of labour and management. The experience with community labour-management committees provides direct parallels for sector councils on issues of mission, funding, and staff. Developments around worker participation and quality systems raise complex issues around employee commitment to the employer and to the union, the role of non-union firms, and ideological battles within the labour movement. Altogether, reviewing the history is not only important because of the parallels with current experience among sector councils, but also because some of the historical developments, especially those around participation and quality, are still unfolding and interacting with the sector councils.

The Challenge of Joint Governance

Sector councils are an example of joint governance at the sector level. Though most research and business press has focused on joint governance at the work-site level, there are key challenges which cut across all levels. The notion of joint governance is quite complex.

At its core, a sector council represents a decision by interdependent stakeholders to make joint rather than separate decisions on one or more issues. Placing issues under joint governance brings opportunities and costs. Four such dynamics are examined here: the complications of joint decision-making given the contrasting contexts from which union and management leaders come; managing internal pressures, which can constrain union and management leaders, but can also be aided by the existence of a joint forum; coordinating across levels, which raises issues of centralization and decentralization; and issues of institutional security, which confront employers and unions, though not always in the same way or to the same degree.[1]

Joint Decision-Making

When labour and management leaders come together in a joint forum they face a subtle challenge: they are all experienced decision makers, but their decision-making experiences are not the same (Cutcher-Gershenfeld, McKersie, and Wever, 1988). In general, managers are used to the dynamics of decision-making in a hierarchical organization where the importance of making the 'right' decision is balanced against the importance of following procedure. For example, a manager may correctly conclude that reduced in-process inventory and empowered work teams will improve product quality, but it would be career suicide to implement such changes without proper sign-off at multiple levels. In general, union leaders are used to the dynamics of decision-making in a political organization where the importance of making the 'right' decision is balanced against the importance of addressing constituent priorities. For example, a union leader might know that it is sensible to let a low-profit margin product be outsourced so as to free up floor space for higher value-added products, but publicly would have to oppose any outsourcing of work.

This is not to say that union leaders and managers are unfamiliar with each other's worlds. Managers are not unfamiliar with politics, for example, but they are used to managing politics below the surface through tacit decisions and subtle signals. Similarly, union leaders are not unfamiliar with hierarchy, but they are used to keeping the issues between local, regional, and national organizations out of the limelight. Combining backgrounds in hierarchical and political contexts creates, at its best, a complementary domain of expertise that is greater than either of the partners. For example, at General Motors' Buick City operations in Flint, Michigan, the joint union-management committee responsible for workplace training had the authority to sign contracts with outside suppliers of training services. What the suppliers encountered were teams of managers and union leaders who brought to the negotiations their accumulated experience at the bargaining table, on the shop floor, and in the strategic business planning – all of which was quite a contrast to the mid-level human resource and purchasing professionals who had previously negotiated with these suppliers. Achieving these synergies depends, of course, on mutual understanding and appreciation of what each party brings to the process.

In the absence of mutual respect, the combination of backgrounds that union and management decision makers bring can be a source of frustration and ineffectiveness. For example, an unpopular administrative decision may technically fall within the purview of a joint forum. If the decision could arguably also be made unilaterally by management, there are times when it is in both parties' interest to have it made unilaterally.[2] Similarly, a plant or facility manager who is seen as responsible for implementing a team-based work system may be rewarded with new capital investment. Even if much of the work in the implementation was done by union leaders or appointees, it is not in their interest to diminish the credit accorded to the manager.

In addition to the complex dynamics of decision-making with parties from two contrasting settings, there are further complications stemming from new cultural norms associated with the joint committee or council. In many cases a norm is established that decisions will be made on a consensus basis. The advantages of the consensus model are multifold. First, it allows all appropriate people to be 'at the table' without having to 'count heads.' Second, the mechanics of census decision-making are less complicated than they might first appear.

The guidelines used by the UAW and Saturn, for example, consider a consensus to be a decision with which everyone is at least 70 per cent comfortable – not necessarily 100 per cent comfortable and not necessarily everyone's first choice. Also, if anyone is going to block the consensus they have to be able to generate at least two viable alternatives. These types of guidelines make consensus not an abstract ideal, but a process skill that can be learned and applied. Third, if a joint forum operates on anything other than a consensus it is at constant risk of one party or the other withdrawing based on the perception that a disproportionate number of decisions are unfavourable to its interests.

Despite the many advantages of the consensus approach, it is not a well-developed skill in most management or union organizations. Indeed, constituents not involved in the joint process will often be highly sceptical of the merits of depending on consensus with 'the other side.' Additionally, parties will occasionally abuse the consensus process by blocking progress on a legitimate but controversial issue, or by agreeing to one thing in a meeting and then denying responsibility outside of the session.

For sector councils there is a further decision-making dynamic to be considered. In addition to the above issues of hierarchical, political, and consensus models for decision-making, the presence of policy makers introduces a different set of bureaucratic and political decision-making processes. For sector councils to make wise decisions, it is essential for the participants to understand and build on the distinctive decision-making competencies that each party brings to the council (Kochan and Osterman, 1994).

Managing Internal Pressures

People serving on a sector council are there in their roles as representatives of others. This simple reality is the key to the strength and potential impact of a sector council, yet it can also be a great source of instability. The primary reason for having a sector council is that people can produce plans or decisions that take into account multiple stakeholder interests – rather than one party making a unilateral decision and then discovering if it is acceptable. To succeed in this process, however, the members of the sector council must simultaneously be true champions of their constituents interests and full partners with the other council members.

Invariably, situations arise where the interests of constituents undercut the contributions that a representative makes to a joint forum.[3] For example, a union leader may be facing election opposition from candidates who argue that they have become too close to management. The union leaders then have a choice – either they can champion their role on the joint forum as serving the members' interests or they can distance themselves from the forum. This dilemma is less problematic in a long-standing forum where the benefits of joint action have been well established, as is the case in many health and safety committees. In a relatively new institutional arrangement, as in the case of many sector councils, this can be a source of instability.

A joint forum doesn't only create internal dilemmas; it can also help resolve some complicated internal issues. For example, the UAW/Ford National Education and Training Center was initially established with the relatively limited mandate of training displaced workers. As the agenda expanded and shifted to focus on the active workforce, the parties found that training dollars sheltered under the joint structure were less vulnerable to budget cuts, than were training dollars located in plant, divisional, or corporate budgets. The center's budget is generated by a formula where a certain amount of cents per hour are set aside for each hour worked (with higher amounts for overtime hours). The presence of a joint structure for training turned out to be a valuable solution to what was a perpetual internal problem for managers concerned about human resources and long-term investment (Ferman, Hoyman, Cutcher-Gershenfeld, and Savoie, 1991).

For sector councils, the internal dynamics are compounded by the fact that there are not only dynamics within an organization or a union, but also across multiple employers and sometimes multiple unions. Thus, there is an increased potential for internal dynamics to have an impact on the work of sector councils. On the downside, the instability of coalitions is added to normal challenges of building internal consensus within an organization. On the upside, the shared experience of working on the sector council and the regular interactions around issues of common concern may facilitate coordination within labour or within management that might not otherwise occur.

Coordinating across Levels

In a number of sector councils there are organizational or facility-level joint activities that serve as a formal or informal counterpart to the work of the council. This is similar to the structure of an area labor-management committee where, in additional to the ALMC, there will be a variety of plant-level joint committees. It is also similar to the structure of national joint training centres in the auto, telecommunications, and other industries, where there are dozens of local committees that operate in coordination with the national centres. Indeed, in the auto industry the funding structure even allows for what is referred to as the 'local nickel,' where five cents per hour of the training surcharge was initially allocated for spending at the discretion of joint plant-level committees.

The challenge in these multi-level arrangements involves the classic dilemma of centralization. With more central control there is increased consistency and coordination. With more decentralization there is more innovation and better adaptation to distinctive local circumstances. In the short run there are invariably direct trade-offs between consistency and innovation, as well as between coordination and local adaptation. In the long run there is usually an ebb and flow between degrees of centralization and degrees of decentralization.

For Canada's sector councils the dilemmas of centralization and decentralization are particularly evident on an issue such as workplace training (Cutcher-Gershenfeld and Ford, 1994). Improving general skills in the workforce is a common policy objective, even though many employers worry that the investment they make in workers serves to increase their mobility. The presence of coordination and even funding at a centralized sector level helps to resolve the dilemma, but the delivery and use of training skills still depends on local application in dozens or even hundreds of workplaces. Ultimately, the effectiveness of the councils depends on an dynamic balance of central coordination and local autonomy.

Institutional Stability

Ultimately a labour-management committee or council is only as strong as its constituent organizations. Today, many unions and employers are confronted with direct threats to their institutional stability (Kochan, Katz, and McKersie, 1986). In some sectors, such as auto supply, employers are nearly as fearful as the unions due to the relentless pruning of the supply base by the original equipment manufacturers. More typically, however, the threats are not distributed equally between employers and unions. In sectors such as textiles or garments, the global economy provides new opportunities for highly mobile employers while unions face a long-term decline in membership.

For sector councils this means that some will be operating in a context of comparative growth, while others will be operating in the face of sector decline. Still others will face mixed settings with niches of decline, growth, or stability. This means that lessons or innovations developed in one sector will not necessarily travel easily to others, either because they are genuinely not applicable or because they are rejected by virtue of coming from a very different context.

In addition to the way sector variation will limit the diffusion of innovation, a more basic challenge is posed by the internal implications of institutional instability. Within unions and employers, such instability may undercut internal consensus about the importance of cooperation at the sector level at precisely the time that such cooperation may be essential.

Elements of a Future Vision

What does the future hold for Canada's sector councils? Clearly some of the early councils have weathered shifts in membership, the economy, and government. At the same time, most of the councils are relatively new organizations. Looking to the future we must first build on a critical lesson from the past. A labour-management council is an empty vessel. It is what is placed in this vessel that matters. The vessel will sink if it is filled with an agenda that is too diffuse, threatening to the interests of key stakeholders, or even just incidental to labour and management priorities. On the other hand it has the potential to take labour, management, and government to places that neither party would reach on their own.

Ultimately this is the primary criterion on which to judge Canada's sector councils: do they produce accomplishments that would not otherwise happen or that would at least be more costly or complicated to achieve in the absence of a sector council? For example, sector coordination of job retraining programs could reduce the length of time that displaced workers are without jobs in comparison to programs sponsored at the company, provincial, or federal levels. In order to provide value in this way, however, it means that the agenda and focus of sector councils will have to evolve and change in response shifting sector priorities. Of course, some issues span multiple sectors and others are specific to sub-sets of a sector. In these cases, sector councils will have to ensure that they have in place coordination mechanisms. Coordination is required with other sector councils and service providers at municipal, provincial, and federal levels. Coordination is also required with plant/facility initiatives.

As union, management, and government officials interact at the sector level there will inevitably be spill-over of these experiences into other settings, as well as a reverse flow of experiences in other settings into sector councils. If there are positive collaborative experiences and increased competency in joint governance, this will undoubtedly spill over into collective bargaining relations and legislative arenas. At the same time, contentious battles at the bargaining table or fierce political fights can just as easily spill over into the sector councils.

Inevitably, life within sector councils will be dominated by a twofold challenge: how to add value by increasing the size of the proverbial pie, and how to avoid unnecessary costs by dividing the same proverbial pie without spilling most of it on the floor. Creating joint gains does not happen automatically – it requires the effective application of process improvement and problem solving skills. Despite the overriding focus of sector councils on common concerns, there will be points of conflict which will require equally skilful application of dispute resolution and interest-based bargaining skills.

So what is the image of the future? It is an image of sector councils with an evolving agenda, grounded in the interests of labour, management, and government. It is an image of sector councils skilled at coordinating initiatives with government agencies at all levels, as well as with union-management efforts at the plant or facility level. It is an image of leaders skilled at learning from their experience on sector councils and applying these experiences more broadly, as well as leaders who are able to insulate the councils from conflicts in other arenas. It is an image of parties who add value by creating mutual gains and at the same time constructively surface and address points of conflict. It is an image of sector councils as dynamic and robust forums – vessels that the parties have filled with meaningful interactions. Complicated as it is, this is the only way that sector councils will become an enduring feature of Canada's industrial relations landscape.

Notes

This chapter is adapted from a presentation at a panel on Canada's sector councils the 1996 annual meetings of the Industrial Relations Research Association. Other presentations at the session have also been revised to be chapters in this book. They were all invaluable as background in preparing this paper.

1 The analysis here draws on a number articles the I have co-authored on the subject, including Cutcher-Gershenfeld, Kochan, and Verma, 1991; Verma and Cutcher-Gershenfeld, 1993.
2 This dynamic is illustrated in the context of labour negotiations in Walton, Cutcher-Gershenfeld, and McKersie, 1994.
3 This involves the classic tension associated with intra-organizational bargaining as presented in Walton and McKersie, 1965.

References

Cutcher-Gershenfeld, Joel. 1985. 'The Emergence of Community Labor-Management Cooperation,' in Warner Woodworth, William Whyte and Chris Meek, eds., *Industrial Democracy: Strategies for Community Economic Revitalization*. Beverly Hills: Sage Publications.

Cutcher-Gershenfeld, Joel, and Kevin Ford. 1994. 'Worker Training in Michigan: A Framework for Public Policy,' in Faculty of Institute for Public Policy and Social Research, eds., *Policy Choices: Framing the Debate for Michigan's Future*. East Lansing: MSU Press.

Cutcher-Gershenfeld, Joel, Thomas Kochan, and Anil Verma. 1991. 'Recent Developments in United States Employee Involvement Initiatives: Erosion or Diffusion,' in Donna Sockell, David Lewin, and David Lipsky, eds., *Advances in Industrial and Labor Relations*. Greenwich, Conn.: JAI Press.

Cutcher-Gershenfeld, Joel, Robert McKersie, and Kirstin Wever. 1988. *The Changing Role of Union Leaders*. Washington, DC: US Department of Labor, BLMR 127.

de Schweinitz, Dorothea. 1949. *Labor and Management in a Common Enterprise*. Cambridge: Harvard University Press.

Douglas, Paul. 1921. 'Shop Committees: Substitute for, or Supplement to, Trade Unions?' *Journal of Political Economy*. February.

Ferman, Louis, Michele Hoyman, Joel Cutcher-Gershenfeld, and Ernest Savoie. 1991. *Joint Training Programs: Union-Management Approach to Preparing Workers for the Future*. Ithaca: Cornell ILR Press.

Gershenfeld, Joel E. 1983. 'QWL: A Historical Perspective,' *Work Life Review*. September.

Gold, Charlotte. 1976. *Employer-Employee Committees and Worker Participation*. Ithaca, NY: NYSSILR.

Gomberg, William. 1967. 'Special Study Committees,' in John Dunlop and Neil Chamberlain, eds., *Frontiers of Collective Bargaining*. New York: Harper and Row.

Jacoby, Sanford. 1983. 'Union-Management Cooperation in the United States: Lessons from the 1920's,' *Industrial and Labor Relations Review* 37, no. 1. October.

Keidel, Robert W. 1976. 'The Development of an Organizational Community Through Theme Appreciation.' Ph.D. diss. University of Pennsylvania.

Kochan, Thomas, Harry Katz, and Robert McKersie. 1986. *The Transformation of American Industrial Relations*. New York: Basic Books.

Kochan, Thomas, and Paul Osterman. 1994. *The Mutual Gains Enterprise: Forging a Winning Partnership Among Labor, Management, and Government*. Boston: Harvard Business School Press.

Leone, Richard D., Michael F. Eleey, David Watkins, and Joel E. Gershenfeld. 1982. *The Operation of Area Labor-Management Committees*. Washington, DC: US Department of Labor.

New York Stock Exchange, Office of Economic Research. 1982. *People and Productivity: A Challenge to Corporate America*. New York: NYSE.

Rankin, Thomas. 1990. *New Forms of Work Organization: The Challenge for North American Unions*. Toronto: University of Toronto Press.

Trist, Eric. 1981. *The Evolution of Socio-Technical Systems*. Toronto: Ontario Ministry of Labour, Ontario Quality of Working Life Centre.

Verma, Anil, and Joel Cutcher-Gershenfeld. 1993. 'Joint Governance in the Workplace: Beyond Union-Management Cooperation and Worker Participation,' in Bruce E.

Kaufman and Morris M. Kleiner, eds., *Employee Representation: Alternatives and Future Directions*. Madison, WI: IRRA.

Walton, Richard. 1980. 'Establishing and Maintaining High Commitment Work Systems,' in J.R.Kimberly and R.H.Miles, eds., *The Organizational Life Cycle*. San Francisco: Jossey-Bass.

Walton, Richard, Joel Cutcher-Gershenfeld, and Robert McKersie. 1994. *Strategic Negotiations: A Theory of Change in Labor-Management Relations*. Boston: Harvard Business School Press.

Walton, Richard, and Robert McKersie. *A Behavioral Theory of Labor Negotiations*. New York: McGraw-Hill.

9

Sector Councils as Models of Shared Governance in Training and Adjustment

CAROL JOYCE HADDAD

It has been said that labour-management relations have entered a new era. Unions are far more likely than ever before to be involved in discussions about the design of work and to be active participants in workplace change (Pomeroy, 1995). There is general agreement among industrial experts that labour-management cooperation is essential to business competitiveness and results in tangible gains for both parties (McDermott, 1994; Kochan and Osterman, 1994).

Yet more often than not, joint labour-management activities are neither extensive nor sustained partnerships (Commission on the Future of Worker-Management Relations, 1995). They tend to focus on short-term, company-oriented goals such as improving product quality, process efficiency, or lowering production costs, and do not expand joint decision-making to a level of industrial democracy. According to a study by Cooke (1990), approximately 86 per cent of joint programs were reported to have been initiated by management, on average most did not actively involve a large percentage of bargaining unit employees, and apart from health and safety committees, quality circles were the most common form of joint activity.

Joint training councils have the potential to raise labour-management cooperation to a new level of democratic governance. Because they concentrate on human resource development, they embrace issues that are of importance to employees and their unions, not only to companies. And by promoting skill advancement and not merely job placement, they take a proactive rather than a reactive posture. Still, unless we examine the decision-making structures and practices of joint training councils, we cannot determine whether they advance the concept of shared governance.

For this reason, I conducted qualitative case studies of three labour-management sector training councils in Canada: the Canadian Steel Trade and Employment Congress (CSTEC), the Sectoral Skills Council of the Electrical and

Electronics Industry (SSC), and the Automotive Parts Sectoral Training Council (APSTC). Central to my inquiry were the following questions: Do council members agree on council goals and priorities across labour-management and company lines? How do council members resolve disagreements and arrive at consensus? And do sector training councils improve training design and delivery because of their bipartite nature? A central research premise was that an understanding of how the councils operate structurally, operationally, and philosophically would reveal the extent to which these bodies serve as models of shared governance.

Structured interviews lasting approximately one hour were conducted with thirty-one council and subcommittee members in 1994–95. A stratified sample of thirty-five was drawn to assure equal representation of labour and management representatives, and to provide variability on council membership tenure, size of company, technological sophistication of company, level of union staff affiliation, union/non-union company affiliation, and gender. Council co-chairs and staff directors were automatically included in the sample, as were some past co-chairs and directors for early council history. While the sample size was small, the respondents selected were key decision-makers at the national level. The interviews were supplemented by direct observation of council meetings, review and analysis of council-generated documents pertaining to council structure, objectives, operational requirements and accomplishments, and review and analysis of published studies and reports on sector councils and labour market policy. Although the study was cross-sectional, the councils studied vary by date of incorporation and level of maturity, thereby providing a quasi-longitudinal view of how decision-making practices evolve over time.

Structural and Operational Features of the Councils

A series of structural and governance features are common across the councils that were studied. First, unions (or employee representatives in non-union firms) have equal membership on council boards and committees at multiple levels – the industry/sector level, the company/firm level, and the plant level. While such joint representation is voluntary, training agreements with federal and provincial governments that serve as the basis of public-sector funding facilitate equal bipartite representation.[1] Thus, there are structural similarities between sector training councils and legally mandated works councils of the type that exist in Germany. A second common feature is that council decisions are made by consensus, and decisions focus on substantive issues such as training program content, as well as on procedural issues such as training program administration. While the scope of decision-making on training and adjustment issues is expanded beyond what would normally occur in a collective bargaining forum, shared input does not extend to all strategic domains of the firm, such as technology investment and choice. Thirdly, firms are represented individually, and operate in collaboration with industry trade associations. The influence of trade associations is felt more strongly in some councils, such as Auto Parts, than in others. Finally, the focus of all of the councils studied is to provide and improve human resource development opportunities for employees in their respective industries.

Notwithstanding these commonalities, the three councils differ significantly in structure, objectives, priorities, and operation. As Table 1 indicates, the Canadian Steel Trade and Employment Congress (CSTEC) was the first of the three councils to be formed. CSTEC was born of twin concerns over US quotas that had been imposed on Canadian steel, and massive layoffs affecting Canadian steel workers. On the heels of the labour relations turbulence of the early 1980s, Gerard Docquier, then national Canadian director of the United Steelworkers of America (USWA) contacted John Allen, chief executive officer of Stelco, to discuss the need to combine forces on issues of mutual interest. Their efforts led to CSTEC's formation in 1986, and to its initial focus on trade, employment, and adjustment issues.[2] In 1992 CSTEC's mandate was extended to include training activities for the currently employed. Although trade issues continue to be a part of CSTEC's focus, the bulk of its work centres on worker training and employment adjustment.

CSTEC's training and adjustment activities are overseen by an eighteen-member joint committee. Worker adjustment services, which include peer counselling, financial and career planning, training referral, small business start-up, and job search/job placement assistance are offered through plant-level joint committees. From 1988 to 1994 sixty-seven such committees provided assistance to over eleven thousand employees – approximately 90 per cent of those laid off in the industry. Some of the assistance has come in the form of training referral, and over 90 per cent of those who have enrolled in training have completed it. CSTEC also maintains a computerized National Job Bank. Approximately 75 per cent of retrained workers have found new, mainly non-steel jobs, with no loss of pay on average.

Training programs for the currently employed are funded by cost-sharing agreements negotiated between CSTEC and federal and provincial governments. Training fund monies may be used to finance categories of training deemed eligible; these include basic skills, steel industry general skills, industry-specific technical skills, on-the-job training that is combined with formal instruction, and certain types of union designed and delivered training. Both hourly and salaried employees are eligible to receive the training. Joint

TABLE 1 Structural Features of Councils Studied.

	CSTEC (Steel)	Sectoral skills (Electrical)	APSTC (Auto parts)
Year incorporated	1986	1990	1991
Membership	27 corporate members; 47 local union members	113 companies*; 7 national unions	26 companies; APMA; CAW
Decision-making bodies	12–member board of directors (L/M); 14-member Steel Trade Committee; 18-member Training & Adjustment Committee	12–member council: 3 subcommittees; Training, Education, & Joint Administration	12–member board of directors (8 voting members); 3 committees: Curriculum, Executive, Evaluation
Administrative coordination	1 non-aligned executive director; 11 additional professional field and support staff	Secretariat consisting of 1 non-aligned director, 1 labour associate, & 1 management associate	2 co-managing directors: 1 chosen by labour & one by management
Major focus	Worker adjustment programs; training for employed workers; trade policy lobbying	'Upside' training for employed workers to maintain/grow jobs	Development and delivery of an Auto Parts Certificate Program (APC)
Employees served	11,000 – adjustment; 23,000 – training	40,137 represented by member firms	1,600 completed 1 week of APC as of spring 1994
Training program administration	Decentralized – via (workplace) Joint Training Committees	Decentralized – via Joint Workplace Training Committees	Centralized – few joint training committees, but local selection of APC participants

Note: data in this table are from February 1995 unless otherwise stated.
*As of December 1996 the SSC had a membership of 220 firms, representing 55,000 employees.

training committees at the workplace level are responsible for all facets of training program administration, including needs assessment, training plan formulation, program evaluation, and budgeting. To maximize the portability of training, CSTEC is currently negotiating transfer agreements with community colleges to obtain credit equivalency/certification for CSTEC courses.

The Sectoral Skills Council of the Canadian Electrical and Electronics Manufacturing Industry (SSC) was officially launched in 1990, although joint activities of the Communications and Electrical Workers of Canada (CWC), the International Brotherhood of Electrical Workers (IBEW), and the Electrical and Electronic Manufacturers' Association of Canada were in place as early as 1987. The initial impetus for these discussions was mutual concern about structural and competitive changes in the industry. It was felt that by working cooperatively to upgrade employee skills, layoffs could be averted and competitiveness of Canadian firms enhanced.

Current council membership represents a broad range of firms – large, small, high-tech, low-tech, unionized, non-union, Canadian-owned, and foreign-owned multinational companies. The Sectoral Skills Council is the most diverse of the councils studied, not only in the types of firms represented, but also in its union membership. As Table 1 indicates, seven different national unions belong to the Council. In addition to the Communications Workers (now known as the Communications, Energy and Paperworkers Union, or CEP) and the IBEW, council members include the USWA, the International Association of Machinists and Aerospace Workers (IAM), the Laborer's International Union, the International Federation of Professional and Technical Employees, and the Canadian Auto Workers Union.

SSC activities centre on training for hourly and salaried employees that falls into the following categories: basic skills and trades upgrading; general (non-job-related) training and education; employee group-directed training; and peer counsellor training for plants facing full or partial closure. Training costs are financed by employers and the federal and provincial governments through a fund representing 1 per cent of payroll for each member firm.[3] One of the distinguishing features of the SSC is its extensive network of joint workplace training committees (JWTCs), which are the route through which workplaces can access training funds. JWTCs assess training needs, plan training programs, recruit participants, and administer training resources. One hundred and forty JWTCs were operating as of 31 January 1995, in both unionized and non-union firms. Committee membership consists of equal numbers of employer and employee representatives.

Council subcommittees are active, and vary in size from eight to sixteen members. The Training Subcommittee oversees the use of the training funds and supports the joint workplace training committees. The Education Subcommittee works with colleges, universities, and high schools to improve their responsiveness to labour and management-articulated industry needs. One of their more recent initiatives is a push for 'universal recognition' of courses by colleges. The Joint Administration Committee works on skilled trades and apprenticeship issues, is developing industry-wide skill standards, and is implementing a certificate program for trades employees that enables upgrading and portability.

The Automotive Parts Sectoral Training Council (APSTC), founded in 1991 by the Canadian Auto Workers Union (CAW) and the Automotive Parts Manufacturers' Association (APMA), is the newest of the three councils studied. The driving force for its formation was a shortage of skilled production personnel to meet industry demands during the growth period of the late 1980s. The CAW also hoped that a sectoral training program would enhance the job security of production employees by providing them with credentials that would be recognized throughout the automotive parts industry. Therefore, the Auto Parts Council concentrated its efforts on the creation and delivery of an auto parts certificate program with an emphasis on generic, portable skills that provide a base for more advanced training. The program is intended to promote awareness of changes in technologies and work systems and of the economic factors driving these changes, to develop foundation skills in communications, computer use and statistical problem solving, and to support workplace participation and continuous learning.

The APSTC differs from CSTEC and the SSC both structurally and philosophically. Instead of having one non-aligned director, whether operating alone (CSTEC) or in conjunction with labour and management associates (SSC), the Auto Parts Council has a dual director structure, one representing management and the other aligned with labour. This reflects a clear delineation of labour and management views. As one union representative stated, 'This wasn't about developing partnerships and competitive coalitions and workplace change. What we were trying to establish was a good and effective training program.' Another difference is the CAW's strongly articulated view that workers should not contribute their own money to training funds. Therefore, the funding formula used provides for a one-third split between employers, provincial governments, and federal governments. The federal funding formula ties the level of industry contributions to the volume of training delivered. Thus, firms are not required to pay membership fees up front, as is the case with other councils. This has posed special problems for APSTC, which has faced a funding shortfall since training delivery has not proceeded as quickly as originally expected.

Two governance features common to all of the sector councils suggest a departure from labour relations as usual. One, which was mentioned at the beginning of this section, is the bipartite representation at all levels of council activity – from national governing bodies to subcommittees to plant-level training committees. This permits co-determination on all issues of policy and program administration, and in interactions with governmental bodies and educational institutions. A second feature is that the sector councils are free to develop organizational structures that best fit their goals, respective institutional needs, and levels of trust, so long as they are bipartite. For example, the APSTC's decision to select aligned co-directors may have reflected low trust as well as philosophical differences guiding labour's and management's vision of skill development. This does not in any way imply an absence of disagreement among labour and management representatives in councils that use single, non-aligned directors and labour and management co-chairs. Rather, it suggests that the sector councils have been particularly innovative in developing joint governance structures that are most appropriate to their particular needs and circumstances, and that allow for true power sharing.

Goal Consensus

Interviewees were asked to identify the top three current priorities for their council, in rank order. Table 2 displays the mean rankings of the top three council priorities identified by labour and management respondents. In CSTEC some differences along labour-management lines are evident, with labour representatives placing greater emphasis on adjustment programs and managers on community college partnerships and steel trade lobbying. However, there are similarities in their prioritization of training for employed workers and adjustment services.

Sectoral Skills Council members and subcommittee members agree on the top two priorities. One is recruiting more firms and members to join the SSC, and expanding the training fund, training programs (both in level of activity and in geographic coverage), and expanding training program accessibility. The second is upgrading employee skill and knowledge, and preparing the workforce. Both groups ascribe slightly lower importance to setting up apprenticeship programs and establishing skills standards. Among subcommittee members some differences emerge, with unionists wanting to limit the recruitment of anti-union companies, and managers wishing to increase the responsiveness of schools to industry needs.

Within the Auto Parts Council, the parties are united in their choice of the top priority: expansion of program delivery, increased employer participation, increased numbers of trainees, and program operation stabilization. Although labour representatives were alone in listing workforce preparation/skills upgrading and equitable access to training as high priorities, both groups gave high ranking to the goal of stabilizing program funding and extending government funding agreements. Thus, despite strong philosophical differences which

TABLE 2   Mean Rankings of Top Three Council Priorities, by Council and Labour-Management Affiliation

Top Three Priorities	Labour	Management
CSTEC:		
Adjustment services/training	1.7	2.9
Expand/improve training for employed workers	2.3	2.8
Steel trade lobbying	4.0	2.8
Lobby for government funding	3.7	3.6
Expand community college partnerships re: training portability & program development	–	1.9
Motivate some employers to sponsor joint training programs	3.3	–
SSC:		
Recruit more firms/members and expand training fund/programs/ activity/accessibility/ geographic coverage	1.5	1.5
Skills upgrading/workforce preparation	1.8	2.7
Set up apprenticeship program/skills standards	3.9	3.8
Maintain government funding	4.1	3.1
Expand community college partnerships re: training portability	–	4.3
Hire/promote more skilled trades employees	4.3	–
Limit recruitment of anti-union companies	4.3	–
Increase school responsiveness to industry needs	–	4.3
APSTC:		
Expand program delivery & employer participation/ increase number of trainees/stabilize operation	2.0	1.9
Stabilize program funding/extend gov't funding	2.8	2.8
Prepare current workforce for changing work environment/skills upgrading	2.0	–
Ensure equitable access to training	2.2	–
Finish the APC curriculum & deliver level 2 on time	–	3.3
Expand training program content	–	4.2
	N = 13	N = 15

Note: lower numbers represent higher degrees of importance. Dashes denote items not listed as priorities by anyone in that group. The table excludes data collected from current and former non-aligned council directors.

TABLE 3   Perceived Goal Consensus

(Percentage responding yes to the question: Do you feel that your management [union] counterparts on the Council/Subcommittee would rank the above goals in the same way that you did?)

	Between labour & management counterparts %	Among labour counterparts %	Among management counterparts %
CSTEC (N = 7)	57	100	50
SSC) (N = 12)	67	100	67
APSTC (N = 8)	88	100	80

are evident in APSTC interactions, labour and management tend to unite around basic council survival and growth issues.

To determine whether council representatives perceive that goal consensus exists across labour-management lines and within their own ranks, interviewees were asked if they believed their management and union counterparts would rank the priorities in the same way that they had. Their responses appear in Table 3. Overall, perceived goal consensus between labour and management is quite high, ranging from 57 per cent in CSTEC to 88 per cent in the Auto Parts Council. The CSTEC figure is a bit misleading due to the low number of respondents and also because the wording of the question asked about rankings, not merely about shared goals. In CSTEC, for example, one management representative explained that if management peers come from a professional training or human resources background they might view 'upside' training as the top priority, whereas those with broader backgrounds might place higher priority on industry-wide trade issues. One reason for the rather high perceived goal consensus in the Auto Parts Council was the shared recognition that many more firms in that sector had to be persuaded to join the council and adopt the auto parts certificate program, since the member firms at the time of this study represented a very small percentage of the number of firms in the industry.[4]

Across all three councils, labour-management differences had more to do with perceptions about rank order and less to do with actual goal divergence. A plant-level union representative to CSTEC explained that while his management counterparts on the council share his goals, their company superiors are less willing to release active workers for training because their plants are operating 'lean.' A management representative to the Sectoral Skills Council who thought that his union counterparts would rank goals in the same way added that labour places more emphasis on worker participation, process training, and equitable access to training. Philosophical labour-management differences emerged as union representatives on the Auto Parts Council elaborated on their responses to the question about perceived management ranking of council priorities. One mentioned that while both parties agreed on skills formation as a short-term goal, management hoped that in the long term they could engage the CAW in cooperative relations and promote a joint work culture, which was not a priority for the CAW. Another noted that while skills upgrading is the main focus for both labour and management, management's emphasis is on maximizing profits while the union's is on retaining jobs within the industry.

The extremely high level of perceived intra-union goal consensus (union representatives' assessment of how their union counterparts would rank priorities) is particularly interesting in light of the fact that seven different national unions comprise the SSC, and that even CSTEC and APSTC union representatives occupy different levels within their unions. Some, for example, are plant-level representatives while others hold national union positions. The differences among management representatives are less surprising, since they come from a variety of firms with different competitive rankings and institutional needs. One manager belonging to CSTEC felt that his peers would rank upside training (for employed workers) above downside (adjustment) training, but he had reversed them in priority because his plant had experienced severe labour force reductions.

In short, the data suggest that labour and management representatives to the sector training councils agree on some fundamental council priorities, even though their philosophical motivations and rank order may differ. The development and administration of relevant and effective training and adjustment programs are key objectives that all parties strive to attain, irrespective of their institutional affiliations. There is also general agreement on the need to maintain healthy, competitive Canadian industries, provided that industry growth is coupled with the maintenance of high-skill jobs. It should be noted that where goal consensus may have existed at the time of this study, this agreement has evolved from a history of discussion and debate from the inception of the councils to the present, as will be evident from the following section on conflict and its resolution.

Conflict Resolution

The high level of goal consensus described above does not imply an absence of conflict. Popular press reports on labour-management cooperation suggest that it is the antithesis of conflict-ridden bargaining, with the parties laying all differences aside for the sake of harmony. The sector councils' decision-making practices present a much more realistic model of joint governance, one in which basic goals are shared, but parties spend a great deal of time working out the details to arrive at decisions that every member can accept.

To examine dispute resolution procedures and the role that council directors play in mediating conflicts that may arise, interviewees were asked first whether disagreements occur on the council/subcommittee, secondly, if so, which issues lead to the greatest disagreement, and thirdly, how disagreements are resolved. In response to the first question, all the CSTEC respondents stated that disagreements do occur, though some modified their answers by adding 'occasionally.' Similarly, APSTC interviewees unanimously answered in the affirmative, some adding 'with regularity' and others minimizing the extent of the conflict. In contrast, eight of the thirteen SSC council and subcommittee members indicated that no disputes of any real consequence occur.

The types of issues at the centre of disputes reflect clear philosophical differences across labour-management lines. In CSTEC, disputes have occurred around the North American Free Trade Agreement (labour opposed and management favoured), labour's demand for an equal role in training program design and administration (the joint governance structures at the national and plant levels afford this opportunity), disagreements over which courses should be eligible for accreditation by community colleges, and, during CSTEC's early years, disputes over adjustment issues. However, the two most contentious issues identified by respondents at the time of the study were the criteria used to fund upside training proposals (training for employed workers) and the content of curriculum. Decisions about whether certain courses fit the broad criteria guidelines must be made at the national level each time a local training proposal is received, and courses do not always fit neatly into prescribed categories. CSTEC's involvement in upside training has come rather recently in the organization's history (formally since 1992), and therefore there is little precedent for decisions on courses designed to meet special needs or cover innovative topics.

An example of course content decision-making emerged at the CSTEC meeting I observed. At that meeting, a staff member presented the skills training proposal of one the CSTEC's member firms. A representative from that firm sits on the Training and Adjustment Committee, and was present at the meeting. A management representative from another company raised questions about the content of a series of courses proposed, namely those on human rights, employee ownership, professional development, and restructuring. His questions had to do with whether the human rights course had been legislated (which would render it ineligible for funding) and whether the employee ownership and restructuring courses were company-specific (the firm requesting the courses is employee-owned). Considerable discussion took place, with the management representative from the firm requesting the courses explaining the intent of the courses and arguing that they met the funding criteria, and the other management representative continuing to raise questions. The director added that the courses were eligible because they would be teaching portable skills, and the only issue to be resolved was whether the courses are for additional or established training. Following more discussion, a vote was taken on whether to approve the staff recommendation to fund development of the courses. The motion in support of the recommendation was carried unanimously.

This discussion demonstrated the impressive degree of attention committee members pay to detail. The questions they asked about all of the training and adjustment proposals brought to the meeting focused on whether the programs clearly met the CSTEC eligibility criteria, and whether they were cost effective. Thus, proposals are most likely to be approved if it can be demonstrated that they are sector-appropriate, and effectively and efficiently delivered – even when the course content is controversial because of ideological labour-management differences. As one manager noted during an interview, 'the Steelworkers have their employee empowerment agenda ... they want to encourage training that develops the ability of the employee to enhance his or her own job,' and some managers regard this as conflicting with the notion of management rights.

When simple discussion and debate prove inadequate, the most common method of dispute resolution in the steel sector council is the use of caucus meetings in which contentious issues are identified and prioritized in separate labour and management meetings which take place the night before the formal meeting of the Training and Adjustment Committee. The committee co-chairs then meet, with the executive director and CSTEC staff present (if further information or advice is requested) to try to arrive at consensus. Issues that cannot be resolved in this way are discussed and debated at the committee meeting, and brought to a formal vote.

Disputes within the SSC have taken place over the percentage of training fund allocations (the percentage of a firm's payroll allocated to the fund, and the question of whether employees should be asked to contribute), skilled trades upgrading and apprenticeship issues, and the purpose and focus of job training (job retention/security versus improved job performance and productivity with fewer job classifications). Regarding fund contributions, the unions wanted companies to contribute 2.5 per cent of payroll to the fund, and the companies favoured a much lower percentage. A compromise was eventually reached at 1 per cent of regular, average payroll. Still, the expectation that one-quarter of this 1 per cent come from employees directly, though never actually put into practice, was opposed by some of the unions on principle. As a result, two of the unions, the Canadian Auto Workers Union and the United Electrical, Radio and Machine Workers of Canada (UE) withdrew from the council. Since that time the council has changed the wording to state that 50 per cent of the fund's monies come from 'private sector contributions,' and the CAW has rejoined the council (the UE membership was absorbed into the CAW).

The disagreement on apprenticeships had to do with the companies' wish to create a new combined trade of automated equipment maintenance and repair specialist for which they would hire external employees. The unions favoured an upgrading of existing journeymen in related trades instead of establishing and recruiting for a new trade. The matter was referred to a special task force which ultimately became the Apprenticeship Subcommittee, where it was finally resolved after two years of study. The union position on this matter prevailed, strengthened in some measure by a letter of endorsement from the Ontario Training and Adjustment Board. Consequently, jointly agreed-to skills standards have been developed to upgrade qualified electricians, industrial mechanics, and millwrights. A Joint Administration Committee (JAC) has been established to develop training modules that implement the agreed-to standards.

According to a union representative, some of the disagreements in the council's earliest days reflected deep divisions along labour-management lines. The name of the council was itself a contentious issue. The first name used, prior to the signing of the Declaration of Trust, was the 'EEMAC (Electrical and Electronic Manufacturers Association of Canada) initiative.' Aware that this recognized employers only, labour representatives developed the title of Sectoral Skills Council of the Canadian Electrical and Electronics Manufacturing Industry (SSC), and although the government began to refer to the group as CEEMI (Canadian Electrical and Electronic Manufacturing Industry), the SSC name prevailed.

One council member representing employers stated that another philosophical difference is that unions focus on training for job retention, while companies focus on it for improved job performance, competitiveness, and a reduction in the number of job classifications. According to a company representative, management would like to see Type II training (individual, non-job related) abolished because it's underutilized (only one tenth of available funds in this category are used), but labour wishes to retain it.

Differences of opinion arose along labour-management lines regarding the selection criteria for the hiring of an industry-education liaison person, according to a union member of the Education Subcommittee. Some union members favoured the appointment of a plant-level employee, regardless of whether that person possessed a university degree. They felt that the focus of any educational activity needs to relate back to the plant floor, and titles and degrees can be obstacles to effective linkage with the average worker. Ultimately, a person with a background in industry was chosen by a tripartite selection committee, consisting of labour, management, and college representatives.

When asked how disagreements are resolved, the majority of interviewees from the SSC used words such as 'discuss' and 'examine in depth'; they indicated that a slow, educational approach rather than a confrontational one is the norm. Sometimes an incremental solution will be adopted for a limited trial period in order to keep the process moving forward. Since standing subcommittees exist, many of the issues discussed in council meetings arise from these committees along with their recommendations. Occasionally the director may step in to suggest that an issue be returned to the appropriate subcommittee for further discussion and recommendations, but he/she does not play the role of mediator. Contentious issues are typically anticipated, and the labour and management secretariat work with their respective co-chairs to resolve these issues in the management or labour caucus meetings which occur outside of the council meetings. While caucus meetings took place more frequently in the early days, they typically occur annually at present. Outside experts are called in occasionally, but this is not a primary method of dispute resolution. As one of the union subcommittee members put it, the most effective way of bridging differences is to 'air concerns, get to know and respect each other, and compromise.' While the council by-laws allow for a vote to be taken when consensus cannot be achieved, this provision has never been used, according to the employers' secretariat.

Within the Auto Parts Council, all of the interviewees cited curriculum content as the issue which has led to the greatest disagreement. Since sections of the auto parts certificate program focus on inherently political issues such as work restructuring, economics, and free trade, ideological disputes during its development were inevitable. Ultimately a framework was developed in which both labour and management points of view would be presented side by side in the classroom, instead of merging the differing viewpoints into a middle-ground, consensus-based position. Also, a team of three professional curriculum developers was hired to work with the curriculum committee in drafting training module language and format.

Another issue that provoked strong disagreement along labour-management lines was that of peer trainers. That dispute revolved around several points. One was the degree to which peer trainers versus professional trainers (such as community college faculty or other trainers) would be used. A related concern was the precise ratio of peer to professional trainers to be used in each classroom. Still another was the question of how to define who could be a peer trainer. Labour was quite clear that peer trainers should come only from the ranks of production workers, while management initially advocated a broader definition that encompassed skilled trades, supervisors, and human resource managers.

Ultimately, it was decided that a team of two instructors would always appear together in the classroom; sometimes this team pairs a professional trainer with a peer trainer, and other times two peer trainers teach the course. Moreover, labour's definition of 'peer' prevailed, since it was recognized that psychological barriers to learning would be minimized only if the peers came from job classifications or levels akin to those of the trainees. Though this issue has been resolved, one of the management representatives expressed the view that non-union firms have been slow to sign onto the council because of their discomfort with unionized production employees training their employees.

Those who were involved in the council from its earliest days described disputes surrounding the hiring of the co-managing directors. The CAW wanted a dual director structure, noting that the council was not about labour-management cooperation, but rather about working in a bipartite manner to develop a sector training model for the auto parts industry. In the words of one of that union's visionaries, 'The clearer you are about separate interests, the more able you will be to actually develop positions that work.' For its part, the management side was facing a change of leadership at the APMA, and this delayed their decision-making process. The more compelling reason for co-directors, though, was that trust between labour and management was low. In the words of one of the management founding members, 'So [when] the issue of could we together surface candidates that we would mutually agree to and feel would represent the Board's desires without leaning too heavily towards management or too heavily towards labour [arose] ... we couldn't.'

Consequently, the CAW approached a university professor with whom they had worked on earlier projects and who had a background in curriculum design and adult learning to serve as labour's co-managing director. She obtained a leave of absence from her faculty position, and was hired by the CAW without the input of the APMA on 1 September 1991. The APMA hired its own co-managing director approximately two months later. The management co-director had different but necessary skills from his labour counterpart; while she was well versed in curriculum development and delivery, his strengths were in the areas of negotiating agreements with the governments, running the internal office, and the logistics of delivering the services. Ironically, the dual director structure had benefits that had not been anticipated. As a management member of the council observed, 'One person could not have done the work.'

Other issues that respondents mentioned as causing disagreement on the council were the marketing of the program, with labour (and at least one management member) contending that management, in particular the APMA, has failed to strongly push the program,[5] the use of workers' personal time to attend classes, and the selection of trainees and trainers.

In the Auto Parts Council, discussion and debate until consensus is reached is the most frequently used method of conflict resolution, and voting is seldom used. Co-chairs intervene where needed, bringing in top-level political leaders from each side if necessary. Co-directors try to anticipate potential problems and bring them to the appropriate standing committees. Subcommittees are used to examine issues in greater depth. Another technique that was mentioned is the development of incremental solutions, such as agreeing to a limited trial period, in order to keep the process moving forward.

Contrary to expectations, this study found across all three of the councils that staff executive directors or co-directors do not play an overt role in mediating disputes, though they sometimes serve as behind-the-scenes facilitators. Another unanticipated outcome was that the discussions that transpired at the meetings I observed for all three of the councils involved some mildly expressed disagreement at times, but overall no overt conflict. This can be explained by the tremendous amount of internal dialogue and deliberation within labour and management ranks prior to council meetings, and by the vast amount of information that is provided by council staff in advance of face-to-face discussions.

A central assumption at the onset of this study was that substantive disagreement among council and committee members is inevitable, since each person represents the interests of very different constituencies, not only from a labour-management perspective, but also based on individual company or union affiliation. The study results support this assumption, and demonstrate that sector training councils have advanced the concept of mature bipartite governance. Because parties are equally represented at all levels of the decision-making structure, they are able to work out differences and arrive at consensus decisions that represent the interests of all parties to the process. It is not only equal numerical representation at every level of the council structure that affirms labour's stature and provides a balance of bargaining power, but also the strategic posture unions assume and the government funding that gives unions an independent source of leverage despite their inability to match company contributions to training funds. Government funding agreements in fact specify bipartite council governance structures at the national and plant levels as mentioned earlier, and this plays a vital role in affirming union legitimacy as co-determination partners.

Contribution to Training Design and Delivery

Sector councils focus not only on training delivery, but on training program *design* – an area that is normally considered a management right. In some cases, design means determining curricular and course content and modes of delivery, but using external training and organizations and consultants to perform needs assessments, develop and deliver training modules. In other cases, especially with the Auto Parts Certificate program, the council retains control over all aspects of curriculum development and delivery.

Sector councils therefore give unions a voice in training issues that fall outside of the scope of what is typically included in collective bargaining agreements, which tend to focus more on equitable access to training than on training content and instructional design. As one union leader noted:

CSTEC ... provides a vehicle for the union to have a say in how the whole [training] thing's going to happen. Without the structure that's there, we'd still be sitting in the back seat saying: 'It's completely management's prerogative. And all we'd be doing would be banging our fist on the table at the local level, saying: We don't think this is right.' And they'll say: 'Well, too bad, we're going to do it anyway.' I think there's a definite structure there that will give us a say in how things will happen overall.

By their involvement in training program design, and not merely program administration, unions have actually made training more effective – even by the admission of company representatives. One high-ranking employer representative to the SSC explained:

Many companies ... don't really get serious about training. They establish budgets ... [but] maybe if there's a business downturn or the margins are getting skinnier, the CEO will say: 'Well, let's reduce it across the board.' What we're doing here is to say that this 1 per cent training fund cannot be touched – it is not subject to business downturns. It is dedicated for training and training alone. This is a big step forward. We are also, through the Joint Workplace Training Committees [say]ing to the companies, 'Could you please [share] your training plan for next year with us, and we will use our 1 per cent to integrate with that plan?' That request forces a discipline that hitherto has not been in many companies, to put together a training plan and budget. I think this is one of the very significant leverages in establishing a training culture.

This sentiment was echoed by another company representative belonging to the same council:

In total, I am absolutely certain [the linkage of council programs to company training strategy] is better than it used to be. That's because there is more attention given to it. Before there was always this great idea that there would be a training plan ... but in terms of a business manager's life it's not his most important activity. Whereas now we have committee[s] that [are] chewing away at it ... It's better than it ever was.

Company officials from the Auto Parts Council added that outside of sector council programs, 'training in this industry is crisis-oriented, not long-range.' Other management and labour representatives observed that although most companies in the auto parts sector lack human resource strategies, the auto parts certificate program has provided production workers with basic learning skills that enable them to master more difficult technical skills.

Because of the creative pedagogical approaches and courses sector councils have developed, they are widely regarded as leaders in curriculum design and training delivery. The Auto Parts Certificate program, for example, embodies principles of adult learning in two important ways. One is that the curriculum is designed to be developmental, so that basic courses serve as a foundation for more advanced learning. Second, the program uses peer trainers, that is, production workers who are selected and trained to deliver program instruction. This is intended to break down psychological barriers to learning by providing instructors who are familiar with trainees' jobs and experiences. CSTEC has developed ten generic training courses in basic skills, steel industry general skills, and specific technical skills. Although the content is universal enough to encourage skill portability, it is highly relevant and directly applicable to the steel industry.

The training offered by sector councils is also cost-effective, even though the comprehensive nature of the auto parts certificate program made it expensive to develop. When courses are designed for general industry use, the costs are shared across all of the companies belonging to the council, and the dollar-for-dollar government matching funds further lower development costs. Training program administration skills are leveraged across the entire sector as well. Joint workplace training committees operating within plants are provided with expertise and materials about how to analyse and respond to training needs. Resources like CSTEC's 'Training Needs Analysis Handbook for Joint Training Committees' reduce the need for individual companies to develop their own needs assessment tools or pay external consultants to do so.

A more recent development that also contributes to lowering training costs is CSTEC's negotiation of a national per diem tuition rate with nineteen colleges across six provinces. This assures a standard cost of $105 for the first ten trainees and $25 for the next five, a lower rate than that previously paid to colleges by companies for employee training. This goes hand-in-hand with the development (by plant joint committees and college faculty) of twenty-six standardized courses leading to a steel industry training program (SITP) certificate and the negotiation of a 'block transfer' agreement that assures recognition and transfer of these courses across any of the nineteen colleges. Obviously, such curricular standardization is not easily accomplished in highly diverse industries such as electrical and electronics.

An important dimension of sector training councils from a design and delivery standpoint is the decentralized system of training program administration that the SSC and CSTEC have in the form of joint workplace training committees. Not only do these committees manage every phase of training program administration, from selection of trainers to evaluation and cost auditing, but employers are also obliged to provide them with relevant information such as existing training tools and plans. In the case of CSTEC, this requirement includes a management assessment of capital expenditures and new technologies to be implemented over the next five years, along with an estimate of the amount and nature of training required as a result of these changes. This is a significant breakthrough for the union, since information of this nature is rarely disclosed to unions so far in advance. In a recent study of CSTEC, surveyed JTC members stressed the importance of including senior-level operations managers in training committee discussions (Ekos, 1995a).

The contribution of sector councils goes beyond training of employed workers; it extends to the development of innovative adjustment programs and approaches. As was mentioned earlier, CSTEC's adjustment services include peer counselling, financial and career planning, training referral, small business start-up, and job search/job placement assistance. These activities are carried out by local adjustment committees – comprised of labour and management representatives – operating at the plant level. The adjustment committees are supported by a Helping Employees Adjust Together (HEAT) team – a group of labour and management representatives who provide peer counselling to laid-off workers and technical assistance to local joint adjustment committees. All are retired or currently employed workers who are hired on a per diem basis. There are approximately ten HEAT teams operating in English-speaking Canada, and eight in Quebec.

Peer counsellors bring a knowledge of the industry to their jobs. This approach to counselling is undoubtedly premised on the assumption that laid-off employees are less likely to experience the psychological humiliation of asking for help when those providing it are peers who can remind them that industry conditions, and not personal failure, are responsible for their plight. On average, CSTEC has referred approximately 50 per cent of the workers it has assisted into training programs; this figure was 65 per cent when the industry was facing a severe downturn in 1992–3. The computerized National Job Bank, which was mentioned earlier, links all CSTEC projects and regional action centres to provide information on workers assisted, prospective employers, and specific employment requests. The re-employment rate of employees on pilot projects using the Job Bank has been about 90 per cent.

CSTEC boasts that it is able to provide adjustment services at a relatively low cost because of program administration fees, and because of its proven ability to negotiate lower training and service rates from external vendors. One figure cited in some recent CSTEC literature is that its adjustment training costs per hour are approximately one-third the cost of government training purchases (CSTEC, 1995).

In summarizing the contribution of the sector councils to training and adjustment services, it should be noted that while this study was not intended to be an evaluation of council effectiveness, respondents were asked to rate their respective council's success in meeting its goals. The vast majority of interviewees, regardless of labour or management affiliation, described them as 'very' to 'extremely successful.' Only in the area of the delivery and marketing of APSTC's auto parts certificate program were the ratings more qualified, though interviews were conducted just prior to an expansion of APSTC marketing activities.

Conclusion

The results of this research suggest a number of ways in which the three sector training councils studied have advanced the practice of joint governance. One is their bipartite structure at the national and plant levels. This assures a co-deterministic approach to strategy and policy as well as administration and practice. A second is the equitable balance of power evident in the relationships between union and management council representatives. A third is the finding that shared vision does not imply an absence of conflict, but in fact evolves when all parties have an opportunity to present, discuss, and debate their concerns. Cooperation and equal participation do not mean capitulation but instead evolve from a position of strength. Finally, the presence of unions on training councils not only improves the design and administration of training and adjustment programs, but also expands unions' scope and degree of influence into areas that have traditionally been the sole purview of management. This is particularly important for unions that lack sufficient numerical strength in a given sector to win major concessions individually. As a member of a smaller union on the Sectoral Skills Council observed:

Labour and management and government have to now come to a new era in their relationships. And I believe that the Council allows that to occur because we are not in there [as individuals], but we are able to tackle situations in a general [way]; thereby common good is coming out of it for all parties. So [in] areas where we would have not necessarily gotten agreement at a particular company, [now], because it's the Council, we can look at in a far better way, and ... come up with a solution that suits and is satisfactory to all. The Council plays a *vital* role in that manner.

Recent problems experienced by the Auto Parts Sectoral Council have caused some observers to question the long-term viability of the council approach, particularly when government support is withdrawn. An anti-union climate in Ontario that has been attributed in part to the policies of Conservative Premier Harris's government has by some accounts emboldened the APMA to notify APSTC of its desire to pull out of the council. While certain individual member companies declared their intention of remaining in the APSTC, it officially collapsed in August of 1996. In questioning whether this situation represents a failure of the joint governance model, it is important to note that on a day-to-day level labour and management representatives to the council worked across their differences to develop a model educational curriculum and a strategy for implementing it. As a former APSTC co-managing director observed, 'The joint governance model worked. For three years, people who in every other arena had a strong adversarial relationship were able to work together on a variety of issues.'

This view is supported by an external evaluation study, which notes that, 'at the level of the Board of Directors, labour and management work together amicably and there is [sic] no hostile or overt labour or management agendas.' (Ekos, 1995b: 17). Overall, the Auto Parts Council's problems had more to do with the difficulty of getting firms to buy into the concept of generic, foundation skills education. Although the Auto Parts Certificate program was highly regarded by adult education experts and past participants, companies in general are often unwilling to release employees and pay for courses that are not highly technical and skill-specific (ABC Canada, 1995). Interviews conducted by a former council administrator and external consultant with CEOs and human resource managers at fifteen auto parts firms just prior to the dissolution of APSTC revealed that the top *admitted* reason for the lack of commitment to continuation of the certificate program was the low status of non-mandatory training on companies' lists of priorities, especially generic training and training for production workers (Brophy, 1996). The fluctuating production demands placed on auto suppliers by original equipment manufacturers increased managers' reluctance to disrupt staffing schedules over the three-year period it would have taken an entire workforce to complete the three-week certificate program (Settle, 1995; Ekos, 1995b). The centralized system of training program development and administration, and the lack of local 'ownership' of the process were also thought to be barriers to plant participation. Lower-than-projected course enrolments placed the finances of the council in jeopardy, based on the funding structure described earlier in this paper.

However, three of the fifteen respondents cited perceptions about union involvement as primary obstacles. One was a perception of a union-dominated training agenda on the council, another was fear of wage and working condition comparisons among workers from different companies that might lead to collective bargaining demands, and the third was fear of negative effects of program participation on labour relations (Brophy, 1996). Thus, there is some evidence to suggest that joint governance is more difficult to sustain when a strong, proactive union and an external anti-union climate embolden marginally committed companies to withdraw tepid support for shared decision-making.

The APSTC story does not minimize the value of joint governance, but it does highlight the importance of government support in facilitating innovative and democratic solutions to industry-wide human resource problems. Some critics argue that if labour and management were truly committed to a human resource development agenda, they would fund programs on their own and not rely upon government monies. Yet government withdrawal would invariably leave small firms and unions behind. And there would be little incentive for companies and unions to share resources and tools that they have paid to develop across an entire sector, or to put forth policies and programs that benefit the industry as a whole. Above all, we know that the best models of joint governance exist in countries in which government plays an active role in encouraging and enabling bipartite and tripartite cooperation. The realities of impending budget cuts both federally[6] and provincially are enough to cause some supporters of sector councils to suggest that their existence and funding be embedded in collective bargaining agreements as a security measure (Warrian, 1996).

Although the results of this study are limited by the small sample size, the depth of the interviews and the consistency of the results advance our knowledge of the decision-making practices of labour-management sector training councils. One clear message that emerges from this research is that council members agree on fundamental, pragmatic objectives. While differences of opinion exist and conflicts are not avoided, these differences are philosophical in nature and relate to the degree of emphasis placed on commonly identified priorities. This is not to minimize the importance of philosophical differences, for they point to fundamentally different world views about such basic matters as management rights versus industrial democracy and worker/union empowerment. In the words of one council director; '[our council] is a vehicle for different parties to pursue respective, legitimate needs. Jointness is not a central objective.' Still, while parties may disagree vehemently on the means to an end, or even on the reasons an issue such as training is given high priority, they are able to unite around vital issues like the importance of upgrading workers' skills, or the need for a US–Canada steel agreement.

Another pattern that is suggested by these findings is that as councils mature, a common vision is more likely to emerge over time. For example, during the early days of the Sectoral Skills Council, simply establishing commitment and a process for joint (labour-management) determination of training priorities and practices was a challenge. Now all of the parties seem to agree on certain key tenets: that skills upgrading is vital to the health of Canada's electrical and electronics industry and to the security and prosperity of its employees, that labour unions' participation in council and JWTC activities adds value to the training design and delivery process, and that the continued financial support of the federal and provincial governments is critical to the council's success.

The interview and meeting observation data suggest that council executive directors play a facilitative role, but not a directive one in dispute resolution. The most common method of dispute resolution across the three councils studied is open, honest discussion and debate. Co-chairs, and in the case of the SSC, labour and management secretariat associates also play important roles, as do the labour and management caucuses in CSTEC. Executive directors help to anticipate potentially divisive issues and provide clarifying information, and may work behind-the-scenes with co-chairs, but it is the parties themselves who ultimately resolve the issues.

It should also be mentioned that there are indeed issues which unite council members. According to one account, early in CSTEC's history a unifying issue was the joining of labour and management representatives to lobby on behalf of trade legislation that would provide fairer access to markets by Canadian steel firms. As this mandate expanded into other areas, the respectful dialogue that had developed between the parties followed. As one interviewee observed, 'Canadians see that their economy and their industries are much more vulnerable than the United States' industries ... There is a national industrial consciousness, and it's a unifying force that calls for a certain kind of leadership ... that furthers some national purpose. CSTEC has become a major player in formulation of public policy.'

When viewed in a comparative sense, Canada's sector joint training councils are unique entities on the industrial relations landscape. Unlike some of the more limited labour-management cooperative efforts in the United States, they tackle substantive, sometime contentious issues and influence areas of decision-making that would normally be off-limits to unions. While they do not approach Sweden's 1970s version of industrial democracy (Hammarström, 1989), they move North American unions more closely towards Germany's co-determination system – not only because of bipartite representation, but also because of government's role in actively facilitating joint structures. However, unlike the German works councils which are often weakened by a lack integration with unions (Havlovic, 1990), organized labour plays a strong and strategic role in Canada's sectoral joint training councils, even though some of the councils include non-union firms and extend their programs to salaried employees. Sector councils clearly advance the practice of democratic decision-making in a vitally important domain, and illustrate the value that labour brings to human resource development efforts.

Notes

The author gratefully acknowledges the research support provided by the Canadian government in the form of a Canadian Studies Faculty Research Award, and by Eastern Michigan University's, Department of Interdisciplinary Technology, Office of Research Development, Canadian Studies Program, and World College. A debt of gratitude is also owed to Andrew Sharpe, Morley Gunderson, Rodney Haddow, Henry Milner, Lynn Brophy, George Nakitsas, and Gregg Murtagh for their valuable comments on earlier versions of this manuscript, and especially to the council members and staff who gave so generously of their time to participate in the study.

1 This is particularly true where councils have organized on an industry-wide basis and where unions have a strong presence in the industry. Some newer councils organized by occupation rather than industry do not operate with equal union representation.
2 CSTEC's original name was the Canadian Steel Trade Congress. The word 'Employment' was added in November of 1987, thereby formally emphasizing the importance of labour employment and adjustment issues and not merely trade issues (Haddad, 1995).
3 Although the funding formula was originally described as a four-way split between employers, employees, the federal government and provincial governments, the employee contribution was in fact never levied. Current literature describes the .5 per cent private sector portion of the fund as a 'workplace' contribution.
4 At the time of this study there was a potential industry population of approximately 425 firms in Ontario alone.
5 It should be noted that the APMA leadership disputed this view, noting that they had invited APSTC representative/co-directors to make presentations at three annual

meetings where high-ranking CEO's were in attendance, as well as at regional meetings. It should be also be noted that the APMA, which is an industry association, cannot direct or compel its member firms to take certain actions. It was further reported that many of the senior managers of branch plants are from the United States and rotate frequently from plant-to-plant across the US–Canadian border.

6 The federal government has expressed its intention of withdrawing cost-share support for training delivery, though some funding for training infrastructure (e.g., curriculum) may continue to be provided.

References

ABC Canada. 1995. 'Case history: training in auto parts.' *Literacy at Work.* December.

Brophy, Lynn. 1996. *Report to APSTC Executive Committee on Viability Research Project.* Markham, ON.: Automotive Parts Sectoral Training Council.

Commission on the Future of Worker-Management Relations. 1995. 'Employee participation and labor-management cooperation in American workplaces.' *Challenge* 38, no. 5, pp. 38–46.

Cooke, William N. 1990. *Labor-Management Cooperation: New Partnerships or Going in Circles?* Kalamazoo, MI: W.E. Upjohn Institute for Employment Research.

CSTEC. 1995. *About CSTEC.* Toronto, ON.: Canadian Steel Trade and Employment Congress.

Ekos Research Associates. 1995a. *Formative Evaluation of the Sectoral partnership Initiative – Case Study Report on the Canadian Steel Trade and Employment Congress.* Ottawa: Human Resources Development Canada.

– 1995b. *Formative Evaluation of the Sectoral partnership Initiative – Case Study Report on the Automotive Parts Sectoral Training Council.* Ottawa: Human Resources Development Canada.

Haddad, Carol J. 1995. *Sectoral Training Partnerships in Canada: Building Consensus through Policy and Practice.* Final Report to the Government of Canada. Ypsilanti, MI: Eastern Michigan University Department of Interdisciplinary Technology.

Hammarström, Olle. 1989. Swedish Industrial Relations,' in G.J. Bamber and R.D. Lansbury, eds., *International and Comparative Industrial Relations.* London: Unwin Hyman.

Havlovic, Steven J. 1990. 'German Works' Councils: A highly evolved institution of industrial democracy,' *Labor Studies Journal* 15, no. 2.

Kochan, Thomas A., and Osterman, Paul. 1994. *The Mutual Gains Enterprise: Forging a Winning Partnership among Labor, Management and Government.* Boston: Harvard University Press.

McDermott, Michael. 1994. 'Unions and Management: The old labels don't stick anymore,' *Journal of Business Strategy*, 15, no. 6, pp. 47–53.

Pomeroy, Fred. 1995. *Canadian Business Review* 22, no. 2, pp. 17–19.

Settle, Antony. 1995. *APSTC Promotion Strategy Development: Report to the Board of Directors.* September.

Warrian, Peter. 1996. 'Sectoral Councils: A Partial Solution to the Crisis of Representation in Wagnerism.' Paper presented at the CSLS conference on the Emergence of Sector Councils in Canada, Montreal, 12–13 January 1996.

10

The Canadian Steel Trade and Employment Congress: Old-fashioned Labour-Management Cooperation or an Innovation in Joint Governance?

ANIL VERMA, KAI LAMERTZ, and
PETER WARRIAN

The idea of joint labour-management decision-making has been suggested for as long as workplaces have existed. Yet their occurrence in practice has been limited at both the sectoral as well as at the more decentralized level of the enterprise or the establishment. The low incidence may be accounted for, at least in part, by the lack of our understanding of the effectiveness of joint decision-making as a rule-making process within industrial relations. While calls for joint decision-making have been numerous, the research literature on its impact on the parties has been thin.

Sector Councils as a form of joint labour-management decision-making provide an excellent opportunity to study the efficacy of this idea. In this paper we examine some aspects of local joint training committees which embody joint labour-management decision-making under a mandate of the Canadian Steel Trade and Employment Congress (CSTEC), one of the more successful councils to be established in Canada in the 1980s. The CSTEC was chosen because it allowed us to examine the outgrowth of sectoral-level cooperation to the establishment level. If it is argued that effective sectoral-level cooperation should ultimately spill over to a more decentralized level, then it becomes all the more important to see if any spillovers are occurring and if they are effective in promoting the interests of both parties.

The skills training program implemented under the auspices of the CSTEC in a variety of sites throughout the steel industry since the late 1980s is a good example of joint union-management decision-making at the establishment level that grew out of cooperation at the sectoral level. Joint labour-management decision-making, also called joint governance when both parties have equal say in decisions, is a significant organizational innovation because it operates within the collective bargaining framework even as it augments traditional labour-management relations (Verma and Cutcher-Gershenfeld, 1993). At the same time it is a significant departure from unilateral managerial decision-making. Since it is a flexible forum for making decisions that satisfies the needs of both management and labour, joint governance promises innovative solutions to the volatile problems facing many organizations in the 1990s. Yet little is known about why some joint governance mechanisms succeed while others fail or remain muted in their ability to bring about change.

By focusing on joint governance at the establishment level this paper addresses the dual need of examining the effectiveness of sector councils as well as of joint governance processes in general. Of course, joint governance at the plant level in our case cannot be separated from its institutional sectoral context. Although we do not examine the sectoral relationships directly, an examination of the plant-level relationships serves as an indirect assessment of the sectoral initiatives. We draw connections wherever appropriate to link the establishment-level joint governance processes to the sectoral efforts.

This study examines plant-level joint training committees (JTCs) set up under CSTEC to make decisions about training needs and the design and implementation of appropriate training programs. It is important to situate the JTCs within the CSTEC context without which it is unlikely that they would have been formed. Accordingly, the adoption and diffusion of these committees and the scope of their work is described in the first section. Next, we develop a conceptual model of how parties would respond to joint decision-making. The third section describes the methodology and the results of the study for which decision-makers from both labour and management were interviewed at seventeen sites. Lastly, we discuss some of the implications of these findings for joint decision-making for workers, managers, union leaders, and public policy-makers.

CSTEC Training: An Overview

Dating back to the mid-1980s, the Canadian Steel Trade and Employment Congress was established as a joint venture of the United Steelworkers of America (USWA) and the Canadian steel companies (Verma and Warrian, 1992). It is governed by a board of directors with labour and business co-chairs and a membership comprising the CEOs of the six largest steel producers and the six senior officers of the union. From 1988 to 1995 CSTEC provided counselling, training, job search and placement services to some twelve thousand laidoff steelworkers. Adjusting for those who left the workforce through retirement, over 80 per cent of all laidoff steelworkers were placed into new jobs, typically through a period of retraining in community colleges.

In 1991 CSTEC took the initiative to extend its mandate in human resource management in the steel industry by expanding its involvement to include training of the current workforce for future technologies and future skill requirements. Through CSTEC the steel companies and the United Steelworkers developed a skill training program, the cost of which is shared with the federal and provincial governments. The proposed funding formula was 1:1, that is one dollar from government for each additional training dollar spent by the industry. In practice, the industry contributed three dollars in additional training for each dollar of government training funds. The objectives of the program were to improve the quality and effectiveness of training and to at least double the amount of training in the industry over three years from 1993 to 1996, to develop industry standards and guidelines, and to develop a system of accreditation and certification to improve the portability and transferability of skills.[1]

The CSTEC had two types of leveraging effects on training as it augmented its downside adjustment activities to include upside training. First, the amount of training, especially in the generic portable skills, increased quite markedly as the numbers shown below indicate. Second, it led to growth of joint decision-making at the plant level in training matters, an area where decisions in the past were made primarily by management alone. This in turn led to wider access to training, especially for workers who did not traditionally benefit from firm-level training.

The 1991 Human Resources Study: A Baseline

In 1991 CSTEC contracted with the Canadian Labour Market and Productivity Centre to conduct a survey of human resource practices and training in the Canadian steel industry. The level of training expenditure of the industry circa 1990 was $31.7 million or 1.8 per cent of total payroll (see Table 1). An estimated 23,360 training courses or modules were offered. Since some employees would have participated in more than one module, the number of persons would be somewhat less. The types of training being given in 1991 were heavily weighted towards legislatively mandated health and safety training, apprenticeships, and technical training for non-bargaining unit staff (see Table 2). Since there was no CSTEC-sponsored training for employees at the time, all of this training was funded and operated by management either because it was mandated by law or because it was seen as important for the efficient operation of the firm.

TABLE 1 Training Expenditure, 1990

	Total Cost	Share of Total Cost
	($ 000s)	(%)
Wages of trainees	24,239	76
Salaries of trainers	4,119	13
Course fees	1,046	3
Consulting services	964	3
Training materials	778	2
Travel, accommodation, etc	348	1
Tuition reimbursement	67	0*
Other expenses	171	1
Total Training Costs	31,731	100
Training Cost / Payroll	1.8%	

Source: CSTEC, Proposal for a Steel Training Partnership (Toronto 1992), p. 13.
*Denotes less than 1%; totals may not add up to 100% due to rounding.

TABLE 2 Types of Training, 1990

	Hours of Training	% of Total
Health & safety, WHIMS	435,916	42
Technical training	240,358	23
Provincial apprenticeship	197,720	19
Company apprenticeship	112,320	11
Computer training	18,978	2
Supervisory training	16,706	2
Quality control	5,639	1
Literacy/numeracy	7,800	1
Tuition reimbursement	460	0
Management training	1,360	*
Team building	1,800	*
Total	1,039,057	

Source: CSTEC, Proposal for a Steel Training Partnership (Toronto 1992), p. 16.

CSTEC-sponsored Training

To be eligible for CSTEC funding, each establishment had to first establish a joint training committee (JTC), made up of equal numbers of local union and management representatives. The JTC surveyed employee and supervisory personnel on training needs to compile training plans for submission to the national Training and Adjustment Committee of CSTEC. 'CSTEC-eligible' training is defined as training that is broad-based and develops portable, generic skills.

TABLE 3 Training Expenditures, in millions of dollars

Industry Training	1993–4	1994–5
Established	$10.03	$23.30
Additional	15.91	7.11
Total	25.95	30.41
Government contributions, federal and provincial	$5.29	$5.59

Legislatively mandated items such as health and safety and government-sponsored apprenticeships are specifically excluded.

During the first year of the upside program ending on 31 March 1994, four-teen local JTCs out of a total of thirty-five established ones presented their training plans. In the second year some twenty-nine plans were submitted on behalf of thirty-six local JTCs. The results were some $26 million of CSTEC-eligible training in the first year and over $30 million in the second year (see Table 3).

To provide a base of comparison, the data from the 1991 Human Resources Survey were split based on the criterion of CSTEC eligibility into CSTEC-eligible and non-CSTEC-eligible categories. This breakdown shows that CSTEC-eligible training expenditure in 1991 was $5.7 million which rose subsequently to $26 million in 1994 and to $30 million in 1995.

Clearly there was a dramatic increase in the amount of portable, generic skills training being offered in the industry. Over 23,000 steel industry employees received CSTEC training in 1993–4 and over 24,000 in 1994–5. When combining the 1991 Human Resources Survey data with eligibility, the result was an equally dramatic change in access and distribution of training. In the earlier period, the preponderance of training expenditures, outside of legislatively mandated health and safety training plus apprenticeships, were going to non-bargaining unit technical and supervisory / managerial employees (see Table 4).

The pattern of results from the first two years of the CSTEC skill training program are clear: a much higher level of overall training effort, joint labour-management decision-making, greater access to training on the part of hourly employees, and a much greater emphasis on foundational skills and work organization. In the second year there was a significant further shift towards non-supervisory employees (production and clerical) and towards greater emphasis on technical skills training.

The real results of the new training effort in the steel industry will only be

TABLE 4 Percentage of Trainees by Occupation

Occupation	1993–4	1994–5
Managerial	3	3
Supervisory	20	8
Production	44	54
Clerical	3	21
Trades	21	6
Technical	8	7
Total	100	100
Types of Training		
Technical Skills	63	75
Foundation Skills	23	16
Work Organization	14	9

Source: CSTEC Training Program, First Year Results 1993–1994, CSTEC Toronto October 1994, Tables 2 and 4.

evident as those skills are put to work on the shop floor. This raises a number of questions about on-going monitoring and success factors for the CSTEC program. Will the greater access to training result in utilization of new forms of work organization? Will the emphasis on basic skills result in a leveraging to higher-order skills? Do improved generic skills enable employees to participate more effectively in work teams and problem-solving in the workplace? The answers to questions such as these are critical to the continued success of CSTEC. In order to identify what works and what does not, we need to understand how organizations that have implemented a CSTEC joint training committee incorporate it into the organizational structure and turn it into an effective decision-making process. If the parties can make such joint decision-making work, it may alter both parties' attitudes and behaviours towards each other in other spheres as well. Accordingly, the rest of this chapter focuses attention on the dynamics of JTCs as joint governance mechanisms.

JTCs under CSTEC: An Exercise in Joint Governance

In this section we develop a conceptual model of the outcomes that one may expect from joint governance, a process which is a radical departure from the dominant form of decision-making in Canadian industry, namely, unilateral managerial decision-making. In order to understand how a joint governance arrangement works and affects organizational processes, it is essential that we capture some of its unique characteristics in a theoretical framework by focusing on how joint governance arrangements may alter interaction and relations between labour and management decision-makers. We examine in particular the introduction of a new decision-maker role (i.e., the JTC member) in the organization, and the implications of this role for cooperative interaction and labour-management relations at the committee and the organizational levels.

Joint governance is unlike other forms of worker participation in decision-making practised in North-America, or elsewhere (Verma and Cutcher-Gershenfeld, 1993). In contrast to common types of employee involvement or labour-management committees, where labour is restricted to an advisory role, under a joint governance arrangement both parties share executive decision-making power. Moreover, such decision-making power is shared equally between labour and management, making joint governance distinct from typical labour representation on boards of directors. In addition, joint governance is formalized through codification in the collective agreement or some other legal arrangement, rather than based on a private, oral agreement between the parties. Another defining characteristic of joint governance is the voluntary nature of the agreement, which indicates a fundamental distinction from legally mandated works councils, such as those in Germany and other European countries. Joint governance can also involve either direct or indirect participation. Finally, in comparison to traditional collective bargaining, joint governance emphasizes continual interaction between labour and management, rather than intermittent sessions of negotiations without continued cooperation in between. In contrast to the collective agreement, which consists primarily of a set of rigid substantive rules, joint governance is a set of procedural rules that is designed for the making of work rules on a flexible basis. Traditional theories of participation in decision-making, which primarily utilize intra-personal variables (cf. Cotton, 1993), are unable to capture the dynamics which make joint governance a unique form of labour-management decision-making. Therefore our theoretical approach will examine how the introduction of joint governance alters the nature of the relationship between labour and management, and how this change is manifest in the roles and interactions of joint governance decision-makers.

Exchange Relations

The unique attributes of joint governance outlined above suggest a fundamental change to the exchange relation between labour and management in the domain of organizational decision-making. There are four elemental forms of exchange relations (Fiske, 1991): communal, hierarchical, egalitarian, or market-oriented. These elemental relational forms are cognitive schemas for initiating and interpreting social interaction (Fiske, Haslam, and Fiske, 1991). Communal relations involve perceptions of common group membership, the pooling and sharing of resources, and decision-making by unanimity. Hierarchical relations involve subordination by one individual to another, the exchange of deference for guardianship, and decision-making by authority. Egalitarian relations revolve around maintaining balance, in-kind exchanges, and decision-making through majority vote. Finally, market-oriented relations involve cost-benefit calculations, exchange based on utility maximization, and decision-making through proportional trade-offs.

For example, collective bargaining is premised on formal, legally mandated 'arm's length' relations that can be described as market-oriented. Traditional employment relations between management and workers are hierarchical, while union membership is more akin to an egalitarian relation. Most importantly, a concrete social relation between two individuals consists of multiple overlapping ideal types because different elementary forms may characterize interaction in different social domains (Fiske, 1991). Thus, two negotiators in collective bargaining may share an egalitarian professional relationship in addition to their market relation during contract talks.

The sharing of power between labour and management within the formal organizational structure of daily workplace decision-making suggests that an egalitarian element has been added to the traditional hierarchical relations between the two parties. In addition, new roles for both labour and management decision-makers are created, which situate both parties as equal partners in a single group context, thus shifting inter-group conflict between them to the intra-group level (cf. Brett and Rognes, 1987; Burt, 1982). Such change may add a communal element to the exchange relationship. Consequently, joint governance decision-making is likely to be perceived more as rooted in reciprocity and common group membership, rather than authority, utility maximization, and inter-group conflict, which characterize hierarchical organization and collective bargaining. In the ensuing section, we propose that these changes to the formal exchange relation between labour and management constitute the creation of a new organizational role. Occupants of this new role must integrate it into the social fabrics of the organization through an enactment process that transforms the way the parties perceive and interact with each other (Fiske et al., 1991; Verma and Cutcher-Gershenfeld, 1993).

Integration of Joint Governance Roles

Our theoretical framework is based on the idea that changes to the exchange relation between labour and management become operative through the introduction of a new organizational role: the joint governance decision-maker. This role must be integrated into the day-to-day activities of those organizational members who occupy the new role and those who interact with these role occupants (Graen, 1976; Katz and Kahn, 1978; Nadel, 1959). Integrating a new role into the social structure of an organization involves the emergence of a common understanding about the purpose and legitimate activities of its role occupants (Biddle, 1986; Graen, 1976; Nadel, 1959). It is through such common understanding that joint governance affects the perceptions and behaviours of organizational members. Therefore, the changes in patterns of interaction among organizational members to which the introduction of joint governance gives rise can be classified into two categories: interaction on the committee that involves only role occupants, and interaction between role occupants and other organizational members that affects organization-wide processes.

JTC Level Interaction

Conceptually, joint governance requires decision-makers to enact a new role that combines the demands of constituency advocate with the responsibilities of a co-manager (Strauss, 1982). These two role elements parallel what Verma and Cutcher-Gershenfeld (1993) have called the combination of conflict and cooperation in joint governance decision-making. The formal addition of communal and egalitarian components to the traditional hierarchical and market-oriented relations between labour and management creates new role demands on decision-makers which they enact through new patterns of interaction that involve both cooperation and conflict.

At the level of the committee, it is the task of decision-makers to develop a new basis for interacting with each other. We propose that this new basis will be characterized by several features. First, we hypothesize that members of the JTC will perceive joint governance decision-making more like exchange among members of one group, rather than between two opposing groups, because each party may divulge information about its preferences without compromising attainment of its goals (Verma and Cutcher-Gershenfeld, 1993). Moreover, as conflict related to group identification between committee members gives way to genuine conflict of interest (Brett and Rognes, 1987; Skinner, 1979), productive controversy and cooperative goals are likely to emerge. Following Tjosvold (1987), we therefore also hypothesize that these two processes affect decision-makers' experiences and lead them to share more information, exchange more resources, and communicate more accurately. This combination of behaviours is likely to resemble a mixture of problem-solving and bargaining, reflecting the underlying merger of conflict and cooperation.

We further hypothesize that interaction on the JTC will foster the development of trust between labour and management decision-makers and serve to harness a constructive conflict that drives innovation and flexibility under joint governance arrangements. The continual nature of JTC interaction may inhibit opportunistic behaviour and thereby lead to the build-up of trust and a reduction in destructive conflict (Nelson, 1989). Furthermore, through trust and cooperation, decision-makers will develop shared norms and belief structures for decision-making interaction on the JTC (Bettenhausen and Murnighan, 1985; Walsh and Fahey, 1986). Such norms do not compromise advocacy of one's constituent interest or lead to group think (Janis, 1971), but instead foster consensus about interaction between the parties without unnecessary conflicts over procedural details. Finally, Verma and Cutcher-Gershenfeld reported that joint governance requires both parties to learn new skills: labour must acquire more administrative expertise, while management must attain better political savvy. We therefore predict that management and labour decision-makers acquire new competencies and learn new skills from each other through their involvement in the JTCs.

Organization-wide Interaction

Decision-makers must not only establish a pattern of interaction with their fellow JTC members, but also integrate the new role with the role system of the entire organization by establishing a basis for interaction with individuals outside the committee. JTC decision-makers rely on their constituencies for information about training needs, implementation, and effectiveness, as well as other resources to carry out their activities. Thus, it is imperative that decision-makers establish stable relations with those constituents by reaching a common understanding about the meaning, operations, and purpose of the committee and its members. Because joint governance is a form of labour-management interaction that takes place close to the shopfloor level (Kochan, Katz, and McKersie, 1986), we hypothesize that one way through which JTC decision-makers integrate their role into the rest of the organization is by strengthening their connections with individuals at this level. We propose that joint governance resembles a bottom-up approach to decision-making that works effectively when decision-makers are extensively linked to other organizational members through cooperative relations that provide information and support.

We further hypothesize that other cooperative ventures may surface because JTC decision-makers will come to view joint governance as the normal mode of decision-making that generalizes to interaction outside the JTC. Thus, they are likely to initiate cooperative, joint decision-making interaction with other organizational members on issues that go beyond the scope of CSTEC. The fact that the elementary relational forms are cognitive social schemas lends support to this proposition because the addition of communal and egalitarian elements makes decision-makers relate more cooperatively to other organizational members. Furthermore, by integrating the new role with the roles and behaviours of individuals outside the committee, JTC decision-makers may propagate a cooperative approach to labour-management interaction throughout the organization.

Feedback from the Trenches

Method

Our research relies on two sets of interview data. In early 1995 Ekos Research Associates conducted seven discussion groups on behalf of Human Resources Development Canada with members of JTCs from fourteen different plants (Evaluation and Data Development Canada, 1995). The results of these focus groups constitute a secondary data set, which was combined with primary data we collected independently through a set of in-depth interviews with JTC members from three additional plants during December 1995. We conducted these interviews in order to verify the Ekos information with data collected through our own methodology. Our semi-structured interviews were based on exploratory methods, and paralleled the interview guide developed for the discussion groups in many ways. Both approaches employed standardized questions that elicited open-ended responses from the interviewees, and allowed for follow-up questions to be posed. In addition, the discussion groups were conducted in person, while we conducted interviews with key informants both over the phone and in person.

Although the two studies differed in scope, there was considerable overlap between the two sets of questions put to the respondents. The Ekos study was much broader, and included many questions on other issues pertaining to the JTCs. In contrast, our questions were derived specifically from our theoretical framework of joint governance, on which we focus in this research. One common key question dealt with possible changes in the roles, responsibilities, and skills the two parties employ in dealing with each other under the new joint arrangements. Second, both set of questions asked about the scope of functions which the JTC performs, and the existence of other cooperative labour-management interaction that may have developed concurrently. A third common inquiry was concerned with the methods of information-gathering and extent of information-sharing among committee members as well as between them and their constituents. Finally, interviewees in both studies were questioned about differences and similarities between JTC decision-making and other methods of labour-management interaction.

In our results section, we present the data according to the two subheadings of role-related interaction in our theoretical model. The reader should keep in mind that these data were obtained through exploratory methodologies and are to serve as elaboration of our theoretical model as well as a basis for future confirmatory research.

Results

JTC Level Interaction

Respondents felt that JTC decision-making represented a significant departure from prior practices that was more focused on problem-solving than competitive negotiations and were less pressured by deadlines or threats of abandonment by either party. Moreover, solutions made by the JTC were judged as broader in scope because they were not affected by trade-offs with other bargaining issues. However, where such issues did intrude into the JTC process, conflict and deferral were the result. In addition, there was evidence that during committee meetings, inter-group barriers between labour and management were less visible, and that conflict was most often resolved through discussions. These data support our hypotheses that joint governance decision-making is characterized primarily by in-group perceptions and a mixture of conflict and cooperation in the relations between decision-makers.

Through their interaction on the joint committee, JTC decision-makers felt that they learned to be more flexible with each other, not only on their own initiative, but also through acquaintance with their opponents' proclivities. In addition, labour and management representatives each brought their unique skills to the decision-making table, and were able to learn from each other's expertise. Because joint governance is a proactive approach to decision-making, the greater involvement of union initiative helped labour representatives acquire a better understanding of skills needed in administrative tasks. Similarly, management learned to deal with the effects on various organizational groups of implementing training policies because training is administered jointly by union and management. Finally, the data supported our hypothesis that continual interaction on the JTC helps decision-makers get to know and trust one another better than intermittent interaction in collective bargaining.

The certification of a bargaining unit often brings with it a shock effect, which is the realization on the part of management of the need to vastly improve working conditions, human resource policies, and employee relations (Slichter, Healy, and Livernash, 1956). Our data support the conclusion that a secondary shock effect follows the introduction of joint governance through JTC decision-making. For example, some managers recognized that the quality of needs analysis and other training activities required significant upgrading, while others noted the importance of integrating training activities with the organization's overall human resource management strategy, and the usefulness of the JTC towards this end. Similarly, there was consensus among respondents that training evaluation was an under-developed and neglected activity that deserved greater attention in all plants.

Training outcomes are also indicative of this shock effect. The data indicate that joint governance led to better tracking of training goals and activities in plants where a cooperative training culture had been in existence prior to the introduction of the JTC. Moreover, in plants where training had been mostly management-driven, the quantity of training increased, new types of training were introduced, and planning of training activities was greatly advanced (Evaluation and Data Development Canada, 1995). While we did not anticipate this secondary effect, it is entirely consistent with our theoretical framework. The fact that management reacts to the JTC with a greater concern about training issues suggests that the addition of cooperative elements in the new roles and relations facilitate the surfacing of cooperative goals. Moreover, management's implicit admission to the inadequacy of prior training practices shows that joint governance relations allow the parties to divulge information without fear of jeopardizing their interests.

Organization-wide Interaction

There was substantial evidence that the quality of relations between union and management outside the JTC is a cornerstone of effective JTC decision-making. The data show that good relations between labour and management on the JTC and successful implementation of joint governance roles tend to develop from good relations in existence prior to the introduction of joint decision-making. In addition, respondents felt that the JTC was a substantial investment in their relationship with the other party, making it more resistant to threats and crises and reinforcing its overall quality. In contrast, existing labour-management relations that were poor and characterized by continual strife posed a barrier to JTC development.

There is substantial evidence that our propositions about the interactions between JTC decision-makers and members of their constituencies outside the JTC are well founded. Interviewees explained that they have better access to information about all relevant aspects of a particular decision from both managers and workers, and that they learn from each other as well as from members of JTCs in other organizations. There was consensus that JTC decision-making is a bottom-up approach to developing training plans and proposals, which improved the quality and effectiveness of training initiatives. Some managers suggested that there was more contact between line managers and the human resources department than previously, and the use of employee surveys for conducting needs analyses was praised by many other respondents. These data indicate that the new roles on the JTC are broadly integrated into social structure, and that as a consequence a greater variety and number of contacts are available and used for gathering information. This conclusion is further supported by the establishment of departmental sub-committees, which are in frequent contact with the organizational JTC on such issues as needs analysis and training feedback.

Another significant consequence of JTC decision-making were spillover effects: the cooperative approach to decision-making was extended to developing training programs and policies that fall outside of the jurisdiction of CSTEC. This is a significant advancement because such cooperation takes place in the absence of government subsidies. In addition, joint governance type arrangements seemed to spread to other areas of decision-making, such as health and safety, technological change, and scheduling. There was also a sense of positive spillover from JTC roles to other decision-making activities, to which committee members were able to export their JTC skills and experiences. Altogether, these effects served to reinforce the cooperative nature of overall labour-management relations, and suggest that the introduction of the JTC represents a significant impetus to an inert thrust towards organization-wide joint governance.

Discussion and Conclusions

What can we conclude about the implications of a joint governance arrangement like CSTEC for organizational processes and the relationship between labour and management? Is the JTC a smokescreen for venting latent animosities, a step forward in the evolution of labour-management cooperation, or does it represent a significant innovation and revolution of the way the parties interact with each other? Furthermore, what are the dynamics of joint labour-management decision-making, and how do they affect organizational processes? If sector councils can facilitate joint labour-management decision-making at the plant and firm level, this contribution may be more significant than the increase in training that CSTEC may have registered.

Joint Governance as Organizational Feedback Process

One possibility is that the parties do not learn anything constructive from JTC decision-making, nor realize any progress in their relations and interaction with each other. Where existing labour-management relations are characterized by strife and competition, joint decision-making only serves as a new arena for engaging in conflict. On the other hand, where existing relations are good, joint governance is no more than another manifestation of already existing cooperation between the parties. A more optimistic view is that joint governance initiates a fundamental transformation of labour-management relations by dismantling inter-group biases, encouraging cooperation, and cultivating trust. According to this view, we would expect the parties to take advantage of their common interests, resolve their latent conflicts, and realize significant improvements in cooperative and productive behaviour at all levels of the organization over time.

While either of these alternatives is possible, we do not think that they adequately reflect what our interview data are telling us. However, ideas from both possibilities can be combined into an alternative scenario that we consider to be the most plausible description of joint governance dynamics. This view holds that good labour-management relations are a necessary foundation for effective JTC decision-making. In the absence of such relations, JTC or other joint governance may be doomed to fail because the parties do not posses the requisite capacity to deal with each other in a cooperative fashion. Under such conditions, joint governance may not even be considered as an opportunity for overcoming conflict and improving existing interactional patterns. Therefore, we conclude that at the point of inception, joint governance is an extension of what labour and management were previously doing. However, where existing relations are good, the set-up of joint decision-making bodies appears to enable and force the parties to develop new roles and learn new skills that augment and reinforce those relations. The analogy that best captures this view is that of college education which cannot be expected to solve problems of illiteracy just as joint governance is not a solution for parties locked in the traditional adversarial relationship. On the other hand, college education may be essential for a high school graduate who wants to build a career in the information economy. Similarly, joint governance may be an essential step for those parties who have developed some rapport but would like to move their relationship to a higher level of mutual adaptation.

We conceive of joint governance as a feedback process which unravels as labour and management learn new skills, firmly integrate joint decision-making into the organization, and develop their partnership over time. Once joint governance has been implemented and is operating successfully, each successive instance of joint decision-making strengthens mutual relations between the parties in an upward spiralling fashion. This feedback process transpires through successful realization of joint interests and cooperative resolution of enduring conflicts. The process culminates in cyclical reinforcement of the cooperative stance the parties have adopted towards each other and solidification of their commitment to the relationship they have built. The growing strength of this relationship would be manifest in several ways, such as the ability to withstand environmental shocks (e.g., a business downturn), the capacity to adopt new technologies or implement organizational change (e.g. new quality standards such as ISO 9000), and the power to overcome relationship crises (e.g., paralysed contract negotiations). We propose that future research can employ some of these criteria to investigate JTC processes and joint governance decision-making in greater detail.

Implications for Theory and Research

We conclude that our initial theoretical model holds considerable promise for pinpointing processes that contribute to the successful unfolding of joint governance feedback cycles. For example, the integration of new roles and associated behaviours into the organization may be critical to the diffusion of cooperative skills and attitudes into other decision-making domains. We can also investigate changes in social exchange relations between JTC decision-makers in order to evaluate the extent to which labour-management relations evolve and mature over time. Finally, there are possibilities for researching the impact of JTC decision-making on shopfloor level attitudes and behaviours within the context of jointly implemented training sessions. If already cooperative labour-management relations grow stronger through joint governance, how is this strength manifest in the experience of everyday work? Do line managers and employees perceive changes in inter-group relations, and if so, do such perceptions lead to changes in how they feel about work and the organization?

An important consideration is the comparability of joint governance to European style works councils, and the consequent applicability of comparative research (e.g., Adams, 1991) to our theory of joint governance. Some may argue that legislated joint decision-making should have effects on organizational processes that are similar to those of a voluntary arrangement because the difference between the two lies merely in the initiation of cooperation. That is, how the introduction of joint governance is accomplished should have little bearing on how it unfolds and affects the organizational processes we have described in our theoretical framework. While this argument is logical, it does not adequately consider the alternative to joint governance in either situation. Where joint governance is legislated, the parties are compelled to engage in a minimal level of cooperation and do not even have the option of abandoning joint decision-making. In contrast, voluntary joint governance can be discontinued at any time if either party wishes to do so. The critical point is that voluntary joint governance is likely to have a different effect on organizational processes than its legislated counterpart because there is no safety net on which its proponents can fall back, whereas the possibility of no cooperation remains a viable vision for its opponents. While our position is clear and the readers are invited to draw their own conclusions, we suggest that research on some of our observed outcomes of joint governance may provide the final resolution of this issue.

In the 1980s a large amount of research documented the process of decision-making in Japanese organizations (Ouchi, 1981; Pascale and Athos, 1981). One of the key findings in this literature was that Japanese companies practised bottom-up decision-making in which employees at the lowest levels were asked for their input on major decisions. This feedback was passed up the line until it reached the top management who made decisions consistent with the feedback thus received. In contrast, American organizations practised top-down decision-making in which decisions are made by top management without any consultation with employees and then communicated downwards for implementation. The American organization, thus, could make decisions relatively quickly, but these organizations often became bogged down in implementing the decisions, as they met with resistance from employees. The Japanese organization, in contrast, took longer to make decisions but once these decisions were made, implementation was much smoother because employees had already bought into the decision. Joint governance, our evidence suggests, is a North American innovation which helps make high-quality decisions similar to the bottom-up system used by Japanese organizations. We found that setting up the joint governance system led to the formation of several networks through which an extensive flow of work-related information took place. A large number of employees had the opportunity for input, and in the process they received and transmitted information about work flow, personal preferences, and so on. Our findings also suggest that even though the CSTEC joint governance arrangement extended formally only to CSTEC-related training, the interactions among the parties spilled over to other training and workplace issues. In this way, joint governance may prove to be the North American equivalent of bottom-up decision-making.

Our results also point to the catalyzing role of sector councils in creating the context for joint governance to take place. If the steel industry had been left to its own devices, one may have seen fewer JTCs. This view also suggests that the extra-firm inputs such as sector councils be integrated into the theoretical models of joint governance. This role for sector councils may, in the long-run, outweigh the immediate benefits of enhanced training.

Policy Implications

In addition to the support which our data have given to our theoretical propositions about relational processes, we have found that a necessary condition for effective JTC decision-making appears to be the prior existence of good labour-management relations. We therefore conclude that joint governance is unlikely to be a good option for resolving conflictual relations between the parties if they have not yet acquired at least some skills for dealing with each other, such as basic problem-solving techniques. In other words, it may be that organizations which want to implement a JTC successfully must exhibit a labour-management relationship that has matured beyond initial hostilities and positional bargaining. The benefits which this relationship can derive from the feedback process of joint governance are potentially very powerful, and make JTC decision-making a unique form of labour-management cooperation. Indeed, a further elaboration of our theory suggests that the introduction of a joint governance arrangement is not only a logical progression of cooperative labour-management relations, but also a necessary step towards securing long-term development of these relations.

A final issue that remains to be addressed is the role of government funding in motivating the establishment of CSTEC and, in particular, the introduction of JTCs at the plant level. The basic question is: Would joint governance occur without the incentives provided by government money for CSTEC-sponsored training? While in the case of CSTEC such funds certainly played a significant role, several joint governance arrangements in North America have transpired in the absence of government subsidies (Verma and Cutcher-Gershenfeld, 1993). Therefore monetary incentives are not a necessary condition for joint governance, nor are they a sufficient condition for joint governance because success may depend on the prior existence of good labour-management relations. Nevertheless, the experience of CSTEC shows that government money can facilitate the start-up of joint labour-management decision-making, and act as a catalyst for the development of plant-level joint governance. As described in this paper, JTC decision-making was not limited to CSTEC-sponsored training and also spilled over to other decision-making domains. This means that the money which government invested may have exceeded its intended returns, and thereby generated significant leverage.

Notes

The authors are grateful to several labour and management representatives for participation in the interviews carried out as part of this study. We also acknowledge partial financial support by the Social Sciences and Humanities Research Council of Canada.

1 CSTEC, *Steel in Our Future – 1995* (Toronto: January 1995), p. 10.

References

Adams, R.J., ed. 1991. *Comparative Industrial Relations*. London: HarperCollins Academic.

Bettenhausen, K., and J.K. Murnighan. 1985. 'The Emergence of Norms in Competitive Decision-making Groups.' *Administrative Science Quarterly* 30, pp. 350–72.

Biddle, B.J. 1986. 'Recent developments in role theory,' *Annual Review of Sociology*, 12, pp. 67–92.

Brett, J.M., and W.K. Rognes. 1987. 'Intergroup Relations in Organizations,' in P.S. Goodman, ed., *Designing Effective Work Groups*. San Francisco: Jossey Bass, pp. 202–36.

Burt, R.S. 1982. *Toward a Structural Theory of Action: Network Models of Social Structure, Perception, and Action*. Cambridge: Harvard University Press.

Cotton, J.L. 1993. *Employee Involvement*. Newbury Park, Cal.: Sage Publications.

Evaluation and Data Development. 1995. 'Formative Evaluation of the Sectoral Partnership Initiative: Case Study Report on the Canadian Steel Trade and Employment Congress (CSTEC). Ottawa: Human Resources Development Canada.

Fiske, A.P. 1991. *Structures of Social Life*. Toronto: Collier Macmillan.

Fiske, A.P., N. Haslam, and S.F. Fiske. 1991. 'Confusing One Person with Another: What Errors Reveal about the Elementary Forms of Social Relations.' *Journal of Personality and Social Psychology* 60, pp. 656–74.

Graen, G. 1976. 'Role-making Processes within Complex Organizations,' in M.D. Dunette, ed., *Handbook of Industrial and Organizational Psychology*. Chicago: Rand McNally, pp. 1201–45.

Janis, I.L. 1971. 'Groupthink,' *Psychology Today* 5, pp. 378–84.

Katz, D., and R.L. Kahn. 1978. *The Social Psychology of Organizations*. New York: Wiley.

Kochan, T.A., H.C. Katz, and R.B. McKersie. 1986. *The Transformation of American Industrial Relations*. New York: Basic Books.

Lamertz, K., and A. Verma. 1995. 'Joint Governance: A Social Networks Approach to Participation in Decision Making between Labour and Management.' Presented at the 1995 annual meeting of the Academy of Management, Vancouver, BC.

Nadel, S.F. 1957. *The Theory of Social Structure*. London: Cohen & West.

Nelson, R.E. 1989. 'The Strength of Strong Ties: Social Networks and Intergroup Conflict in Organizations,' *Academy of Management Journal* 32, pp. 377–401.

Ouchi, W.G. 1981. *Theory Z*. Reading, MA: Addison-Wesley.

Pascale, R.T., and A.G. Athos. 1981. *The Art of Japanese Management*. New York: Simon & Schuster.

Skinner, M.R. 1979. 'The Social Psychology of Intergroup Conflict,' in G.M. Stephenson and C.J. Brotherton, eds., *Industrial Relations: A Social Psychological Approach*. Toronto: John Wiley & Sons, pp. 75–94.

Slichter, S., J. Healy, and R. Livernash. 1956. *The Impact of Collective Bargaining on Management*. Washington, DC: Brookings Institution.

Strauss, G. 1982. 'Workers Participation in Management: An International Perspective,' in B.M. Staw and L.L. Cummings, eds., *Research in Organizational Behavior,* vol. 4, pp. 173–265.

Tjosvold, D. 1987. 'Participation: A Closer Look at its Dynamics,' *Journal of Management* 13, pp. 739–50.

Verma, A., and J. Cutcher-Gershenfeld. 1993. 'Joint Governance in the Workplace: Beyond Union-Management Cooperation and Worker Participation,' in B.E. Kaufman and M.M. Kleiner, eds., *Employee Representation: Alternatives and Future Directions*. Madison, Wis.: Industrial Relations Research Association, pp. 179–234.

Verma, Anil, and Peter Warrian. 1992. 'Industrial Relations in the Canadian Steel Industry,' in Richard P. Chaykowski and Anil Verma, eds., *Industrial Relations in Canadian Industry*. Toronto: Holt, Rinehart and Winston.

Walsh, J.P., and L. Fahey. 1986. 'The Role of Negotiated Belief Structures in Strategy Making,' *Journal of Management* 12, pp. 325–38.

PART V
EVALUATION OF SECTOR COUNCILS

11

Program Evaluation Criteria Applied to Sector Councils

MORLEY GUNDERSON and ANDREW SHARPE

Evaluating sector councils is extremely difficult because they have a multiplicity of objectives and forms. As well, they are still in their infancy in Canada, and hence are still evolving. In this paper we apply a set of generic program evaluation criteria to sector councils and evaluate them largely as an adjustment mechanism, intended to deal with both downside and upside labour situations. The paper begins with a discussion of interrelated adjustment pressures for which sector councils are a response. It then discusses the importance of using a set of program criteria to evaluate initiatives such as sector councils. The generic program evaluation criteria are then briefly set out and applied to the sector councils. A summary table is provided in the concluding section, highlighting the pros and cons of sector councils as set out by the criteria.

Program Evaluation Criteria

The program evaluation criteria used here are generic in the sense that they could be used to evaluate any other adjustment mechanism or program, such as unemployment insurance or trade protection. They provide a checklist of the wide range of criteria that should be considered in evaluating programs. They narrow the debate by separating the issue of objectives from the evaluation of the effectiveness of the program in meeting those objectives. In many cases the parties may simply 'agree to disagree' over the appropriateness of a particular criterion, and this narrows the zone of disagreement over whether the program is successful. Clearly setting out the evaluation criteria also highlights the difficult trade-offs that are involved when programs are called upon to meet a wide range of often conflicting objectives. Invariably, doing better at achieving one objective conflicts with achieving some others. Enunciating these trade-offs helps not only in evaluating the program but also in suggesting improvements that may mitigate the trade-offs.

In setting out the program evaluation criteria it is important to emphasize that there is no agreement about the appropriateness or relevance of each and every criterion. Furthermore, the ordering used here is for expositional purposes rather than to imply a degree of priority. In each case, the program evaluation criteria are briefly explained, followed by a discussion of the pros and cons of sectoral councils in meeting the criteria. The discussion is meant to be illustrative rather than exhaustive. A thorough review of whether sectoral councils meet the program evaluation criteria would require evidence on the effect of sectoral councils compared to other adjustment strategies. Such an evaluation is beyond the scope of the present analysis.

Target Efficiency

A program is considered efficient if it assists as many persons in the target group as much as possible, without having the benefits (and hence the costs of the program) spill over into the hands of the non-target groups. To assess the success of a program of course, requires identification of the target group (e.g., persons laid off). Sectoral councils have the potential to be efficient since they can define the target groups that are most important to the industry (e.g., permanently laid-off workers, or workers in need of upgrading to retain their jobs). Being 'close to home' in the delivery of the programs and in identifying needs, they can also direct resources to the target groups and minimize spill-overs into non-target groups who do not need the assistance. Of course, as with any program delivery mechanism, some target group members may still be missed, and benefits may spill over into the hands of others given the difficulties of identifying the designated groups. Administrative and other expenses are often involved, and this must be traded off against achieving the objective of target efficiency.

Allocative Efficiency

A program is considered efficient if it encourages the effective allocation of resources, which usually means in the direction of, and not against, market forces. In the labour adjustment area this usually means diverting resources from declining sectors or needs to expanding ones. Of particular importance is the ability to reallocate from sectors experiencing plant closings or mass layoffs to those experiencing skill shortages or prolonged vacancies. Active adjustment programs (e.g., training, mobility, job creation) are generally considered as having greater potential to achieve allocative efficiency than passive income maintenance programs (e.g., unemployment insurance, social assistance). In essence, active adjustment programs facilitate adjustment in the direction of market forces, while passive ones can thwart that adjustment process by encouraging people to remain in declining sectors.

Sectoral councils have the potential to deliver a set of active adjustment programs that are allocatively efficient as they can divert labour from declining to expanding opportunities. Such councils can identify places where there is a potential match between, for example, a redundant worker and an unfilled vacancy. They can also design the matching procedure that best fits the particular circumstances of that industry, whether it be retraining for a new job within the industry, assistance in job search, or retirement.

However, allocative efficiency may require reallocation *across* sectors, and since sectoral councils by definition focus on adjustment within a sector, legitimate questions can be raised about their ability to deal with adjustments across sectors. Furthermore, if displaced workers have sector-specific skills, then information is needed on how at least part of that can best be deployed in other sectors. While sector councils may know their own industry best, they may not know the needs of other industries. Obviously the extent to which this is a real as opposed to a potential problem depends upon such factors as coordination across sectoral councils, which skills are industry specific, and how councils can obtain information about other sectors.

Sector councils can enhance allocative or market efficiency by dealing with the free-rider problem that may exist with respect to training. Individual firms may be reluctant to train workers in generally usable skills that are useful to other firms in the industry for fear of losing their trained workers to other firms that may entice them away rather than train their own workers. While individual workers may have an incentive to pay for their own training in such circumstances because they will receive a higher wage, they may be inhibited from doing so because of financial constraints and because of the uncertainty of the returns from their investments given the real possibilities of job loss over which they have little control. In such circumstances, sector councils may promote generic training that is useful in that particular industry, which in turn, may enhance productivity and allocative efficiency.

This potential strength of sector councils may also belie a potential weakness. Some firms in an industry may be reluctant to pay into a common pool for industry-based training because they may lose any competitive advantage they may have on the basis of a high-performance, trained workforce. The solution is for the sector council to support generic industry-based training, leaving it up to individual firms to engage in proprietary training that can give them a competitive edge. This balancing act can be difficult to establish, however, because it is often hard to delineate generic industry-based training from proprietary firm-specific training.

Sector councils can also give rise to another set of problems in that they can lead to rent-seeking activities (Finlayson, this volume) rather than initiatives that enhance allocative efficiency by offsetting potential market failures in areas such as training. Given their political attractiveness, and their use as a vehicle for off-loading government programs, they may simply extract government funds for activities that would have occurred in any case. If the activities are not economically viable, they may still receive the tacit (albeit not financial support) from their own industry, as long as the funds are coming from elsewhere. This highlights the need for governments to evaluate the effects of sector councils, if continued financial support of any substance is forthcoming.

Distributive Equity

Distributive equity refers to the extent to which a program can deal with the issues of equity and fairness. There are two dimensions of such equity: vertical equity, or the extent to which a program distributes disproportionately to those most in need; and horizontal equity, or the extent to which people in similar circumstances are treated in a similar fashion. An equity-oriented program is also considered desirable if it distributes its benefits in a fashion that does not stigmatize the disadvantaged or destroy their self-respect.

Market mechanisms seldom pay attention to distributive equity, unless it also has an efficiency rationale. For example, providing a degree of job security can be efficient if it reduces resistance to efficient technological change or trade liberalization. Providing a degree of equality in the wage structure (even if it conflicts with principles of rewarding individual merit) may foster team production that may be efficient. In general, however, equity issues often conflict with efficiency issues, and the question simply becomes one of determining the degree of the trade-off and the price that people are willing to pay to achieve equity objectives.

In the labour adjustment area, there is no theoretical reason to believe that moving towards vertical equity would conflict with efficiency objectives. The relative measure of efficiency is *value added*, and there is no necessary reason that the value added from, say, training a low-skilled, low-wage worker is any less than the value added from training a high-skilled worker. Low-skilled workers may be on the increasing returns portion of their learning curve, albeit the characteristics that made them low-wage workers in the first place may make it difficult for them to absorb the training. Ultimately, however, the degree of conflict, if any, between equity and efficiency issues depend on circumstances. Even if there is a mild conflict, internal morale problems that could lead to inefficiencies are unlikely to arise if the benefits of an adjustment program disproportionately go to the more disadvantaged groups in the industry.

Of course, there is always a danger that any institution, be it a government, a union, or a sectoral council, can be used by the more advantaged members of society to further their own ends. This almost automatically happens with the market mechanism, but advantaged individuals can work any system to their own ends. Within a sectoral adjustment strategy, for example, they may be better informed of the options and more skilled at applying for programs and making themselves eligible for them.

With respect to horizontal equity (the equal treatment of equals), sectoral councils as an adjustment mechanism may have the problem that two otherwise identical individuals may receive very different treatment if one industry has a sectoral council and another does not, or at least not an effective one. This can be exacerbated at the industry level if the industries most in need of adjustment assistance cannot muster the resources to provide adjustment assistance. Of course, inter-industry differences exist in various dimensions of the employment relationship, such as wages, fringe benefits, working conditions, union coverage, and legislative protection. Differences in the availability of sectoral councils may be just another of these factors, albeit that may be small consolation to an individual experiencing a severe adjustment problem. Hopefully, if the councils prove successful, they will be emulated across other industries, at least in those industries where that success is also likely to work.

Administrative Efficiency

The administrative costs of delivering services can use up resources that are therefore not available as transfer payments to recipients or to provide the actual adjustment assistance such as training. Some costs, however, can enhance the ability of the program to meet its objectives – by ensuring a more efficient delivery system, by ensuring that benefits go to the target groups without spilling over into the hands of others, or by ensuring that certain equity objectives are met. Sectoral councils can save on administrative costs by having a minimum of core personnel and by tapping into the existing extensive knowledge of the industry in informal ways. By having a more grass-roots, bottom-up orientation, they are not automatically saddled with the bureaucracy that often comes with top-down decision-making.

Of course, this very strength begets a potential weakness. The effective running of an organization often requires a certain minimum of support and a degree of security of that support. Otherwise only short-run time horizons may prevail and resources may be devoted to seeking support rather than to delivering services. Cutting fat in an organizational structure is appropriate, as long as it does not get into cutting muscle and leave an emaciated structure.

Flexible, Adaptable, Reversible, and Self-sustaining

Programs are generally considered desirable if they can be flexible and adaptable to changing circumstances, and even reverse their direction or self-destruct should the needs dissipate. If the need for the program should continue, then it should become self-sufficient or at least move in that direction. There is a danger that programs can develop a bureaucratic structure that gives them a life of their own, independent of the original needs for the program. Programs can even change to serve the interests of the managers of the programs rather than the original clientele. In the extreme, program managers may manufacture the demand for their services; Say's law (supply creates its own demand) can apply in the bureaucratic arena. Sectoral councils have the potential to be very adaptable organizational structures, given their decentralized, bottoms-up orientation, and can change as the adjustment needs of their specific industry change. Furthermore, there will always be adjustment issues at the industry level and within the workplaces of the different organizations within the industry; hence, sectoral committees have no great incentive to manufacture needs to justify their existence.

With respect to ultimate self-sufficency of sector councils, there is more of a question mark. To the extent that sector councils enhance allocative or market efficiency, they should ultimately survive without government support, since the benefits of what they provide exceed the costs. In essence, the industry itself should be willing to pay, albeit coordination problems can make it difficult to devise the appropriate payment scheme, especially if there are a large number of firms in the industry. Few of the sector councils are currently self-sufficient, and some informal survey evidence[1] indicated that only two could become self-sufficient.

While the self-sufficiency of sector councils is certainly in doubt, initiatives are currently underway through Human Resource Development Canada to market and sell certain Canadian labour relations and human resource programs abroad, for example, as part of World Bank contracts.[2] Sector council strategies could certainly be part of that initiative, given the interest in them as cooperative joint labour-managment initiatives. There is some concern that we could be 'shooting ourselves in the foot' by selling our competitive edge, if it were based on such sectoral initiatives. Nevertheless, such initiatives can ultimately be imitated for free in any case. Since sector councils have been labelled a Canadian invention it may make sense to market the invention and use the return to help the councils become self-sufficient.

The adaptability of sector councils is illustrated by the Software Human Resource Council, which brokered a teaching program for its industry using a variety of institutions – a university, a CEGEP, a community college, and a private training firm.[3] Furthermore, the common curriculum is owned and hence marketable by the council. That council is also pressing for international standards, given the importance of international mobility in that industry.

Involvement of Stakeholders

In general, programs are likely to work better if they have significant stakeholder involvement in all phases, including the design and implementation aspects. As stated by one observer, 'Sector councils created *for* an industry will not last; they need to be created *by* the industry.'[4] Clearly the individuals closest to the problem are likely to know how best to craft solutions, whether the issues are associated with downside or upside adjustments. Furthermore, persons who 'take ownership of the problem' are likely to be more willing to support its implementation and to devote time and effort into ensuring its success. They are unable to blame the program's shortcomings on the fact that it was imposed from the outside. Even if the program ultimately fails, it is easier for the parties to accept and understand that failure when they have been involved in seeing its problems throughout all stages. Involving the stakeholder in all phases also means that they have had opportunities to make changes early in the process, and are not simply presented with a program that is difficult to implement because these problems were not foreseen at the design stage.

Rightly or wrongly, in many aspects of industrial relations the process becomes as important as the outcome, and being involved in the process becomes an end in itself and not simply a means to an end. Furthermore, interaction in areas of adjustment can also foster cooperation and consensus building, and this may have positive spill-over benefits to other aspects of the employment relationship. Certainly, it is likely to lead to solutions that are more workable, or at least easier to live with.

Sectoral councils are likely to score high in this dimension of stakeholder involvement. They tend to be decentralized, grass-roots, bottoms-up structures, with an emphasis on cooperative solutions. In setting standards within the industry, stakeholders can be particularly important because they obviously are most knowledgeable about the desired standards and degrees of harmonization. All stakeholders can be involved, including employers, employees and their representatives, governments, equity groups, and those who deliver education and training services. Sector councils also tend to promote joint labour-management cooperation and hence they may foster cooperation in other areas. Even if that does not ensue, at least lines of communication may be opened up.

However, being so close to the issues of their own particular sector, councils may fail to 'see the forest for the trees.' They may not see their problems in the broader context of adjustment issues that are occurring throughout the economy, and may therefore disregard solutions outside of the confines of their own industry. Certainly, as a minimum, their own responses should be coordinated with the responses of other sectors, as well as with broader economic and social issues. There is a danger that a sectoral approach could become myopic, and that lessons are not learned from the experiences of other sectors.

Political Acceptability

Programs are more likely to be successful if they have a high degree of political acceptability and hence broader community support. This will attract additional support and possibly resources. In contrast, 'going against the wind' is apt to add frustrations to a process that is sufficiently difficult without further obstacles.

Sectoral councils are likely to score high in this dimension. They involve numerous ingredients that are conducive to the current political winds: decentralized, grass-roots, solutions suited to the particular needs of each group; private sector involvement; reduced dependence upon governments for solutions; and an emphasis on cooperation and consensus-building. Furthermore, they are part of the strong current emphasis on active adjustment assistance rather than passive income maintenance.

Again, in these very strengths may be the seeds of potential problems. Governments may find sectoral committees appealing because they provide a mechanism for off-loading government responsibilities, even though they do not give up the corresponding power and resources to carry out those responsibilities. This can be especially appealing when governments are trying to reduce their budgets in various areas. Furthermore, sector councils can run into problems of political acceptability if their roles conflict with those of existing industry associations. Such employer associations are under severe budget constraints and would not welcome encroachments into their jurisdictions as representatives for the industry.

Attention to Design and Implementation Detail

Successful programs require not only appropriate visions and goals, but also proper attention to technical details of design and implementation. The expression 'the devil is in the detail' certainly applies to the design of adjustment programs, and well-meaning programs can flounder because of poor details in their design, implementation, and administration. Sectoral adjustment strategies should potentially score high in this category because the programs can be designed and implemented with the specific needs of the industry in mind. But what works for one industry or region may not work for another; sector councils may be appropriate for some industries, but not for others. Where they exist, sector councils can provide a 'one-stop-shopping' service to enable workers to access a wide range of adjustment assistance programs, customized to their particular needs.

National programs, in contrast, may be too uniform, designed for the average situation – but no-one is the average. They may also be designed more with political purposes in mind – constantly repackaging an array of existing programs with new acronyms so that political credit can be given for announcing a new initiative. Furthermore, if the array of programs is so bewildering, savings can be had because people do not know of them. While sector councils have an advantage in this regard, individual councils may not have sufficient resources to properly design and implement a successful adjustment strategy. Duplication of effort may occur, unless there is considerable information-sharing and perhaps pooling of resources to deal with common design and implementation issues.

Summary Evaluation

Sector councils overall have the potential to score high in terms of meeting many of the program evaluation criteria outlined for a successful adjustment strategy. Whether that potential has been met would require actual evaluation information that is beyond the scope of this analysis. At the risk of oversimplification, Table 1 summarizes the program evaluation criteria and highlights the main strengths and weaknesses of sector councils with respect to each of those criteria.

The greatest potential problem may be whether councils can facilitate adjustment *across* industries and overcome any tendency to have too narrow a focus. To the extent that these emerge as actual problems, however, they are amenable to correction through such mechanisms as coordination of activities and information-sharing. The extent to which self-sufficiency is a problem may emerge in the near future, when government support is likely to dissipate. As well, possible conflicts with existing industry associations may arise.

Sector councils also have clear strengths. These pertain mainly to their

TABLE 1 Summary of Strengths and Weaknesses of Sector Councils

Evaluation criteria	Strengths	Weaknesses
Target efficiency	– Can define and focus on target groups and spill-overs to others	– May miss some groups and have spill-overs to others
Allocative efficiency	– Can facilitate adjustment in the direction of market forces and reallocate from contracting to expanding subsectors – Can customize procedures – Can deal with free-rider problem within industry	– May be ineffective in reallocating across sectors, from declining to expanding ones – May provide uniform training that conflicts with objectives of some firms whose competitive advantage is in training – May focus on rent seeking
Distributive equity	– Can identify needy groups and ensure equal treatment of equals – Can negotiate equity-efficiency trade-offs	– Advantaged can control system – Similar workers in industries without councils may be bypassed
Administrative efficiency	– Can function with minimal administrative costs	– May have insufficient support to function properly
Flexible, adaptable, reversible, and self-sustaining	– Tuned to changing industry needs given decentralized grass-roots structure – Adaptable to new needs	– Self-sufficiency a concern, albeit some initiatives to generate revenues
Politically acceptable	– Have many of the characteristics that are politically in vogue	– May be used by governments to off-load responsibilities – May conflict with industry associations
Design and implementation details	– Can customize to the specific needs of each industry – Can provide one-stop service	– May have insufficient resources to design proper programs – Risk of some duplication

decentralized, nature, and their ability to involve stakeholders and customize solutions for their own industry. They can be a potential vehicle to enhance training and standards that are common to the industry, and to provide a one-stop service in a fashion that minimizes administrative costs. However, does the extent to which the apparent success of some existing councils merely reflect the initial enthusiasm and goodwill that often surrounds a new endeavour? Sustaining that enthusiasm when the honeymoon is over may be another matter, especially if government financial support dissipates.

Nevertheless, the potential strengths of sector councils makes them a viable contender to deal with the new adjustment issues that are arising in this new economic and political climate. They certainly merit additional attention to determine whether they are just another passing fad, or whether they will turn out to be a unique Canadian innovation to complement or be a substitute for other adjustment mechanisms – and perhaps even to become a Canadian export.

Notes

1 Information provided by Gérard Docquier at the Fourth Annual Sectors Conference, Montreal, 11–12 January 1996.
2 Ibid., discussion at the international activities workshop. Conference.
3 Ibid., information provided by Paul Swinwood, president of the Software Human Resource Council.
4 Ibid., statement by Lenore Burton.

PART VI
SECTOR COUNCILS, CORPORATISM, AND
INDUSTRIAL RELATIONS

12

Sector Councils and Sectoral Corporatism: Viable? Desirable?

MICHAEL M. ATKINSON and
CASSANDRA W. PERVIN

The idea that sector councils represent a new governance arrangement in the training field seems largely uncontested. Until recently the training of industrial workers has been governed principally by a combination of market and hierarchy.[1] Individual firms made their own training decisions subject to the incentives provided by government programs designed to complement or leverage private investment. In recent years a new governance arrangement has emerged, in which business and labour organizations, using public funds, are given considerable autonomy to formulate and implement training policy at either the plant or the sectoral level.

But what kind of governance arrangement is this? We will argue in this chapter that sector councils are neo-corporatist bodies whose emergence represents the replacement of market and hierarchy with networks and associations as the dominant governance mechanisms. Replacement may be too strong a word. Not only are markets and hierarchies still in evidence in the development of training policies in many industrial sectors, but sector councils may be transitory organizational forms, unable to satisfy political and economic elites or to gather support among critical constituent groups. In the second part of this chapter, drawing on interviews conducted in the spring and summer of 1995, we assess the viability of sectoral corporatism in the training field, paying particular attention to three sector councils: the Canadian Steel Trade and Employment Congress (CSTEC), the Sectoral Skills Council of the Electrical/Electronics Industry (SSC), and the Automotive Parts Sectoral Training Council (APSTC).[2]

The third part of the chapter is devoted to the issue of desirability. We ask whether sectoral corporatism, as exemplified in these sector training bodies, is a development that should be welcomed or resisted. This discussion takes us beyond efficiency concerns, or the capacity of sector training councils to contribute to labour-management relations, to a discussion of how corporatist bodies articulate with the norms of democracy. Implicit in this treatment is the view that sector councils are political creatures that must be assessed using political criteria. Our assessment leads us to conclude that on balance corporatist arrangements are supportive of democratic norms and capable of extending democratic practice beyond conventional political forums.

Are Sector Training Councils Corporatist Bodies?

For some readers, the term 'corporatism' will conjure up images of hierarchical associations, based on functional representation, which are employed by the state to generate social consensus and facilitate political control. The corporatist regimes of Italy and Portugal during the interwar period represent the classic cases. However, it is not this authoritarian version of corporatism, with its roots in Catholicism and nationalism, that is being discussed here. Neo-corporatism, the focus of this chapter, represents an extrapolation of the general model of corporatism, but without its conspicuously illiberal, non-voluntary, character. The principal goal of neo-corporatism is to organize and orchestrate the productive forces in the economy such that the particularistic demands of what have come to be called special interests are subject to a strong measure of negotiation and bargaining. The intended result is a high level of consent for authoritative decisions. The principal instruments of corporatism are private, usually voluntary, interest associations which act as partners of the state in both the formulation and implementation of public policy (Schmitter, 1982).

This policy focus, and the emphasis on associational bargaining, distinguishes neo-corporatism from its earlier incarnation as a system societal organization, but it does nothing to distinguish it from other forms of interest intermediation, particularly pressure pluralism. In fact, the literature on neo-corporatism (which we will refer to as 'corporatism' at this point) has developed under the sceptical eye of those who see the interpenetration of the state and organized interests (central to the corporatist model) as nothing more than a version of pluralism (Jordan, 1981). Pluralism, with its emphasis on a myriad of groups in society, overlapping memberships, potential groups, countervailing power and, yes, bargaining among different societal groupings, certainly seems to share some of the features of corporatist intermediation. Could it be just one more denomination in the pluralist church (Williamson, 1985: 138)?

Corporatist theorists have responded in the negative, employing a structural definition of corporatism intended to delineate it clearly from other forms of interest intermediation (Schmitter, 1974). In the context of policy-making, this structural definition has emphasized three elements: peak or centralized associations which enjoy something resembling a representational monopoly of critical interests; linkages between the state and these interest associations which yield the latter recognition by, and privileged access to, the state; and the social partnership of business and labour in the formulation and implementation of public policy (often in tripartite forums) in exchange for ensuring the control and compliance of association members (adapted from Lehmbruch, 1984: 61).

We will use this structural definition as the starting point in a discussion of training councils, but it must be acknowledged that definitional debates continue to plague corporatist theorizing and that structural definitions only carry us so far. At bottom, corporatism is a means of exerting political control over social and economic processes by channelling and mediating conflict. The question of how this control is exercised and for whose benefit is not something with which a structural checklist can adequately cope. Structure should tell us whether this is, in fact, a species of corporatism that we have here, but we will not solve, by definition, questions of political power.

The structural checklists proposed by corporatist theorists are typically aimed at the macro-political level, where the usual subjects of negotiations are wages and prices and the participants are peak associations of business and labour organized on a national basis (Katzenstein, 1984: 26–30). Thus, incomes policy emerged early as the quintessential topic of corporatist theorizing, and whole systems were evaluated on the degree to which they engaged in national bargaining over wage and price issues (Scharpf, 1991). The idea that corporatism might exist at the sub-system or sectoral level developed more slowly as researchers became increasingly aware of the rather imposing organizational prerequisites of corporatism on the national scale (Held, 1987: 218). It seemed that at the meso level, fractions of business and labour, not simply 'business' and 'labour' writ large, could be readily organized into corporatist policy networks without disturbing national political institutions organized on a territorial basis (Cawson, 1985).

At the meso or sectoral level (we use these terms interchangeably), the purpose of corporatism remains the same as at the macro level – to mediate political differences and achieve consensus among major producer groups on economic goals (Atkinson and Coleman, 1985: 27) – but the focus of negotiation is much narrower and its visibility much reduced. Meso-level corporatism involves the 'fusion of the processes of interest representation, decision-making and policy implementation with respect to a more restrictive range of issues than the "system-steering" concerns of macro-corporatism' (Cawson, 1985:11). A more restricted range of goals enhances the chances of agreeing on an agenda and making concrete progress on its items. As well as being more narrowly focused, sectoral corporatism 'tends to be much more stable because of the greater degree of convergence of the interests involved' (Lehmbruch, 1984: 63).

Definitionally speaking, the structural requirements of meso-corporatism are also less imposing. Whereas macro-corporatism requires peak associations – that is, associations of associations – at the level of industrial sectors only a single association or union may exist. Meso-corporatism requires, instead, that associations organize most of the industry. As Alan Cawson points out, this is not 'the same degree of associational capacity on a class basis that is a prerequisite for macro-corporatism' (1985: 14). Arrangements at the sectoral level between the state and organized interests are likely to be more informal than at the macro level, and to arise from a shared common interest in seeking state assistance in response to a sector-specific issue. Sectors characterized by 'traditional industries particularly if they are major employers, industries facing serious foreign competition, and new industries held to be of strategic economic importance are also likely candidates for intervention and meso-arrangements' (Williamson, 1989: 162). And while macro-corporatism is sometimes equated with tripartism, at the meso level the interests involved are not always business and labour: meso-corporatism includes cooperation among fractions of business for the planning of sectoral development (Cawson, 1986: 76; Atkinson and Coleman, 1989b).

While movement to the sectoral level has been accompanied by an increasing elasticity in definitional requirements, it has not meant their abandonment. Note, in particular, that one of the distinguishing features of corporatism is its reliance on the state to establish boundaries (including the definition of sectors), identify the participants in policy dialogues, establish representational requirements, and delegate responsibility to corporatist bodies. The state may be a silent partner, but it is a partner, complete with bureaucratic interests. The result of the partnership, if it is successful, is a level of effective policy implementation that is typically absent from pluralist arrangements.

Once again stressing structure, we will define meso-corporatism as a policy network in which the state recognizes the principle of equality in the representation of partners in the network and the partners agree to respect this equality principle; in which business and labour organizations that participate are relatively centralized, enjoy a monopoly in interest representation, and exert a measure of control over their members; and in which the involvement of social partners in the policy process is characterized by a large element of participation, not simply advocacy. Do the sector councils qualify as meso-corporatist policy networks using these criteria? Let's consider our three cases.

All three of the sector councils we have studied are organized according to the principal of equal representation of interests. In the case of CSTEC and the SSC, business and labour representatives have equal representation at the national level, as well as on subcommittees and workplace training committees.

The only position which is not equally shared is that of the executive director, an appointment based on business/labour collaboration. In the case of APSTC, the council and committees all involved equal representation of business and labour. In addition, the executive director position was also shared: one representative from the CAW and another from the Automobile Parts Manufacturers' Association (APMA) were co-directors.

The meso-corporatist model expects each council to rest on a firm associational base, where the associations organize most of the sector and participate openly and formally in decision-making. Of the three councils we examined, only one, APSTC, is founded on the open participation of two organizations, one representing business (the Automobile Parts Manufacturers' Association) and one representing labour (the Canadian Auto Workers). The SSC and CSTEC have both business and labour representation, but not in the form of single representative associations. CSTEC's labour representation is orchestrated by the United Steel Workers, but business representation is achieved by the direct participation of a large number of steel-producing companies, including Algoma Steel, Ivaco, Sidebec-Dosco, Dofasco, and Stelco. The industry association, the Canadian Steel Producers Association, does not organize the industry for these purposes and has no role in the sector council.

The opposite applies in the case of SSC. Here the council has enjoyed, and almost certainly has required, the active support of the industry's business association, the Electrical and Electronics Manufacturers' Association of Canada (EEMAC). Labour, by contrast, is not organized by a single union, and much of the industry operates without unionized sites. Unions involved in the SSC include: the Communication, Energy and Paperworkers Union (CEP), the Canadian Auto Workers (CAW), the International Brotherhood of Electrical Workers (IBEW), the United Steel Workers of America (USWA), the International Association of Machinists and Aerospace Workers (IAM), the International Federation of Professional and Technical Employees (IFPTE), the United Electrical, Radio and Machine Workers of Canada, and the Laborer's International Union (LIU).

The absence of singular representative bodies underpinning these sector councils clearly challenges the claim that sector councils conform to the definitional requirements of meso-corporatism. To the extent that councils exist and operate independently of direct associational involvement, it seems difficult to argue that the sector is mobilized behind policy created in the councils. Ironically, however, of the three councils we have examined, the one that has had the most difficulty securing cooperation and compliance of its members for sector council policy is APSTC, where the representational requirements have been met most thoroughly. Both CSTEC and SSC enjoy considerable support for the training initiatives taken to this point. In the case of CSTEC, the cooperation and direct participation of the industry's largest producers has substituted for associational involvement; in SSC's case, the plant-based organization of training programs has neatly circumvented the requirement for industry-spanning associational bargaining. Both cases illustrate the point made earlier, that structural definitions of corporatism miss process and power issues. In the cases outlined here, the sector is mobilized in unconventional ways, but it is mobilized behind the principles of policy collaboration, the third structural criterion.

In pluralist writings, interest groups are most often depicted as supplicants, lobbyists, and information suppliers to decision makers. There may be occasions when the state turns over policy implementation to administratively capable groups (Lowi, 1979), but not to mediate class interests or to plan the future of the sector. Meso-corporatist arrangements envisage a qualitatively different role for associations or, more precisely, for the corporatist bodies these associations create. Policy advocacy gives way to policy participation, a process Coleman describes in terms of '(1) formulation of the guiding principles or general rules of the policy; (2) formulation of the actual text of a law or directive; and/ or (3) formulation of the operationalization of the general rules and legal text' (1968: 50ff). Similarly, implementation involves active control, supervision, and sanctioning of those bodies or individuals charged with applying the policy.

All three of the councils we have examined were established to participate in policy-making in the sense suggested above. The state would provide a part of the necessary funding and much of the infrastructure necessary to identify potential participants in training efforts, but would not actively direct the training enterprise. All three councils were expected to design training programs that would meet each industry's specific needs. Training could be supplied in a host of different ways – through colleges or a myriad of private trainers – but the objectives and standards were to be established within the context of the council. Once again, it is somewhat ironic that the council that best satisfies the other structural criteria for meso-corporatism, APSTC, has had the most difficulty achieving these goals. In the case of CSTEC and the SSC, policy is formulated at the national level and implemented at the plant level through joint workplace training committees. At APSTC, policy was formulated and implemented by the national council only; plant level involvement was nonexistent. Although APSTC members did play a role in the formulation of policy, implementation was another matter. Relatively few workers were ever exposed to the training opportunities provided, and APSTC never secured the commitment of its members to allow workers to meet the training levels it established.

Clearly these sector councils meet some of the structural criteria for meso-corporatism much better than others. The absence of strong, policy-capable, business associations in one case, and strong, singular unions in another, raises doubts about how well these councils conform to corporatist criteria. Moreover, other, newer sector councils have also experienced difficulties meeting one or more of our criteria. For instance, the requirement of representational equity has proven very difficult to meet in sectors without organized labour. It would be inappropriate, and ill-advised, to generalize from a few councils to the entire population.

That said, the most successful (at least in terms of longevity) of the councils have found their way around these difficulties and have established and maintained a sufficiently secure status that both federal and provincial governments are entirely content to treat them as if they speak for the industry. This recognition depends in large measure on a willingness to accept the equality criterion. The question now is: Can meso-corporatist bodies, even ones that are structural mutants, survive in a distinctly unsympathetic political environment?

Viability of Sector Training Councils

Canada has had no shortage of corporatist political thought. From Mackenzie King's musings about labour and business cooperation in *Industry and Humanity*, to the group government notions of the United Farmers movement, through the Catholic-inspired corporatism of the Union Nationale, to the Trudeau government's *Agenda for Cooperation*, Canadian politicians have toyed with corporatist political projects. While some of these ideas might be described as home grown, rooted somehow in Canada's tory or feudal past, since the 1970s the impetus for corporatism has come mostly from abroad, especially from those countries that appear to have transcended the class antagonisms of modern capitalism by establishing joint business and labour planning bodies. Indicative of the borrowing and shaping of corporatist ideas is the pattern of systematic economic summitry adopted by the Parti Québécois in the 1976–85 period and its current program, which is strongly influenced by Scandinavian-style social corporatism.

Whether locally produced or imported, corporatism has not enjoyed much practical success in Canada (with the exception of some sectors of agriculture). The translation of corporatist ideas into corporatist bodies and then into creative political cooperation has proven enormously difficult. There are several explanations for this failure, only three of which need be mentioned here. First, there is the whole question of the match between corporatist ideas and the problems they are intended to address. Corporatist thought is premised on the possibility and desirability of class compromise. The assumption is that corporatist bodies, consisting of labour and business representatives, will somehow be able to overcome the class antagonisms generated by capitalism and usher in a new era of peace and planning. Exactly how corporatist structures can actually accomplish this feat is unclear. In reviewing Canadian proponents of corporatist solutions, Panitch observes that '[T]hey all suffer from the failure to explain how the antagonism and conflict that they observe in reality will actually come to be resolved voluntarily without a fundamental change in the social structure that the theories themselves see as the cause of conflict,' (1977: 56). Business and labour, in this reading, may have prudential reasons for cooperation, but cooperation does not resolve fundamental antagonisms, and those who propose corporatist solutions in the hope that it will are deluding themselves.

Second, there is the argument that neither business nor labour in Canada is adequately organized to participate in corporatist forums. The level of unionization is too low to sustain labour's position in policy disputes and labour's central organization, the Canadian Labour Congress, is not empowered to engage in collective bargaining on behalf of labour as a whole. Business is likewise decentralized in terms of its political organization (Coleman, 1988: ch. 5) and possessed of a firm-centred culture that abhors any collaboration that might impinge on managerial prerogatives (Atkinson and Coleman, 1989b: ch. 2). As a result, major areas of public policy that are subject to nation-wide bargaining in other systems – pensions, day care, supplementary health benefits – in Canada are either mandated by the state, imposed by individual firms, or subject to political processes quite different from the creative, state-sponsored cooperation that corporatists espouse (Haddow, 1994: 209).

Finally, there is the added complication of Canadian political institutions, both parliamentary and federal. These institutions are organized using majoritarian and unanimity decision rules, neither of which, in the Canadian case, have been especially conducive to successful cooperation. Temporary majorities at both levels engage in prolonged political conflict, both with one another and with institutionalized oppositions. Where conflictual strategies are privileged, cooperative outcomes are rare. In the case of training policy in particular, a fragmented state in which two orders of government have been engaged in a prolonged jurisdictional dispute has done nothing to facilitate corporatist collaboration. Corporatism places a large premium on stability and the orderly conduct of negotiations. There is nothing orderly, or predictable, about the evolution of Canadian federalism and no reason for the parties to corporatist discussions to believe that agreements will be honoured and that governments will sustain their commitment to corporatist forums.[3]

Under these circumstances, viable corporatist bodies will be those that are able to evolve and sustain themselves without continuous financial support and bureaucratic coddling by the state. If the viability of sector councils were to rest entirely on Canada's capacity to sustain macro-corporatist bodies, then their prospects would be bleak. But, as we have already suggested in the previous section, the political requirements for macro-corporatism are not identical to, nor as imposing as, those for meso-corporatism. Moreover, meso-corporatist entities do not presume or require the presence of macro-corporatism. So, what do they require? We will argue that the viability of sectoral corporatism depends on four conditions: the nature of the policy at issue; the structure of conflict in the sector; the role of the state in the origins of these bodies; and the scope of the corporatist contract. Once again, we consider the three sector councils discussed earlier in light of these conditions.

Issue Content

Corporatism is more viable if it is attempted in areas where there are large potential gains to cooperation, and these gains do not require substantial concessions by either side. Training, particularly employed-based training, qualifies as an issue that is quite conducive to cooperative strategies. In the first place, no one seems to dispute the size of the potential gains from cooperation. Workers benefit because they get training which will improve their chances of job security, employers benefit from well-trained workers, and the state benefits, if nothing else, from the positive externalities associated with an educated workforce. By extension, the costs of failure to cooperate on training initiatives are high and immediate, especially if the sectors involved are subject to significant international competition. To the extent that other policy instruments, such as trade barriers or regulatory requirements, are unavailable to shield the sector, investment in training takes on an added attraction.

But cooperation cannot come at too high a price. Paul Quirk (1989: 913) has argued that as long as parties to a cooperative solution are able to achieve their goals through compromise or trade-offs, then the prospects for cooperation remain high. Once they are obliged to engage in compensation, where an agreement depends on concessions on unrelated matters, or reorientation, where original positions must be abandoned entirely, then cooperative outcomes are much less likely. In the three councils we examined, compromise in particular, and trade-offs on occasion, were the means chosen to effect agreements. The mandate of the councils – to focus on training issues only – avoids the possibility of compensation strategies, and any reorientation that has occurred within the councils has been a joint product of negotiation, not the subject of imposition by one side.

The Structure of the Conflict

Corporatism works best when the social partners are not themselves divided, in this case when business and labour both come to the table relatively united. Most of the literature on the structural conditions for corporatism implicitly endorses the view that a proliferation of voices and positions is anathema to agreement. In all three councils examined, those interviewed affirmed that business and labour normally demonstrate a high level of agreement during council meetings but that difficulties often arise *within* the business and labour sides. Business must determine how much training is proprietary and what types of training can be openly discussed with representatives from other companies. On the labour side, different unions (and sometimes no union at all) can produce different strategies and different agendas. These kinds of internal divisions are what prompt calls for a 'highly mobilized business community,' or centralized labour representation, which may, in turn require high levels of industrial concentration or low levels of foreign ownership (Atkinson and Coleman, 1989a: 54).

In the cases we examined, a high level of industrial concentration in the steel sector and the presence of a single, strong union almost certainly facilitated the initial sectoral initiative. In the case of the electrical and electronics industry, the proliferation of firms and the absence of a single union meant that for cooperation to work, training programs had to be developed for the plant level. A grass-roots structure, in which workplaces in effect volunteer for participation in training programs, has removed the necessity for industry-wide agreement on every initiative.

In the automobile parts sector, the structure of conflict has not been conducive to cooperation. In the first place, a high level of foreign ownership in the sector meant that any sector council would be confronted with the problem of providing training funds to foreign-owned firms. Although the workers in these firms are Canadians who pay Canadian taxes and hence have a legitimate claim to publicly funded training, the council decided to limit membership to Canadian-owned firms. As a result of this decision, the Automobile Parts Manufacturers' Association, which represents the entire industry, was seriously weakened as a partner.

Moreover, neither the association nor the CAW appeared particularly committed to defining training issues in terms that transcended traditional political cleavages. The CAW insisted on management's responsibility to train its workforce and treated sector councils as an extension of the traditional, adversarial, collective bargaining process extended to the realm of training. The only difference, from the union's point of view, was that instead of bargaining at the plant or firm level, labour now bargains at the sectoral level. For its part, business was unwilling to commit to a cooperative approach to training beyond very basic requirements. It was never entirely clear that firms in the automotive parts sector could be persuaded that corporatist arrangements would be sustained. If their interests could be served more effectively by waiting out the NDP's mandate, rather than negotiating trade-offs on training policy with social partners, then there was no particular point in investing heavily in a new structure. Symbolic motivations played a large role here, with both parties intent upon defining training questions in traditional left-right terms, a penchant that makes cooperation highly unlikely (Quirk, 1989: 915).

The Role of the State

Sectoral corporatism is more viable if it rests on a perceived need to cooperate rather than on state-imposed collaboration. The state will always play a role in sponsoring corporatist bodies and judging their effectiveness, but if a council has been created as a result of challenges to the growth of the sector – technological advances, increased competition from foreign companies, or globalization of the means of production – the likelihood that business and labour will prolong their partnership if financial support is withdrawn is greater than if the initiative was entirely state-directed. Crises that affect the very livelihood of an industry are particularly conducive to the creation of meso-corporatist structures (Williamson, 1989: 162). And these structures can emerge unconsciously – that is, without a blueprint or a promise of state support. In contrast, where business and labour are urged by the state to join the council, and do so principally to receive training at a lower cost, the likelihood of persistence in the absence of financial support is much less. In short, motivation matters and the less the state has to do with supplying that motivation, the greater the prospects for viability.

The steel industry's sector council began with virtually no prompting from the state. In 1985, following an industry conference that brought business and labour together to discuss trade issues, the steel-producing companies and the USWA approached the federal government for the funding of downside adjustment programs in anticipation of a steep decline in the number of workers employed in the steel industry. Thus the impetus for CSTEC was a serious industry problem, diagnosed at the sectoral level, and resulting in a coordinated response by both business and labour. The financial assistance of the state was vital in the early stages, but since 1992, when CSTEC turned to upside adjustment issues, it has become increasingly clear that business is willing to fund the program even in the absence of federal support. Although funding arrangements for the council stipulate a 50:50 split between government and industry contributions, in actual practice business contributions have been much larger, in the order of four dollars for every one dollar of federal funds.

In the case of SSC, the council was created following a human resources study conducted by Employment and Immigration Canada. In 1987 business, represented by EEMAC, and labour, represented by the IBEW and CWC, met to discuss the results of this study and concluded that the industry suffered from a skills deficit. Spurred by the report's conclusions, representatives of the industry approached the federal and provincial governments to assist the industry in forming a council to address the training needs of the sector. The result was the establishment of a joint labour and business training council on 11 July 1990. As in the case of CSTEC, business and labour cooperated in the creation of the sector council and were partnered by choice from its inception.

APSTC was a state-driven initiative from the outset. Emboldened by the initial success of CSTEC and SSC, the federal government, or more precisely Human Resources Development Canada (HRDC), approached representatives from the automotive parts manufacturing sector to establish a sector council that would assist in the skills upgrading of the sector's workers. Indicative of the fact that this was a state initiative, it took business and labour almost a year to establish the centrepiece of the council's programming, the auto parts certificate. Carol Haddad's survey of APSTC members suggests that concerns over this program did not diminish as time went on (Haddad, this volume). Design questions aside, it seems clear that the CAW's preference for a program that emphasized generic skills intended to enhance the job security of its members did not match the motivation of business participants who were more interested in programs devoted to improving worker productivity. Businesses responded with an unwillingness to commit their workers to the second phase of the certificate. Clearly, the lack of business and labour buy-in from the inception of the councils led not only to continuous conflict between the partners, but also to the lack of genuine commitment in terms of formulating and implementing policy.

Scope of the Corporatist Contract

The term 'corporatist contract' refers to the subjects of negotiation between the social partners; 'scope' refers to the range and variety of those subjects covered by negotiation. The broader the scope of subjects, and the greater the opportunity to participate in decisions regarding them, the more viable sectoral corporatism will be. Training that is focused on a single set of skills, delivered to a narrow band of workers, and limited in terms of time horizons, has a narrow scope. Evaluating scope involves an assessment of who is trained, how they are trained, where they are trained, and for what purposes. Such an assessment would take us far beyond the purposes of this paper, but it is useful to point out, in the context of the councils we have been examining, that some agreements contemplate a much broader array of training opportunities than others. Moreover, some councils are willing to move the training issue onto the plant floor where participation in decision-making about the content and appropriateness of the training provided is no longer limited to elites.

APSTC drew up a relatively narrow corporatist contract. It provided the sector with only two levels of training programs. Initial plans to provide three levels were shelved when business made it clear it was reluctant to take workers off of the line for that much (or that type of) training. APSTC was never involved in apprenticeship initiatives, the development of standards for the industry, or other kinds of activities that complement and reinforce the training enterprise. CSTEC and SSC, on the other hand, offer a broad spectrum of programs that cover everything from basic skills training to advanced college and university credits. Furthermore, both CSTEC and SSC offer programs geared not only to the skills of workers in the sector, but also to the educational needs of the industry as a whole. These initiatives include negotiations with colleges and universities to develop curriculum that meets the expectations of employers and, in CSTEC's case, broader adult education initiatives (Prior Learning Recognition), in SSC's case the development of industry standards.

Participation in the corporatist contract refers to the extent to which all levels of the industry participate. Although APSTC had the advantage of two peak associations represented on council, their ability to achieve genuine participation at any level was very limited. APSTC did not have a high level of firm/workplace participation. Business and labour were loosely involved in the umbrella council with some participation on subcouncils, but APSTC did not offer plant-level participation. This created a real difficulty for the council in terms of getting business and labour to push workers through the Level I and II training programs.

CSTEC and the SSC have been much more successful in establishing and working with workplace committees. All of CSTEC's training activities are administered and coordinated through joint labour-management training committees (JTCs) co-chaired by business and labour representatives. Every member work site has a JTC responsible for the allocation of training funds, needs assessments, training plan formulation, program evaluation, and budgeting. The involvement of employers and employees from the plant level increases understanding of the types of programs the sector needs and contributes to an atmosphere of continuous innovation based on the board, the committees, and the JTC's increasing level of experience.

The core of the SSC is their joint workplace training committees (JWTCs). Each JWTC develops a specific corporate training plan and a JWTC must be in place at a workplace before it can begin to receive funding from the council through the training trust fund. The JWTC's role is to assess the training needs of the work site and identify gaps, to create training programs and establish priorities among them, and to recruit participants, deliver training programs, and administer the training resources. Each site that joins the SSC creates a JWTC. If a plant is unionized, the structure of the JWTC is equal management and union representation; in sites where the company is not unionized, employees are recruited to represent labour on the committee.[4] The key to the success of the JWTCs has been their ability to enable workplaces in the industry to 'access government subsidized training funds, while at the same time, offering them an opportunity to shape their training programs jointly with their workers' (Wolfe and Martin, this volume).

We have argued in this section that whether or not the cultural and institutional landscape of Canadian politics is hostile to corporatism, at the meso or sectoral level it is possible to develop corporatist initiatives with a relatively narrow set of objectives, thus avoiding the need to establish a class compromise on such highly disputatious issues as incomes and prices. The success of sector councils depends less on macro constraints, and much more on the characteristics of the sector and the nature of the policy problem. In that regard, the progress made by some sector councils should encourage others to believe that sectoral corporatism is indeed viable.

Should Sectoral Corporatism Be Encouraged?

Sectoral corporatism may be viable, but is it desirable? There are two types of arguments in favour, or against, corporatism: functional and normative. Functional arguments focus on the contribution that corporatist arrangements make to the solution of public policy problems, frequently cast in terms of the performance of the economy: Can corporatism improve competition? Does it produce demonstrable efficiency gains? Normative arguments stress the contribution that corporatism can make to the realization of political values, frequently those associated with democracy. For example, do corporatist arrangements increase political equality? Do they enhance accountability? As Claus Offe has pointed out, critics tend to be more favourably disposed to corporatism on functional grounds, less favourably disposed on normative grounds (1955: 119). Is this fair?

Functional Arguments

Estimating the net contribution of sector councils to productivity is a highly speculative business, but it is certainly possible to argue that sector councils represent an improvement, in functional terms, over bureaucratic solutions to training problems. It was a growing dissatisfaction with the hierarchical approach that led to sector councils in the first place. It has been argued, for example, that the federal government's practice of purchasing seats in community colleges provides training that is attuned to the political needs of government but disconnected from the labour market and the training needs of workers (Haddow, 1995: 342–3). If training dollars are directed by councils of workers and business, then the state has an additional opportunity to reduce its own bureaucracy while capitalizing on the expertise of those close to the problem. And because the training provided emerges from negotiation, not state direction, there is some prima facie reason to believe that agreements will be better enforced. Workers are more likely to receive the training that has been contracted for if the contractors are constantly monitoring its delivery.

Still, these arguments remain in the realm of principle. No comparative studies have been done on the productivity gains of moving from pluralist to corporatist arrangements in the training field. For one thing, there are simply too many confounding, and usually unmeasured, variables that bear on success. For example, the advent of sector councils in Canada is coincident with a change in the goals of public policy. The main task of sector councils is to train those who are already employed.[5] This is a far narrower policy objective than the training of the entire workforce, plus those who have yet to enter it. And frankly, it is a far easier one. Not only can programs be focused on those who already have the minimum skills to function in the labour market, but they can be linked to investment decisions of firms. Whether the shift in policy goals predates the growth of the sector council idea or the other way around, we should be aware that comparing sectoral corporatism, on the one hand, to state direction or pressure pluralism, on the other, is not altogether fair if the former is directed at a more tractable problem than the latter.

Where corporatism has been compared to other policy networks it has been at the macro level and in terms of its contribution to economic growth, low levels of inflation, and low levels of unemployment. Here the results are often favourable, with corporatist systems exhibiting higher levels of growth and a more favourable trade-off between inflation and unemployment. Defenders of corporatism argue that as long as the participants in these arrangements are large, encompassing groups, they have fewer incentives to free ride on the sacrifices of others and hence are more likely to make short-term sacrifices that contribute to the public good. Reductions in transaction costs, including costs of information gathering and enforcement, lead to overall efficiency gains. At least this is the theory. The fact is that comparing large systems and large processes is risky. While regression models suggest that countries that have embraced corporatist arrangements typically fair better on a conventional set of economic indices, there are large residuals and many unmeasured variables (eg., Alvarez et al., 1991). Moreover, while it is tempting to appropriate to the meso level gains that appear to have been made at the macro level, it would seem wise to await more definitive empirical results before drawing too firm conclusions.

Normative Arguments

In the literature on group politics, normative arguments against corporatism far outweigh normative arguments in favour. The most compelling arguments against corporatism have their roots in the fear of faction. Factions, it is assumed, will employ their resources in a single-minded pursuit of self-interest. In benign versions of this tendency, a political invisible hand aggregates this competitive behaviour and produces outcomes that are policy optimal. But it is far more likely that factions motivated by self-interest will forgo opportunities for cooperation and mutual gain, or will combine with other factions to impose losses on third parties. It is this latter fear that grips critics of corporatism. After all, corporatist arrangements are exclusionary by definition: that is what makes them attractive in terms of policy resolution. Intense interests, like business and labour, are included, but diffuse interests – consumers or taxpayers – are left out. The temptation for the former to impose self-regarding solutions on the latter would seem to be awfully strong.

Notice, however, that a willingness to exploit collaboration to the disadvantage of others presumes a competitive strategy. In this scenario, the factional parties conspire, they do not compromise, trade-off, or redefine their goals. Do corporatist arrangements inevitably produce conspiracy? In the case of training policy, one might argue that corporatism will help generate a conspiracy in which labour and business induce an overinvestment in training, or an investment in a type of training that suits their narrow interests but not the needs of a broader society. How realistic are these fears? Much depends on the ability and willingness of state officials to identify a range of acceptable outcomes (Cohen and Rogers, 1995: 72). Corporatist arrangements, it must be remembered, imply that the state sets the broad rules of the game and monitors the ensuing agreements. So, for example, the government's requirement that training dollars spent by sector councils be devoted to generic, not firm-specific, skills, decreases the capacity of business and labour to invest in short-term, proprietary training at the expense of mobile skills. And while it is the taxpayer, and not the consumer, who is most vulnerable to collusion, the state does hold the purse strings and hence the capacity to set an upward bound on expenditures. Corporatist arrangements are not licences to impose solutions.

Beyond the immediate fears of factional collusion lies the more general concern that corporatist bodies will undermine the traditional institutions of popular sovereignty, namely political parties, elections, and legislatures. These institutions are constructed around the ideal of an autonomous and equal citizenry whose preferences are aggregated on a territorial basis and whose public policy is debated in deliberative assemblies. Of course, these institutions also make room for elite politics, privileged access, and command-oriented bureaucracies, but this does not gainsay the fact that they are rooted in the will of the people. It is much more difficult to make the same claim for corporatism, especially at the meso level where it is typically separated from party politics and therefore from any direct connection to the outcomes of electoral struggle. Meso-corporatist arrangements, because they feature functional, not territorial representation, offer a distribution of benefits that cannot be easily disaggregated on territorial grounds or used to advance the interests or policy agendas of women and minority groups.

But we must be realistic about this argument. In the first place, apart from macro-economic policy, and incomes policy in particular, there have been very few areas of public policy subject to corporatist-style bargaining (Held, 1987: 218), even in countries with an apparent penchant for this form of representation. And where corporatist arrangements do exist, in the training area for example, it can hardly be argued that they have deprived parliamentarians of the opportunity to debate or even decide on the direction of public policy. The state bureaucracies charged with overseeing training policy retain the right to shift responsibilities from one government to the next, set the rules for the allocation of training dollars, and establish overall training budgets. And while there has been little inclination to do so to this point, it is not inconceivable that the state will require sector councils to reflect a broader range of interests than just business and labour, especially if training becomes a central feature of social welfare policy.

There is another reason to doubt that corporatism will ultimately undermine popular sovereignty. Simply because corporatist arrangements rest on the vitality of interest associations does not mean they are at odds with democratic politics. Far from abhorring associative action, modern democracies thrive on it, if only because it is by joining together that citizens can form and express opinions. As Offe puts it, 'People have "voice" only to the extent that they merge their political resources into associative action' (1995: 121). Of course, corporatism implies much more than voice. Corporatist entities, as we have already seen, are distinguished by their responsibility for the implementation of public policy and for ensuring conformity on the part of group members. But this kind of delegation of responsibility exists outside of corporatism, in clientele pluralist arrangements where state bureaucracies entrust program administration to private associations. Groups endowed with this authority are more powerful than their counterparts who merely lobby, but they are not necessarily corporatist.[6] Corporatism presumes the capacity to engage in multipartite negotiation devoted to mediating economic interests and planning the development of a sector. In short, we should not consider the incorporation of groups into the policy process as either an aberration in democratic politics, or as the hallmark of corporatism.

Let us turn, in conclusion, to normative arguments favourable to corporatism. These arguments suggest that, far from detracting from the practice of democratic politics, corporatist arrangements actually contribute to it. This is not an easy argument to make given that, as we have already seen, the viability of corporatism depends in some measure on preserving the elitist character of its internal bargaining processes. In the context of democratic theory, elitism is normally tolerated, not celebrated. But elitism itself need not be judged undesirable; the real issue is the basis on which, or the rules under which, elites interact.

On this score, it is argued that corporatism helps reset the political balance by providing for an equal representation of key interests on decision-making counsels. If investments in training were treated as the sole prerogative of business, rather than being subject to negotiation in forums premised on equal representation, then it seems clear that the preservation of power inequities would be virtually guaranteed. To the degree that democratic processes are premised on political equality, corporatism advances democracy by requiring that the contest for power take place under conditions that redress existing imbalances (Mansbridge, 1995: 135). Redress them perfectly? No. Corporatist arrangements merely bring the contest for power under public control, that is under the auspices and monitoring of the state. This itself is a guarantee of nothing. What is required is a state capable of articulating interests that are separate from those of the parties to corporatist forums. These state interests must include a strong predisposition towards political equality as a good in itself. The idea that the state's authority must have a moral basis has always been central to corporatist thought (Williamson, 1985: 194 and passim). To the extent that this moral basis favours democratic norms, including, but not limited to, political equality, then corporatism can be associated with the advance of democracy.

It might be argued that this advance will inevitably be limited because corporatist arrangements invariably focus on the major economic cleavages in society, ignoring other aspects of political identity and leaving weaker, more diffused interests without an invitation to the corporatist party. Here too the state is in a position to respond (albeit somewhat imperfectly). As long as the state exists separate from, and superior to, corporatist bodies, then it can bestow (or withhold) a semi-public, authorized status on those interest associations drawn into corporatist forums. Philippe Schmitter has suggested that such associations be granted a charter and with it a coveted status, such as 'exclusive bargaining agent' (1995: 174). In return for the privileges of policy participation that such a status would bring, the state can insist on a measure of internal democracy and a 'fact-regarding, other-regarding, future-regarding attitude.' Nothing of the sort has been tried with sector councils, perhaps because their legitimacy has yet to be challenged. If and when that happens, it may be necessary and advantageous to arrange an open debate about the criteria for public status and about which interests deserve to be included in the construction of corporatist bargaining forums.

The second normative argument in favour of sectoral corporatism concerns what happens in these forums. Allies of corporatism argue that when opposing interests deliberately organize to confront a policy problem, they begin the process of educating one another, that is, producing information that generates innovation and ultimately changes preferences. It is the latter step that is considered crucial (Mansbridge, 1995: 137–43). Groups can be counted on to produce information and their interaction will often generate innovations. It is information and innovation that often resolve collective bargaining impasses. But changing preferences requires changing not only the rules of the game, but the game itself. Familiar, non-cooperative games, such as Prisoner's Dilemma and Chicken, are replaced by a cooperative game, sometimes called Battle of the Sexes, in which the parties are not only intent upon securing their own interest, but in helping their adversaries secure theirs (Scharpf, 1989).

Fritz Scharpf argues that this shift is accompanied by a change in policy-making style whereby 'bargaining' is replaced by 'problem solving.' Jane Mansbridge characterizes the new process as negotiation and observes that: 'in negotiation, the parties involved not only manoeuvre for advantageous positions but try to understand what the other really wants' (1985: 140–1). This is not the negotiation with which most labour-management observers are familiar, but one in which group leaders are transformed from agents of individual interests to instruments of collective identify formation (Streeck and Schmitter, 1984:16). Paradoxically, the capacity to form such an identity seems to require, at least initially, genuine respect for differences. It is only then that a new identity, that of the corporatist body itself, can emerge, complete with interests that may be at variance with those of any one of its constituent groups.

While evidence of preference transformation is hard to come by in the sector councils, we have seldom constructed research designs with the intention of finding it. Easier to observe (but not necessarily document) is the change in culture that sector councils have produced. They have established rules for the funding of projects which in turn have fostered a sense of industry-wide training standards. Their mere existence represents a clear alternative to the strategy of deliberate underinvestment in training by individual firms or the strategy of insisting that training is the responsibility solely of employers. Corporatist arrangements nourish a culture of obligation to the point that elites involved in these entities can sometimes be accused of what Kalt and Zupan (1984) call 'ideological shirking,' that is, using the time and effort paid for by groups to promote the public rather than group's interest. We know of no such accusations in the councils we studied, perhaps because in the most successful entities the leadership simultaneously represents business and labour. In any event, the transformation of elite preferences is a claim often made on behalf of corporatism and is worthy of careful empirical examination.

Conclusion

Three questions were posed at the outset of this chapter: Are sector councils corporatist bodies? Are sector councils viable structures? Are sector councils desirable? We have endeavoured to answer these questions using political criteria. While sector councils might be viewed as more efficient than traditional means of delivering training, and capable of contributing to improved industrial relations, the viability and desirability of sector training councils must also be evaluated in terms of their contribution to the governance of particular sectors.

It seems fair to conclude that, with some qualifications, CSTEC, SSC, and APSTC represent neo-corporatist structures, if only in embryo. Equal partnership is the working principle on all levels of these councils and each is characterized by a high degree of policy participation. The degree of associational involvement is decidedly mixed, but we have suggested that even in the absence of classic interest intermediation, these councils have been able to draw on representatives of business and labour in a manner that allows them to act on behalf of the sector as a whole. Plainly, sector councils are stronger, and more decidedly corporatist, to the degree that they rest on a firm associational base, but when that base is weak, the bodies that emerge can still exhibit the other qualities normally associated with corporatist entities.

Not all sector councils are viable. Of the three we examined, one, APSTC, is no longer in existence. The factors we have identified as contributing to the viability of sectoral corporatism can doubtless be expanded and refined. The point is that the viability of sectoral corporatist bodies is something determined at the sectoral level employing criteria based on the characteristics of the sector and the organizational attributes of these bodies themselves. Viability is partly a structural issue, in the sense of organization, but it also depends on power and process variables that no amount of structural tinkering can effect. The fact that some of these councils have been more successful than others should spur us to identify more precisely, and with a wider set of cases, the most important contributing factors.

Are sector councils desirable? Even if the councils are able to obtain business and labour cooperation and begin training employed workers within their sector, is this something we should welcome? Without endorsing corporatism as a solution to problems in all sectors, or to the political impasses that confront Canadian governments, it should be acknowledged that sector councils offer an opportunity for business and labour to cooperate without compromising larger political positions. With the state no longer willing or able to support training programs on its own, it becomes increasingly important to include other labour market interests in the policy-making process. However, relationships cannot be built overnight; for a corporatist initiative to succeed business, labour, and government must have the time to develop their relationships and work out their differences. Part of the promise of corporatist policy networks is their capacity to induce shared beliefs and understandings. This is a long-term project, but one which is critical for the establishment of a training culture in Canada.

Notes

The authors would like to thank Neil Bradford, William Coleman, and Andrew Sharpe for their helpful comments on an earlier version of this paper.

1 Mechanisms of governance include hierarchy, markets, networks, associations and clans. Each employs a set of rules that secures compliance and governs relations among economic actors. It is sometimes argued, from this perspective, that economic performance improves to the extent that an appropriate mix of these mechanisms, or an appropriate governance regime, is deployed in response to the particular problems or pressures each sector faces (Lindberg, et al., 1991; Atkinson and Coleman, 1989a).

2 These councils were chosen because they represent the oldest and most established sector training councils in Canada. The research for this chapter relies heavily on personal interviews and materials provided by government officials and sector council managers. Nineteen open-ended interviews were conducted, five with federal officials, five with provincial officials, three with business managers, three with labour representatives, four with sector council managers, and one with an academic. Since completing these interviews, APSTC has been dissolved, which accounts for our use of the past tense in discussing this particular council on its own, but the present tense when discussing all three together.

3 This point has been driven home by the recent treatment of labour force development boards. Four years after establishing the Canadian Labour Force Development Board

in 1991, the federal government downsized the board and reduced its mandate. Similarly, the governments of Ontario and British Columbia recently terminated their provincial labour adjustment boards.

4 According to an executive member of the SSC, most of the newer members to the council are non-unionized plants with fewer than fifty employees.

5 Recently, at the prompting of the federal government, sector councils have been experimenting with programs designed to facilitate the acquisition of specific skills by young people.

6 As Williamson observes: 'Evidence of participation in, or acquisition of, the exercise of public authority by interest associations should not *per se* be regarded as corporatism' (1985: 192).

References

Alvarez, Michael R., Geoffrey Garrett, and Peter Lange. 1991. 'Government Partnership, Labor Organization and Macroeconomic Performance.' *American Political Science Review* 85:539–56.

Atkinson, Michael M., and William D. Coleman. 1985. 'Corporatism and Industrial Policy,' in Alan Cawson, ed., *Organized Interests and the State: Studies in Meso Corporatism*. London: Sage Publications.

– 1989a. 'Strong States and Weak States: Sectoral Policy Networks in Advanced Capitalist Economies.' *British Journal of Political Science* 19:47–67.

– 1989b. *State, Business, and Industrial Change in Canada*. Toronto: University of Toronto Press.

Cawson, Alan. 1985. 'Varieties of Corporatism: The Importance of the Meso-level of Interest Intermediation,' in Alan Cawson, ed., *Organized Interests and the State: Studies in Meso Corporatism*. London: Sage Publications.

– 1986. *Corporatism and Political Theory*. New York: Basil Blackwell.

Cohen, Joshua, and Joel Rogers. 1995. *Associations and Democracy*. New York: Verso.

Coleman, William. 1988. *Business and Politics: A Study of Collective Action*. Kingston and Montreal: McGill-Queen's University Press.

Haddad, Carol. 1995. *Sectoral Training Partnerships in Canada: Building Consensus through Policy and Practice*. Final Report to the Government of Canada. Canadian Studies Research Award.

Haddow, Rodney. 1994. 'Canada's Experiment with Labour Market Neocorporatism,' in Keith G. Banting and Charles M. Beach, eds., *Labour Market Polarization and Social Reform*. Kingston: School of Policy Studies, Queen's University.

– 1995. 'Federalism and Training Policy in Canada: Institutional Barriers to Economic Adjustment.' in François Rocher and Miriam Smith, eds., *New Trends in Canadian Federalism*. Peterborough: Broadview Press.

Held, David. 1987. *Models of Democracy.* Palo Alto: Stanford University Press.

Jordan, A. Grant. 1981. 'Iron Triangles, Wooly Corporatism and Elastic Nets: Images of the Policy Process.' *Journal of Public Policy* 1:109–13.

Kalt, Joseph, and Mark A. Zupan.1984. 'Capture and Ideology in the Economic Theory of Politics.' *American Economic Review* 74:279–300.

Katzenstein, Peter J. 1984. *Corporatism and Change: Austria, Switzerland, and the Politics of Industry.* Ithaca: Cornell University Press.

Lehmbruch, Gerhard. 1984. 'Concertation and the Structure of Corporatist Networks,' in John H. Goldthorpe, ed., *Order and Conflict in Contemporary Capitalism.* Oxford: Oxford University Press.

Lindberg, Leon N., John L. Campbell, and J. Rogers Hollingsworth. 1991. 'Economic Governance and Analysis of Structural Change in the American Economy,' in John L. Campbell et al., eds., *Governance of the American Economy.* New York: Cambridge University Press.

Lowi, Theodore. 1979. *The End of Liberalism.* 2nd ed. Norton.

Mansbridge, Jane. 1995. 'A Deliberative Perspective on Neocorporatism,' in Joshua Cohen and Joel Rogers, eds., *Associations and Democracy.* New York: Verso.

Offe, Claus. 1995. 'Some Skeptical Considerations on the Malleability of Representative Institutions,' in Joshua Cohen and Joel Rogers, eds., *Associations and Democracy.* New York: Verso.

Panitch, Leo. 1977. 'Corporatism in Canada.' *Studies in Political Economy: A Socialist Review* 1:43–92.

Quirk, Paul J. 1989. 'The Cooperative Resolution of Policy Conflict.' *American Political Science Review* 83:905–21.

Scharpf, Fritz W. 1989. 'Decisions Rules, Decision Styles and Policy Choices.' *Journal of Theoretical Politics,* 1:149–79.

– 1991. *Crisis and Choice in European Social Democracy.* Ithaca: Cornell University Press.

Schmitter, Philippe. 1974. 'Still the Century of Corporatism?' *Review of Politics* 36: 85–131.

– 1982. 'Reflection on Where the Theory of Neo-Corporatism Has Gone and Where the Praxis of Neo-Corporatism May be Going,' in Gerhard Lehmbruch and Phillipe Schmitter, eds., *Patterns of Corporatist Policy-Making.* London: Sage Publications.

– 1995. 'The Irony of Modern Democracy and the Viability of Efforts to Reform Its Practice,' in Joshua Cohen and Joel Rogers, eds., *Associations and Democracy.* New York: Verso.

Streeck, Wolfgang, and Philippe Schmitter. 1984. *Community, Market, State – And Associations?: The Prospective Contribution of Interest Governance to Social Order.* European University Institute Working Papers. Florence: European University Institute.

Williamson, Peter J. 1985. *Varieties of Corporatism: A Conceptual Discussion.*
   Cambridge: Cambridge University Press.
– 1989. *Corporatism in Perspective: An Introductory Guide to Corporatist Theory.*
   London: Sage Publications.

13

The Role of Sector Initiatives in the Canadian Industrial Relations System

RICHARD P. CHAYKOWSKI

At the macro-economic level, it is generally acknowledged that successful human capital formation supports productivity growth and hence national economic competitiveness (Thurow, 1992). Yet there are concerns that the existing institutional arrangements in Canada and the United States in the areas of general education, skills training, and labour force transitions are poorly matched to the requirements of emerging industries and high-performance workplaces (Betcherman et al., 1994; Appelbaum and Batt, 1994). Policies aimed at developing new institutional arrangements in the labour market must not only account for a broad range of economic and social considerations, but must also adapt to an industrial relations environment that is clearly very dynamic.

Several sector councils were first formed in Canada in the late 1980s. Since that time, numerous councils and activities have been established across a broad spectrum of industries. They are unique because, in highly unionized industries, they require formal labour-management cooperation at a broader level than that which was originally envisaged under the traditional Wagnerian system of industrial relations. Since the current industrial relations system is highly decentralized, it favours the development of union-management relationships at the establishment level. As such, in relation to the industrial relations system, sector councils represent a significant new institutional arrangement in the area of human capital formation.

The degree of success and longevity they have attained to date suggest that they are worthy of serious consideration, both as a viable institutional arrangement for supporting human capital development and as a potential model for labour-management cooperation. The extent to which sector councils are able to endure as new institutional feature of the labour market and industrial relations system will, in part, depend on the success of their design and adaptability in producing desirable outcomes. One purpose of this paper is to outline how the development of sector councils relates to the existing industrial relations system in Canada.

However, in view of the increasing economic integration of the Canadian and American economies, the recent decline of American unions may have implications for the types of industrial relations institutions and labour practices that will succeed in either country. While acknowledging the distinct characteristics of the Canadian and American systems of industrial relations, they do have a common heritage and they continue to share important features and approaches to labour relations. This paper also explores the extent of joint labour-management approaches to training and labour adjustment issues in the United States.

In the first section I begin with a discussion of the changes in macro-economic conditions and workplace systems that suggest a role for joint labour-management sector councils in human capital development. The following section considers the role of the councils in the Canadian industrial relations system. Next, I consider how joint firm and union involvement in human resource issues has evolved in the United States and come to some preliminary conclusions regarding the role and function of sector councils in the Canadian and American industrial relations systems. Finally, I discuss how joint industry councils constitute a new industrial relations strategic choice regarding training and adjustment issues.

Sector Councils in the Context of Macro-economic and Firm-level Changes

Current Canadian labour market policy on human capital formation is a response to the emerging economic and organizational developments. While support for sector councils may be viewed as one element of government policy, the councils have roles at both the industry (or sector) and firm levels. They interface with the industrial relations system at both of these levels.

Training, Labour Market Adjustment, and Labour Policy

Perhaps the overarching labour market consideration is that, as global markets evolve, the positive relationship between human resources development and economic competitiveness will become increasingly important (Thurow, 1992; Harris and Watson, 1993). The basic argument underlying this proposition is that those nations' that are better able to enhance the quality and quantity of their human capital stock will be more productive; the policy implication is that labour market policies ought to emphasize active labour market measures that enhance (re)training and education. From a national perspective, the enhancement of education and training is also seen as a primary means of easing the impacts of labour force transitions caused by both downside and upside firm adjustments associated with evolving markets and industrial restructuring (Riddell, 1995).

In Canada, legislative jurisdiction over education resides exclusively with the provincial governments. Historically, though, both the provincial and federal governments have been active in training and adjustment programs. Given provincial jurisidiction in these areas, the substantial role that the federal government has developed in human resources (e.g., training) is largely a consequence of its considerable financial leverage. However, it is important to emphasize that provincial governments are actively involved in a variety of labour market programs involving training and adjustment, and that by the 1990s the federal government had begun to devolve such programs to the provinces.

The federal Canadian Jobs Strategy of 1985 provides a good example of a government labour market program that included some form of direct training or training incentives intended for both unemployed and employed persons and that has the overall objective of improving the efficiency of the labour market (Riddell, 1995; Meltz, 1990).[1] More recently, federal initiatives (e.g., the Employment Insurance Act) have become further focused on training.

One challenge to this type of conventional human resources policy is that, whether one considers workers who are dislocated as a result of industrial restructuring or firm downsizing, or workers facing increased demand for advanced skills as a result of technological advances and product market growth, the implications for the workforce typically vary considerably across sectors. Consequently, the economy-wide government programs that support education and training may not provide sufficient flexibility in responding to the requirements of individual firms, unions, or workers in a particular industry. These considerations have led policy-makers to re-evaluate conventional programs and institutional arrangements for advancing human capital formation. A fundamental strength of the sector council approach is its ability to accommodate the distinctive human resource requirements of specific industries. In this sense, it represents a shift in government policy in support of a new institutional arrangement in the labour market.

Canadian sector councils also constitute an important exception to other governmental approaches in that they operate on the basis of firm, union, and non-union employee representation and are responsible for the conduct of the programs that are developed. As such, the activities of the councils are initially supported by government grants. Under this model, the role of the government is that of an honest broker (Appelbaum and Batt, 1994); this is critical in helping to establish a credible cooperative labour-management decision-making structure where none existed before. In the case of sector councils, the Canadian government essentially underwrites the start-up costs of the new arrangement and sanctions a form of labour-management cooperation at a sectoral level. Where sector councils involve unions, they in effect become a part of the industrial relations system although, at the industry level, they represent a new form of institutional arrangement.

Firm-level Developments and Sector Councils

At the establishment level, the increased competitive pressures brought about by such forces as the globalization of product markets, the deregulation of domestic industries, and the development and diffusion of advanced technologies has led to a profound transformation of production systems and organizational structures. This has had far-reaching implications for both human capital requirements and the adjustment of labour.

In the context of the industrial relations system, these pressures have led to a range of labour relations responses. Behavioural responses have ranged from increasing efforts at union-management cooperation over workplace issues (e.g., related to technological change) to increased adversarialism. Cooperative initiatives typically focus on the formation of joint labour-management committees. Not surprisingly, collective bargaining has focused on job security and adjustment issues. Typically, the objectives include retraining workers for new jobs within the firm or providing workers with severance packages. Whether or not collective bargaining has adequately focused on upside training needs is less certain.

Rapid and ongoing technological change in production systems has affected skill levels as well as the need for workers to adapt to new skill requirements. From a competitiveness perspective, of particular interest are emerging 'high-performance' work systems. These new organizational arrangements typically combine advanced production technologies with new, more flexible and more participative forms of work organization, and require high-skill workers with the capability to learn continuously (Marshall, 1992:292–5; Appelbaum and Batt, 1994).[2] In both Canada and the United States, it appears that as yet only a small minority of firms can be characterized as having a high-performance workplace (Appelbaum and Batt 1994; Betcherman et al., 1994).[3] Yet the ability to foster and diffuse the key characteristics of the high-performance workplace is viewed as a key element of future industrial competitiveness.

Appelbaum and Batt identify five broad areas of policy alternatives aimed at promoting high-performance work systems in the American workplace; the three that are most relevant to sector councils are:

- strategies to develop institutionally based training programs that are flexible and responsive to emerging workplace requirements;
- promotion of both employee-management and union-management cooperation through workplace councils that address a range of issues, among which could be training;
- encouragement of inter-firm cooperation in several business-related areas, including training (1994:161–9).

The idea that government may have a role in supporting inter-firm joint initiatives to achieve these types of objectives is echoed in the policy recommendations forwarded by Betcherman et al. (1994:102) for Canada. In either the American or Canadian case, the partners may gain from economies in the provision of training activities and benefit from an ongoing exchange of best practices that serve to support the development of high performance work systems. Sector councils provide these advantages and have the added benefit of explicitly and formally embracing worker participation (through union or non-union employee representation) in the process.[4]

Several councils have effectively established workplace joint committees, but the sectoral approach is an inherently macro-economic institutional arrangement. A remaining challenge is to embed the role of sector councils more formally within the existing system of labour relations in order better to connect the activities of the councils with the conduct of labour relations at the firm level.

The Industrial Relations System and Sector Councils

Although sector councils are essentially industry-level institutional arrangements, they provide a forum for union-management consultation and cooperation and their activities are aimed at many of the same outcomes that are generated through the conduct of industrial relations at the establishment level. While sector councils are not involved in the conduct of labour relations per se (e.g., bargaining over employment outcomes), as they evolve, their activities increasingly influence and interact with the more established outputs of the industrial relations system, particularly in the area of human resources.

Figure 1 provides a basic framework for considering the relationship of sector councils to the conduct of industrial relations at the establishment level. In the following section I begin by outlining the major components of the framework: the environment, joint activity at the industry level, and the conduct of industrial relations at the firm level. This is followed by a discussion of some of the important dimensions of the interface between sector councils and industrial relations. This framework will form a basis for considering the implications of the current arrangement between sector councils and industrial relations.

Sector Councils: Distinct but Related to Industrial Relations

The Environmental Context

Both sector councils and firm-level labour relations operate within the same broad environmental context, although the particular social, political, and economic factors at work at each level may be quite distinct. For example, individual firms and unions typically accept the current state of the labour market as fixed in conducting a given round of negotiations. This makes sense in cases where a particular firm and local union are only one pair among many in their relevant product and labour markets. In the long run, the outcomes of collective bargaining may feed back to affect future conditions in the labour market. In contrast, since the purpose of sector councils is to affect labour market outcomes in the area of human resources, the outcomes of sector council activities are expected to have a direct effect on the broader labour market in an industry.

Therefore, environmental factors such as the state of the labour and product markets, public policy, or the nature of technological advances set a common context. But since sector councils and individual firms and union locals function at different levels, the relationship of each to the various environmental factors is typically quite different.

Joint Activity at the Sector Level

The framework depicted in Figure 1 associates sector councils with a broad level of labour market activity. Institutionally, these councils function essentially as bipartite bodies, with representation from among the major unions, employers, or employer associations in an industry. In industries with a significant unionized component, sector councils are a forum for union-management cooperation.

Across industries, the number of employers and unions represented in sector activities can vary widely. For example, there are one union, six individual corporations, and six employer associations in the consumer electronic and appliance service industry council. But the CAW, the Communications, Energy and Paperworkers Union of Canada, the International Brotherhood of Electrical Workers, and the United Steelworkers of America, and six individual corporations make up the electrical and electronics manufacturing industry council, known as the Sectoral Skills Council of the Electrical/Electronic Industry (HRDC, 1995).

The standard approach is for the federal government to provide support for

FIGURE 1 Industrial Relations and the Sectoral–Establishment Level Interface

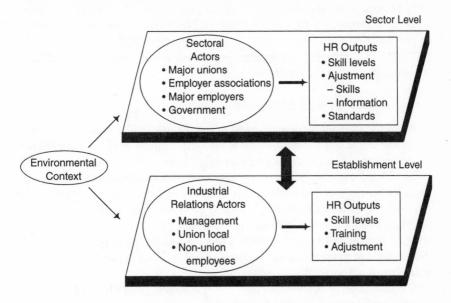

sectoral initiatives through limited-term funding; but government involvement is also undertaken by provincial governments. The Ontario government has been involved in the Auto Parts Sectoral Training Council, whereas in the consumer electronic and appliance service industry the Alberta, New Brunswick, and Ontario governments have all been involved. In contrast, in the electrical and electronics manufacturing industry, government plays more of a facilitative role.

The overall objectives of the councils are to improve the skill levels of workers (often through training), facilitate labour adjustments, and develop standards and certification. Specific human resource goals include: developing training programs/curricula (e.g., aircraft repair and service, auto parts, electrical and electronics manufacturing); establishing standards (e.g., aircraft repair and service, auto repair and service, consumer electronic and appliance service; electrical and electronics manufacturing, steel, tourism and hospitality, truck transport); instituting training certification (e.g., consumer electronic and appliance service; software; tourism and hospitality; truck transport); and developing internship programs (e.g., auto repair and service; tourism and hospitality).

The Sector Skills Council (SSC) in the electrical and electronic manufacturing industry has been noted for its success in upside skills training, while the Canadian Steel Trade and Employment Congress (CSTEC) has successfully focused on retraining workers displaced in the steel industry. Sector council outputs, such as setting standards or developing certification programs, essentially set parameters within which individual firms and unions are encouraged to operate. However, other outputs, such as retraining displaced workers (e.g., CSTEC), or developing apprenticeship and internship programs (e.g., SSC), require direct linkages to establishments.

Industrial Relations at the Establishment Level

Skill levels, training, and adjustment programs are important aspects of the terms and conditions of employment at the establishment level and have been a long-standing subject of collective bargaining in unionized firms. Examples of issues related to on-the-job training and apprenticeship programs include the basis for access and financial support. Since many large unionized employers have developed their own internal training programs, supply has not traditionally been a major concern, although in some industries there has been a problem with the poaching of trained workers. From the employee perspective, much of this on-the-job training has not been transferable, often because the company training was not accredited.

The outcomes of individual collective bargaining generally depend on the relative bargaining power of the individual parties. Even so, in the areas of training and adjustment packages, collective bargaining would only be expected to lead to cross-establishment parity in outcomes in industries where there was a history of strong patterning of collective agreements (e.g., autos or steel). However, across many industries there appears to have been a general decline in the patterning of contracts, as settlements have increasingly come to reflect the particular circumstances of individual firms. Consequently, individual bargaining settlements would not be expected to yield progress on key human resource issues such as industry standards, certification, or industry-wide adjustment.

With respect to the industrial relations system, the available international research evidence suggests that the incidence of training under unionism is at least as much, and is possibly greater, than in the absence of unions.[5] In unionized establishments in Canada, matters relating to (re)training, the impacts of technology on skills or job security, and employment downsizing have largely been an outcome of the established collective bargaining process. In 1992, among collective agreements covering five hundred or more employees in the private sector, the proportion of contracts with clauses dealing with education or training varied considerably (Chaykowski and Lewis, 1994: 20, Table 2): 13 per cent were concerned with general education leave, 19 per cent with job-related education leave; 20 per cent with the right to retraining related to technological change; 54 per cent with on-the-job training, and 55 per cent with apprenticeship training.

These types of collective bargaining clauses are generally well established across sectors. Aside from such substantive contractual outcomes, there has also been interest in union-management cooperation dealing with governance issues in the areas of training and adjustment. From an industrial relations perspective, human resource issues (e.g., retraining in response to adjustment, upskilling) tend to be inherently integrative. In other words, there are prospects for mutual gains for both employers and unions. Although there is little systematic evidence about the nature and extent of joint labour-management training activities across sectors, examples of these types of efforts are appearing in Canada (e.g., the Communications, Energy and Paperworkers Union and Bell Canada). In the United States, joint union-management training initiatives have been negotiated in such industries as autos, steel, and telecommunications (Savoie, 1985).[6]

Whether these outcomes are formally negotiated through collective bargaining or instituted and regulated by cooperative union-management action, they represent traditional outputs of a mature system of industrial relations (Dunlop, 1958). They are essentially establishment-centred, which matches well with a view of competitive labour and product markets in which firms regularly adopt best practices and employees have access to relevant information about (and support for) relevant skills development. But this approach may not be optimal in the presence of market imperfections and externalities; there is mounting evidence that there is inadequate diffusion of best workplace practices, that workers have insufficient access to financial markets for human capital investments, and that existing institutions do not adequately match the emerging demand-side requirements of the labour market (Appelbaum and Batt 1994; Betcherman et al., 1994).

Moreover, as industrial restructuring has progressed, protecting job security has become a major union priority across sectors. Heightened concern over job security has led to collective bargaining objectives such as improved severance packages, enhanced resources for retraining programs, and adjustment services. It has also prompted unions to explore new approaches to addressing these issues, including sector councils.

The Linkage between Sector Councils and Industrial Relations

As discussed subsequently, the industries in which councils have been formed have quite distinct industrial relations characteristics, including the extent of unionization, the number of major employers and unions that are involved in sectoral activities, and the conduct of labour relations (including joint activities).

Each of these dimensions defines one aspect of the linkage between the operation of the industrial relations system at the establishment level and sector councils at the industry level. Moreover, the characteristics of these dimensions are expected to have a major impact on the activities and success of the councils.

Sector Councils and the Extent of Unionization

Among industries in which sector councils have either already been formed or are under development, the extent of unionization varies considerably.[7] For example, in 1992, within Canadian manufacturing, union density ranged widely: 68.7 per cent in pulp and paper, 43.0 per cent in electrical and electronics manufacturing, 27.7 per cent in textiles, and 19.3 per cent in printing.[8] Sector councils have been formed in the fish harvesting and seafood processing industries, where union density in the broader fishing sector was around 53.5 per cent. In mining and telecommunications, where sector councils were only being developed in the mid-1990s, union density was 29.4 per cent and 60.5 per cent, respectively.

In some industries the level of unionization is extremely low and union participation is essentially absent. Although sector councils are only at the stage of being considered in both the financial services and the oil and gas industries, there seems to be little role in either for organized labour. In the case of financial services this is not surprising, since union density in the broader financial sector was only 4.7 per cent in 1992.

The formation of sector councils therefore does not appear to be a function of the extent of unionization in an industry; in fact, many councils have been formed in sectors that are primarily non-union, so it would appear that a high degree of unionization is neither a necessary nor sufficient condition for the development of the councils. Rather, the major issue associated with the extent of unionization is the need to reconcile the representation needs of unionized and non-unionized workers on sector councils. Non-union representation can be a contentious issue, especially in industries where non-union employers do not recognize a role for established unions. The role of non-union representation vis-à-vis the organized component of the industry poses a significant challenge for the functional success of councils.

The Effect of the Composition of Sector councils

At the sectoral level, achieving a consensus on appropriate human resource initiatives becomes not only an issue of reconciling management versus union positions, but also one of harmonizing the objectives of many individual stakeholders. That is, one may reasonably expect as much diversity in interests across employers and unions, respectively, as between management and labour. Particularly in industries in which there are many different unions and firms, but only one or two that are dominant, the challenge is to build linkages among all of the organizations.

On the employer side, an industry with many firms that are highly competitive in their labour markets may be reluctant to cooperate, while some companies may view themselves as sufficiently large to enable them to meet all of their own human resource requirements independently. Where the extent of industrial concentration in an industry is expected to have a major impact on the level of participation in the council or on its ability to develop consensus positions, the challenge is to demonstrate that joint human resource activities will make each firm better off.

There may also be potential issues associated with the effect of union rivalries on cooperative initiatives. For example, in the mining industry the United Steelworkers of America and the Communication, Energy and Paperworkers Union have been the dominant unions. However, as recently as 1995, the CAW has entered the mining industry and has become a member of the founding board of directors of the newly proposed Mining Industry Training and Adjustment Council (MITAC).[9] While these two unions may find it possible to cooperate on general human resource issues at an industry level, friction caused by ongoing competition among these unions or through conflicting industrial relations priorities could spill over to affect the level of cooperation among these unions at the sector council. More generally, if irreconcilable differences exist among labour representatives to such an extent that a union declines to participate, then the likely outcome is that some segment of the industry labour force will not be included in the sector councils' programs.

Linking Sector Councils and the Conduct of Labour-Management Relations

One might expect firms and unions that have more cooperative (i.e., less adversarial) relationships in the conduct of their labour relations to be more likely to support sectoral arrangements and, once involved, to be more successful. These participants will be expected to have developed the behavioural approach and skills required in joint undertakings and to focus on the integrative nature of human resource activities. The experience of the CSTEC suggests that union-management cooperation at the sectoral level is a direct function of firm-level union-management relations:

One requirement of the CSTEC model is that a common basis or will to cooperate exist between management and labour at the sectoral level ... This cooperation cannot be predicted and tensions between management and labour as a result of collective agreement negotiations strike situations, and the adjustment process itself often make a joint sectoral effort difficult to maintain. (Ekos Research Associates, 1991:16)

In the case of the steel industry, this connection between the activities of the council and the state of industrial relations in the industry is facilitated by the high level of unionization and industrial concentration in the industry: the United Steelworkers of America is the dominant union in the industry, while the top three firms produce roughly 70 per cent of total output (Verma 1992).[10]

The CSTEC experience suggests a strong causal relationship between the tenor of labour-management relations and the level of cooperation at the sectoral level. But if the programs developed by sector councils are to be effective, they must somehow balance the need for their programs to be substantively linked back to the establishment level, with the need to avoid conflicting with the conduct (and outcomes) of labour relations at the establishment level. The struggle to achieve this balance is reflected in the experiences and findings reported in the human resource studies of a cross-section of industries in which sectoral activities are being developed:[11]

- The human resource study for the mining industry identified the need for a sector council to separate its work from local issues generally, and from collective bargaining issues specifically, but said that local stakeholders should be consulted about the work of council (Price Waterhouse, 1993b:ix–x).
- In the pulp and paper industry, the importance of developing linkages between the local level and the industry were explicitly acknowledged: 'Any significant changes in the industry must be worked out between management and labour representatives at both the mill level and on a wider basis' (Price Waterhouse, 1994:113).
- In the broadcasting industry, the issue of developing multi-skilling was identified as an issue that, while determined through individual contracts, had implications across collective agreements:

Multi-skilling ... also has implications for jobs covered by more than one collective agreement. For example, one individual might be expected to drive a truck, align the microwave or satellite dish, turn the equipment on, point the camera, go back to the truck and start the equipment. Historically these duties may have represented two or three jobs under different collective agreements. Today they may be one. (Peat Marwick Stevenson & Kellogg 1993:101).

- In the British Columbia wood products industry, there was an explicit recognition that sectoral-level initiatives must be consistent with establishment-level practice:

Joint participation of unions and companies on apprenticeship boards is critical to the development of appropriate trades training. Companies and unions can also review their agreements on access to apprenticeship training ... to review entry requirements and ways to upgrade individuals to qualify for apprenticeship openings. They also need to review agreements on seniority requirements and their application to entry requirements for apprenticeship positions. (Ernst & Young 1992:77)

Approaches taken in the electrical/electronics manufacturing and mining industries, respectively, have more formally embraced the need to establish direct and substantive linkages between the programs of the councils and the workplace level. In the former case, the strategy has been to link the SSC to the workplace level by funding the work of joint workplace training committees.[12] In the latter case, the proposal to establish the MITAC includes a provision to formally connect the sector council to the establishment:

Members of MITAC will establish a Joint Workplace Training Committee (JWTC). The purpose of the JWTC is to develop human resource development needs and to provide the primary link between the workplace and the Council. In unionized workplaces, JWTCs will be composed equally of representatives of management and of the union and will be co-chaired. (MITAC, n.d.:20)

This proposal is among the most far-reaching, particularly because of the large number of firms in the industry. The approach of linking union-management workplace committees to joint sector council activities recognizes that, under the current industrial relations system, the terms and conditions of employment are, first and foremost, determined through collective bargaining at the enterprise level.

Joint Activities and the American Industrial Relations System

In the United States, interest in joint union-management programs, particularly in the human resource area, has been focused on the firm level, where they have usually been an outcome of collective bargaining (see Savoie, 1985; Ferman, Hoyman, and Cutcher-Gershenfeld, 1990). Savoie and Cutcher-Gershenfeld point out that if joint training programs are to be successful, they cannot be developed independently of collective bargaining (1991:210).

Significant joint training initiatives emerged in the early 1980s in such industries as autos, steel and telecommunications, although the programs negotiated between the United Auto Workers and both Ford and General Motors are particularly noted for their scope and apparent success (Savoie, 1985). In most cases, joint approaches to training are a product of the industrial relations system: 'The joint training efforts in larger firms are usually first defined at the collective bargaining table where contractual provisions establish the programs, specify governance and coverage, and provide some financial formula to cover the cost of program operations.'[13]

Ferman, Hoyman, and Cutcher-Gershenfeld identify a number of potentially divisive issues that may arise in the development of joint programs, including determining the source and allocation of program funding; ensuring that other types of training (that are not included in a joint program) are not undermined; and determining the extent of joint decision-making (1990: 179–82). Agreeing upon resource allocations and the extent of shared decision-making are inherently distributive bargaining issues, which is precisely why joint programs are typically established through collective bargaining.

In the United States, there are few examples of joint union-management initiatives undertaken on a multi-firm or cross-union basis. Broader approaches to human resource issues have recently emerged in Michigan and Wisconsin.

In the late 1980s in Michigan, the state government decided to attempt to model a new program to deal with worker dislocation after the Canadian Industrial Adjustment Service. The idea was to ease the labour market transitions of workers displaced by a plant closing by supporting the establishment of an establishment-level labour-management joint adjustment committee (JAC). The role of the committee would be to develop an adjustment program that included training and counselling services. The Michigan program was viewed as a policy success, but it appears to remain focused on responding to individual plant closings, where the role of government is to support these initiatives.

Another recently established program aimed at addressing emerging human resource needs in the labour market is the Wisconsin Regional Training Partnership (WRTP). The WRTP is a regional tripartite organization (labour, management, government) that includes major employers and unions. To date, its activities have developed in two program areas (Rogers, 1994:404–5): a Help In Re-Employment (HIRE) program directed at assisting displaced workers in the Milwaukee area; and, a Wisconsin Manufacturing Training Consortium (WMTC) which concentrates on addressing human resource issues in the Milwaukee metalworking industry. These programs appear to be successful and there is a desire to expand them beyond Milwaukee and the metalworking industry, although as yet there has been little progress on this objective.

Where macro-level joint human resource initiatives have begun to emerge, they may best be described as regional programs. They appear to address primarily the issue of labour market adjustment, typically including facilitating job search and placement, entry into training programs, and job and personal counselling (Rogers, 1994:404; Baker, 1991:138–40). In the area of training, the Wisconsin WRTP has many of the same human resource objectives as do Canadian sector councils.

What accounts for the differential development of broader joint initiatives in the United States and Canada? Two systemic factors likely account for much of the difference. First, Canadian public policy at the federal level has been explicitly supportive of sectoral initiatives. It would appear that the extent of government support evident in Canada is not likely to occur in the United States, with its stronger tradition of resistance to government involvement in the private sector.

Second, Cutcher-Gershenfeld and Hoyman point out that joint labour-management activities may be construed as constituting 'employer-dominated' committees, especially in non-union settings (1991:244). This is a particular example of the more general issue in current American labour relations policy of the appropriateness of various forms of employee participation; it is a critical issue that received special attention in the 1994 *Fact Finding Report of the Commission on the Future of Worker-Management Relations* (Dunlop Commission).[14] While some observers have advocated loosening restrictions on joint activities, it is clear that American labour policy is not currently oriented towards supporting joint initiatives; neither does there appear to be any strong interest in reshaping current policy in a manner that might support such initiatives and unionism alike.

Another factor concerns the difference in the evolution of the Canadian and American industrial relations systems. In Canada, the presence of strong and involved unions has been a major factor in the establishment and success of sectoral initiatives. The decline of the American labour movement in many of its traditional industrial bases has weakened the prospects for unions to play a role either in influencing labour policy or in serving as an institutional linkage across establishments in an industry. Therefore, the deunionization of American industry is likely to inhibit the establishment of joint sectoral activities.

Sector Councils as a New Strategic Choice on Training and Adjustment Issues

In the context of a Canadian industrial relations system that is inherently adversarial in its nature, joint labour-management sector councils confer distinct advantages to both parties. First, they provide a forum in which the parties can address issues of mutual concern away from the typically conflictual setting of the collective bargaining table. Second, they are focused on resolving human resource issues (particularly training and adjustment concerns) that, while affecting an industry, also yield tangible benefits to both parties at the establishment level. While the incentives for individual firms and unions to cooperate on long-run or systemic human resource issues may, generally, be too small, the broader scope of labour-management cooperation through sector councils may lend itself to achieving such objectives (e.g., economies in the delivery of training; the diffusion of best practices). The fact that, in the short run, the conduct of labour relations at the firm level may not be highly coordinated with cooperative sectoral level activites may be an advantage – by providing flexibility at the establishment level and by encouraging establishment-specific adjustments.

By fostering labour-management cooperation, sectoral initiatives constitute a factor that tends to reduce adversarialism and hence the costs of conducting labour relations. Further, sector councils can provide long-term support for industry training and workforce adjustment requirements that complements the outcomes that emerge from the collective bargaining process at the firm level. To the extent that particular sector councils are successful in developing workplace joint labour-management activities, this complementarity would be expected to be strengthened.

Although developed at the industry level, sectoral human resource initiatives impact at the establishment level, where they must interface with the established industrial relations system. From a strategic choice perspective, the participation of unions, management, and government in sectoral-level joint activities constitutes a major departure from traditional industrial relations activities and decision-making (Kochan, Katz, and McKersie, 1994). Through their involvement in sector councils, firms and unions have expanded their industrial relations and human resources strategies beyond a narrow focus on workplace and collective bargaining outcomes at the establishment level towards a broader, and possibly longer-term, approach that includes inter-firm (inter-union) cooperation.

In so doing, the unions and firms involved have pursued a distinct strategic path. This cooperation may involve the pooling of resources, the sharing of information, and the joint management of institutional structures in the areas of training and workforce adjustment. In some cases, it may involve creating a new web of linkages between joint training committees at the establishment level with a single joint sector council. This shift in strategic decision-making may be expected to parallel a shift in other, possibly related, business strategies.

For the government, the policy of financially supporting and encouraging sector councils also constitutes a movement beyond conventional policies.

From the perspective of advancing industrial relations policy, formal support for sector councils is important because it further legitimizes the notion of labour-management partnerships and it enlarges the scope of cooperative industrial relations to the industry level. In turn, the involvement of strong unions in the operation of sector councils ought to increase the likelihood of success in addressing longer-term, industry-wide human resource issues.

In the American industrial relations scene, where most joint labour-management training initiatives are firm-specific, Cutcher-Gershenfeld and Hoyman suggest that simply adopting a successful joint program from another organization is not likely to be appropriate where it has been the outcome of a particular collective bargaining experience (1991:241). By extension, sectoral initiatives would be expected to have the most success in an industry when they serve as broader institutional arrangements within which the parties may craft specific programs that match the requirements of their own union-management relationship. The experience of Canadian sector councils would appear to take this into account.

There are two broad issues that merit further research and about which we now have very little or no research evidence. First, it would be useful to conduct systematic case studies in order to assess the effect of the strength of unionism and the maturity of collective bargaining in an industry on the development and success of sector councils. Indeed, insight into this issue would likely help us to understand better the differential development of sectoral initiatives in Canada and the United States. Second, we need to know more about the extent and nature of the linkages between the human resource initiatives undertaken by sector councils and collective bargaining outcomes in the areas of workplace training and workforce adjustment. This would provide a better understanding of whether the outputs of these two processes complement each other. Taken together, gaining insight into these two areas would further our understanding of the role of sector councils in the industrial relations system.

Notes

The author gratefully acknowledges the benefit of comments and suggestions from Morley Gunderson, Andrew Sharpe, and anonymous referees, as well as comments from participants in the Sectors Councils Conference in Montreal.

1 Specifically, the 1985 Canadian Jobs Strategy was a set of program that included: a job entry program aimed at facilitating transitions into work; a job development program that endeavoured to enhance employment prospects; a program designed to

reduce skill shortages; a skills investment program that targeted the labour market adjustment needs of persons already in the labour force. In addition, the federal government has moved to increase the level of training financed through the unemployment insurance system (Riddell, 1995: 160, 161, Table 7).

2 Appelbaum and Batt (1994) distinguish two emerging American models of 'lean' and 'team' production, and contrast the evolution of these work systems with production systems that have been established internationally, including the Japanese lean production, Swedish socio-technical, Italian flexible specialization, and German diversified quality production systems. Appelbaum and Batt (1994) depict the American models as distinct from the other national systems. While related to each other along several dimensions, the American systems are evolving and in transition.

3 The evidence on the prevalence of different types of work systems is only now emerging in the United States and remains extremely limited in Canada.

4 Betcherman et al (1994: 102) also recommend government support for sector councils and various training boards.

5 See Tan et al (1992) for an empirical analysis of training in the United States, Great Britain, and Australia; and Brown (1990) or a review of empirical research studies on training in the private sector in the United States.

6 As examples, joint training programs are now well established between the UAW and both Ford and GM, the UAW and International Harvester, the USWA and Jones and Laughlin, and the CWA and Bell operating companies (Savoie, 1985:536–8; Pascoe and Collins, 1985).

7 All union density figures are reported for 1992.

8 Manufacturing had an overall union density of roughly 35.2 per cent (Statistics Canada, 1994:38; Appendix 1.5).

9 Even so, the United Steelworkers continue to dominate MITAC.

10 Of the twelve firms producing steel in Canada in 1990, all except Dofasco Inc. were unionized and, among the unionized firms, two were represented by the CSN (i.e., the CNTU), and ten by the United Steelworkers (Verma, 1992).

11 These human resource studies were typically commissioned by the federal government in order to assist the stakeholders in determining industry requirements before proceeding with plans to establish a joint sector council.

12 Approximately 150 joint workplace training committees have been linked to the SSC through its training fund.

13 Ferman, Hoyman and Cutcher-Gershenfeld (1990:163) acknowledge that, in small firms, a joint training program may not have been established as a result of collective bargaining. While the program may not be contractual, it may still be viewed as an (informal) product of the conduct of labour relations.

14 This became a major issue in the recent *Electromation* (1992) case in which the firm

created joint worker-management committees which were subsequently challenged by the Teamsters as an unfair labour practice under section 8(a)(2) of the National Labour Relations Act (USDL/USDC, 1994:53, 54).

References

Appelbaum, Eileen, and Rosemary Batt. 1994. *The New American Workplace*. Ithaca, NY: ILR Press.

Baker, Richard. 1991. 'Joint State-Level Responses to Worker Dislocation,' in L. Ferman, M. Hoyman, J. Cutcher-Gershenfeld, and E. Savoie, eds., *Joint Training Programs: A Union-Management Approach to Preparing Workers for the Future*. Ithaca, NY: ILR Press, Cornell University, 129–51.

Betcherman, Gordon, Kathryn McMullen, Norm Leckie, and Christina Caron. 1994. *The Canadian Workplace in Transition*. Kingston: IRC Press, Queen's University.

Brown, Charles. 1990. 'Empirical Evidence on Private Training,' in L. Bassi and D. Crawford, eds., *Research in Labor Economics*. Vol. 11. Greenwich, Conn.: JAI Press Inc, 97–113.

Canadian Labour Market and Productivity Centre (CLMPC). 1993a. *Canada: Meeting the Challenge of Change*. Ottawa: CLMPC.

– 1993b. *1991 National Training Survey*. Ottawa: CLMPC.

Chaykowski, Richard, and Brian Lewis. 1994. *A Review of Canadian and American Training Practices*. Kingston: IRC Press, Queen's University.

Cutcher-Gershenfeld, Joel, and Michele Hoyman. 1991. 'Public Policy and Research Implications of Joint Training Programs,' in L. Ferman, M. Hoyman, J. Cutcher-Gershenfeld, and E. Savoie, eds., *Joint Training Programs: A Union-Management Approach to Preparing Workers for the Future*. Ithaca, NY: ILR Press, Cornell University, 229–51.

Dunlop, John. 1958. *Industrial Relations Systems*. New York: Holt, Rinehart and Winston.

Ehrenberg, Ronald. 1994. *Labor Markets and Integrating National Economies*. Washington DC: Brookings Institution.

Ekos Research Associates. 1991. *Program Evaluation Study of the Canadian Steel Trade and Employment Congress*. Final Report. Ottawa: Ekos Research.

– n.d. *Sound of the Future: Human Resource Issues in Music and Sound Recording*. Ottawa: Ekos Research.

Ernst and Young. 1992. *Human Resources in the British Columbia Wood Products Industry* (Summer).

Ferman, Louis, Michele Hoyman, and Joel Cutcher-Gershenfeld. 1990. 'Joint Union-Management Training Programs: A Synthesis in the Evolution of Jointism and Training,' in L. Ferman, M. Hoyman, J. Cutcher-Gershenfeld, and E. Savoie, eds., *New Developments in Worker Training: A Legacy for the 1990s*. Madison, WI: Industrial Relations Research Association, 157–89.

Harris, Richard, and William Watson. 1993. 'Three Visions of Competitiveness: Porter, Reich and Thurow on Economic Growth and Policy,' in T. Courchene and D. Purvis, eds., *Productivity, Growth, and Canada's International Competitiveness*. Kingston: John Deutsch Institute, Queen's University.

Human Resources Development Canada (HRDC). 1995. *Sectoral Activities: Update Report*. (Spring 1995). Catalogue LM-283–06–95.

Kochan, Thomas, Harry Katz, and Robert McKersie. 1994. *The Transformation of American Industrial Relations*. Ithaca, NY: ILR Press.

Marshall, Ray. 1992. 'Work Organization, Unions and Economic Performance,' in L. Mishel and P. Voos, eds., *Unions and Economic Competitiveness*. Armonk, NY: M.E. Sharpe, 287–315.

Meltz, Noah. 1990. 'The Evolution of Worker Training: The Canadian Experience,' in L. Ferman, M. Hoyman, J. Cutcher-Gershenfeld, and E. Savoie, eds., *New Developments in Worker Training: A Legacy for the 1990s*. Madison, WI: Industrial Relations Research Association, 283–307.

Pascoe, Thomas, and Richard Collins. 1985. 'UAW-Ford Employee Development and Training Program: Overview of Operations and Structure,' in B. Dennis, ed., *Proceedings of the 1985 Spring Meeting , April 18–19* (Detroit, MI) Industrial Relations Research Association. Madison, WI: Industrial Relations Research Association, 519–26.

Peat Marwick Stevenson & Kellogg. 1993. *Human Resources in the Canadian Broadcasting Industry* (January).

Price Waterhouse. 1993a. *Human Resources and Labour Canada: Labour Market Outlook and Sectoral Analysis of People, Performance, and Partnerships. Common Themes in Sector Studies*. Final Report. Mimeographed.

– 1993b. *Breaking New Ground: Human Resource Challenges and Opportunities in the Canadian Mining Industry* (Summer).

– 1994. *The Canadian Pulp and Paper Industry: A Focus on Human Resources*.

Riddell, Craig. 1995. 'Human Capital Formation in Canada: Recent Developments and Policy Responses,' in K. Banting and C. Beach, eds., *Labour Market Polarization and Social Policy Reform*. Kingston: School of Policy Studies, Queen's University, 125–72.

Rogers, Joel. 1994. 'The Wisconsin Regional Training Partnership: A National Model for Regional Modernization Efforts?' in P. Voos, ed., *Proceedings of the Forty-Sixth Annual Meeting*, Industrial Relations Research Association. Madison, WI: Industrial Relations Research Association, 403–11.

Savoie, Ernest. 1985. 'Current Developments and Future Agenda in Union-Management

Cooperation in Training and Retraining of Workers,' in B. Dennis, ed., *Proceedings of the 1985 Spring Meeting, April 18–19* (Detroit, MI) Industrial Relations Research Association. Madison, WI: Industrial Relations Research Association, 535–47.

Savoie, Ernest, and Joel Cutcher-Gershenfeld. 1991. 'The Governance of Joint Training Initiatives,' in L. Ferman, M. Hoyman, J. Cutcher-Gershenfeld, and E. Savoie, eds., *Joint Training Programs: A Union-Management Approach to Preparing Workers for the Future*. Ithaca, NY: ILR Press, Cornell University, 207–27.

Sharpe, Andrew. 1990. 'Training the Work Force: A Challenge Facing Canada in the '90s.' *Perspectives in Labour and Income* 2, no.4 (Winter), 21–31.

Statistics Canada. 1994. *Corporations and Labour Unions Returns Act. Part II – Labour Unions 1992.* (November) Catalogue 71–202.

Tan, Hong, Bruce Chapman, Christine Peterson, and Alison Booth. 1992. 'Youth Training in the United States, Great Britain, and Australia,' in R. Ehrenberg, ed., *Research in Labor Economics*. Vol. 13, Greenwich, CT: JAI Press, 63–99.

Thurow, Lester. 1992. *Head to Head*. New York: William Morrow.

United States Department of Labor and United States Department of Commerce. (USDL/USDC). 1994. *Fact Finding Report of the Commission on the Future of Worker-Management Relations*.

Verma, Anil. 1992. 'Industrial Relations in the Canadian Steel Industry,' in R. Chaykowski and A. Verma, eds., *Industrial Relations in Canadian Industry*. Toronto: Holt Rinehart and Winston.

Conclusion: Issues and Lessons from the Sector Council Experience

MORLEY GUNDERSON and ANDREW SHARPE

Drawing upon the preceding chapters of the volume, this concluding chapter provides a discussion of a number of issues confronting sector councils and the overall lessons of the sector council experience. It also highlights the accomplishments of the councils, develops the general principles for building successful ones, and discusses their future.

Accomplishments of Sector Councils

Sector councils in Canada have many accomplishments to their credit, and they have laid the foundation for the attainment of a number of important goals likely to have wider benefits for society. They have helped to foster a climate of trust based on a mutual desire and ability to resolve problems between business and labour. Such cooperation can expand from areas of initial concern, such as training, to other areas, such as the introduction of technological change or workplace practices which may also benefit from joint consultation outside the framework of collective bargaining.

Sector councils have promoted more effective development and delivery of labour market programs. The experience of Canadian Steel Trade and Employment Congress (CSTEC) has shown that downside adjustment programs can be more effective when they are delivered by persons with grass-roots knowledge and experience in the downsized sector (Ekos, 1991). Similarly, experience with the Sectoral Skills Council (SSC) shows how consistent rules and approaches to training can be developed once applied more generally on an efficient, cost effective basis at a sectoral level.

Sector councils have further successes to their credit, such as the development and implementation of better public policy through the provision of joint advice and recommendations to government by sectoral organizations; the development of new labour market mechanisms and institutions to deal with specific labour market issues (the training fund established by the SSC represents a particularly innovative manner of dealing with the need for skills upgrading in the electrical/electronics industry), and finally, the laying of the foundation for bipartite initiatives at broader levels which will be in the interest of business and labour.

Some Issues in the Further Development of Sectoral Initiatives

The development of successful sectoral initiatives is a long, complex, and at times difficult process, fraught with many pitfalls. Given differences in views between business and labour and at times within the business and labour constituencies themselves, it is not surprising that convincing business and labour to work together can be challenging. The role of government in the process also merits discussion. This section, which draws on the insights contained in the papers in this volume, briefly lays out some of the issues which continue to be debated by business and labour in the development of sectoral initiatives.

Employee Representation in Non-unionized Sectors

An important issue in the establishment of bipartite initiatives in sectors with large numbers of non-unionized workers is the question of who speaks for the non-unionized workforce. Unions argue that they should represent all workers; employers argue that non-unionized employees should decide how they wish to be represented. When non-unionized employees are given representation, the parity relationship between organized labour and employers is forfeited, although equality between employees (unionized and non-unionized) and employers is maintained.

Role of Non-Labour and Business Groups

A related issue is the role of groups other than business and labour in the development of sectoral initiatives. Some argue that sectoral issues can go beyond the purview of business and labour and that groups which have a direct interest in developments in a particular sector should be represented in a decision-making capacity. For example, it could be argued that women's organizations should play a role in initiatives in sectors with a large female presence, or where they are under-represented in the workforce. Equally, native groups should be represented in any initiative involving sectors employing large numbers of aboriginal persons. Education institutions that provide training and retraining to workers in a particular sector may also merit being involved as decision-makers. While no one denies the desirability of input for such groups, some argue that they should not be given formal representation in sectoral initiatives. It is felt that such representation may lessen the feeling of ownership that business and labour have of the initiative and thus reduce their commitment to its success.

Definitions of a Sector

One issue which comes up at times is the question of definition. Sectors are normally defined by the Standard Industrial Classification (SIC) and data are gathered using these definitions. But for a variety of reasons, SIC sectoral definitions may not always be appropriate. Indeed, around one-third of the councils are based on occupational categories and non-SIC defined industries. It may be better for business and labour to agree on a sectoral definition which reflects their reality. The demarcation of sectoral boundaries may be particularly important for policy issues such as standard-setting.

Role of Government Funding

The funding of sector councils has generated considerable debate. Most councils have been financed by Human Resources Development Canada. The federal government has indicated, however, that it is not prepared to underwrite these councils indefinitely and that it would like them to take steps to secure other sources of financing, in particular, financial contributions from business and labour. Indeed, current policy is to fund councils for only three years, with support progressively declining over the period. Government argues that a true commitment on the part of business and labour to sectoral initiatives requires some financial support.

Labour, however, has indicated a reluctance to make a major financial commitment to sectoral initiatives (at least in cash; contributions in kind are more acceptable), largely because it feels its financial resources are stretched too thin to permit such contributions. In addition, certain labour leaders have been particularly adamant that unions should not contribute to the funding of any training initiatives undertaken by sectoral organizations. It is felt that this is the responsibility of the employer, or government.

It can be noted that sector councils might be considered a public good. Individual firms might never undertake the types of activities sector councils engage in because of the poaching problems and other constraints, even though these activities would be highly desirable for society at large. From this point of view, some government funding of sector councils may be merited.

Expansion beyond Human Resource Issues

Sector councils, particularly those that have had an impact at the workplace, have largely limited themselves to human resource and adjustment issues. An important question is whether councils can deal with other workplace concerns, such as technological change, work practices, or worker participation schemes. Some argue that these issues are best left to the collective bargaining process because they are often firm-specific. Others argue that a sectoral approach may foster innovations or have cost advantages that can benefit both labour market partners. For example, a code for the implementation of new technologies agreed to by business and labour at the sectoral level, and adhered to by all firms and unions in the sector, may facilitate the diffusion of best practice technologies and promote increased productivity. It may also set a general standard to be reflected in other ways, including through collective agreements.

Relation between Sector Councils and National Bipartite Initiatives

A related issue involves the relationship between sector business-labour councils and national bipartite initiatives. Some argue that successful ventures at the sectoral level may lead to similar successes at the national level. Once it has been demonstrated that business and labour can develop new and effective institutions at the sectoral level to deal with labour market issues, for example, it is significantly easier to do follow up at the national level. The experience of CSTEC, the SSC, and other sectoral initiatives are said to have in part inspired the creation of the Canadian Labour Force Development Board. Sector councils are believed to represent an important step towards building a new business-labour approach to labour market issues (Kumar and Coates, 1991). Others argue that the demonstration effect of sectoral successes on national initiatives may be limited because the interests of business and labour are much more divergent at the national than at the sectoral level.

Lessons from the Sector Council Experience

This section puts forward five lessons from the Canadian sector council experience that are believed to be particularly important.

• Sector councils fulfill a public good role, as certain activities, such as the design and mounting of training programs, are better undertaken at the sector rather than the firm level.
• Sector councils should be seen not as a replacement for collective bargaining

but rather as a development that can transform the traditional collective bargaining system.

- The relative success of sector councils at the industry level compared to labour force development boards at the provincial level suggests sectoral approaches to labour market issues may be more effective than geographical approaches.
- The great diversity of sector councils' structures and activities is a strength, as it reflects grass-roots involvement.
- Sector councils are not a panacea and have a number of important limitations.

Sector Councils Have Important Public Good Aspects

Government financial support has been crucial for the development of sector councils, but the continuation of government funding for sector councils beyond a three-year start-up period is uncertain. But if some of the activities of sector councils constitute a public good for society at large that would not be provided without government support, a case could be made for continued government financial assistance.

A number of sector council activities provide benefits well beyond the sector which would not be fully undertaken without government subsidy. Smith in his article in this volume identifies four specific market failures that sector councils can address: underprovision of labour market information; inability of private sector actors to agree to standards; free-riding by non-innovators on labour-management on innovations; and an undersupply of training due to poaching and high curriculum development costs. Osberg, Wien, and Grude argue that there is too little recognition that cooperation among producers can be socially productive (1995:30). Small firms may not have the resources to design and mount effective training programs. These activities may be most effectively carried out at the sectoral level through the direct involvement of both employers and employees

Sector Councils Can Transform, Not Replace, Collective Bargaining

The objective of sector councils is not to replace the traditional collective bargaining structures as they pertain to compensation and working conditions. Indeed, employer and union sector council representatives tend to avoid these divisive issues and focus on more common-ground issues such as training. But the emergence of sector councils can have an indirect, positive effect on the functioning of the collective bargaining system. As Haddad has shown in her article in this volume, the development of joint governance structures at both the workplace and sectoral level changes the attitudes and perceptions of management and workers towards one another. A shared understanding and a climate of trust develop that over time increases consensual behaviour and reduces adversarial behaviour, although the latter is never completely eliminated.

Countries with cooperative business-labour relations have tended to enjoy superior economic performance compared to countries where business-labour relations are more adversarial. Germany, Austria, Sweden, and Japan are often pointed to as examples of countries where business-labour cooperation has paid dividends. The emergence of sector councils in Canada represents an increase in the extent of business-labour cooperation, and may contribute to improved economic performance.

Of course, other factors, such as macro-economic variables (interest rates and exchange rates), international competition, and technological change, are undoubtedly more important for economic performance than business-labour cooperation. Nevertheless, all roads to improved performance should be taken, even narrow and bumpy ones. Kochan and Osterman, in *The Mutual Gains Enterprise*, have made the case that a mutual gains policy framework is needed that goes beyond the regulation of conflict to support practices and policies facilitating innovations in employment relations. Equally, Piore in *Beyond Individualism*, stresses the importance of fostering trust and cooperation in society through the establishment of institutions that bring together members of different groups for a common purpose. We believe the Canadian experience with sector councils represents a step in this direction.

Sector Councils versus Labour Force Development Boards

In the late 1980s and early 1990s, two new institutional structures emerged for the development and implementation of labour market policy: sector councils and labour force development boards. The federal government has facilitated the establishment of over twenty national sector councils. The Quebec government through the Société québécoise du développement de la main-d'oeuvre (SQDM) is currently attempting to establish twenty-five sector councils in Quebec. Other provincial governments, particularly Ontario and British Columbia, have also indicated a preference for a sectoral approach to labour market issues.

The federal government in 1991 established the multi-partite Canadian Labour Force Development Board (CLFDB) to advise it on labour market policy (McFayden, 1997). Through the CLFDB, provincial labour force development boards were established in Newfoundland, Nova Scotia, New Brunswick, and Sakatchewan, and to a lesser extent British Columbia. Provincial boards developed independently of the federal initiative in Quebec through the Société québécoise du développement de la main-d'oeuvre and in Ontario through the Ontario Training and Adjustment Board. Alberta, Manitoba, Prince Edward Island, and the two territories chose not to establish boards.

The development of sector councils in Canada has not suffered any major setbacks recently and can point to a number of concrete accomplishments, including the setting up of training trust funds (SSC), the operation of highly regarded adjustment programs (CSTEC), the elaboration of industry standards (CARS), or the establishment of a training institution (CAMAQ). No established councils have shut their doors, although certain sectors such as construction have not expressed interest in establishing a council.

In contrast, the development of labour force development boards in Canada has experienced a number of difficulties (Haddow and Sharpe, 1997). First, in those provinces that did chose to establish boards, a number of them have either been downsized or closed. In March 1995 the federal government cut the size of the CLFDB in half, reducing its quasi-decision-making role to that of a purely advisory body. Also in 1995, the Newfoundland Labour Force Development Board closed. In April 1996 the Ontario government shut down OTAB, a move that was virtually ignored by the media. The Nova Scotia Labour Force Development Board has also been closed. Indeed, labour force development boards have yet to be able to point to many tangible accomplishments.

This brief assessment of sector councils and labour force development boards raises the obvious question of what accounts for the superior performance of sector councils. Grass-roots support, which is a key determinant in the success of a new labour market institutional structure, appears to be greater for sector councils than for labour force development boards. This suggests that employers and employees identify more closely with their sector or industry than with their provincial jurisdiction when it comes to addressing labour market issues and consider the sectoral approach more relevant than a geographical one.

Sector Council Diversity Constitutes a Strength

Sector councils are very diverse in both characteristics and operations, as manifested by different types of employee representation (both unions and employee associations), different foci (some councils have an occupational rather than a sectoral focus), and different activities (upside and downside adjustment programs, curriculum development, certification, establishment of training standards, and so on). It is thus difficult to speak of a 'typical' sector council.

This diversity reflects the grass-roots nature of the councils. It is the actual labour market partners that determine the mandate of the council and define the organizational structure of the council. This means that business and labour take ownership of the process and have a stake in the success of the enterprise. A recipe for failure would be to have government define in advance the parameters of what sector councils look like and how they should function.

Limitations of Sector Councils

Sector councils, while certainly an important part of the economic restructuring and adjustment process, should not, however, be seen as a panacea. There are a number of weaknesses and inherent limits to the role these councils can play.

- Inconsistencies may exist between the common sectoral interests of business and labour and the overall national interest. Examples are generally not found in the human resource development area, but may occur in areas such as tax policy, trade policy, and resource management where specific sectoral policy proposals may constitute a zero-sum game between the sector and the rest of the economy. For example, tax policy changes to facilitate adjustment or favour the development of a particular sector may mean less revenue for the rest of the economy. Trade protection for a particular sector may mean higher prices for other sectors.
- Sector councils may be unable to move beyond issues such as training.
- Structural impediments may inhibit the establishment of sectoral initiatives in certain sectors. In these cases, national initiatives would be needed.
- Sector councils, by focusing on adjustment issues *within* a sector, may inhibit necessary adjustment *across* sectors, especially from declining to expanding ones.
- A limited number of policy levers are available to business and labour at the sectoral level. Certain problems may require policy solutions well beyond the ambit of business and labour in that particular sector. The problem of insufficient demand, which leads to fewer jobs, is one example of a situation where forces well beyond the control of the sector are responsible for its problems. There may be a danger that emphasis on a sectoral approach to solving the problems faced by a particular sector will transfer responsibility from the national level to the sectoral level. This may reduce the pressure at the national level for more effective policies, even though it is at this level that the problem may lie. Supply-side policies at the sectoral level may not be substitutes for demand-side policies at the national level.

General Principles for Building Effective Sector Councils

An examination of the accumulated experience in the building of sectoral initiatives in Canada over the past decade allows one to identify a number of general principles for building effective sector councils.

1/ Labour and business must act as equals in the process of building sector councils. This principle is particularly important to labour because unions often feel that business does not consider them a legitimate and equal partner in the workplace. Where unions must constantly defend their right to represent workers and must fight for their very existence against employers who would prefer a non-unionized workforce, there is little possibility of employers and unions working productively together. While the concerns of business and labour differ and neither party behaves in an altruistic manner, each side must recognize the legitimacy of the other's goals and objectives and realize that they can jointly develop solutions to their respective concerns.

2/ Sector councils must complement the collective bargaining framework and should avoid dealing with issues better suited to collective bargaining. The role of sector councils is not to replace collective bargaining but rather to complement it.

3/ The agenda of sector councils must be driven by business and labour, not third parties such as government, even if government is providing funding. Building a successful sectoral initiative requires commitment from business and labour. The most effective way to develop this commitment is to ensure that business and labour have a sense of ownership of the initiative, and set the agenda. The role of government should be that of facilitator or observer, not active participant.

4/ The decision-making process in sector councils must be joint in nature and based on mutual recognition of the concerns of each party. Given the equal representation of business and labour, each party in effect has veto power. For this reason only policies and directions that have the support of both parties can be implemented.

5/ Sector councils should develop strong linkages to the workplace. Without such linkages the activities of the sector organizations may bear little relation to the needs of business and labour at the workplace level. Grass-roots support may then be lost. Delivery of labour market services and administration of sectoral training funds are examples of activities which have a strong workplace focus. Such activities in turn build grass-roots support for other sectoral programs which bear less directly on the workplace.

An additional aspect of the linkages between the sector councils and the workplace is that the sectoral initiatives should attempt to replicate or at least foster at the workplace level the joint business-labour structures, based on parity of representation, developed at the sectoral level. This can be done through the establishment of business-labour workplace committees responsible for the delivery or administration of labour market services or programs.

6/ Adequate resources must be made available for the development of sector councils. The establishment and staffing of a secretariat require financial resources which often the labour market partners, particularly labour, are not in a position to contribute. Third-party assistance, generally from government, is often required.

7/ Expectations of business and labour concerning the outcome of sector councils should be kept at relatively low levels, particularly in the beginning. Because of significant differences in views and attitudes and because of both the limited experience of both partners in dealing with each other outside the collective bargaining framework, progress in building sector councils can be slow. Two steps forward are often followed by one or more steps backward. For this reason it is wise not to foster expectations that the process will quickly lead to significant and quantifiable benefits for all parties involved. If such expectations are not met, the initiative might unravel.

8/ An important factor which has contributed to the success of sector councils such as CSTEC and the SSC has been strong leadership. The quality of leadership can in many cases be the determining factor in whether a sector council is established. Leadership is critical in starting the dialogue in setting up the initiatives, in ensuring that each constituency feels its interests are being met, and in keeping the process going through both good times and bad. Labour and business leaders are not acting in an altruistic manner when they enter into sectoral initiatives. They know that their own interests can be furthered by working with each other. Crucial for the success of sector councils is the emergence of leaders who recognize the potential of sectoral initiatives to serve their constituency's interests, and who have the ability to convince their colleagues of this.

The Future of Sector Councils

Alternative Scenarios

The outlook for sector councils appears bright, but it is by no means assured. At the conference on the emergence of sector councils in January 1996, where the initial versions of the papers in this volume were presented, Gordon Betcherman, of Ekos Research Associates and the Canadian Policy Research Networks, put forward a number of scenarios for the future of sector councils. This section draws upon his presentation.

Five scenarios for the future of sector councils can be envisaged. At one extreme is the pessimistic view that sector councils will end up nothing more than a fad or a 'flavour of the month.' According to this scenario, the councils are currently flourishing largely because of government support, but would decline and eventually disappear if government financial assistance were to dry up. Factors supporting this view include the federal government's stated position of not providing funding to sector councils beyond the third year of operation and of devolving its current responsibilities in the area of training to the provinces.

At the other extreme is a scenario where sector councils replace enterprise-based institutions in a wide range of areas. According to this view, the advantages of sector councils are recognized by both employers and employees, resulting in their rapid expansion. Sector councils develop a representational role for non-unionized workers, (i.e., by setting wage guidelines), and serve as a forum for industry-wide collective bargaining for unionized workers.

Three intermediate scenarios can also be identified. In the first, a limited role for sector councils develops in the narrow area of manpower issues. For example, business and labour work together to determine sectoral skill requirements and conduct needs assessment studies. Sectoral initiatives benefit both employers and employees through risk pooling. Traditional collective bargaining is not threatened by sector council development as the two institutions fulfill completely separate functions.

In a second intermediate scenario, an uneasy alliance between sector councils and collective bargaining emerges. While business and labour realize benefits from participation in certain council activities, the councils never become truly effective. The parties still feel ambiguous about their relationship with one another within the framework of the council and are reluctant to give up their long-established collective bargaining processes

In the third intermediate scenario, probably the most promising one, the traditional model of collective bargaining is enhanced through the development of sector councils. The collaboration of business and labour on human resources issues in the councils builds trust that spills over to broader labour-management relationships, making it more harmonious, as evidenced by a decline in grievances and strikes. Unions are by no means replaced by the councils. Rather business and labour attitudes change and their relationship expands beyond the traditional ambit of collective bargaining over compensation and working conditions to include other issues approached from a joint problem-solving, mutual gains perspective.

While there is a wide variance in the sector council experience, with certain councils operating effectively and others encountering difficulty, the first and second intermediate scenarios best characterize the current situation. The challenge facing sector councils is to move to the third intermediate scenario.

The Employment Insurance Act

Labour market policy in Canada has recently undergone a major change with the passage of Bill C-12, an act which creates a new employment insurance system and replaces the Unemployment Insurance Act and the National Training Act. According to the federal government, the act is designed to 'strengthen work incentives, help workers adjust to economic change through reinvestment in back-to-work benefits, and secure $1.2 billion in saving by 2001–02' (Government of Canada, 1996:3). The act has two parts: redesigned income benefits which provide temporary support for approximately 2.4 million claimants a year while they look for work; and active employment benefits for 400,000 unemployed workers a year, tailored to meet the needs of individuals and local circumstances, with an emphasis on flexibility and employment. The bill also proposed a new partnership with the provinces aimed at increasing effectiveness and eliminating duplication in the labour market area. The federal government is withdrawing from labour market training. Since it has been the federal government that has supported sector councils, devolution of responsibility for labour market training to the provinces may have important implications for the councils, which are national in scope. It is unclear whether the funds allocated to the Sectoral Partnership Initiative, which have been used to fund the councils, will be turned over to the provinces. If the provinces assume responsibility for funding council activities, the national orientation of the councils will be jeopardized. Councils whose focus is in the poorer provinces, such as the Canadian Council of Professional Fish Harvesters, may encounter funding problems as these provinces may not have adequate resources to fund their activities.

Conclusion

This volume provides a wide range of perspectives on the emergence of sector councils in Canada. The overall conclusion is that this experience has been a positive one for both business and labour. In contrast to the general experience at firm and workplace level and at the aggregate economy level, where business and labour often are at loggerheads over particular issues, the sectoral level has seen new and effective forms of joint decision-making. Sector councils represent a true innovation in the area of business-labour cooperation in Canada.

There is much to learn, both for Canada and for other countries, from this experience for a broader understanding of the forces at work in the overall industrial relations system.

References

Docquier, Gerard, and Strategic Planning Associates. 1996. *Marketing Canada's Sector Council Expertise in a Global Context*. Report prepared for Human Resources Development Canada-International Services, 31 January.

Ekos Research Associates Inc. 1991. *Program Evaluation Study of the Canadian Steel Trade and Employment Congress: Final Report (Phase I)*. Prepared for Employment and Immigration Canada.

Government of Canada. 1996. *A Guide to Bill C-12: Employment Insurance*. May.

Haddow, Rodney. 1997a. 'The Emergence of Labour Force Development Boards in New Brunswick and Nova Scotia,' in Andrew Sharpe and Rodney Haddow, eds., *Social Partnerships for Training: Canada's Experiment with Labour Force Development Boards*. Kingston: Queen's University School of Policy Studies, Caledon Institute of Social Policy and Centre for the Study of Living Standards.

– 1997b. 'Saskatchewan: Reforming Labour Market Governance in a Cold Climate,' in Andrew Sharpe and Rodney Haddow, eds., *Social Partnerships for Training: Canada's Experiment with Labour Force Development Boards*. Kingston: Queen's University School of Policy Studies, Caledon Institute of Social Policy and Centre for the Study of Living Standards.

Haddow, Rodney, and Andrew Sharpe. 1997. 'Canada's Experiment with Labour Force Development Boards in Canada: An Introduction,' in Andrew Sharpe and Rodney Haddow, eds., *Social Partnerships for Training: Canada's Experiment with Labour Force Development Boards*. Kingston: Queen's University School of Policy Studies, Caledon Institute of Social Policy and Centre for the Study of Living Standards.

Hommen, Leif. 1997. 'The British Columbia Labour Force Development Board: Delivering Consensus,' in Andrew Sharpe and Rodney Haddow, eds., *Social Partnerships for Training: Canada's Experiment with Labour Force Development Boards*. Kingston: Queen's University School of Policy Studies, Caledon Institute of Social Policy and Centre for the Study of Living Standards.

Human Resources Development Canada. 1996a. 'Case Study Report on the Forum for International Trade Training (FITT).' Formative Evaluation of the Sectoral Partnership, Evaluation and Data Development, Human Resources Development Canada.

– 1996b. 'Case Study Report on the Canadian Automotive Repair and Service (CARS) Council.' Ibid.

– 1996c. 'Case Study Report on the Canadian Aviation Maintenance Council.' Ibid.

- 1996d. 'Case Study Report on the Automotive Parts Sectoral Training Council.' Ibid.
- 1996e. 'Case Study Report on the Canadian Council for Human Resources in the Environment Industry.' Ibid.
- 1996f. 'Case Study Report on Impression 2000 Graphic Arts Training Council.' Ibid.
- 1996g. 'Case Study Report on the Canadian Professional Logistics Institute.' Ibid., March.
- 1996h. 'Case Study Report on the Canadian Steel Trade and Employment Congress (CSTEC).' Ibid.
- 1996i. 'Case Study Report on the Software Human Resource Council.' Ibid.
- 1996j. 'Case Study Report on the Horticultural Human Resource Council (HRDC).' Ibid.
- 1996k. 'Case Study Report on the Canadian Tourism Human Resource Council (CTHRC).' Ibid.
- 1996l. *Sectoral Activities: Update Report*. Spring.
- 1996m. 'Management Report' Formative Evaluation of the Sectoral Partnership. September.
Johnson, Andrew. 1997. 'La Société Québécoise du Développement de la Main-d'oeuvre,' in Andrew Sharpe and Rodney Haddow, eds., *Social Partnerships for Training: Canada's Experiment with Labour Force Development Boards*. Kingston: Queen's University School of Policy Studies, Caledon Institute of Social Policy and Centre for the Study of Living Standards.
Kochan, T., and P. Osterman. 1994. *The Mutual Gains Enterprise: Forging a Winning Partnership among Labor, Management and Government*. Boston: Harvard Business School Press.
Kumar, P., and M.L. Coates. 1991. *Industrial Relations in 1991: Trends and Emerging Issues*. Kingston: Queen's University, Current Industrial Relations Scene, Industrial Relations Centre.
Osberg, Lars, Fred Wien, and Jan Grude. 1995. *Vanishing Jobs: Canada's Changing Workplaces*. Toronto: James Lorimer.
Piore, Michael. 1995. *Beyond Individualism*. Cambridge: Harvard University Press.
Sharpe, Andrew. 1992. 'The Role of Business-Labour Sectoral Initiatives in Economic Restructuring,' *Quarterly Labour Market and Productivity Review* 1–2, Canadian Labour Market and Productivity Centre.
Wolfe, David. 1997. 'The Evolving Institutional Framework for Labour Force Development in Ontario: The Ontario Training and Adjustment Board,' in Andrew Sharpe and Rodney Haddow, eds., *Social Partnerships for Training: Canada's Experiment with Labour Force Development Boards*. Kingston: Queen's University School of Policy Studies, Caledon Institute of Social Policy and Centre for the Study of Living Standards.

Contributors

Michael M. Atkinson is a professor of political science and vice-president (academic) at the University of Saskatchewan.

Neil Bradford is an assistant professor in the Department of Political Science at Huron College, University of Western Ontario.

Jean Charest is an assistant professor at the École des relations industrielles, Université de Montréal.

Richard P. Chaykowski is an associate professor at the School of Industrial Relations at Queen's University.

Joel Cutcher-Gershenfeld is an associate professor at the School of Labor and Industrial Relations at Michigan State University and visiting scholar in the Program on Negotiations at Harvard Law School.

Jock A. Finlayson is vice-president, policy, at the Business Council of British Columbia.

Gary Fletcher is the former director of the Sector Studies Division at Human Resources Development Canada.

Morley Gunderson is a professor at the Centre for Industrial Relations and the Department of Economics at the University of Toronto.

Carol Joyce Haddad is a professor in the Department of Interdisciplinary Technology at Eastern Michigan University in Ypsilanti, Michigan.

Kevin Hayes is senior economist at the Canadian Labour Congress, with responsibility for labour market policy.

Kai Lamertz is a graduate student in the Faculty of Management at the University of Toronto.

D'Arcy Martin is a national representative for the Communications, Energy, and Paperworkers Union.

Cassandra W. Pervin is a graduate student in political science at McMaster University.

Andrew Sharpe is executive director of the Ottawa-based Centre for the Study of Living Standards.

Douglas A. Smith is a professor of economics at Carleton University.

Anil Verma is a professor at the Faculty of Management and Centre for Industrial Relations at the University of Toronto.

Peter Warrian is a senior research fellow at the Centre of International Studies at the University of Toronto. From 1989 to 1992 he served as executive director of the Canadian Steel Trade and Employment Congress.

David A. Wolfe is an associate professor in the Department of Political Science at the University of Toronto.